Social History of Africa

MEMOIRS
OF THE MAELSTROM

D1453849

Recent Titles in
Social History of Africa Series
Series Editors: Allen Isaacman and Jean Allman

MEMOIRS
OF THE MAELSTROM

A SENEGALESE ORAL HISTORY
OF THE FIRST WORLD WAR

Joe Lunn

HEINEMANN
Portsmouth, NH

JAMES CURREY
Oxford

DAVID PHILIP
Cape Town

Heinemann
361 Hanover Street
Portsmouth, NH 03801-3912
www.heinemann.com

James Currey Ltd.
73 Botley Road
Oxford OX2 0BS
United Kingdom

David Philip Publishers (Pty) Ltd.
208 Werdmuller Centre
Claremont 7708
South Africa

Offices and agents throughout the world

ISBN 0–325–00139–1 (Heinemann cloth)
ISBN 0–325–00138–3 (Heinemann paper)
ISBN 0–85255–688–8 (James Currey cloth)
ISBN 0–85255–638–1 (James Currey paper)

British Library Cataloguing in Publication Data
Lunn, Joe
Memoirs of the maelstrom : a Senegalese oral history of the First World War.—(Social history of Africa series)
1. World War, 1914–1918—Participation, Senegalese   2. World War, 1914–1918—Personal narratives, Senegalese
I. Title
940.3'0899663

ISBN 0–85255–638–1 (James Currey paper)
ISBN 0–85255–688–8 (James Currey cloth)

Library of Congress Cataloging-in-Publication Data
Lunn, Joe.
Memoirs of the maelstrom : a Senegalese oral history of the First World War / Joe Lunn.
p.   cm.— (Social history of Africa, 1099–8098)
Includes bibliographical references and index.
ISBN 0–325–00139–1 (alk. paper)
ISBN 0–325–00138–3 (pbk. : alk. paper)
1. World War, 1914–1918.   2. World War, 1914–1918—Senegal.   3. World War, 1914–1918—Personal narratives, Senegalese.   4. Oral history.   5. France. Armee. Tirailleurs senegalais—History.   6. France. Armee—Colonial forces—History—19th century.   7. France. Armee—Colonial forces—History—20th century.   8. Africa, French-speaking West—Race relations.   9. Africa, French-speaking West—History, Military.   I. Title.   II. Series.
D811.A2   L85   1999
940.3—dc21   99–29405

Paperback cover photo: Biram Mbodji Tine. Photograph by the author.

Printed in the United States of America on acid-free paper.

Docutech RRD 2009

*In memory of my father, William Dixon Lunn (1923–1978),
whose last words to me were a request for a copy
of the as yet unrecorded interviews
on which this book is based.*

CONTENTS

ILLUSTRATIONS

PHOTOGRAPHS

ACKNOWLEDGMENTS

A study of this nature, which was conducted in Senegal and France and compiled in the United States and in England over a span of fifteen years, necessarily owes much to many people. It is a pleasure to acknowledge my personal debt to those who have assisted me in this endeavor, without whose help this work would not have been possible.

Jan Vansina, professor emeritus of history and anthropology at the University of Wisconsin–Madison, ranks foremost among those whom I wish to thank for their professional guidance. He trained me as an oral historian, served as my major professor, critiqued with care the dissertation on which this book is based, and offered much welcomed advice about its publication. His astonishing breadth of knowledge about Africa as well as Europe proved invaluable in directing this wide-ranging inquiry, while his unfailing enthusiasm, patience, and humor throughout the process were deeply appreciated. In short, it is inconceivable that this work could have been completed in its present form without his assistance, and I feel indebted to him far beyond my ability to adequately acknowledge.

Two other professors also deserve special acknowledgment. Robert A. Nye, formerly at the University of Oklahoma and currently at Oregon State University, and the late George L. Mosse, of the University of Wisconsin–Madison, were sources of intellectual inspiration and guidance during my graduate education. They also offered me the benefit of their critiques of chapters of this work and provided particularly helpful professional advice and support on numerous occasions.

Several other historians have also assisted me during various stages of this project. I would like to thank my dear friend, Elizabeth Williams, Oklahoma State University, both for her encouragement and her reading of this manuscript. Special acknowledgment is also due to Jim Searing,

University of Illinois–Chicago, with whom I have exchanged ideas about this project since we were conducting field research together in Senegal and who has read drafts of this work with care and offered valuable suggestions for revision. Thanks are also due to William B. Cohen, Myron Echenberg, Martin Klein, Charles Balesi, and Alice Conklin, who have provided critical evaluations that have substantially improved the quality of this work. I have also profited from discussions with other Africanists—notably Melvin Page, Malcolm Thompson, and Nancy Lawler—who have explored similar subjects using methodological approaches that were much the same as my own.

This project would also have been impossible without the financial support of several granting agencies. I would like to thank the French Ministry of Culture for awarding me a *Bourse Châteaubriand* to conduct dissertation research in France during the 1981–1982 academic year; the Fulbright Program for a Doctoral Dissertation Fellowship that enabled me to pursue research in Senegal, 1982–1983; the University of Michigan, for a Horace H. Rackham Grant and Research Fellowship, which supported research in France in 1996 and a summer's writing; and the University of Michigan–Dearborn for a Faculty Research Grant to fund archival research in Paris.

My research was abetted by the assistance of numerous archivists and librarians. In France, I would like to thank the staffs of the Archives de la Guerre; the Archives nationales; the Archives nationales, Section d'outre-mer; the Bibliothèque de l'Institut de France; the Bibliothèque nationale de France; and the Centre Militaire d'Information et Documentation: outre-mer. I am grateful to the late Général Henri Lapierre for assistance with the archives at CMIDOM, and also to Général Charles Mangin for giving me permission to consult the Papiers Mangin at the Archives nationales. In Senegal, I would like to express my appreciation to the staffs of the Archives nationales du Sénégal and the Institut Fondamentale de l'Afrique Noire. I am also indebted to the helpful staff members at the Memorial Library of the University of Wisconsin, the African Studies Library of Cambridge University; and the Graduate Library of the University of Michigan.

The long process of compiling the oral histories in Senegal necessarily entails debts to many people. Without the assistance of the associations of the *anciens combattants* in the various regions of the country, locating the veterans on whom this study is based would have been impossible. In this regard, however, I am particularly indebted to Souleymane Doumouya of the Cape Vert Association. Special thanks are reserved for William Ndiaye and Douada Fall, who served as interpreters for me throughout my field research. William, moreover, has become a lifelong friend who has deepened my understanding of Senegalese society. Finally, I would like to thank all the men and women whom I interviewed for welcoming a stranger into their midst and sharing their life's memories with him. This was especially true for the families of Ousmane Diagne, Yoro Diaw, Nar Diouf, Mamadou Djigo, Demba Mboup, Abdoulaye Ndiaye, Sera Ndiaye, and Masserigne Soumare, who accorded me an exceptional degree of hospitality.

My research was also facilitated by a number of others. In Paris, my friends Bob Bullock and Françoise Navasse, as well as Donna Evleth, provided critical assistance. While in Senegal, I was helped by Barbara Shear, Mike White, Oumou Ndiaye, and Hal Glucksberg. I also want to thank the innumerable Peace Corps volunteers, local veterans' association officials, and Senegalese families who found room for William or Douda and me when we were conducting interviews far from home.

A number of individuals have offered essential help during the production stage of this project. In particular, I would like to thank Simon Buck, Sebastian Barclay, Susan Richmond, and Donna Wasserman. I also would like to express my gratitude to Jean Allman and Alan Isaacman, editors of Heinemann's Social History of Africa Series, for their advice and guidance, and to Jim Lance and Lynn Zelem for their assistance in preparing the manuscript.

Special appreciation goes to the many friends who offered constant support through this endeavor, including Michael McManus, Robert Mayer, Alan Wasserman, and Paul Barclay. Special thanks also goes to Judy Cochran, Graduate Secretary of the History Department at the University of Wisconsin–Madison.

It is to my family, however, that I owe the most. I would like to thank my mother and my brother Bill for their ongoing support and encouragement during this long process. To my daughters, Sarah and Laura, I wish to express my gratitude for their understanding and patience while I was preoccupied with this project, for bravely adapting to the numerous cultural changes my work has required them to make, and for the inexpressible joy they have brought to my life. My debt to my wife, Marsha, is greater still. She has been the person most intimately involved in this work over the years, and her courage, perseverance, and belief in me has been a continual source of inspiration. More specifically, she has also provided intellectual stimulation, critical commentary, editorial expertise, and financial support throughout the writing of this book—all while pursuing her own demanding career as an historian of science. In short, I would like to thank her for deciding to explore the wider world with me so many years ago, and for choosing to share her life with me.

Finally, I wish to express my gratitude to my father for being the exceptional man that he was, and for providing the primary source of determination to complete this undertaking in the face of many obstacles. As in all aspects of my life, he encouraged me in my decision to become an historian and exhibited a keen interest in this particular project. When I was first preparing to depart for Africa, his last words to me, in response to my jocular inquiry about what gift I should bring him, were that he would like "a copy of the tapes" on which this work is based. Unfortunately his sudden and all too early death prohibited the fulfillment of this desire. I hope that in some small measure this work will honor his memory and his abiding interest and faith in me.

INTRODUCTION

Even though my leg aches today [from the
shrapnel wound I received in France],
my heart and my tongue wish to speak.

Demba Mboup, 15 April 1983

Although the circumstances that afforded Demba Mboup an opportunity to speak about his experiences during the First World War were unusual, his participation in the conflict was not. He was but one of over 140,000 West Africans who were recruited into the French army and served as combatants on the western front between 1914 and 1918. This temporary, enforced migration of Africans to Europe—unprecedented at the time and never since surpassed in scale over a comparable duration—carried profound implications for African as well as French society that ranged far beyond the outcome on the battlefields. The broader impact of this unique wartime encounter, as well as the ways in which it affected the lives of the individual soldiers involved, is the theme of this work.

Emphasis is placed on the African experience. More specifically, this study focuses on Senegal, which provides an illuminating vantage point for assessing the full range of the war's impact on West Africans. The oldest of the colonies in the French Federation, Senegal was the most thoroughly integrated into the European administrative network and export economy in 1914. There the recruitment burdens imposed by the French were also the heaviest, the response to them the most diverse, and the political and social implications arising from the soldiers' service overseas most pronounced.

Indeed, the Senegalese experience sheds light on experiences common to all West Africans during this period. It offers insights into the character of the prewar colonial order and the images the French inspired in the minds of those they had recently conquered. It demonstrates how the colonial recruitment drives were conducted, as well as the response these drives evoked among Africans. And, most significantly, this work illuminates the nature of the soldiers' service on the western front and shows how the interplay between the experience in the army, the ordeal during combat, and closer contacts with Europeans altered many of the soldiers' previous attitudes about themselves, their society, and the French. As such, this study elucidates important aspects of the recent African past by using the crucial watershed of the First World War as a frame of reference.

This work is not, then, simply a military history of the impact of World War I on Senegal. Because French wartime recruitment demands were so extensive—affecting over half of the able-bodied men of military age in the colony—the war influenced not only the lives of the soldiers sent to France but also virtually all groups in Senegal: men and women, young and old, aristocrats and slaves, Muslims and "Ceddo," urban citizens as well as rural colonial subjects. The diverse reactions occasioned by the novel dictates of the colonial regime afford a unique opportunity to explore Senegalese society from multiple vantage points and at a crucial juncture. Like Frederick Cooper's study of colonization and decolonization, this work similarly strives to recover "the consciousness and actions of ordinary people . . . instead of reducing the colonial subject to a stick figure in a drama written elsewhere."[1] As such, this book aims to provide a broader understanding of colonialism by shedding light on the social history of Africans at the midpoint between the French conquest and the reclamation of political independence.

Although emphasizing the diverse experiences of the Senegalese, such an inquiry also necessarily explores significant aspects of French history. It offers a compelling insight into the application of race theory by the French military in the organization and utilization of African troops, and the consequences this had for the individuals involved. It also shows how the interaction between new public images of Africans disseminated as a result of the war, as well as the closer personal contacts that this made possible, helped to alter previous French stereotypes about Africans.

Memoirs of the Maelstrom relies on a distinctive methodology. Although the participation of West Africans in the First World War has been assessed by a number of eminent scholars—including Marc Michel, *L'Appel à l'Afrique* (1982); Myron Echenberg, *Colonial Conscripts* (1991); and Charles Balesi, *From Adversaries to Comrades-in-Arms* (1979), among others—their works, although breaking new ground and representing enduring historical contributions to this subject, nevertheless suffer from a methodological constraint. Based predominantly on French archival and published sources, these studies shed little light on the lived reality of the war for Africans. This work seeks to circumvent the limitations inherent in this approach by making extensive use of oral history.

Unlike Europeans, who left a vast body of literature recounting their experiences during the First World War, West Africans did not record what the war meant for them. Indeed, aside from Bakary Diallo's *Force Bonté* (1926), no contemporary African memoirs about the war were ever written or published.[2] The historiographical constraints posed by the paucity of African written sources has long been recognized by scholars, dating back to Shelby Cullom Davis's pioneering work of 1934 and including Michel and Echenberg.[3]

By adding the testimony of some 85 African veterans and witnesses on the period between 1914 and 1918, my work provides a more comprehensive view of the meaning of the war for West Africans than has hitherto been attempted. In so doing, it duplicates the methodology employed by other African historians—notably Melvin Page for Malawi during the First World War and Nancy Lawler for the Ivory Coast during the Second.[4] In short, this study adds Senegalese voices to what has perforce been a discourse defined in large measure by the observations (and omissions) of European witnesses and hence sheds new light on, and offers a new perspective of, this crucial phase of the West African past.

The oral histories were compiled in Senegal between September 1982 and July 1983. Confronted by an unexpectedly large number of nearly 150 surviving veterans—who were located through the *Office des Anciens Combattants du Sénégal*, which administered quarterly veterans' pensions from the French government—I engaged in a process of selection. Though random in many respects, this procedure was also influenced by both conscious decisions and unforeseen factors. There was, for example, a widely varying number of potential respondents in different regions. Aiming to obtain a sample from as wide a geographic area as possible, I selected veterans at random in those regions where the veterans were most numerous; in areas where they were fewer in number, an effort was made to contact all surviving ex-servicemen. Other factors, including whether individuals were in residence when contacted and the state of their physical and mental health, also played a role in the selection process.

In addition to locating the veterans, linguistic and logistical difficulties had to be surmounted. Seeking to conduct the interviews in the primary languages of the respondents, I relied on the intermediary of interpreters.[5] In all but two instances, either William Ndiaye or Daouda Fall served in this capacity throughout the entire series of interviews.[6]

Though working from a general research design that sought to explore specific aspects of the informants' wartime experiences, the interviews were conducted in an open-ended fashion. This technique involved initially posing very broad questions and then asking the respondents to elaborate in greater detail about particular aspects of the answers they gave. In so doing, I strove to avoid raising themes unless they had previously been mentioned by the informants, thereby enabling them to structure the content of their interviews as much as possible. I also consciously eschewed using a questionnaire type of format during these sessions. Only rarely, and at the conclusion of interviews, were questions of particular interest to me raised if they had not been touched on in the course of the conversation.[7]

Of the 85 interviews conducted, 74 were recorded: 57 with veterans (including 35 *tirailleurs*, 15 *originaires*, and 7 from the *Banlieue de Dakar*), 16 with witnesses, and one oral tradition (see "Oral Histories" under Sources). Recorded interviews eventually reached some 200 hours in length. (Copies of the tapes are on deposit at the Archives of Traditional Music and Folklore at Indiana University and the Archives de la République du Sénégal in Dakar.) I also compiled ledgers, organized by categories of information, which provided the basis for recognizing trends as well as synthesizing the testimony of individuals.

Interpreting archival as well as oral source material is occasionally difficult for the historian. The French archival records (and other published materials) are generally used here to provide an overview of events, while the oral histories present a personal perspective of how Africans viewed the war. The written record, though extensive, was compiled by a comparatively small number of individuals, most of whom often sought to advance their careers by complying with the wishes of their superiors. Hence, the reports sometimes exaggerate, downplay, or omit significant pieces of information. The oral histories also need to be examined with a critical eye; they sometimes suffer from a lack of chronological specificity or, when personally sensitive information (e.g., the servile origins of family ancestry) was being concealed, from contradictions, omissions, or implausible explanations about specific points.[8] I have attempted to avoid the pitfalls inherent in using these source materials by evaluating the available information within its historical context and seeking to corroborate or question the testimony whenever possible through recourse to other sources.[9] In general, however, the oral and written records have been used in an equivalent fashion. This stems from my belief that the testimony of a peasant from Khinine, for example, was usually as reliable about events witnessed in his village as that of a Governor General reporting to the Minister of Colonies about the results of a recent recruitment drive in Senegal.

The oral histories are also used collectively to indicate trends within Senegalese society that French sources do not document. However, it should be emphasized that the recorded interviews on which these observations are based do not constitute a valid sample in the statistical meaning of the term. They are far too few in number to provide an acceptable margin of error. Longevity alone, among octogenarians, was ultimately the key to a respondent's being included in the survey, and even those who were interviewed were not always selected on the basis of uniformly random principles.

Nevertheless, the oral histories do offer important insights. Collective trends are readily discernible. When these trends are explicitly attested to by several different respondents and corroborated by the actions or situations of other informants in the vast majority of cases, the reliability of such information seems secure.

The research methodology of synthesizing oral and written sources is difficult to pursue but exceptionally rewarding. Since the appearance of Jan Vansina's pioneering work *De la tradition orale* (1961), the acceptance by scholars of oral sources has come a long way.[10] Indeed, following the appearance of the *International Journal of Oral History* and an increasing number of other periodicals, the technique of oral history has graduated from being an experimental methodology into a well-developed discipline. In the context of the present study, the advantages of recourse to oral history are readily apparent. While the French archives offer an indispensable overview of events, the oral histories supplement this by providing a no less valuable view from below. This affords a rich and multifaceted perspective of the past that encompasses social, political, military, and intellectual history as well as the history of mentalities.

The first three chapters of the book are set in Senegal and explore the diverse African responses to the French wartime recruitment drives. Chapter 1 sets the tone by appraising the impact of colonial rule on African life before 1914 and Senegalese images of the French. While the extent of African contact with the French as well as their local influence on Senegalese life varied significantly throughout the colony, Europeans inspired fear because of their unjust and ruthless exercise of authority, and hence were to be avoided. Chapters 2 and 3 examine the dramatically different ways in which the Senegalese reacted to the call-up of their young men. In rural Senegal between 1914 and 1917, French demands were novel and terrifying, and Africans responded by sacrificing those deemed most expendable. Also explored are the methods of appropriating recruits and the scale of French demands: in more remote areas of the colony the roundup of men harkened back to slave raids in the past, while in scale the numbers of Senegalese exported overseas between 1914 and 1918 was substantially larger than the eighteenth-century trans-Atlantic slave trade had ever been during a similar period. In dramatic contrast to the situation that existed in rural Senegal, Chapter 3 surveys the quest of urban Africans (the *originaires* of the Four Communes) to acquire French citizenship, and it explores how military service in the war came to be equated with a movement to secure these political rights. It describes how the communal deputy, Blaise Diagne, in securing passage of the Diagne Laws of 1915–1916 and during his recruitment mission of 1918, sought to redefine the meaning of the war for Africans into a means of obtaining civic rights.

The next three chapters assess the nature of the soldiers' experiences in Europe during the war. Regardless of when the soldiers were recruited or whether they came from rural or urban areas, their introduction to military life, explored in Chapter 4, transcended the bounds of customary experience. Despite the hierarchical character of military life, it was paradoxically more egalitarian in many respects than either the Senegalese society or the French colonial order from which the recruits came. This chapter also examines the fiscal cost to the metropole of raising and sustaining a West African army during the war. I argue that, public pronouncements about pursuing an ostensible "civilizing mission" in Africa notwithstanding, French wartime expenditures probably exceeded all other outlays during the previous quarter century of French rule in Senegal combined.[11]

Chapter 5 seeks to revise current understanding of the deployment of Senegalese troops during the war by reinterpreting archival data, and it challenges earlier conclusions reached by Michel, Balesi, and Echenberg, among others. Linking French tactical doctrine in combat to older, racial assumptions about Africans, I argue that Senegalese soldiers were primarily used as shock troops; indeed, during the last two years of the war, many generals sought to spare French lives by sacrificing African ones. This is supported by showing that Senegalese combat losses while at the Front after 1916 were nearly three times greater than those of French soldiers. African impressions of trench warfare, as well as their reasons for fighting and the psychological supports that sustained them through their ordeal, are also graphically described. Chapter 6 concludes the European section of the book by probing the soldiers' perceptions of the French, as well as metropolitan views of the Senegalese, during encounters behind the lines. The reciprocal images of each group were initially informed by the colonial context, but these perceptions were gradually altered as a result of official policy and increased personal interaction. While the extent of this change in mentalities varied significantly in both cases, the war nevertheless brought about a more humane image of the "Other" than had previously existed and prefigured an eventual movement toward more egalitarian humanism.

Chapter 7 examines the soldiers' return to Senegal after the war and their subsequent reintegration into society. It indicates that while many veterans resumed their lives much as before, others—especially the *originaires* from the communes as well as particular groups of *tirailleurs*—found their lives dramatically altered by their wartime service. The new mentality some manifested found political expression in the thwarted attempt between 1919 and 1923 to extend civic rights enjoyed in the communes to the rest of Senegal. Also highlighted are several postwar social trends, most notably the migratory patterns among the soldiers: *tirailleurs* who did not return to their homes became permanent exiles, while the *originaires*, after often obtaining employment in the French sector of the economy elsewhere in West Africa, nevertheless eventually returned to their former residences.

The Postscript develops these themes by offering the soldiers' interpretations of the legacy of their wartime service, which testifies to the multidimensional meaning of the struggle in which they, as young men, found themselves engaged. These recollections exemplify the fashion in which the oral histories convey a sense of the human dimensions of the war for Africans—what people thought, how they felt, and how their mentalities were changed by their experiences. When combined with written sources, they provide a compelling insight into the catastrophic European maelstrom in which the Senegalese found themselves engulfed after 1914, by recounting how men like Demba Mboup interpreted the fate that befell them.

NOTES

[1] Frederick Cooper, *Decolonization and African Society: The Labor Question in French and British Africa* (Cambridge: Cambridge University Press, 1996), p. 9.

[2] Bakary Diallo, *Force Bonté* (Paris: Rieder, 1926). See also Guy Ossito Midiohouan, "Le Tirailleur Sénégalais du fusil a la plume: La fortune de *Force-Bonté* de Bakary Diallo," in *"Tirailleurs Sénégalais": Zur Bildlichen und Literarischen Darstellung Afrikanischer Soldaten im Dienste Frankreichs—Présentations Littéraires et Figuratives de Soldats africains au Service de la France*, ed. János Riesz and Joachim Schultz (Frankfurt am Main: Peter Lang, 1989), pp. 133–51.

[3] Shelby Cullom Davis, *Reservoirs of Men: A History of the Black Troops of French West Africa* (Ph.D. thesis, University of Geneva, 1934); rpt. ed. (Westport, CT: Negro Universities Press, 1970), pp. 12–13; Marc Michel, *L'Appel à l'Afrique: Contributions et réactions à l'effort de guerre en A.O.F. (1914–1919)* (Paris: Publications de la Sorbonne, 1982), p. 391; and Myron Echenberg, *Colonial Conscripts: The "Tirailleurs Sénégalais" in French West Africa, 1857–1960* (Portsmouth, NH: Heinemann/London: James Currey, 1991), p. 1.

[4] See Melvin E. Page, "Malawians in the Great War and After, 1914–1925," (Ph.D. diss.: Michigan State University, 1977); and Melvin E. Page, "Malawians and the Great War: Oral History in the Reconstruction of Africa's Recent Past," *Oral History Review* 8 (1980), pp. 49–61. Nancy Ellen Lawler, *Soldiers of Misfortune: Ivoirien Tirailleurs of World War II* (Athens: Ohio University Press, 1992).

[5] The interviews were conducted primarily in Wolof, Serer, or Pulaar. A few of the informants, however, were Jola, Soninke, or Malinke speakers.

[6] William Ndiaye worked for the Senegalese Ministry of Culture and had previously served as a translator collecting oral traditions throughout the country. Daouda Fall was a student at the English Language Institute in Dakar and was president of the Pekine Association of English Language Speakers.

[7] These field techniques were based on training by Jan Vansina. For a discussion of these techniques by his former students, see Carolyn Keyes Adenaike and Jan Vansina, eds., *In Pursuit of History: Fieldwork in Africa* (Portsmouth, NH: Heinemann/Oxford: James Currey, 1996).

[8] On the reluctance, for example, of former slaves to reveal their servile origins when being interviewed, see Martin A. Klein, "Studying the History of Those Who Would Rather Forget: Oral History and the Experience of Slavery," *History in Africa* 16 (1989), pp. 209–17.

[9] Unresolved contradictions nevertheless still arise. For example, when interviewed in 1982, Abdoulaye Ndiaye gave *"originaire"* as his prewar status, while in a 1998 interview with Philip Bernard, he claimed to have been a *sujet* (see "Le dernier de la 'Force Noire,'" *Le Monde*, 12 novembre 1998). In any event, although Ndiaye's personal account is contradictory, his factual descriptions coincide in their particulars with the testimony given by numerous other *originaire* and *sujet* respondents.

[10] Jan Vansina, *De la tradition orale* (Sciences de l'homme, Annales no. 36) (Tervuren: Musée royal de l'Afrique centrale, 1961).

[11] On the French civilizing mission, see Alice L. Conklin, *A Mission to Civilize: The Republican Idea of Empire in France and West Africa, 1895–1930* (Stanford: Stanford University Press, 1997).

1

THE VISION OF THE VANQUISHED: MEMORIES OF THE PREWAR COLONIAL ORDER

An assessment of the far-ranging impact of the First World War on Senegal, as well as its profound influence on the lives of all those who were sent to Europe to serve as combatants, must commence with an appreciation of the prewar colonial order. Senegalese reactions to the demands made on them between 1914 and 1918 were conditioned by the immediate African past—with its legacy of alien conquest and domination—as a point of reference. Moreover, those soldiers who participated directly in the conflict shared from the outset a novel perspective within African society. Unlike their elder kinsmen whose outlooks were formed in precolonial times and who experienced the trauma of the conquest firsthand, they were drawn exclusively from the first generation of Senegalese to grow to adulthood under the French regime.[1] As such, their attitudes toward the war and their subsequent interpretations of their ordeal overseas reflected a novel cultural configuration of long-standing African values and assumptions, which frequently sought accommodation with the new and often disconcerting realities of European rule. Thus, it is against a backdrop of recent French domination superimposed on the conventions of an older order that both the soldiers' reactions to the war, as well as its broader implications for Senegalese society, must be gauged.

In order to appreciate the nuances of the prewar colonial situation and the influence that the French presence had on the Senegalese, it is essential to incorporate an African perspective. The oral histories on which this study is based embody the collective historical consciousness of 85

Senegalese witnesses from the period. Their testimony affords a unique means for presenting an interpretation of the past as they recalled it.[2] Through recourse to this record, it will be possible to address this subject from two vantage points. First, what were the tangible effects of the imposition of colonial rule on the Senegalese, and how may we characterize the nature of their relations with the French? Second, and perhaps more important, how did the Senegalese interpret the collective catastrophe that befell them in the late nineteenth century, and what imagery did the French conquerors evoke in their minds? A discussion of these questions will illuminate the dynamics of the prewar colonial order and delve into the mentality of the vanquished. This, in turn, will provide an essential point of reference for assessing Senegalese reactions to the unprecedented wartime demands that were made on them.

THE IMPACT OF COLONIAL RULE ON AFRICAN LIFE

The ways in which French rule impinged on the Senegalese corresponded to the extent of the European presence, and hence their degree of control, within particular areas of the colony. Although on the whole French influence remained tangential throughout the prewar period, it nevertheless varied significantly within particular locales. These, broadly speaking, can be divided into three categories: the rural hinterland, where the vast majority of the African population lived and where the French presence was virtually nonexistent; isolated administrative and commercial outposts in the interior, where handfuls of Frenchmen sought to maintain tenuous links with the nodal points of colonial authority and with trade along the Atlantic seaboard; and the as yet small European urban centers along the coast—the so-called Four Communes of Senegal comprising Gorée, St. Louis, Rufisque, and Dakar—which, despite serving as the nexus of French power and influence as well as their presence, nevertheless remained predominantly inhabited by Africans. By examining the prevailing conditions in each of these distinctive areas, it is possible to gauge the physical dimensions of the European impact on African life and impart an idea of the parameters of contact that existed between the colonizers and the colonized during the years immediately preceding the outbreak of the war.

Rural Villages

In the rural villages of the interior, where an estimated 90 to 95 percent of the Senegalese population lived, the tangible effects of the imposition of the colonial regime were most circumscribed. There European

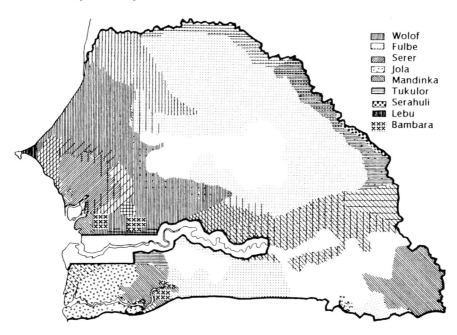

Wolof
Fulbe
Serer
Jola
Mandinka
Tukulor
Serahuli
Lebu
Bambara

MAP 1.1   Ethnographic Map of Senegal
Source: Based on map from Ministry of Planning and Cooperation, Government of the Republic of Senegal, *Atlas pour l'aménagement du territoire* (Dakar: Nouvelles éditions africaines, 1977).

authority was exercised indirectly through African clients. Since the introduction of extensive cash cropping for export to the metropole—the distinguishing feature of the colonial economy—was only beginning to take root in many areas, French influence on prevailing Senegalese social norms was slight. And yet, because of their capacity to bring incontestable coercive power to bear, their influence on African existence, when they sought to enforce compliance with their wishes, was far from negligible.

French political authority in the hinterland was exercised through African provincial or cantonal chiefs, who were overseen by a European district administrator (*commandant de cercle*) and were responsible for executing colonial directives affecting the local inhabitants through the medium of village chiefs beneath them. Appointment to a major chieftaincy required French approval and was ultimately dictated by expediency. Cantonal chiefs were chosen from among families of ancient ruling

KEY

- - - - CERCLE BOUNDARY
········· RAILWAY
  △   COMMUNE
  ⊠   DISTRICT (CERCLE) CAPITAL
  ○   FRENCH ADMINISTRATIVE RESIDENCE

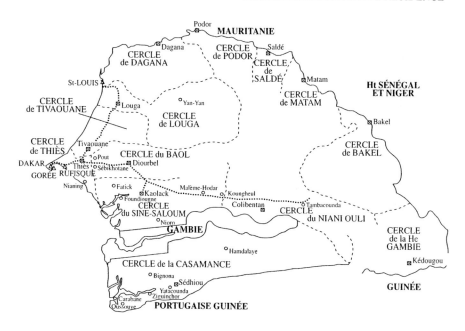

Map 1.2   Senegal in 1914: Administrative Divisions

Source: Archives nationales du Sénégal: 1 G 359. *Politique et administration général: Circonscriptions administratif du Sénégal, 1908–1920.*

elites, in conformity with customary practices, when this proved convenient, or from among the pool of trusted French auxiliaries—such as former soldiers or interpreters—when it was not. In all instances, however, obedience to French commands and the ability to enforce compliance with them were prerequisites for retaining office.[3]

French demands on the countryside were threefold. Their most important concern was the collection of the "head tax" to support the costs of maintaining the colonial administration. Describing how the system functioned, Mahmout Demba recalled that after compiling "lists" of the number of residents in each village:

The *chef de canton* used to send the *chef de village* to collect the taxes. . . . [And] they used to pay by head—the father had to pay, the mother, the children, [and so forth]. They used to give the money to the *chef de village*, and the *chef de village* [gave it] to the *chef de canton*, and the *chef de canton* to the *commandant de cercle*. . . . [And] they only accepted [French] money. If you didn't have [any] money, you had to sell one of your cows or something like that, but you had to pay the taxes in money. . . . Each [time], after you paid your taxes, you used to receive a receipt for the money you had given.[4]

Though tax rates varied according to locale and continued to rise throughout the prewar period (reaching an average of 4 francs per head in 1914), the burden, while representing a significant outlay of disposable income, was seldom considered onerous.[5]

In addition to being required to pay taxes in the "pieces of silver" introduced by the French, the colonial authorities also requisitioned African labor. The institution of *travaux forcés*—whereby rural Senegalese were liable to work (at least ostensibly) for eight days per year on government projects—was used primarily for constructing the colony's communications infrastructure, on which both the consolidation of French political control as well as the growth of export economy depended. In practice, the workload fluctuated according to local imperatives, and men were commandeered for as long as necessary to build and maintain roads or, less frequently, to help construct railways in those areas where they were being laid.[6]

French administrators also often demanded satisfaction of their sexual desires, and to this end chiefs were frequently compelled to provide the local *commandants* with concubines. Recalling the degradation of these women and the impotence of the Senegalese in the face of such orders, Boubacar Gueye recounted: "When they arrived as *commandants de cercle*, the French administrators used to tell a village chief to bring about ten women [to their residence]. They used to choose from among these women two or three to spend time with. . . . And after a few months, when they finished with these women, they used to change [them] and take others to their home."[7]

Aside from the exactions of taxes and labor and the expropriation of women by the French, the impact of the colonial regime in rural areas was most apparent in the growth of the export economy. This transformation, however, occurred gradually and was stimulated indirectly. French currency—which was not only a prerequisite for paying taxes but also essential for purchasing an assortment of imported items ranging from food and cooking utensils to cloth—was most readily obtained through the sale of cash crops. As a result, most peasants, while continuing to grow enough millet or rice to feed their families, also began to devote increasing labor to cultivating other, less essential crops such as peanuts, which were more marketable.[8]

The system of commercial exchange in the countryside (like the functioning of the rural administration) depended on African middlemen, who provided the crucial link between the peasant producers and the transportation network that carried their crops to the coast. Usually employed either directly or indirectly as sub-traders by the major import-export firms, they conducted transactions in the villages or acted as intermediaries between Senegalese farmers and French traders in the commercial outposts of the interior. The power to set basic rates of exchange, however, normally rested in the hands of the larger French companies, which sought to maximize their profits by standardizing the prices paid to the Senegalese for their produce. The upshot in the case of peanuts, for example, was that despite increased toil by the peasantry, and notwithstanding considerable fluctuations in both the metropolitan market and the size of the colony's crop, the price paid to rural farmers remained static at 5 francs per 100 kilos throughout the prewar period.[9]

French domination also marginally impinged on Senegalese social institutions. Though they were generally loath to become involved in internal African affairs (which were little understood by them), the French made a few exceptions to this rule. The institution of domestic servitude, for example, was gradually abolished in Senegal. By the first decade of the twentieth century, slavery was effectively outlawed in all colonial towns, and although it continued to persist in many areas of the countryside—especially where the use of servile bondsmen to cultivate cash crops favored French economic interests—it was, nevertheless, on the wane there too.[10] Also, among those ethnic groups, such as the Bambara, that practiced scarification as a means of accentuating collective social identity, such rituals—which also exemplified courage in the face of pain—were prohibited because of disputes arising with the authorities about their propriety.[11]

Irrespective of the nature of French demands, compliance was exacted through the use or threat of coercion. For comparatively minor infractions—such as the lack of proper deference for European officials or failure to pay taxes or perform labor services as scheduled—beatings, followed by fines or imprisonment (which were sanctioned by the code of administrative "justice" known as the *indigénat*), were the norm. In the case of more serious offenses—such as the murder of a European administrator arising from a dispute provoked by him—those responsible were not only executed, but their heads and limbs were severed and publicly displayed as a grim warning to all of the penalty for such misdeed.[12] Under such circumstances, the Senegalese felt "powerless" to contest French authority and, regardless of the rectitude of their commands, were "forced" to submit to the colonizers' will.[13]

Direct contacts between the rural population and their French overlords were, however, extremely rare. In most villages, the inhabitants literally "never saw" Europeans, and their dealings with the agents of the colonial regime were restricted to infrequent visits by the *chefs de canton*, or African *commerçants*. Exceptions to this norm were unusual but did occur now and again. French traders sometimes ventured into less remote villages to conduct commercial transactions, while colonial officials, who were usually in transit between regional administrative centers, also occasionally appeared. In either case, interaction with Europeans was brief, superficial, and, in the latter instance, usually conducted by them in an imperious manner. Horses, donkeys, or porters were commandeered to carry baggage; sheep or goats were taken from farmers, slaughtered, and eaten; and, despite local resentment at such impositions, "no one could say anything" against the French.[14]

The only other occasion when Africans encountered Europeans—and this was when most laid eyes on them for the first time—was during rare trips to French towns to sell their crops. Such journeys usually occurred at end of the harvest, and the character of Senegalese contacts with European *colons* was both circumscribed and ephemeral. Indeed, aside from hasty transactions (usually conducted through interpreters) with French traders and occasional glimpses or chance encounters with other European inhabitants, interaction between the two groups seldom took place at all. As a result, even though the colonial order impinged on their lives in numerous ways, most rural Senegalese experienced very little personal contact with Europeans and, hence, had only the vaguest of notions about what their new overlords were like.[15]

Colonial Towns of the Interior

For those Africans living in the colonial towns of the interior, the situation was somewhat different. They were subject to most of the same demands as their kinsmen in the villages and continued to conduct their lives in much the same manner, but since they also resided in close proximity to the *colons*, they had more opportunity to observe them firsthand. As a result, they were better placed to assess the character of the colonial order.

The French towns in the Senegalese hinterland (i.e., Thiès, Louga, Kaolack, Tambacounda, etc.) were often recent creations, and because they were designed to serve specific needs, they evolved in particular ways. Many began as isolated military outposts founded during the conquest to support troop movements and overawe a hostile populace. With the advent of the colonial regime, their former role gradually became subordinated, and they expanded to assume new functions. They became the regional centers of French political authority in the countryside while also linking the rural economy—via the ever-expanding communications infrastructure—to the *entrepôts* for overseas export on the coast. As such, the nature of their development reflected the sequence of French imperatives exemplified in their choice of construction priorities. In the case of Louga, which was a Muslim Wolof village before the arrival of the railhead in 1886, the following pattern occurred. After the completion of the railroad linking it to St. Louis and Dakar, the building of a station to service the line was given precedence. When this was finished in 1888, it was followed, in turn, by the erection of a permanent residence for the *commandant*, a police station, a post office, and a hospital. As these outposts gradually developed into towns, other French buildings were added, including commercial houses for the major import-export firms such as Maurel et Prom and Peyrissac, a few primary schools, and, in larger centers like Thiès, a *hôtel de ville*.[16]

French structures, however, remained comparatively few in number, and the colonial towns—which seldom contained more than one or two thousand residents—inevitably exhibited a distinctively African character. This was evidenced not only in prevailing architectural styles (where thatch predominated over lumber and stone) but also in the composition of the population. The expatriate presence in such locales was sparse and usually consisted of a handful of administrators, several dozen "agents" of the larger commercial houses or other "independent" traders, and, occasionally, some European soldiers. Collectively, these almost never amounted to more than a few score inhabitants and, compared to the Senegalese with whom they resided, they remained numerically insignificant.[17]

The French were acutely aware of their isolated situation and, aside from imposing their customary demands for taxes and labor and pursuing their commercial endeavors, they were primarily concerned with maintaining "order" among the Senegalese. Relying on African policemen and *gardes de cercle* (who were recruited from alien ethnic groups and notorious for their brutality) to intimidate the local inhabitants, they also sought to regulate Senegalese activities by imposing evening curfews and prohibiting all public gatherings without official authorization.[18] Furthermore, although limited social interaction with Africans was occasionally tolerated—most notably during public festivals—the French normally maintained their distance from the Senegalese and demanded constant deference from them. Africans were slapped at the slightest provocation, beaten for failing to remove their hats at the approach of European officials, whipped by malicious *commandants* for offenses such as impeding the movement of their horses, and offered derisory compensation when French negligence caused injury, such as the death of their children. Such behavior was designed to impress on the populace the exalted status of the *colons*, who, irrespective of their comportment, inevitably remained beyond reproach for abusing Africans.[19]

Under such circumstances, the nature of the contacts between the Senegalese and the expatriate community were perforce constricted. Even though kept to a minimum and conducted under conditions of subservience at best, some more extensive contact did exist. Africans who were employed by the French (as domestics, shop assistants, construction workers, sub-traders, etc.) or who were able to attend one of their primary schools were in intermittent touch with them and often acquired a rudimentary knowledge of their language, customs, and institutions.[20] Such situations were, however, atypical. For most Africans even these limited occasions for interaction remained foreclosed, and, aside from infrequent commercial relations with the Europeans, they had very little truck with them. Indeed, despite the closer proximity of the urban Senegalese to the *colons*, the specter of their presence was often so menacing that many fled from them on sight.[21] The tenor of the times, and the fundamental perversity of Eurafrican relations in the French towns, is perhaps best exemplified by an incident that occurred in Louga, which was recalled by a resident, Abdoulaye Ndiaye:

> One Sunday, at the house next to ours—which was a commercial house [then]—a "*Tubab*" [Frenchman] was on the balcony with his wife. A Senegalese was walking by wearing a tarboosh on one side of his head. . . . And the *Tubab* said to his wife, "I can shoot the hat [off his head] with my hunting rifle." But when he fired, he missed the hat and the bullet struck the man in his forehead and killed him. And after the incident, all of the family of the [dead] man came [to the house], and they wanted to fight with the *Tubab*. But the policemen were there to prevent them from climbing [onto the balcony]. And after that, the *Tubab* [was allowed] to leave [Louga] and was sent to Dakar, and we never knew what became of him.[22]

The Four Communes

Excluding such acts of nonchalant criminality, the impact of the French presence was felt most keenly by those Africans living in the Four Communes of Senegal. Although Dakar, Rufisque, St. Louis, and Gorée contained only 3 to 6 percent of the total indigenous population during the prewar period, they were home to about 85 percent of the colony's European inhabitants. As a consequence, they were the areas where the most frequent contacts between the Senegalese and the French occurred. Moreover, under the terms of the metropolitan legislation that granted the communes municipal status in 1872, most African residents were arbitrarily accorded a unique civic standing that subsequently differentiated them from their rural counterparts. As "*originaires*" of the communes, they were entitled to vote in municipal and legislative elections and allowed access to French courts—rights that were prohibited to the vast majority of Senegalese "*sujets*" who were born in the more recently conquered territories of the interior. Furthermore, in addition to being immune from the *indigénat*, they were also exempted from the "head" tax (until 1912) and from corvée labor obligations. Though these "privileges" were resented by the colonial authorities (who sought to abrogate them after 1910) and rural Africans alike, their significance has often been exaggerated.[23] Prior to 1914, they were of little practical consequence. Legal distinctions notwithstanding, the tenor of the *originaires'* relations with the French was not qualitatively dissimilar to that experienced by other Africans elsewhere in the colony. And despite their more pervasive presence in the communes, the influence of the Europeans and their institutions on the prevailing patterns of Senegalese existence often remained slight.

Throughout the prewar era, the communes represented the nodal points of French political and economic power in the colony. Though small in population (St. Louis and Dakar, which were the largest communes, never numbered more than 25,000 inhabitants), they were nevertheless diverse and differed from each other in important respects. The tiny island of Gorée in the lee of Cape Vert was the oldest area of European habitation in Senegal. Founded as a fort and slave factory in the seventeenth century, it had long since lost its former significance. St. Louis, at the mouth of the Senegal, was established later in the seventeenth century, and before the construction of the railways it served as the primary *entrepôt* for French commercial and military activity in the African interior. Although its previous importance as a trading center was steadily declining, it remained the capital of colonial Senegal. It was also distinguished by the fact that its municipal institutions were not dominated by the French but by their "*métis*" (or "creole") allies, who, though of Eurafrican descent, disdained the Senegalese. The newer municipalities of Rufisque and Dakar were the focal points of recent European settlement, and by the early twentieth century had become the most important centers of French colonial activity. Rufisque, whose wharves were literally connected via rail to the peanut basin in the interior, served as the commercial nexus of the European export economy. Dakar, which was elevated to the status of the capital for French West Africa in 1902, was not only the seat of federal political authority, but its economic significance was rapidly increasing as well. As such, it was the fastest growing commune and contained the highest proportion of European residents.[24]

Despite the greater concentration of expatriates in the communes than anywhere else in Senegal, their numbers (which never exceeded 9 percent of the municipal population in Dakar and were less than 4 percent elsewhere) remained small. This salient feature of communal existence goes far toward explaining why even there the European impact on prevailing patterns of African existence (though not necessarily on their lives) was still marginal. The organization of Senegalese communal society exhibited most of the same characteristics that were found in the countryside. Bonds of family and extended kinship networks provided the focal points for allegiance among most *originaires*, and residential collectives within the urban areas (and in the villages in the outlying suburbs) still invested authority to make group decisions in customary ways. Although precolonial hereditary status was usually less important as an arbiter of social prestige in the communes than in rural areas, it too nonetheless continued to be an influential factor governing internal African relations.[25]

Moreover, even with the growth of the colonial economy, these transformations as yet had little effect on the ways in which most *originaires* earned their livelihoods. Though a select few managed to secure comparatively lucrative jobs in the French sector that obviated their need to work the land, the vast majority of the Senegalese were not employed by Europeans and continued to derive their existence from farming or fishing exactly as their forebears had done.[26] And even among those who did work for the French in positions of relative responsibility—such as administrative functionaries and commercial middlemen—most still supplemented their meager incomes by these traditional means.[27] The European impact on Senegalese conventions was further restricted because of religious differences. Nearly all African communards were Muslims and, as such, they were frequently wary of the corrupting influence of French institutions on their religious beliefs, which they often sought to avoid by such means as prohibiting their children from attending local primary schools.[28]

Yet, the European presence was not without effect on the lives of the *originaires*. Exacting compliance with the wishes of the colonial regime depended in the communes, as it did throughout the rest of Senegal, on the use of African auxiliaries. These were composed of the municipal police forces or, when their numbers proved insufficient to quell major disturbances, companies of African *tirailleurs*, which garrisoned the colony.[29]

Aside from maintaining European "prestige" and collecting municipal taxes to help fund local government, the primary French preoccupation in the communes—at least insofar as it affected the African *habitants*— was with public health. Because of their greater population density, the communes were, prior to 1914, the most disease-ridden areas of the colony, and the authorities were obsessed with preventing the spread of contagion. In addition to imposing little understood sanitary regulations on the populace (such as prohibiting urination in public places, enforced by fines and imprisonment if ignored), the French took sweeping countermeasures when epidemics broke out. African homes in the communes and outlying suburban villages were indiscriminately put to the torch, their residents were removed and quarantined for prolonged periods under armed guard, and the bodies of their loved ones were burned in violation of Muslim burial practices. In the case of more severe outbreaks—such as the epidemic of plague in Dakar in 1914—many of the Senegalese living in the city center (the *Plateau*) had their lands confiscated by the French. They were forcibly removed at gunpoint to an outlying district, known as the Medina, which subsequently became designated as the African quarter.[30]

Residential as well as other forms of systematic segregation notwithstanding, contacts between the *originaires* and the French occurred more often in the communes than anywhere else in Senegal. There was a considerable range of variation in the extent and parameters of these encounters. Those employed in jobs requiring literacy in French (such as medical assistants, civil servants, teachers, etc.) or who, despite the occasional misgivings of their parents, managed to obtain a primary certificate, had sustained contacts with Europeans and their institutions. As such, they were usually more extensively acculturated than other *originaires*.[31] These instances were, however, comparatively rare, and for most Africans concourse with the French was much more restricted. Those employed by the *colons* in more menial positions (such as porters, carpenters, mechanics, stevedores, etc.) or who catered to their material needs in other ways often had no more than a cursory knowledge of their language and customs, and the extent of their association was minimal.[32] For the vast majority of the other *originaires*, relations were normally confined to infrequent commercial exchanges or chance encounters, if even that.[33]

Yet despite the variation in the range of their contacts and their respective degrees of acculturation, the fundamental character of the encounters of *originaires* with Europeans was remarkably similar. Though a few, and usually those who had been befriended by a French *patron*, remembered being on "good terms" with the *colons*, the reverse was far more often the case. Nearly all Senegalese recalled the prewar period as a time of profound inequality and viewed the arrogant comportment of the French with indignation and resentment. As Abdoulaye Diaw recalled: "They [the French] had [all] the power. And they acted like [people] who had power, and they did whatever they wanted. And we couldn't do anything, because they were the owners of the communes."[34]

Such overweening behavior was made all the more objectionable by the racism of the *colons*, who collectively subordinated Africans to Europeans in all circumstances.[35] Indeed, notwithstanding the ostensible rights of *originaires*, the French assertion of their racial primacy over the so-called "niggers," as well as their control of the apparatus of municipal coercion placed them, at least in disputes with the Senegalese, effectively above the law: "If you had trouble, with a 'white' man and you went to the police, they would [keep] you there in jail [without even asking the reasons for the incident]. [But] they would release the 'white' man . . . even though the 'white' man was guilty."[36] Under such conditions, the central hallmark of French rule in the view of most *originaires* was that there was "no justice."[37]

The exalted status of Europeans and their immunity from accountability for their actions led to widespread abuses in the communes no less than in the villages. Senegalese were struck by *colons* for attempting to fend off the attacks of their dogs; bludgeoned by the police if they dared to dispute the word of a Frenchman; maimed by the horses of European officials when they were caught in their path; arrested and exiled at the whim of the colonial authorities; and pistol-whipped to death by sadistic settlers.[38] Such outrages, which the *originaires* were powerless to prevent, graphically convey the prevailing ethos among the French during the era. And irrespective of the context of their encounters or the extent of their acculturation, most Senegalese remained deeply wary of Europeans and, indeed, sought to keep their contacts with them to a minimum.[39] Thus, despite their greater proximity to the *colons* in the communes, African interaction with them there was, on the whole, very limited. While the *originaires* as a group were more familiar with the French than their rural counterparts, their enhanced knowledge of their European overlords and their ways was only acquired at the cost of constant deference and frequent abuse.

Thus the impact of the colonial regime on African life, and the extent of Senegalese contacts with their conquerors, overall remained limited. Yet, despite its peripheral character, the impact of the French regime was far from insignificant. This was most apparent in the exercise of European political authority, which was notable for its brutality. The corresponding sense of powerlessness of Africans in the face of recurring French demands and repression was perhaps the most salient feature of the prewar colonial order. Continually manifested in physical degradation, it also carried profound psychological implications as well. By exploring the mentality engendered by alien domination—examining in particular how the Senegalese interpreted the fate that befell them and the specific images that the French conquerors evoked in their minds—it is possible to gaze on the face of French colonialism through African eyes, and thereby to offer a vision of the vanquished on the eve of the First World War.

THE SENEGALESE IMAGE OF THE FRENCH

The physical impact of the French colonial regime on Senegalese life was readily perceptible and often quantifiable. Less tangible, but no less real, was the psychological impact of alien domination on Africans. How the Senegalese interpreted the overthrow of the precolonial order, and how it influenced their image of themselves as well as of the French, are more elusive but equally important questions. These issues can be broached from two perspectives. First, what explanations did Africans offer for their subjugation by Europeans, and how did they interpret the fate that befell them? Second, what images did the French evoke in their minds, and how did they characterize the attitudes of Europeans toward them?

Interpretations of the Conquest

Senegalese perceptions roughly corresponded to the extent of their contact with the French. Assessments of the reasons for their subjugation and its significance were, however, a different matter.[40] African interpretations of the conquest were usually influenced, not by physical proximity to the *colons*, but rather by their historical point of reference. These references may be distinguished from more conventional accounts, which focused primarily on the resistance of the precolonial kingdoms to the French and the specific factors that contributed to their defeat, and those that adopted a Muslim perspective, which sought to explain the collective catastrophe that overwhelmed Africans in a religious context.

Explanations for the conquest that centered on the demise of the Senegambian kingdoms were most frequently advanced by those whose families had previously served the ancient ruling lineages—members of the hereditary aristocracy, their armed retainers, and especially their *griots*. These accounts, though varying according to the particulars of each situation, nevertheless stressed a series of common themes about the nature of the encounter between Africans and Europeans. The French were repeatedly characterized as avaricious, duplicitous, and powerful—traits that were juxtaposed against Senegalese integrity, naiveté, and bravery. In these interpretations French aggression was motivated primarily by greed and the desire for material profit: viewing the interior from the confines of their coastal enclaves, they wanted to "own the country" in order "to exploit the land and the people."[41] Europeans, at least initially, pursued these objectives by deceitful and often treacherous means: gifts—such as alcohol that was "so strong that a drop of it would wither a leaf"—were presented as tokens of false friendship; treaty negotiations—over the construction of telegraph lines, for instance—were conducted in bad faith; and African leaders who were ostensibly invited to St. Louis as honored guests of the government were seized and imprisoned.[42]

In the face of such machinations, some Senegalese leaders admittedly committed serious blunders in their dealings with the French. The naiveté of one Damel (in part owing to the linguistic barriers that made comprehension of European designs so difficult for Africans) is conveyed in a *griot*'s advice to him, the humor of which disguises the later bitter consequences of his folly:

> Samba Laobe was the Damel of Kayor. And when the French were negotiating with him, he used to always answer "*oui*" [but, in very bad French]. And a *griot* told him: "Damel, it is very dangerous to always say '*oui*,' '*oui*,' [to the French], because someday you will say 'o-o-o-i-e!' [which is when something hurts you]. . . . It is better to say '*non*,' '*non*,' from time to time because these men are your '*noon*' ['enemies' in Wolof]."[43]

Ultimately, however, it was the technological superiority of the French, rather than their guile or African gullibility, that made the conquest inevitable: "The *Tubabs* got their power from their cannon, [and only that] enabled them to dominate the people here."[44]

Indeed, despite the heroic defiance of a series of Senegalese leaders—including Lat Dior, Albury Ndiaye, and Umar Kann—whose courage and tenacity were glorified in oral tradition, their resistance to the French was foredoomed because the odds they faced were hopeless.[45] Yet their unwillingness to bow to the inevitable, and the assertion of African dignity this represented, was also cited to explain the subsequent character of the colonial order. Because of their perseverance and the difficulty experienced by the French during the conquest in subduing them, "revenge was in the heart of the 'white' man." This desire for retribution persisted into "the next generation," and it accounted for the ongoing maltreatment of the Senegalese at the hands of their new colonial masters.[46] Moreover, despite their later occasional protestations of friendship especially in commercial dealings, Africans were counseled always to be wary of the French because their fundamental character traits remained unaltered. As the Wolof proverb warned the people: "[The French] gave with the left [defiled] hand, [but] they took with the right." [laughter][47]

Muslim interpretations of the conquest differed from those advanced by apologists for the *ancien régime* in several significant respects. Although these accounts too stressed the irresistibility of French "power" and the "hard times" that followed on the heels of defeat, the loss of Senegambian sovereignty was ultimately construed as a "manifestation of Allah's will."[48] As such, the reality of alien domination needed to be accepted, although the degradation that accompanied it in the temporal world could be ameliorated by seeking spiritual consolation.

In this scheme, Amadu Bamba, founder and leader of the Mouride brotherhood, figured especially prominently. Because of Bamba's apparent triumph in the face of French persecution (he was twice exiled between 1895 and 1903 but subsequently allowed to return on both occasions), his followers interpreted this as a sign of his divine grace and, hence, of his spiritual ascendancy over the colonial authorities.[49] His moral stature in African eyes was further enhanced by his insistence on the fundamental equality of all believers before Allah, which offered a compelling counterpoint to the racist claims of Europeans and their denigration of the Senegalese. Recalling the prejudices of the *colons* and the influence of Bamba's teachings, one Mouride observed: "At that time, the 'black' man didn't mean anything [to the French]—they didn't have any respect for us. . . . [But we learned that] all the races are equal, because . . . we have all been created by God. Some [are] 'white'; some [are] 'black.' But [because you are 'black'] doesn't mean you are a fool; you are a human being."[50] Convictions of this kind, as well as the confident expectation of eventual justice from a righteous God in the hereafter, served to assuage the palpable injustice of the colonial order. Such beliefs, like the oral traditions that sought to ease the pain of subjugation by glorifying Senegalese resistance to the French, expressed the fundamental need of peoples in times of extreme crisis to reassert their collective worth before those who strove to deny it.

Images of the French

Although African interpretations of the conquest differed in significant ways, they generally agreed in their negative characterizations of the colonizers. Yet despite this basic similarity, the Senegalese image of the French was far from uniform.[51] It varied considerably over time and according to locale, which, in turn, reflected the extent of exposure to Europeans. In extremely isolated areas, the physical and cultural differences between the two groups appeared to be most extreme. Aside from the obvious but startling difference in their pigmentation, other aspects of the French appearance—such as the trousers they wore—struck Africans as exceptionally odd.[52] Furthermore, in addition to speaking in an incomprehensible tongue, they also "made signs on paper," which some had never seen done before.[53] Under such circumstances, many—like others elsewhere in the world at the initial moment of contact with Europeans—questioned whether they were human at all. Some decided that they were not and, seeking to comprehend their essence within the context of pre-Islamic belief systems, assigned a cosmological significance to them. In such schemes, the French were equated with one of the "malevolent spirits"—which were also "always 'white'" in appearance and "did bad things like killing people."[54] As a result, in some remoter villages, the African image of Europeans assumed spiritual dimensions that inevitably elicited abject fear.[55]

In most areas of the countryside, however, the Senegalese regarded Europeans in a much different light. Though usually having very little contact with them, and often being astonished by the dissimilarities in their behavior and physical appearance when they did, they nevertheless looked on the French as discernibly human. Evidence of this was, however, sometimes acquired in peculiar ways. Recounting an incident from his youth, Daba Dembele recalled: "When the *Tubabs* came to the countryside and went to the toilet, we used to go and [look in the latrine after they had finished]. [And we found out]: 'Oh, it's the same shit as ours!' [And we] used to say: 'The *Tubabs* are very white, but they have very dark shit!'" [laughter.][56]

Although ceasing to be viewed as spiritual aberrations, the specter of Europeans nevertheless continued to inspire deep-seated apprehension because of the incontestable power they wielded over Africans.[57] As a consequence, most Senegalese regarded the French in a political light and employed metaphors consistent with this conception to characterize them. They were alternately depicted as "acting like kings," as "the owners of the country," or as those who "were colonizing us."[58] While the choice of terms varied, the essence of the relationship they conveyed remained the same. The gulf that separated the Senegalese from their European conquerors was vast, and alien rule was notable in the eyes of those who were subjected to it, both for its profound inequality and for its pervasive injustice.

In those areas, such as the communes, where maximum contact between the Senegalese and the French occurred, the political imagery that prevailed elsewhere sometimes also took on social overtones. In this scheme, the position of Africans in their dealings with Europeans was likened to the situation of those who were accorded least status in the precolonial social hierarchies: "We were considered almost like 'slaves' because we had no rights, [and there was] no justice."[59] Thus, even though the image of the French was usually least daunting among those who were in closest contact with them, their increased proximity led to a heightened awareness of the servile character of their relations with the *colons*.

Irrespective of the general images that Europeans evoked in their minds, the underlying assumptions expressed in these characterizations stressed the impotence of the Senegalese in the face of their colonial masters and the ongoing degradation they experienced as a result. Although some ambivalence occasionally existed—individual Frenchmen might be classed as "very good men" or be regarded favorably for their patronage—even these exceptions conveyed an acute awareness of the fundamental disparity that existed in all relations between Africans and Europeans.[60] Moreover, such examples were rare, and the prevailing paradigm among the colonized with regard to the colonizers was far more negative. This may be most clearly expressed in a table of equivalents, which, as a composite of Senegalese views, conveys their collective conceptions of the French.

The French were regarded by the Senegalese as:

"spirits"

"devils"

"kings"

"chiefs"

"regulating us"

"colonizing us"

"the owners of the country."[61]

The French were characterized by the Senegalese as:

"powerful"

"clever"

"duplicitous" (or tricky)

"greedy" (or exploitative)

"vengeful"

"racists."[62]

The French referred to the Senegalese as:

"dirty"

"niggers"

"dirty niggers"

who were:

"without knowledge"

"ignorant"

"stupid"

"fools"

"crazy."[63]

The French treated the Senegalese:

"without respect"

"unjustly"

"very bad[ly]"

"like slaves"

"however they wanted."[64]

The sight of Frenchmen made the Senegalese:

"very afraid"

"run away."[65]

These images offer a bleak insight into the tenor of colonial rule and the profound psychological impact it had on the Senegalese. Indeed, the vision of the French was so deeply ingrained in the African psyche that it was incorporated into the interpretative symbolism of their dreams. Images appearing in dreams were believed to foretell the future, and they were normally accorded either a positive or negative meaning. For example, the ocean, birds in flight, having or being given a fish, going to a marabout, or stepping in excrement all portended varying degrees of good fortune. Conversely, laughter or joy, a hen, a bull, or riding a camel betokened dire consequences ranging from shedding tears to death. Although the meanings attached to particular images sometimes varied depending on the circumstances, the basic attributes of the symbols almost always remained constant. Thus, lions, for instance, always signified violence and very great danger, but their connotation was less ominous in times of peace than in war, when they inevitably foretold death or a serious wound.

The exceptions to this rule were dreams involving human aberrations (with abnormal eyes, fangs, etc.) or Mauritanians or Europeans. These figures were ambiguous and, depending on their behavior, conveyed one of two extremely different meanings. For example, if Europeans behaved generously (e.g., presenting gifts, shaking hands, conversing amiably), they were interpreted in a highly favorable light and, indeed, equated with "the Prophet." Alternatively, if they were beating Africans, holding weapons, or mistreating them in other ways, they were viewed as a sign of "the Devil," which augured great evil.[66]

The combination of Europeans with aberrant figures and Mauritanians illuminates the deep-seated apprehension the Senegalese felt for the French. All three images denoted power relationships (one spiritual and, in the case of the Moors and the French, historic) in which domination was, had been, or was thought to be exercised over the Senegalese. As such, these likenesses inspired a mixture of awe and dread that, because of the power they betokened and their unpredictable character, might portend either extraordinary good luck or terrible misfortune.

After 1914, several of the symbols associated with Europeans in the interpretation of Senegalese dreams assumed tangible form. With the outbreak of hostilities overseas, the French appeared before the Senegalese in the guise of friendship and bearing gifts. But, ironically, the present they proffered was a rifle—not to abuse them with, as had happened in their nightmares, but for them to take across the ocean and kill other Europeans. Irrespective of the contradictory imagery involved, most of those who received the murderous offering of the French knew all too well which hand it was given with; it was presented with the left hand and not with the right.

NOTES

[1] Although the colony of Senegal was an artificial construction, the precolonial physical boundaries of Senegambia were broadly demarked and the people of this region displayed a generally "homogeneous culture" and "common style of history." Hence, the term "Senegalese" has been used to denominate the inhabitants of this area in precolonial times. See Philip D. Curtin, *Economic Change in Precolonial Africa: Senegambia in the Era of the Slave Trade* (Madison: University of Wisconsin Press, 1975), pp. 6–7.

[2] A register of the respondents interviewed is included in the Sources. For an explanation of the methods employed in conducting interviews with them, see the Introduction. Copies of the audiocassette interviews are housed in the Archives of Traditional Music and Folklore, Indiana University, Bloomington, and the Archives de la République du Sénégal in Dakar. References to these in the notes include the name of the individual and the number and side of the cassette.

[3] On the French administrative system in the Protectorate, see Michael Crowder, "The Administration of French West Africa," *Tarikh* 4 (1969), pp. 59–71; and Pierre Alexandre, "Chiefs, *Commandants* and Clerks: Their Relationship from Conquest to Decolonisation in French West Africa," in *West African Chiefs: Their Changing Status under Colonial Rule and Independence*, ed. Michael Crowder (New York: Africana Publishing Corp., 1970), pp. 2–13, 24–78. On the backgrounds of the chiefs, see: Henri Brunschwig, *Noirs et Blancs dans l'Afrique noire Française, ou comment le colonisé devint colonisateur (1870–1914)* (Paris: Flammarion, 1983), pp. 125–35.

[4] Mahmout Demba: 1A.

[5] On tax rates by *cercle* in 1914, see "Statistiques de la population de 1914," *Archives nationales: Section Outre-Mer* (hereafter: *AN:OM*): 14 MI 1110.

[6] On corvée labor, see William B. Cohen, *Rulers of Empire: The French Colonial Service in Africa* (Stanford: Hoover Institution Press, 1971), pp. 57–83.

[7] Boubacar Gueye: 2A. See also: Alexandre, "Chiefs, Commandants, and Clerks," pp. 2–13.

[8] On the need for French currency and the increasing expenditure of labor on cash-cropping to obtain it, see Sheldon Gellar, *Structural Changes and Colonial Dependency: Senegal, 1885–1945* (Beverly Hills and London: Sage Publications, 1976), pp. 49–66.

[9] On the increasing domination of the colonial economy by larger firms, see: A. G. Hopkins, *An Economic History of West Africa* (London: Longmans, 1973), pp. 167–225. On the commercial exchange system in Sine-Saloum, see: Martin A. Klein, "Colonial Rule and Structural Change: The Case of Sine-Saloum," in *The Political Economy of Underdevelopment: Dependence in Senegal*, ed. Rita Cruise O'Brien (Beverly Hills: Sage Publications, 1979), pp. 65–99; and Martin A. Klein, *Slavery and Colonial Rule in French West Africa* (Cambridge: Cambridge University Press, 1998), pp. 94–141, 197–251. For annual international fluctuations in the price of peanuts, see Xavier Guiraud, *L'Arachide sénégalais: Monographie d'economie coloniale* (Paris: Librairie Technique et Economique, 1937), table, p. 37. For prices paid in the interior and descriptions of the system of commercial exchange, see: Ndematy Mbaye: 1B; Nar Diouf: 1A; Amar Seck: 1A; Sera Ndiaye: 1A; Amadou Yassin: 1A; and Demba Mboup: 1A.

[10] On the gradual decline of domestic servitude, see: J. L. Boutillier, "Les captifs en AOF (1903–1905)," *Bulletin de l'Institut Fondamental de l'Afrique Noire*, Sér. B, 30 (1968), pp. 508–29; Philip D. Curtin, "The Abolition of the Slave Trade from Senegambia," in *The Abolition of the Atlantic Slave Trade: Origins and Effects in Europe, Africa, and the Americas*, ed. David Eltin and James Walvin (Madison: University of Wisconsin Press, 1981), pp. 83–98; Andrew F. Clark, "Slavery and Its Demise in the Upper Senegal River Valley," *Slavery and Abolition* 15 (1994), pp. 51–71; Martin A. Klein, "Slavery and Emancipation in French West Africa," in *Breaking the Chains: Slavery, Bondage, and Emancipation in Modern Africa and Asia* (Madison: University of Wisconsin Press, 1993), pp. 171–96; Andrew F. Clark, "Freedom Villages in the Upper Senegal Valley, 1887–1910: A Reassessment," *Slavery and Abolition* 16 (1995), pp. 311–30; and Klein, *Slavery and Colonial Rule in French West Africa*, pp. 126–40.

[11] Cohen, *Rulers of Empire*, pp. 57–83.

[12] Ibid. For a discussion of the so-called "Chautemps Affair" based on French archival records, see: James F. Searing, "Accommodation and Resistance: Chiefs, Muslim Leaders, and Politicians in Colonial Senegal, 1890–1934" (Ph.D. Diss.: Princeton Uni-

versity, 1985), pp. 199–208. For Senegalese accounts of this incident, which ended in the public mutilation of the body of the purported murderer of a French administrator in Thiès, see: Demba Mboup: 1A, 1B; and Yoro Diaw: 2B.

[13] Galaye Gueye: 2A; Soudou Laye: 2A.

[14] The quotations are from: Samba Diouf: 2A; and Gamou Wade: 1B, respectively. See also: Adiouma Ndiaye: 1B; Nar Diouf: 1A; Yoro Diaw: 1A; and Souleye Samba Ndiaye: 2A.

[15] Diouli Missine: 2A; Malal Gassala: 1A; Issap Niang: 1A; Amar Seck: 1A; and Biram Mbodji Tine: 1A.

[16] For detailed descriptions of the French colonial towns during specific years, see *Annuaire du Gouvernement Général de l'A.O.F.* (Paris: Emile Larose, 1914), pp. 664–80. On the sequence of construction in Louga, see: Abdoulaye Ndiaye: 3B, 4A. For other descriptions of the early evolution of French towns, see also: Nar Diouf: 1A; Abdoulaye Ndiaye (Z): 1A; Masserigne Soumare: 3B, 4B; and Demba Mboup: 1A, 4A.

[17] Estimates of the numbers of Senegalese inhabitants, as well as precise figures for European residents (itemized by occupation), are found in the yearly *Annuaire du Gouvernement Général de l'A.O.F.*

[18] Brunschwig, *Noirs et Blancs*, pp. 13–86. See also: Soudou Laye: 2A; Abdoulaye Ndiaye (Z): 1B.

[19] Abdoulaye Gassama: 1B; Demba Mboup: 13A; Abdoulaye Ndiaye (Z): 1A; Boubacar Gueye: 2A; and Abdoulaye Ndiaye: 3B. The first incidence of a Senegalese chief being acquitted for striking a European (when the evidence suggested that the Frenchman struck the first blow) only occurred after the outbreak of the First World War. See: Searing, "Accommodation and Resistance," pp. 448–51.

[20] For examples, see: Demba Mboup, Daour Gueye, Abdoulaye Ndiaye, and Masserigne Soumare.

[21] Amadou Yassin: 1A; Abdoulaye Ndiaye: 1A; and Boubacar Gueye: 2A.

[22] Abdoulaye Ndiaye: 4A.

[23] For population data in the communes, see, for example: "Statistique de la population de 1914," *ANOM*: 14 MI 1110; and the prewar *Annuaires*. On the civic status of the "*originaires*," see: Michael Crowder, *Senegal: A Study of French Assimilation Policy*, 2d rev. ed. (London: Methuen & Co., 1967), pp. 7–35; G. Wesley Johnson, Jr., *The Emergence of Black Politics in Senegal: The Struggle for Power in the Four Communes, 1900–1920* (Stanford: Stanford University Press, 1971), pp. 3–92; and François Zuccarelli, *La vie politique Sénégalaise (1789–1940)* (Paris: Le Centre des Hautes Etudes sur l'Afrique et l'Asie Modernes, 1987), pp. 9–58.

[24] For descriptions of the communes (as well as maps and photographs of each of these communities), see: *Annuaire du Gouvernement Général de l'A.O.F.*, 1913–1914, pp. 138–48 and *passim*. On the *métis* community in St. Louis, see: Johnson, *The Emergence of Black Politics in Senegal*, pp. 106–23. For prewar descriptions of Gorée, St. Louis, and Rufisque, see also, respectively: Coumba Niane: 1A; Doudou Ndao: 2A; Abdoulaye Diaw: 2A; Boubacar Gueye: 1B; and Ndematy Mbaye: 1A.

[25] On Senegalese communal society, see: Ousmane Diagne: 1A; Mandaw Mbaye: 1A; Momar Candji: 1B; Daour Gueye, 4A; and Demba Mboup: 7A. On the gradual decline of hereditary status as an arbiter of social prestige in the communes, see also: G. Wesley Johnson, Jr., "The Senegalese Urban Elite, 1900–1945," in *Africa and the West: Intellectual Responses to European Culture*, ed. Philip D. Curtin (Madison: University of Wisconsin Press, 1972), pp. 139–88.

[26] For references to occupations—including professional soldiers and sailors, some administrative functionaries, and medical assistants—that permitted their holders to dispense with farming, see: Abdoulaye Ndiaye: 1A, 1B; Jacques William: 1A; Abdoulaye Diaw: 3A; and Coumba Niane: 1A.

[27] See, for example, Ousmane Diagne: 1A, 2B; Ndematy Mbaye: 1B; Daour Gueye: 1A; and Mamadou Djigo: 1B.

[28] Ndematy Mbaye: 1B, 2A. On the reservations of Senegalese Muslims about French primary education, see also: Searing, "Accommodation and Resistance," pp. 364–400.

[29] On African police, see Brunschwig, *Noirs et Blancs*, pp. 135–49.

[30] Amar Seck: 1B; Mody Sow: 1B, 2A; Bandia Magaye (unrecorded interview); and Abdoulaye Ndiaye: 1B. On epidemics and the forcible removal of Senegalese in 1914 to the Medina, see also: Raymond F. Betts, "The Establishment of the Medina in Dakar, Senegal, 1914," *Africa* 41 (1971), pp. 143-52; Elikia M'Bokolo, "Peste et société urbaine à Dakar: l'épidémie de 1914," *Cahiers d'Etudes Africaines* 22 (1982), pp. 13–46; and M. J. Calvet and C. Ragon, *Aperçu des origines et du développement de Dakar* (Dakar: Ambassade de France, 1982), pp. 71–72.

[31] For examples, see: Coumba Niane: 1A; Abdoulaye Diaw: 3A; Thiecouta Diallo: 1B; Ousmane Diagne: 1A, 3A; Boubacar Gueye: 1B; Ndematy Mbaye: 1B; and Abdoulaye Ndiaye: 1A. See also: Johnson, "The Senegalese Urban Elite," pp. 139–87.

[32] Galaye Gueye: 1B; Abdoulaye Ndiaye, 4A; Niaki Gueye 1A, Jacques William: 2A; and Thiecouta Diallo: 2B.

[33] Abdoulaye Diaw: 2A.

[34] Abdoulaye Diaw: 2A. On the rare favorable characterizations of Senegalese and French relations in the communes, see: Momar Candji: 2B; and Abdoulaye Gassama: 1B.

[35] This charge was voiced by Boubacar Gueye: 1B.

[36] Demba Mboup: 13A. For virtually identical descriptions of similar incidents, see: Boubacar Gueye: 1B; Mbaye Khary Diagne, 4A; and Amar Seck, 4B.

[37] Boubacar Gueye: 1B. For a preliminary assessment of the civil court system in Dakar during this period, see: Richard Roberts, "Text and Testimony in the Tribunal de Première Instance, Dakar, during the Early Twentieth Century," *Journal of African History* 31 (1990), pp. 447–63.

[38] See: Abdoulaye Ndiaye: 3A; Mbaye Khary Diagne, 4A; and Mamadou Djigo: 1B.

[39] On this point, see especially Abdoulaye Diaw: 2A.

[40] The secondary literature on the French conquest is extensive, but very few works examine the Senegalese perspective. Those that treat the experience within a broader historical context, often by synthesizing archival and oral sources, include: Boubacar Barry, *Senegambia and the Atlantic Slave Trade* (Cambridge: Cambridge University Press, 1998); Mamadou Diouf, *Le Kajoor au XIX^c siècle: Pouvoir, ceddo et conquête coloniale* (Paris: Karthala, 1990); Martin A. Klein, *Islam and Imperialism in Senegal: Sine-Saloum, 1847–1914* (Edinburgh: Edinburgh University Press, 1968); David Robinson, *Chiefs and Clerics: Abdul Bokar Kan and Futa Toro, 1853–1891* (Oxford: Oxford University Press, 1975); and Christian Roche, *Histoire de la Casamance: Conquête et résistance, 1950–1920* (Paris: Editions Karthala, 1985).

[41] The quotations are from Galaye Gueye: 1B, and Amar Seck: 4B, respectively.

[42] Demba Mboup: 2B, 3A; 2B, 3A; 1B. The first two references are to the negotiations between Biram Ngone Latir and Louis Faidherbe during the late 1850s over the installation of a telegraph line through Kayor. The last reference is to the fate of Samba Yaya Faal, who, after his betrayal by the French, committed suicide in 1883.

[43] Abdou Karim Gaye, 5B. Samba Laobe Fal, the subject of the anecdote, was killed by a French officer in 1886.

[44] Galaye Gueye: 2A.

[45] See: Demba Mboup: 3A, 8A, 13A; Doudou Ndao: 1A; Galaye Gueye: 1B; and Yoro Diaw: 2B.

[46] Demba Mboup: 13A.

[47] Abdoulaye Ndiaye: 4A. As with the *griot*'s pun about "oui" and "non," this adage also conveys a double meaning. The left hand, which was used to clean the body after excretion, was regarded as defiled and was never employed in social situations. To be offered something with the left hand, therefore, affords a humorous insight into the Senegalese perception of the highly dubious character of all exchanges entered into with the French.

[48] The quotations are from: Abdou Karim Gaye, 5B; Galaye Gueye: 2A; and Abdou Karim Gaye, 5B, respectively.

[49] Ibrahima Thiam: 2A; Bara Seck: 3A. See also: Oumar Ba, *Amadou Bamba face aux autorités coloniales (1889–1927)* (Abbeville: F. Paillart, 1982), pp. 22–126.

[50] Ibrahima Thiam: 3A.

[51] Secondary sources that explore Senegalese views of Europeans are rare. For an interpretation of Senegalese reactions to the French that focuses on the intellectual response of the literary elite during the interwar period, see: William B. Cohen, "French Racism and Its African Impact," in *Double Impact: France and West Africa in the Age of Imperialism*, ed. G. Wesley Johnson, Jr. (Westport, CT, and London: Greenwood Press: 1985). For African images of Europeans (from East Africa, the Congo, and Soudan/Guinée) in oral literature, see Veronika Görög-Karady, *Noirs et Blancs: Leur image dans la literature orale Africaine: Etude anthologie* (Paris: SELAF, 1976).

[52] Yoro Diaw: 1A; Abdoulaye Ndiaye: 2B.

[53] Daba Dembele: 3A.

[54] Daba Dembele: 3A. Dembele's assessment reflects the ancient belief system of the Bambara. For other references to Europeans as "spirits," see: Kande Kamara, 1.1.7, cited in: Joe Harris Lunn, "Kande Kamara Speaks: An Oral History of the West African Experience in France 1914–18," in *Africa and the First World War*, ed. Melvin Page (London: Macmillan, 1987), p. 31.

[55] Daba Dembele: 3A.

[56] Daba Dembele: 3A.

[57] Soudou Laye: 2A.

[58] The quotations are from: Mamadou Djigo: 1B; Doudou Ndao: 1A; and Aliou Dioma: 1B, respectively.

[59] Boubacar Gueye: 1B. For similar characterizations, see: Demba Mboup: 3A; and Amar Seck, 4B.

[60] For example, see: Demba Mboup: 10A; Momar Candji: 2B.

[61] Respondents quoted include: Daba Dembele: 3A; Kande Kamara: 1,1; Daba Dembele: 3A; Mamadou Djigo: 1B; Boubacar Gueye: 2A; Nar Diouf: 2A; Galaye Gueye: 2A; Aliou Dioma: 1B; Demba Mboup: 3A; Doudou Ndao: 1A; Nar Diouf: 2A; Adiouma Ndiaye: 1A; Galaye Gueye: 1B and 2A; Pierre Diaw: 2A; and Malal Gassala: 2B.

[62] Respondents quoted include: Soudou Laye: 2A; Pierre Diaw: 2A; Galaye Gueye: 2A; Abdoulaye Ndiaye: 4A; Demba Mboup: 1A and 1B; Abdoulaye Ndiaye: 4A; Galaye Gueye: 1B; Galaye Gueye: 1B and 2A; Abdoulaye Ndiaye: 4A; Amar Seck: 4B; Demba Mboup: 3A; Boubacar Gueye: 1B; and Ousmane Diagne: 4A.

[63] Respondents quoted include: Daba Dembele: 3A; Daour Gueye: 1A; Mbaye Khary Diagne: 4A; Ibrahima Thiam: 2B; Pierre Diaw: 2A; Amar Seck: 4B; Ibrahima Thiam: 2B; Amar Seck: 4B; and Amar Seck: 4B.

[64] Respondents quoted include: Pierre Diaw: 2A; Amar Seck: 4B; Ibrahima Thiam: 3A; Boubacar Gueye: 1B and 2A; Soudou Laye: 2A; Ousmane Diagne: 2B; Demba Mboup: 3A; Amar Seck: 4B; Boubacar Gueye: 2A; Adiouma Ndiaye: 1A; Gamou Wade: 1B; Amar Seck: 4B; Pierre Diaw: 2A; Soudou Laye: 2A; and Mamadou Djigo: 1B.

[65] Respondents quoted include: Nar Diouf: 2A; Adiouma Ndiaye: 1B; Abdoulaye Ndiaye (Z): 1B; Daba Dembele: 3A; Mamadou Djigo: 1B; Boubacar Gueye: 2A; Abdoulaye Ndiaye (Z): 1A; Sera Ndiaye: 1A and 4A; Daba Dembele: 1A; and Adiouma Ndiaye: 1B.

[66] These examples are based on Wolof interpretations of dreams, but they are valid for other Senegambian ethnic groups, including the Bambara and the Serahuli. See: Demba Mboup: 5B, 8B, 9A, 9B, and 10A. For other references to the prophetic interpretation of dreams (among the Lebu and Serahuli, respectively), see: Momar Cisse: 1B; and Masserigne Soumare: 3B. For dream interpretation among West African Muslims, see also: Lamin Sanneh, *The Crown and the Turban: Muslims and West African Pluralism* (Boulder, CO: Westview Press, 1997), pp. 39–42

2

THE TAX IN BLOOD:
MILITARY RECRUITMENT IN
RURAL SENEGAL,
1914–1917

With the outbreak of the First World War in Europe, the imperatives of the French colonial regime shifted dramatically. During the previous quarter century, the French were primarily concerned with the consolidation of their political authority and the development of an export economy in the colonies. After 1914, priority was given to raising thousands of African recruits to augment the military strength of the beleaguered metropole. In Senegal as elsewhere in French West Africa, this novel demand carried profound repercussions. In the rural areas of the colony—the "Protectorate"—the ever-increasing demands for men were universally regarded, at least prior to 1918, as the most onerous burden yet imposed by the colonial authorities, and they elicited a gamut of responses ranging from reluctant compliance to armed resistance. Although Senegalese reactions to enforced recruitment varied considerably depending on individual circumstances and locale, almost everywhere they encompassed the most dire forebodings for those who were compelled to enter the army and the outrage of others at the magnitude of the human sacrifice they were required to make. Nor were these feelings ill founded. Indeed, as comparisons between wartime recruitment levels and the volume of the eighteenth-century trans-Atlantic slave trade make clear, the French quest for soldiers soon came to represent the most intense expropriation of manpower for service overseas in the history of Senegambia.

THE ADMINISTRATION OF RECRUITMENT
IN THE PROTECTORATE, 1914–1917

Phases

With the onset of hostilities in Europe, the expanded recruitment of West Africans set in motion two years earlier by the government's Decree of 7 February 1912 gradually began to increase.[1] In rural Senegal as elsewhere in the French Federation, the raising of colonial levies between 1914 and 1917 fell into three distinct phases, which corresponded to exigencies of the military situation in France as well as to domestic administrative concerns in the colonies. In August 1914, the government's initial effort to augment existing forces by creating a reserve of 20,000 additional soldiers remained incomplete: only 16,000 had been enrolled in 1912 and 1913, and of these only about 2,000 came from Senegal.[2] At the initiative of Governor General William Ponty, however, recruitment was gradually stepped up throughout West Africa. In the Senegalese Protectorate, a series of three "exceptional" drives, which were sanctioned by the Ministry of Colonies and the Ministry of War, succeeded in raising by October 1915 an additional 3,350 men for service overseas.[3]

After the staggering losses suffered by the army during the first 15 months of the war—over 50 percent of all French casualties suffered during the war occurred during this period—the metropolitan government, recognizing that the struggle would be both bloody and prolonged, and deeply concerned about the shortage of French "effectives," undertook to raise in the colonies a massive additional levy of soldiers.[4] Though receiving only the reluctant endorsement of the new Governor General Marie-François Clozel, and against the vigorous opposition of the Lieutenant Governor of Senegal Raphael Antonetti, the government, by Decrees of 9 and 14 October, set new provisions for implementing the policy in West Africa.[5] In the great recruitment drive that was conducted between October 1915 and April 1916, over 7,500 men were enrolled in rural Senegal.[6] Although the French encountered little effective opposition in the colony, the unprecedented scale of these demands elsewhere in the Federation provoked widespread and protracted revolts that were suppressed only with difficulty by a hard-pressed colonial administration.[7]

In the wake of these insurrections, and despite the gravity of the military situation on the western front, the government acceded to the advice of the governor general and substantially reduced the scale of African recruitment. During the next year and a half (November 1916 to April 1917), only one "exceptional" drive was authorized in the Federation. As a result, the Senegalese contingent, which continued to be supplemented by its "ordinary" quota of recruits, nevertheless fell in numbers during

Table 2.1   Recruitment in Rural Senegal, August 1914–November 1917

Phase		Totals
Phase I: August 1914–October 1915		
August–October 1914		1,350
January–May 1915		1,050
May–October 1915		800
"Volunteers"		150
	Total:	3,350
Phase II: October 1915–April 1916		
October 1915–April 1916		7,506
Phase III: April 1916–November 1917		
April–November 1916		300
November 1916–April 1917		1,783
May–November 1917		400
	Total:	2,483
Total Recruitment:		
August 1914–November 1917		13,339

this period, like those in the rest of West Africa, to a total of less than 2,500 men.[8] Amid a background of ongoing unrest in the colonies provoked by these exactions (even though diminished) and the discrediting of the foremost advocate of the policy, General Charles Mangin, in the aftermath of the debacle at the Chemin des Dames, the fall of Alexandre Ribot's government in September led to a new, albeit brief, consensus about the futility of pursuing further recruitment.[9] Enjoying the enthusiastic support of the commercial lobby (which had long opposed recruitment because of its adverse effects on the colonial economies), the recently appointed governor general, Joost Van Vollenhoven, argued that A.O.F. could best contribute to the national defense through the export of its material resources rather than its men.[10] Denouncing the previous policy in uncompromising terms—calling it a "utopian" idea that had assumed the form of a "man hunt" since the beginning of the war and, if pursued further, "would set the country aflame" and thereby wreak havoc on France's long-term colonization efforts—Van Vollenhoven managed to obtain a temporary suspension of compulsory recruitment in October 1917.[11] Thus, during the first three years of the war and before the policy slipped into abeyance, rural Senegal provided slightly over 13,000 men for the defense of *la patrie* (see Table 2.1).[12]

French Recruitment Methods

The means by which these men were raised reflected the hierarchical nature of the colonial administration in West Africa as well as the degree of control the French exerted over particular areas of rural Senegal. After the views of the major *responsibles* were taken into account, African recruitment levels were finally determined in Paris by the Ministries of Colonies and War and then passed down the Federation's administrative ladder to the governor general in Dakar, who, in turn, apportioned the numbers required among specific colonies. In Senegal, the lieutenant governor again subdivided the quota expected of the colony among the *commandants* in each of the Protectorate's thirteen *cercles*.

The weight of this burden was distributed unevenly from the outset. It coincided with the extent of the French presence in the colony, and hence with their potential capacity to apply coercion, in specific regions. In the four densely populated *cercles* of central Senegal—which were also most integrated into the French export economy, were serviced by a comparatively extensive rail and communications infrastructure, contained the largest number of French officials, and were administered as a separate military district—recruitment levies (reckoned as a percentage of the total population) were heaviest.[13] In comparison to the more peripheral and less densely inhabited areas of the colony—which included the *cercles* along the Fleuve in the north, the Casamance in the south, and those in sparsely populated eastern Senegal—the quotas demanded in central Senegal between 1914 and 1917 were nearly twice as high as they were for the rest of the Protectorate (see Table 2.2).[14]

Within the *cercles*, the *commandants* again apportioned the local recruitment quotas expected of them among the respective provincial and cantonal chiefs (and sometimes other notables) under their jurisdiction. These men, in turn, bore ultimate responsibility for presenting the requisite number of bodies before the French Recruiting Commissions, which determined whether the prospective soldiers were "apt" or "inapt" for service. Normally composed of a *commandant*, a military officer, and a French doctor (who were often in short supply and frequently incompetent), as well as several assistants and interpreters, these so-called "mobile" commissions (thirteen of which were in operation by the end of the war) usually administered the most cursory types of physical examinations. Eyesight was reckoned by the ability to distinguish fingers at 10 meters, while motor coordination was scrutinized by watching the young men leap in the air. Nevertheless, despite a minimum weight requirement

Table 2.2 Distribution of Recruitment by *Cercle* in Rural Senegal, 1914–1917

Central Senegal: "District for the Defense of the Fortress of Dakar"

Cercle	Population	Numbers Recruited	Percentage of Population
Sine-Saloum	189,053	3,179	1.68
Tivaouane	109,920	1,339	1.22
Diourbel	159,922	1,438	0.90
Thiès	100,434	765	0.76
Banlieue des Quatre Communes	35,807[a]	992	2.77
Total	595,136	7,713	1.30

Northern, Eastern, and Southern Senegal:
"Military and Territorial Subdivision of Senegal"

Cercle	Population	Numbers Recruited	Percentage of Population
Niani Ouli	47,086[b]	282	0.84
Haute Gambie		114	
Matam	65,665	550	0.83
Louga	94,520	757	0.80
Podor	74,263	500	0.67
Bakel	36,515	240	0.66
Dagana	41,748	260	0.62
Saldé	36,258	223	0.62
Casamance	196,406	1,050	0.53
Total	592,461	3,976	0.67
Origin Unrecorded		1,650	
Total	1,187,597	13,339	1.12

[a] Recruits from the Banlieue des Quatre Communes have been included within the District for the Defense of the Fortress of Dakar because, with the exception of those from St. Louis, they fell within its jurisdiction.

[b] Population figures for Niani Ouli and Haute Gambie represent the combined total for the two *cercles*. They were not listed separately in the 1921 census owing to their merger in the new *cercle* of Tamba-Counda.

Sources: For recruitment: *ANS:* Affaires militaires: 4 D 65; 4 D 55; 4 D 54; 4 D 49; 4 D 68; 4 D 73; and 2 D 69. Population figures for the *cercles* are based on the 1921 census, which was the most comprehensive and reasonably accurate one to date. See *Annuaire du Governement Général de l'Afrique Occidentale française, 1922* (Paris: Emile Larose Libraire, 1922), pp. 65–66, 368–81.

of only 46 kilos (101 pounds), and accepting those with a wide range of physical infirmities—including mutilated or missing fingers (provided their absence did not make it "impossible" for the prospective recruits to fire a rifle)—only about 25 to 30 percent of the Senegalese presented were usually deemed physically fit for military service.[15] As a result, the chiefs were normally required to bring at least three times the number of men ultimately expected of them for inspection by the commissions.[16]

Aside from dispensing enlistment bounties to those inducted and offering "material benefits" (officially reckoned at 15 to 25 francs per head after 1915) to chiefs and other African "agents" who demonstrated exemplary "zeal" in the execution of their duties, the French administrators remained, at least in theory, uninvolved in the actual recruitment process, which was to be conducted strictly in accordance with "local custom."[17] In practice, of course, at least insofar as the *commandants* were responsible for enforcing the policy, this formula remained an official fiction from the beginning. The *commandants* coerced recalcitrant chiefs with fines and imprisonment of up to 1,000 francs and five years and sanctioned repressive countermeasures against all those who were reluctant or unwilling to comply with their demands.[18] What this French administrative dictum did imply, however, was a formal indifference to the methods employed to raise men and a willingness to turn a blind eye to the most flagrant types of abuse. Indeed, far from remaining unaware of what was occurring beyond the gates of their compounds, most *commandants*, no less than their superiors in St. Louis and Dakar, condoned many of the more unsavory practices that took place there.[19] As their reports—which chronicle incidents of self-mutilation, mass flight, and occasional armed resistance—make abundantly clear, they were quite conscious of the broader impact that the recruitment policy had on the Senegalese.[20]

Though some French officials objected to the deleterious effects of the recruitment policy on the colony, or to the fashion in which it was sometimes conducted—which was all too reminiscent of the "slave trade"—most continued to blow with the prevailing political wind and, at least prior to the ascendency of Van Vollenhoven, were unwilling to condemn it unequivocally.[21] Moreover, irrespective of any personal reservations that existed among the French officials, the colonial administration continued throughout the war to comply with whatever demands were made of it by the metropole.[22] Indeed, some displayed remarkable callousness in attempting to satisfy the dictates from above; as one *commandant* assured the lieutenant governor in 1916, continued recruitment was certainly possible among the "savages" in the Casamance provided he was furnished with the additional troops he had requested to implement it.[23]

Yet despite being broadly aware of the consequences of the policy, and occasionally differing about the advisability of continuing it, the French re-

mained largely ignorant about how individual Africans perceived the demands
that were placed on them and how they chose to cope with their situation.
This too is reflected in the French reports, which, though providing an administrative overview of the implementation of the recruitment policy, shed
little light on the lived reality of the experience for the Senegalese. Exactly
how young men came to be selected for military service within their villages, and the tragic dimensions such a fate often assumed in their minds as
well as those of their loved ones, have long remained obscure because the
French records are understandably moot on the subject. This omission can
be rectified by considering the consequences of the wartime recruitment policy
as viewed through African eyes.

THE SENEGALESE REACTION

Senegalese Recruitment Methods

The methods used by the French to impose the new "tax in blood," as
well as the range of African responses to it, vividly illuminate the impact of
the wartime recruitment drives on the Senegalese. Aside from a mere handful of often reluctant "volunteers," the vast majority of Africans recruited
between 1914 and 1917 had "no choice" in the matter of their induction.[24]
Young men were raised by the colonial authorities by a variety of means that
reflected the largely improvised nature of the recruitment system. On occasion in areas near army garrisons, French officers, accompanied by military
escorts, enlisted Africans directly.[25] Such instances were, however, extremely
rare. Much more commonly, the colonial administration relied, as it did when
exacting other demands, on an array of African intermediaries to impose its
will. As a result, most Senegalese were recruited in one of three other ways:
through their village chief's compliance with the dictates of their *chef de
canton*; through the admonitions of their marabouts; or by outright capture,
through armed raids by either the retainers of the cantonal chiefs or by other
African recruiting "agents" working directly for the French.[26]

In the villages, the local chiefs filled the quotas expected of them by a
variety of means. "Lotteries" were sometimes held in the early days of recruitment, with the unlucky winners being reluctantly sacrificed to satisfy
the obligations of the collective unit.[27] Elsewhere, and usually when only a
few recruits were as yet demanded from a village, domestic slaves, the "very
poor," or alternatively one of the chief's sons might be sent.[28] But as the
wartime calls for men grew, other expedients were devised. Frequently, the
ultimate burden of decision was shifted from the village chiefs to the heads
of compounds, who were each periodically required to designate "one son
per family" to present before the Recruiting Commissions.[29] Finally, but only
restrictedly and usually belatedly, "lists" of all those of "the age to enter the

army" in the village were compiled for use by the *chefs de canton* to determine who was eligible to present to the French.[30]

Among the Mourides, whose disciples were often beyond the pale of chiefly
authority and who, at least initially, were deemed of doubtful military utility
by the French because of their sullen spiritual detachment, a similar but nevertheless distinctive system was employed. Complying with the instructions
of Amadu Bamba (who, like the Tidjaniya leader Malik Sy, eventually bowed
to French pressure in 1915 and agreed to sanction recruitment), marabouts
fulfilled the function of the *chefs de canton*.[31] These men, including Ibra
Fall, a former *ceddo* convert and one of Bamba's most prominent followers,
in turn provided recruits in the designated numbers from among their *Talibe*.[32]

Finally, in areas where recruitment proved exceptionally difficult, especially on the fringes of colonial authority (i.e., along the Senegal, in the
Casamance, and particularly along the northern border of the Gambia in eastern Saloum and Niani Ouli) "surprise" raids equated with "man hunts" were
conducted by auxiliaries of the French in an effort to capture young men.[33]
Sometimes composed of the retainers of the *chefs de canton* (*dag* in Wolof)
or, alternatively, of other locally recruited "agents" (who were usually
"Malinke" and employed in areas where chiefly authority was, as yet, un-
consolidated), these men, or more often those they served in the former case,
normally received a "gift" of up to 25 francs for each "recruit" they caught.[34]
The unfortunates they seized were frequently bound, linked with "ropes around
their necks," and marched in coffles to points of assembly for presentation to
the French Recruiting Commissions.[35]

Aside from those who were physically captured, compliance with the
French demands was exacted through fear of retribution. Recalcitrant village
chiefs who obstructed or were remiss in executing the policy were imprisoned throughout Senegal.[36] Moreover, in a measure designed to have sobering effects on prospective recruits, the fathers, parents, or other relatives of
potential recruits were sometimes seized as hostages if they sought to evade
enlistment. As one *tirailleur* from Sine-Saloum, Biram Mbodji Tine, recalled:

> Many of the young men fled from the village [when the *chef de canton*
> came to take soldiers]. [But] they used to arrest their fathers [if] they [did
> not] come back. [And] often their mothers used to say to their sons [when
> they returned from the countryside for food]: "You know that your name
> has been written [down by the *chef de canton*] and [yet] you ran away.
> And now your father has been arrested and he will be taken [to] prison. So
> go and enter the army." And often they used to go and enter the army [so
> that] their fathers [would be] released.[37]

In more remote areas of the colony, where even these deterrents occasionally proved ineffective, the French resorted to still harsher methods.

There reprisals were not restricted to individuals but were also directed against collectives. Crops and livestock were seized or destroyed, homes were indiscriminately put to the torch, and villagers—often irrespective of whether they were innocent bystanders, parents taken as hostages, or armed resisters—were killed or executed by soldiers.[38]

The omnipresent threat of such ruthless countermeasures, if not actual recourse to them, was an absolute prerequisite for commandeering soldiers because of the dread the new recruitment policy evoked in the minds of the Senegalese. None of the other burdens imposed by the colonial regime—not the head tax, corvée labor, nor the injustice of the *indigénat*—bore so heavily on the populace as did the prospect of service overseas. The collective anguish it prompted was succinctly summarized by the lament of one mother to a French officer: "You have already taken all that I have, and now you are taking my only son!"[39]

Terror of enlistment was prompted by the anticipated fate of the soldiers. Some recruits, deriving consolation from the encouragement of their fathers or from marabouts, hoped they might survive the war and one day see their homeland again.[40] Most Senegalese, however, felt that the soldiers "would never return" and that induction into the army amounted to a sentence of "certain death."[41] Indeed, when young men departed from their villages, they were sometimes considered as "already dead," and the anxiety of those who remained was so great that mothers suffered miscarriages, children were given the names of those who would never be seen again, people spoke of their desire "to kill the *Tubabs*," and "in every district you heard people crying."[42]

The Senegalese Response

Senegalese reactions to the exactions imposed on them in the face of such dire premonitions varied. A handful, motivated either by the French bounties or other personal considerations, willingly enlisted.[43] Others, and especially those who were "ordered" by their Mouride marabouts to enter the army, accepted their fate without opposition, which was interpreted as the "will of Allah."[44] After receiving the benediction of Amadu Bamba—with his compelling admonition to: "Go! . . . and come back!"—they complied with differing degrees of enthusiasm to the temporal demands made on them by their marabouts and the French.[45] The overwhelming majority of those who acceded to the wishes of the colonial authorities, however, did so only with greatest reluctance and the most profound misgivings. Knowing themselves to be powerless to "resist the *Tubabs*" and not "dar[ing] to refuse" their commands, most of the Senegalese rural collectives responded to the harsh realities they confronted by grudgingly sacrificing those deemed most expendable.[46]

Although ascribed social status within the community came into play
as a factor in their decisions because both domestic slaves and "strangers" were sometimes offered as substitutes, this alone does not appear to
have been the decisive determinant: from the war's outset recruits were
also drawn from among the free peasantry, the endogamous casts, and the
aristocracy as well.[47] Perhaps a better gauge of the Senegalese response
is offered by the criterion "absence of parents" at the time of the recruit's
induction. Well over half of all the soldiers interviewed were missing either
one or both of their parents when they were compelled to enter the army.[48]
Although this may reflect natural demographic diminution, the trend is
further exemplified by the relative status within their respective families
of those who were sent.[49] Among the wealthy, the sons of second, third,
or fourth wives were selected in preference to those of the first wife.[50]
Finally, among those soldiers whose families were composed of a single
father and mother, eldest sons were usually protected whenever possible.
If the family had two or more sons of military age, in virtually all instances a younger brother was sacrificed to preserve the presence of the
eldest at home.[51] Recalling the grim logic behind such astonishingly painful decisions, Sera Ndiaye, a Wolof veteran, explained how he came to
be chosen:

> In each family they only took one young man, never two. And my father
> decided that I should go and enter the army instead of my elder brother.
> Because, he told me: "If I die, your elder brother could care for the family,
> but you are too young for that." That's why he sent me into the army. I was
> not happy to go, [but] because I was very close to my father . . . I felt
> obliged to.[52]

Those who were selected to go were prepared by their families for the
ordeal that awaited them as best they could. Depending on their religious
predilections, prayers were delivered in their behalf or, alternatively, cer-
emonial baths and other ritual observances were performed in the hope
of preserving their lives.[53] Moreover, almost without exception, all were
presented with protective charms to ward off the coming dangers they
would face overseas.[54]

Though very few were pleased about their fate—"[it is] never good for
someone to tell you to 'come and die,'" as Yoro Diaw tersely put it—most
recruits reluctantly complied with the decisions of their families and collectives.[55] This occurred not only because of their youth, their sense of obedience and devotion to their elders, and their concerns about French reprisals
against them, but also for a series of other, less tangible reasons. Male codes
of honor—exemplified by the Wolof concept of *jom*—and the explicit fear
that failure to perform the duties expected of other men would reduce them

to the status of "women" motivated some.[56] For others, especially those who were accompanied into the army by peers from their villages, the personal disgrace entailed in flight or, even worse, the ridicule that their families might be subjected to if they did so, made such a course of action unthinkable.[57] Under such circumstance, death, which many were convinced awaited them, was literally deemed preferable to dishonor. Indeed, the widow of one soldier, Aminata Ngom, lamented, "[my husband] died because he didn't want to run away."[58]

Nevertheless, in the face of such daunting sacrifices, not all Senegalese complied with the French requisitions of young men. Their resistance to the recruitment policy assumed two forms: avoidance of the French demands or, when this proved impossible, defiance of them. Avoidance of the draft might be accomplished by one of several means. For the wealthy or well connected, it was sometimes possible to obtain exemption from the army through the patronage of a French employer, by bribing a *chef de canton*, securing a replacement, or through the lucky expedient of having an obliging kinsman act as interpreter when the recruits were being selected.[59] A second possibility was to fail the French medical examination and thus be designated unfit. The use of herbal concoctions designed to create the illusion of illness—*paftan* leaves crushed into powder were used to discolor eyes, while *palme de cajou* combined with grain created swollen sores when applied to the face and feet— was widespread throughout Senegal, and resort to such measures sometimes fooled the French doctors.[60]

By far, however, the most common way of attempting to avoid enlistment was through flight. Indeed, it is probably true that for every soldier recruited in rural Senegal between 1914 and 1917, another potential inductee fled the colony to seek refuge in foreign territories.[61] Recourse to this option appears to have been determined to a major extent by the relative proximity of an individual to sanctuary. In the more densely populated areas of central Senegal, where recruitment levies were heaviest, this course of action was more difficult to accomplish. There were few nearby havens and the countryside was continually combed by chiefly retainers searching for fugitives.[62] Moreover, flight farther afield often entailed separation from kinsmen as well as enhanced risk of capture.[63] In the more sparsely inhabited regions of the Fleuve and eastern Senegal, flight from the village to the comparative safety of the countryside was more common. There, potential recruits temporarily sought refuge in the "bush" until the Recruitment Commissions had exacted their tolls or, alternatively, crossed over into Mauritania, where the French exercised but scant control.[64] Finally, in those areas such as Saloum, Niani-Ouli, and the Casamance, which bordered on either British Gambia or Portuguese Guinea where recruits were not being levied, avoidance assumed the dimensions of a major exodus. Describing the situation near Sedhiou in the Casamance, Coumba Kebe remembered:

Many, many young men used to run away [whenever the recruiting "agents" were seen near the village]. [And] when they ran, they used to go to a [Mandinka] village called Wai—it was [in Guinea-Bissau]. And whenever you crossed the frontier, no one was allowed to touch you. . . . And on the road to this village, there was a bridge. And eventually, the bridge broke down because of the [number] of men that were crossing over it.[65]

Indeed, in these outlying districts, not just potential recruits but sometimes entire families fled to seek sanctuary with kinsmen beyond the range of French authority.[66]

More active types of resistance to the French policy took three forms. In more remote areas of the colony, the French recruiters were sometimes opposed by force of arms. In isolated parts of the countryside, where fugitives hid, small groups of soldiers were occasionally ambushed by those they sought to apprehend.[67] Elsewhere, but especially in the Casamance, defiance periodically assumed the dimensions of collective resistance. Such incidents, however, were rare, and in the latter case they were restricted to the village level and quickly suppressed by the army. Usually born of spontaneous fury against the demands placed on them for young men, these outbreaks also exhibited a certain naiveté about the coercive capacity of the French. Souan Gor Diatta recalled the fighting outside his village:

When the *Tubabs* first came [to recruit soldiers], there was resistance. But the people of the village only had very old rifles—you had to put powder in them and a ball—"muskets." But they took their muskets to fight with the *Tubabs*. But when they began to fight—when [the soldiers opened fire and] they saw that the *Tubabs* had very modern rifles—they decided to run away. But some of them were killed before they ran.[68]

An alternative means of defiance was desertion from the army soon after induction. Because of fears about the consequences of capture—"[they would] beat you so severely that you would never try to escape again"[69]—or reprisals against their parents even if they eluded being apprehended, this course of action was only taken with the direst misgivings.[70] Nevertheless, desertion occurred comparatively frequently among the Senegalese, and it is significant to note that it was most common among Fulbe pastoralists, whose families were the least susceptible to administrative retaliation.[71] Finally, among those recruits who had abandoned all hope, a last desperate gesture of defiance against the fate that had befallen them was suicide. Though few took their own lives, men did kill themselves in the training camps, and others plunged into the sea from the decks of their transport ships as they lost sight of their homeland on their way to France.[72]

LA CHASSE À L'HOMME

As this catalogue of flight, desertion, and occasional armed resistance makes abundantly clear, the Senegalese universally regarded compulsory military service as the most oppressive demand yet imposed by the colonial authorities. In this respect, far from representing a return (under French aegis) to the martial ethos of the precolonial past (as prewar advocates of the recruitment policy asserted), for most Senegalese the reverse was true. Metropolitan claims about the ostensible benefits arising from *la paix française* notwithstanding, the French wartime demands led to an unprecedented militarization of Senegalese society.

Although precise figures on the size of precolonial Senegambian armies are lacking, the main Senegambian states could field between 1,000 and 5,000 mounted men in emergencies.[73] These armies, which usually conducted comparatively brief campaigns and were never mobilized simultaneously, were probably collectively smaller than the nearly 29,000 Senegalese soldiers mobilized by the French army during the war for terms of up to six years. Hence, by the end of the First World War, there were more Senegalese continuously under arms than ever before. It is also indisputable that the French indiscriminately enlisted men from large sections of the population—*griots*, most domestic slaves, and much of the free peasantry—who had never previously been called on to participate in Senegambian conflicts.[74]

Aside from the erroneous (but militarily expedient) assumptions underlying the policy, which stressed the "warlike" character of the African "races" in Senegal, its implementation graphically exemplifies the character of the French regime during the first quarter century of colonial rule. The distribution of the local recruitment burden in Senegal was uneven and inequitable from the beginning. It was heaviest in the more densely populated *cercles* of central Senegal, where about half of the colony's inhabitants provided nearly two-thirds of all pre-1918 recruits.[75] This occurred because Senegal's "peanut basin" was more thoroughly integrated into the colonial administrative, economic, and communications network than the outlying districts of the Protectorate. Though originally intended to facilitate the export of groundnuts, this infrastructure was easily converted to accommodate the expatriation of soldiers.[76] Moreover, these *cercles* also roughly corresponded to those areas where the precolonial social hierarchies among the Wolof and Serer were most stratified and the ancient aristocracy (or their Mouride successors) continued to exercise the greatest sway.

The methods employed by the French to raise recruits, though frequently improvised, were notable for their brutality. Lacking the bureaucratic sophistication that was a prerequisite for raising large conscript armies in Europe, they fell back on a series of other expedients. These frequently accorded with long-standing African methods of appropriating manpower, but the key to the system was based on the omnipresent threat of French reprisals. In areas where reluctant compliance was the norm, the threat of sanctions against anyone obstructing the policy—ranging from *chefs de canton* to the recruits themselves—generally proved effective. But where noncompliance or active resistance was more common, especially on the fringes of colonial authority, French auxiliaries resorted to methods that were virtually indistinguishable from the slave raids of previous generations. In these areas, the practices used to garner soldiers—including surprise raids on villages, the forcible seizure of young men, marching them bound in coffles to the Recruiting Commissions, the payment of premiums to those responsible for their capture, or, alternatively, the misappropriation of enlistment bounties—recalled all too vividly the recently outlawed "trade in human flesh."[77]

Although recruitment methods varied considerably in Senegal, the analogy with the slave trade is far from apocryphal: in fact, in some respects recruitment was worse. In terms of scale, the magnitude of French wartime recruitment in Senegal was much larger than the European slave trade had ever been. During the first three years of the war, possibly more rural Senegalese were exported to fight overseas than during the peak decade of the eighteenth-century trade by all British, French, Portuguese, and Dutch carriers combined (see Table 2.3). Furthermore, if the wartime levy for the entire colony is taken into account (see Chapter 3), the disparity between the scale of wartime recruitment and the slave trade is even more pronounced. Indeed, the numbers of those sent abroad between 1914 and 1918—which amounted to some 29,000 men—probably exceeded all the slaves shipped in French holds from Senegambia to the New World during the entire eighteenth century.[78] Finally, in central Senegal, where rural recruitment was most intensive, the average annual export of soldiers during the war may have been ten times as great as that for slaves during the eighteenth century (see Table 2.4).[79]

Although the Senegalese were unaware of the historical dimensions of the demands placed on them, references to the slave trade were common. Most equated the advent of French rule with the gradual abolition of the slave trade and domestic servitude. Even among those who recounted the forcible seizure of recruits, a distinction was drawn between these practices and those of earlier times because, as Daba Dembele emphasized, "the French didn't sell anybody."[80] Yet for those who had suffered from slave raids in the past as well as the more recent exactions of the French, the parallel between the two experiences appeared much closer. There was, however, one significant difference: previously local villagers had been able to "resist" the attacks of those who sought to capture them; they were "powerless" to do so against the French and their agents.[81]

This view is compelling. In method and scale, if not necessarily in the minds of most of its victims, the recruitment policy provokes sobering paral-

Table 2.3 Scale of French Military Recruitment Compared to the Trans-Atlantic Slave Trade: Senegalese/Senegambians Exported Overseas

---

Senegambian Slaves Exported, 1700–1800:
Range of Adjusted Decadal Estimates[a]

1700–1710	6,133 – 7,410
1711–1720[b]	10,300–12,086
1721–1730[b]	7,500–17,510
1731–1740[b]	8,733–19,070
1741–1750	8,333–11,666
1751–1760	7,500–10,033
1761–1770	4,700 – 9,196
1771–1780	4,033 – 8,133
1781–1790	5,080 – 7,366
1791–1800	2,066 – 6,107

Rural Senegalese Recruited

1914–1917	13,339

Senegalese Recruited

1914–1918	28,902

[a] Decadal estimates are based on Curtin's calculation that two-thirds of the slaves exported from Senegambia during the 18th century came from east of the headwaters of the Senegal and Gambia rivers. They have been reduced by two-thirds to convey a sense of the comparative scales of the slave trade and recruitment. For the purposes of comparison, I have accepted Curtin's guess, based on the 1960 census, that the population of Senegambia in the 18th century was about 1,500,000 and assumed that the populations during the two periods were roughly equivalent to that in the 1921 census (1,200,000).

[b] Richardson's figures for these decades represent a considerable upward revision of Curtin's estimates for the scale of the British (though not the French) trade in Senegambia. However, Richardson cautions that his findings about English exports, which otherwise generally accord with Curtin's for the period 1741–1800, may "exaggerate the level of the British trade with Senegambia in the early part of the century."

Sources: Curtin 1975, 1: 187; Lovejoy 1983; and Richardson 1989, Table 7. For recruitment sources, see Tables 2.2 and 3.1.

---

lels with the trans-Atlantic slave trade. Although obvious distinctions existed between the two systems, we should note several similarities. Both systems expropriated African labor for use overseas. In the case of slaves, this was for the duration of their natural lives instead of from three to six years (assuming the soldiers survived). But the mortality rates of soldiers during their period of service (between 20 and 25 percent of those sent abroad)

Table 2.4 Scale of French Military Recruitment Compared to the Trans-Atlantic Slave Trade, 1700–1800: Central Senegal[a]

Senegambian Slaves Exported: Estimates by State

	Years	Annual Averages
Kayor, Baol, Sinn		
	1700–1750	300–400
	1760–1790	200–300
Kayor, Baol		
	1700–1800	200–300[b]
Walo, Kayor, Baol, Sinn, Saloum		
	1700–1800	344[c]

Senegalese Recruited from the *Cercles* of Thiès, Tivaouane, Diourbel, and Sine-Saloum

	1914–1918	3,006

[a] Due to recent emigration into the "peanut basin" of Central Senegal, the population of the region was probably higher in the early 20th century than it was in the 18th, though not substantially so.

[b] Searing subdivides his estimates for the 18th century between the first and second half. Becker and Martin offer this as a minimum estimate that should be supplemented by the (unspecified) number of slaves diverted by interlopers through Portugal to British traders along the Gambia.

[c] This is my estimate rather than Curtin's; it is derived from his total for the volume of 18th century slave exports from Senegambia and his sampling of the ethnic origins and states from which they came. The figure is within the range of estimates offered for central Senegambia by Searing and Becker and Martin.

Sources: Searing 1993, pp. 31–33; Becker and Martin 1975, pp. 278–83; Curtin 1975, 1: 164, 184–85, 188.

were likely considerably higher than that of slaves during comparable periods. The geographic origins and proportion of recruits exported via Senegalese ports also bear a striking similarity to the slave trade. While approximately two-thirds of the slaves exported from Senegambia during the eighteenth century came from east of the headwaters of the Senegal and Gambia Rivers, not less than 65 percent and perhaps as many as 75 percent of all soldiers embarking from Dakar or St. Louis were recruited in southern Mauritania or Haut-Sénégal et Niger.[82] Furthermore, although the slave trade usually placed a premium on the export of able-bodied men (often in a ratio of two-to-one compared with women, if not higher in Senegambia), the recruitment policy did so exclusively.[83] Consequently, between 1914 and 1919 (when the survivors returned), wartime service resulted in a much greater proportional loss of the most productive element of the Senegalese labor force than the slave trade ever had.

Indices of social disruption also bear on the question. Although the level of violence (and death) accompanying the acquisition of slaves was greater than that of recruits in Senegal, this was probably not the case in other areas of A.O.F. where revolts occurred. In the *cercle* of Bobo-Dioulaso for instance, the ratio in 1916 of those killed to those recruited appears to have been on the order of at least six-to-one.[84] Moreover, although comparative data is lacking, the scale of external flight from Senegal as a result of the policy (which, prior to 1917, was probably on the order of one refugee to one recruit) may have approximated the extent of interregional migration prompted by the slave trade in Senegambia.

Indeed, in terms of combat deaths alone, the losses sustained by the Senegalese during the four years of the war were substantially higher than the annual average of all Senegambians exported overseas by the British and French for a comparable period during the eighteenth century. Combat deaths were 4,600 at a minimum and probably considerably higher, while estimates of the annual average of Senegambian slaves exported range between 600 and 840.[85] In this regard, there is considerable justification in viewing the wartime recruitment of soldiers as the last, the largest, and the most inescapable "man hunt" in the history of Senegambia.[86]

Senegalese reactions to the calamity that befell them between 1914 and 1917 closely resembled their responses to analogous situations in earlier periods of crisis. When evasion proved impossible, an imperative was placed on preserving the collective at all costs. To this end, those with low social status—domestic slaves and those separated from or bereft of kinsmen—were frequently (but not exclusively) sent into the army. As the wartime demands for soldiers grew, however, even this expedient proved increasingly exhausted. Then, those able-bodied men deemed most expendable by the social organism—those lacking parental protection and younger siblings serving as substitutes for their elder brothers—were most often sacrificed.

By late 1917, the coercive character of French recruitment methods, which provoked a massive exodus to foreign colonies and widespread revolts elsewhere in the Federation, came to be recognized as dysfunctional, and the policy was temporarily suspended. When it was resumed six months later, it was conducted under dramatically different circumstances. Then, the metropolitan government was obliged to offer the first significant concessions to Africans since the advent of colonial rule, and an emphasis was placed on persuasion rather than coercion as a means of recruiting men.

This shift in policy—which was anticipated by political developments in the Four Communes (see Chapter 3)—carried profound, if paradoxical, implications. Prior to 1918, the requisitioning of young men in the Protectorate had been devoid of ideological rationale and frequently assumed the dimensions of an aberrant throwback to the worst depravations of the past; thereafter it became suffused with novel aspirations for the future expressed by Senegalese communards, which, but for the unforeseen circumstances created by the war, would have been inconceivable. In this regard, French wartime concessions and the transformation of the meaning of the conflict for many Africans from an odious "tax in blood" into a "war to obtain rights" inaugurated nothing less than a fundamental redefinition of the relations that had previously existed between the colonizers and the colonized. As such, it effectively brought to a close an era in Senegalese history that dated from the onset of the French conquest, if not long before.

NOTES

[1] On the metropolitan debate over the promulgation of this decree, see: Marc Michel, "Un mythe: la 'Force Noire' avant 1914," *Relations Internationales* 1 (1974), pp. 38–90; and Joe Lunn, "'Les races guerrières': Racial Preconceptions in the French Military about West African Soldiers during the First World War," *Journal of Contemporary History* 34, 4 (1999). For the provisions of the decree, see: *Journal Officiel de la République Française* (Paris: Imprimerie national, 1912), pp. 1347–48.

[2] Figures on the numbers of Senegalese recruited during this period vary between 1,955 and 2,160 men. See: *ANS*: Affaires militaires: 4 D 73 and 4 D 55.

[3] *ANS*: Affaires militaires: 4 D 65 and 4 D 55.

[4] According to the government's official postwar inquiry, 918,000 out of an eventual total of 1,798,000 losses (dead, missing, and prisoners) suffered by the French army, or 51 percent, occurred between August 1914 and November 1915. See "Rapport Marin," *Journal Officiel de la République Française, Documents parlementaires*, 1920, t. 2, annexe 633, p. 74.

[5] *ANS*: Affaires militaires: 4 D 55.

[6] For the new provisions of these decrees—including recruitment (at least theoretically only on a "voluntary" basis), increased enlistment bounties of 200 francs, and the allocation of 500,000 francs to be dispensed as "gifts" to those responsible for presenting recruits—see: *Journal Officiel de la République Française*, 1915, pp. 7286, 7519–20. For the numbers recruited, see: *ANS*: Affaires militaires: 4 D 65 and 4 D 54.

[7] For summaries of the various "incidents" that occurred as a result of recruitment in the *cercles* in Senegal between 1914 and 1916, see: *ANS*: Affaires militaires: 4 D 65. The first major revolt against recruitment took place between February and March 1915 among the Bambara of Beledougou; this was followed the next year by a much larger rebellion in West Volta, which involved half a million people and took eight months to crush. See Jean Herbert, "Révoltes en Haute-Volta de 1914 à 1919," *Notes et Etudes Voltaïques*, July–September 1970, pp. 3–54; Blamy Gnankambary, "La révolte bobo de 1916 dans le cercle du Dedougou," *Notes et Etudes Voltaïques*, July–September 1970, pp. 56–87. For the suppression of these revolts, see: "Rapport sur les operations militaires en A.O.F. pendant la guerre 1914–1918," *Centre militaire d'information et de documentation: Outre-Mer* [hereafter *CMIDOM*]: Rapports: AOF-INT-C III-27-C.

[8] *ANS*: Affaires militaires: 4 D 73 and 4 D 69.

[9] Northern Dahomey remained in revolt between April 1916 and April 1917. See: Luc Garcia, "Les mouvements de résistance au Dahomey (1914–1917)," *Cahiers d'Etudes Africaines* 37 (1970), pp. 144–78; Helen d'Almeida-Topor, "Les populations dahoméennes et le recrutement militaire pendant la première Guerre mondiale," *Revue Française d'Histoire d'Outre-Mer* 60 (1973), pp. 196–241. Mangin, who commanded the 6th Army in the offensive, was initially made the scapegoat for the disaster and relieved of his command in May. He was reinstated seven months later by Clemenceau. Ribot's government, which had sanctioned the ill-fated attack at the Chemin des Dames and bore official accountability for the "mutinies" in the French army that ensued, was briefly replaced by that of Paul Painlevé. More specifically, André Maginot, who had supported further recruitment as Minister of Colonies, was replaced by René Besmard, who did not.

[10] In Senegal, for example, the local groundnut trade, which accounted for 50 percent of the value of all of A.O.F.'s exports in 1913, declined dramatically during the war. Harvests that reached 303,000 metric tons in 1914 plummeted to an average of only 142,000 tons between 1915 and 1917—a fall of more than 53 percent. See Xavier Guiraud, *L'Arachide sénégalais: Monographie d'economie coloniale* (Paris: Librairie Technique et Economique, 1937), table, p. 37. For a summary of the grievances of the *colons*, see: *ANS*: Affaires militaires: 4 D 73.

[11] *ANS*: Affaires militaires: 4 D 72 and 4 D 73.

[12] *ANS*: Affaires militaires: 4 D 65; 4 D 55; 4 D 73; and 4 D 69. All such estimates must remain inexact: the local French bureaucracy was rudimentary, and clerical errors appearing in the *cercle* figures were occasionally duplicated in the reports of the lieutenant governors, while discrepancies also sometimes arose between the colonial reports and later ministerial summaries.

[13] For prewar population densities see Charles Becker, "Les Effets demographiques de la traite des esclaves en Sénégambie: Esquisse d'une histoire des peuplements du XVIIe à la fin du XIXe siècle," *De la Traite à l'esclavage. Actes du Colloque international sur la traite des Noirs, Nantes 1985*, vol. 2: *XVIIIe–XIXe siècles*, ed. Serge Daget (Paris: L'Harmattan, 1988), pp. 106–07. For the military organization of the Federation, which dated from 1911, see: *ANS*: Affaires militaires: 4 D 32.

[14] On the distribution of the recruitment burden throughout Senegal for the duration of the war, see Table 3.1.

[15] This statistic, which no doubt reflects the efforts of some chiefs to shield members of their communities from the draft and of potential inductees to evade it, nonetheless offers a telling insight into the physical condition of much of the population, which had recently been ravaged by both famine and epidemics. For the percentage of "inapts" in Senegal, which was reckoned at 71.2 percent of those examined by the recruiting commissions during the war, see Baron des Lyons de Feuchins, "Rapport fait au nom de la Commission de l'Armée," *Journal Officiel de la République Française, Documents Parlementaires, Chambre*, 29 juillet 1924, annexe 335, p. 1307. For periodic reports on the percentage of "inapts," which were reckoned at 70 to 80 percent during the recruitment drives between August 1914 and October 1915, and at 75 percent for those between October 1915 and April 1916, see: *ANS*: Affaires militaires: 4 D 65 and 4 D 49. For the medical instructions to the doctors in the commissions, as well as the list of maladies (including tuberculosis, syphilis, elephantiasis, and leprosy) that secured exemption, see: *ANS*: Affaires militaires: 4 D 81. On the shortage of doctors for the recruiting commissions, as well as the incompetence of some of the physicians who served, see: *ANS*: Affaires militaires: 4 D 81; 4 D 88; and 4 D 89.

[16] *ANS*: Affaires militaires: 4 D 35.

[17] Bounties, which amounted to 200 francs by 1915 (or the approximate sale price of 4 tons of peanuts), represented "astronomical" wealth by average peasant standards. They also roughly coincided with the prewar purchase prices of "captifs" in many areas of A.O.F. and, on occasion, were dispensed directly to the "fathers" of recruits who presented them for induction instead of to the soldiers. See *ANS*: Affaires militaires: 4 D 71. *"Cadeaux"* and *"encouragements divers"* had been used since at least 1912 to stimulate recruitment. The practice, though initially discouraged, was officially sanctioned in 1915. See *ANS*: Affaires militaires: 4 D 35; 4 D 55; and 4 D 65. For the distancing of French administrators from recruitment, see *Journal Officiel de la République Française*, 1912, p. 1348, and *ANS*: Affaires militaires: 4 D 35.

[18] *ANS*: Affaires militaires: 4 D 43, 4 D 55, and 4 D 77; *ANS*: Archives des cercles (Casamance), 2 D 5-2.

[19] In November 1915, for example, Lieutenant Governor Antonetti explicitly instructed his *commandants* to advise the chiefs to seize "strangers" in their *cantons* first to reduce the recruitment burden on the local inhabitants. He also advised that those attempting to flee be "severely beaten" when apprehended as an example to others. *ANS*: Affaires militaires: 4 D 55.

[20] See, for example: *ANS*: Affaires militaires: 4 D 49 and 4 D 55.

[21] For analogies between recruitment and the slave trade by Van Vollenhoven among others, see: *ANS*: Affaires militaires: 4 D 72; 4 D 70; *ANS*: Affaires politiques: 2 G 17-4.

[22] Despite his earlier protests, even Van Vollenhoven made it clear that he was willing to undertake the additional recruitment drive subsequently demanded by Clemenceau in 1918. See Chapter 3.

[23] *ANS*: Archives des cercles (Casamance), 2 D 5-2; and Archives militaires: 4 D 77.

[24] The percentage of genuine "volunteers" in Senegal for this period was probably less than 5 percent. Lieutenant Governor Antonetti reckoned that it varied between 3 per 1,000 up to 7 or 8 percent during the recruitment drive conducted between October 1915 and April 1916. See *ANS*: Affaires militaires: 4 D 49. Among the pre-1918 veterans interviewed, only four claimed to be "volunteers," and in each case there were mitigating circumstances. See Doudou Ndao (1A and 1B); Abdou Karim Gaye (1B, 2A, 2B, 3A, and 5B); Sickh Yero Sy (1B); and Galaye Gueye (1B).

[25] Sickh Yero Sy: 1B and 2A; Antoine Diouf: 1A.

[26] Although resentment was occasionally expressed against village and cantonal chiefs about the role they played in raising recruits, this appears to have been exceptional and usually restricted to those who exercised their powers unfairly (Gamou Wade: 1A). On the whole, most Senegalese recognized that the *chefs de canton* personally opposed the policy but had "no choice" about complying with French "orders" (Sambou Ndiaye: 1A; Saer Anta Loum: 1A). As a result, their prestige, like that of the marabouts involved in recruitment (Bara Seck: 3A), does not appear to have suffered unduly.

[27] Malal Gassala: 1A; Mamadou Ndiaye: 1A. Both references to village "lotteries" were mentioned by sedentary Fulbe living along the Fleuve in the *cercles* of Matam and Podor.

[28] See, respectively: Thiam Nding (1A and 2A), who was a *captif* and sent to fill the village quota at the behest of his aristocratic "uncle" in Jolof; Soudou Laye (1A), who recounts the roundup of the poor performing "forced labor" in Baol early in the war; and

Nar Diouf (1B) and Yoro Diaw (1A), who were the younger sons of village chiefs in the *cercles* of Thiès and Louga and entered the army early in 1915.

[29] This practice was widespread in Senegal and was conducted among the Wolof, the Serer, the Lebu, and the sedentary Fulbe. For pre-1918 references to it, see: Yoro Diaw: 1A; Biram Mbodji Tine: 1A; Mandiaye Ndiaye: 1A; Sera Ndiaye: 1B; Sambou Ndiaye: 1A; Samba Diouf: 1A; and Mamadou Ndiaye: 1A.

[30] Recruitment lists, usually derived from tax rolls, were nonexistent when the policy was first implemented in 1912. For example, see: *ANS*: Affaires militaires: 4 D 35. Despite subsequent French efforts to compile such rosters, these initiatives, generally undertaken only later in the war, often proved desultory. Among the *tirailleurs* who referred to the presence of their names on "lists," only one—Diouli Missine (1915)—was recruited before 1917. See Diouli Missine: 1A; Samba Diouf (1917): 1A; Nouma Ndiaye (1917): 2A; Mahmout Demba (1917): 1A; Amar Seck (1918): 1B; and Samba Diop (1918): 1B and 2B. On the whole, the colonial bureaucracy in the countryside remained rudimentary, and even in the communes, where records of births were ostensibly recorded at the city hall, attempts to use them during the recruitment of *originaires* in 1915 to 1916 proved an administrative nightmare. By 1926, the use of recruitment lists (based on census lists for the male population) by *commandants de cercle* became standardized throughout A.O.F. See Myron Echenberg, *Colonial Conscripts: The "Tirailleurs Sénégalais" in French West Africa, 1857–1960* (Portsmouth, NH: Heinemann/London: James Currey, 1991), p. 51.

[31] Bamba's "loyalty" to the French cause was commended by the colonial administration, while his followers were subsequently rewarded with the grant of extensive tracts of land in eastern Senegal. See: *ANS*: Affaires politiques: 17 G 39; and Donald B. Cruise O'Brien, *Saints and Politicians: Essays in the Organisation of a Senegalese Peasant Society* (Cambridge: Cambridge University Press, 1975), p. 47.

[32] For descriptions of the recruitment system among the Mourides, as well as the respective roles of Bamba, Fall, and other marabouts, see: Bara Seck: 1B and 2A; Amadou Yassin 1B; Momar Khary Niang: 1B and 2A; Ibrahima Thiam: 1A, 1B, and 2A; Makhoudia Ndiaye: 1A, 1B, and 2A; and Thiam Nding: 4A.

[33] *La chasse à l'homme* was the phrase employed by several French officials to describe the nature of these activities. For examples, see: *ANS*: Affaires militaires: 4 D 72 and 4 D 73.

[34] For surprise raids by chiefly retainers, see: Sambou Ndiaye: 1A; Samba Diop: 3A; Mamadou Ndiaye: 1A; Soudou Laye: 1A; Malang Fati: 1A and 1B; Adiouma Ndiaye, 1B; and Issap Niang: 1A. For recruiting "agents" (which sometimes included *gardes de cercle* and are only referred to in the Casamance), see: Abdoulaye Ndiaye (Z): 1A; Coumba Kebe: 1A and B. For compensation rates, which ranged between 15 and 25 francs, as well as the circumstances surrounding the shooting of several "agents" in the Casamance, see: *ANS*: Affaires militaires: 4 D 55; 4 D 65; and 4 D 49.

[35] Abdoulaye Ndiaye (Z): 1A; Soudou Laye: 1A; Samba Diop: 3A; and Allou Ditta: 1A. Identical methods were used in Mali; see: Daba Dembele: 1A.

[36] Gamou Wade (1A), whose uncle was a chief in the *cercle* of Dagana, was arrested when his son fled the village. The fathers (or in one instance uncle) of three *tirailleurs*, who were village chiefs, were also threatened with imprisonment if they did not provide a son (or nephew) for the army (see Nar Diouf: 1B; Yoro Diaw: 1A; and Galaye Gueye: 1B). For further accounts of sanctions against chiefs, see: *ANS*: Affaires militaires: 4 D 55.

[37] Biram Mbodji Tine: 1A. Similar references to the seizure of hostages are mentioned by: Aminata Ngom: 1A; Samba Diop: 2B; Mamadou Ndiaye: 1A; Allou Ditta: 1A; Issap Niang: 1A; and Coumba Kebe: 1B. In the case of Ngom, her uncle was taken. See also Diouli Missine (1B), who, as his parents' only son, was advised by them to "run away"; he refused to do so because he feared they would be imprisoned if he did.

[38] Adiouma Ndiaye: 1A; Issap Niang: 1A; Souan Gor Diatta: 1B; Coumba Kebe: 1A and 1B; and Allou Ditta: 1A and B. Though the seizure or destruction of property took place in several *cercles*, all references to the killing of villagers occurred in the Casamance. See also: *ANS*: Archives des cercles (Casamance), 2 D 52.

[39] Fatou Diop: unrecorded interview (notes, 14 March 1983). Aside from concern for the safety of their sons, the absence of recruits also sometimes wreaked an economic hardship on families, where not enough able-bodied young men remained to help till the land. See: Gamou Wade: 1A; Karamako Cisse: 1A; and Samba Diop: 3A, whose elderly father had to use the bounty his son sent him to hire workers to help cultivate his fields.

[40] Sera Ndiaye: 1B; Bara Seck: 1B.

[41] Yoro Diaw: 1A; Diouli Missine: 1B; Adiouma Ndiaye: 1A; and Sera Ndiaye: 1B. Such forebodings were often exacerbated by the absence of any news from those who had been recruited previously. Both the French and the *chefs de canton* frequently sought, at least initially, to restrict the flow of information from France because of their fears about the adverse effects that the soldiers' letters and their descriptions of the character of the fighting would have on subsequent recruitment (Nouma Ndiaye: 2B; Sera Ndiaye: 5B). Also, see: *ANS*: Affaires militaires: 4 D 70.

[42] Seydou Amadou Thiam, 1A; Gamou Wade: 1B; Coumba Kebe: 2A; and Souna Gor Diatta: 1B. Also see: *ANS*: Affaires militaires: 4 D 55, which describes the funeral dirges that were sung in some areas for those departing.

[43] Perhaps Abdou Karim Gaye (1B) and also Sickh Yero Sy (1B) enlisted.

[44] Bara Seck: 1B; Momar Khary Niang: 2A.

[45] Amadou Yassin: 1B; Bara Seck: 1B and 2A; and Momar Khary Niang: 1B and 2A. Bamba's admonition also conveyed an implicit symbolic meaning; he had twice been sent into exile by the French (in 1895 and 1903) and returned safely to Senegal on both occasions.

[46] Masserigne Soumare, 4B; Coumba Kebe: 2A. Yoro Diaw: 1B; Mahmout Demba: 1A; and Diouli Missine: 1B.

[47] Thiam Nding: 1A and 2A; Mamadou Ndiaye: 1A and B; Coumba Kebe: 1A; Soudou Laye: 1A; and Abdoulaye Ndiaye (Z): 1A. On the latter point, see Doudou Ndao: 1B; and Soudou Laye: 1A. Overall, among the 26 pre-1918 *tirailleurs* interviewed, the distribution by social group was as follows: aristocrats: 2 (8 percent); free peasants: 12 (48 percent); endogamous castes: 3 (12 percent); domestic slaves or those of servile origin (including *ceddo*): 5 (20 percent); uncertain: 3 (12 percent). Although too small to be statistically valid, this sample nevertheless roughly corresponds with the likely composition of Senegalese society at the time (i.e., approximately 5–10 percent aristocrats, 50–60 percent free peasants, perhaps 10 percent castes, and 25 percent of servile origin, with this last group in decline).

[48] Among those referring to their mothers and fathers, 54 percent were missing either one or both parents at the time of their induction (six were missing a mother, four a father, and three both mother and father; two did not indicate whether their parents were present).

[49] The absence of accurate, detailed demographic information makes this impossible to ascertain.

[50] Among the four *tirailleurs* interviewed whose fathers had more than one wife, each was a son from a later marriage.

[51] This practice was widespread in Senegal, occurring among the Wolof, the Serer, the Lebu, and the sedentary Fulbe. Among those interviewed who had families with two or more sons of military age, a younger one was sent instead of the eldest in all but two instances. These were Abdou Karim Gaye (3A), whose elder brother was an *originaire* rather than a *sujet* and therefore obliged to perform military service as well, and Nouma Ndiaye (2A), who, though the eldest son and recently married, offered to go in place of his younger brother.

[52] Sera Ndiaye: 1B. See also: Biram Mbodji Tine: 1A; Mandiaye Ndiaye: 1A; Seydou Amadou Thiam: 1A; Sambou Ndiaye: 1A; Momar Cisse: 1A; Samba Diouf: 1A; and Mamadou Ndiaye: 1A. Mamadou Ndiaye, a sedentary Fulbe and the eldest son in his family, eventually had three younger brothers sent in his place.

[53] Diouli Missine: 2A; Seydou Amadou Thiam: 1A; Coumba Niane: 1A; Sera Ndiaye: 1B; Biram Mbodji Tine: 1B; and Nouma Ndiaye: 1B.

[54] Charms, including "St. Joseph" [St. Christopher?] medals among Christians, were normally purchased from marabouts, made by elder kinsmen, or, if the recruits were of *ceddo* or aristocratic descent, sometimes passed down within the family from earlier generations. For especially detailed descriptions of how the charms were made, their protective properties, and the prohibitions that would render them ineffective, see: Daour Gueye: 3A; Sera Ndiaye: 1B; Biram Mbodji Tine: 1B and 2A; Nouma Ndiaye 1B; Mody Sow: 1B; Momar Cisse: 1A and 1B; and Yoro Diaw: 1B. For "St. Joseph" medals, see: Antoine Diouf: 1A.

[55] Yoro Diaw: 1A.

[56] Abdou Karim Gaye: 1B, 2A, and 6A; Mandiaye Ndiaye: 1A and B; and Doudou Ndao: 1A and 4A.

[57] Malal Gassala: 2B; Souleye Samba Ndiaye: 1A; and Mahmout Demba: 1B.

[58] Aminata Ngom: 1A.

[59] Karamako Cisse (1B and 2A), who was a skilled railway worker, obtained an exemption at the request of his *chef de département*. For bribes, see: Mamadou Ndiaye: 1A; Sera Ndiaye: 6A; and Karamako Cisse: 1A. Replacements could be obtained in the Casamance for 500 francs, or roughly three times the French enlistment bounty. See: Abdoulaye Ndiaye (Z): 1A. Souan Gor Diatta (1A and B) was designated to replace a "Peuhl" who had been judged "fit" after the man's relative, who was an interpreter for the French, convinced them that Diatta should be chosen instead.

[60] *Paftan* leaves were used in the Fouta, while *palme de cajou* was used in the Casamance (Mahmout Demba: 1B; Souan Gor Diatta: 2A). See also the instructions to the medical personnel accompanying the Recruiting Commissions, which explicitly warned them to beware of those "simulating" illness. *ANS*: Affaires militaires: 4 D 81.

[61] Although estimates by the colonial authorities represent little more than informed guesses, they do indicate that the scale of flight to foreign colonies was substantial. In Senegal, the governor general calculated that 15,000 able-bodied men (out of 61,500 from A.O.F.) had left the colony by the beginning of 1917 (*ANS*: Affaires militaires: 4 D 88 (145)). If this figure is even approximately accurate, it indicates that for every soldier recruited in rural Senegal between 1914 and 1917 (i.e., about 13,500), another man fled the colony to seek sanctuary in foreign territories.

[62] Samba Diop: 2A; Soudou Laye: 1A; and Abdou Karim Gaye: 1B. An additional hazard was predatory animals: in some rural areas men fleeing their villages were devoured by lions. Daba Dembele: 1A.

[63] Momar Khary Niang: 2B.

[64] Sickh Yero Sy: 2A; Mamadou Ndiaye: 1A; Diouli Missine: 1B; Gamou Wade: 1A; and Karamako Cisse: 1B.

[65] Coumba Kebe: 1B.

[66] Souan Gor Diatta (1A and B) escaped recruitment by fleeing from his village in the lower Casamance to live with relatives in the Gambia. Upon his ill-advised return home six months later, however, he was arrested and imprisoned. For other descriptions of flight in these areas, see: Allou Ditta: 1A; Adiouma Ndiaye: 1A; Abdoulaye Ndiaye (Z): 1A; Malang Fati: 1A; Issap Niang: 1A; and Karamako Cisse: 1A.

[67] Samba Diop: 2B; Mamadou Ndiaye: 1A. The incidents occurred in Saloum and Podor.

[68] Souan Gor Diatta: 1B. For the fighting at Diembereng, see also: Allou Ditta: 1A. For French reports on local resistance in Senegal, including accounts of the incidents referred to, see: *ANS*: Affaires militaires: 4 D 55; 4 D 65; and Archives des cercles (Casamance), 2 D 5-2, and (Sine-Saloum), 2 D 8-6.

[69] Amar Seck: 3A.

[70] For the imprisonment of the fathers or relatives of deserters, see: Nar Diouf: 2A; Sera Ndiaye: 1B and 2A.

[71] Prior to 1918, deserters were more numerous in Senegal and Guinea than elsewhere in A.O.F. *ANS*: Affaires militaires: 4 D 88. Overall, desertion rates among those recruited between October 1915 and April 1916 were about 8 percent for the Federation. See: Marc Michel, *L'Appel à l'Afrique: Contributions et réactions à l'effort de guerre en A.O.F. (1914–1919)* (Paris: Publications de la Sorbonne, 1982), pp. 85–86. For the prominence of Peuhls among those deserting, see: *ANS*: Affaires militaires: 4 D 55; 4 D 65; 4 D 80; and Archives des cercles (Louga), 2 D 9-20. *Tirailleurs* frequently mentioned incidents of desertion; like the administrative records, they indicated it was most common among Fulbe pastoralists. On the whole, desertion seems to have been influenced by the parents' attitudes (or marabouts, if they were Mourides). If parents sanctioned their son's entry into the army, they did not try to desert; if they had not, or he was taken by force, young men were much more prone to desert. Mandiaye Ndiaye: 1B; Bara Seck: 1B; Amar Seck: 2B; and Sera Ndiaye: 1B and 2A.

[72] Thiam Nding: 2B; Diouli Missine (2A) witnessed the suicides of several Bambara who, touched by songs that reminded them of their "country," leapt from the ship into the sea. Also see: *ANS*: Archives des cercles (Louga), 2 D 9-20. Suicide rates among the *tirailleurs* continued to be a source of French concern during the interwar period. See *AG*: Journaux de marche et d'opérations (J.M.O.), 26N 869 and 26 N 871; and Anthony Clayton, *France, Soldiers, and Africa* (London: Brassey's Defence Publishers, 1988), p. 351.

[73] Philip Curtin, *Economic Change in Precolonial Africa: Senegambia in the Era of the Slave Trade* (Madison: University of Wisconsin Press, 1975), p. 221. Martin Klein estimates that armies in the Wolof states during the eighteenth century probably never exceeded 4,000 soldiers. See Martin Klein, "The Impact of the Atlantic Slave Trade on the Societies of the Western Sudan," *Social Science History* 14 (1990), p. 238.

[74] For detailed descriptions of the role of *griots* in Senegambian warfare and their status as non-combatants, see: Demba Mboup: 2A, 2B, 7A, 7B, and 8A; and Coumba

Kebe: 2A. See also Lucie Gallistel Colvin, "International Relations in Precolonial Senegambia," *Présence Africaine* 93 (1975), pp. 215–30.

[75] The four *cercles* of Thiès, Tivaouane, Diourbel, and Sine-Saloum, plus the *"Banlieue"* of the Four Communes, comprised 50.1 percent of the Protectorate's population in 1921; between 1914 and 1917 these areas furnished 66.0 percent of all recruits whose origins are known, or about double those raised elsewhere in the colony. If the population and recruitment figures for the communes, as well as those for the 1918 recruitment drive, are included, the proportions shift to slightly more than half of the population (51.1 percent) furnishing over three-quarters (75.9 percent) of all soldiers. Though these areas were the most densely populated in Senegal, this factor alone was not decisive in determining the weight of recruitment burdens. Elsewhere in A.O.F., where population density was even greater (e.g., among the Mossi in Haut-Sénégal et Niger), recruitment levels were comparatively low. For recruitment figures in the rest of the Federation, see: Marc Michel, *L'Appel à l'Afrique*, table, p. 556.

[76] Elsewhere in A.O.F., the areas of most intensive recruitment also generally evidenced railroad lines.

[77] Alfred Guignard to Marie-François Clozel, 8 October 1915. *AN*: 149 AP 11 (Papiers Mangin). The slave trade had been outlawed in Senegal in 1905, but it persisted in some areas thereafter (Thiam Nding: 1B). On the character of precolonial slave raids in Senegambia, see James F. Searing, *West African Slavery and Atlantic Commerce: The Senegal River Valley, 1700–1860* (Cambridge: Cambridge University Press, 1993), pp. 28–38. On the gradual ending of slavery as a domestic institution in Senegal, owing in part to the impact of military recruitment during the First World War, see Andrew F. Clark, "Slavery and Its Demise in the Upper Senegal Valley, West Africa, 1890–1920," *Slavery and Abolition* 15 (1994), pp. 51–71.

[78] According to Curtin, a total of some 77,600 slaves were exported in French ships between 1711 and 1810, only a third of whom were Senegambians. Hence, slightly fewer than 26,000 Senegalese were transported overseas throughout this period, compared with more than 29,000 between 1914 and 1918. See Curtin, *Economic Change in Precolonial Africa*, table, p. 164, and pp. 187, 333. Jean Mettas's subsequent research accords closely with Curtin's original estimate, calculating French slave exports from Senegambia between 1700 and 1799 at 83,860. See Jean Mettas, *Répertoire des expéditions négrières françaises au xviiie siècle*, ed. Serge Daget, 2 vols. (Paris: Société française d'histoire d'outre-mer, 1978–84). See also: Robert Stein, "Measuring the French Slave Trade, 1713–1792/3," *Journal of African History* 19 (1978), pp. 515–21; and Becker, "Les Effets demographiques de la traite des esclaves en Sénégambie," pp. 70–110.

[79] For annual estimates of slave exports, see Searing, *West African Slavery and Atlantic Commerce*, pp. 31–33; Charles Becker and Victor Martin, "Kayor et Baol: Royaumes sénégalais et traite des esclaves au XVIIIe siècle," *Revue Française d'histoire d'Outre-Mer* 62 (1975), pp. 278–83; and Curtin, *Economic Change in Precolonial Africa*, pp. 164, 184–85, 188. On sources for the recruitment figures, see Table 3.1.

[80] See, for example, Thiam Nding: 1B; Demba Mboup: 8B; Coumba Kebe: 2A. The quotation is from Daba Dembele: 2A.

[81] Adiouma Ndiaye: 1A. Kande Kamara, a Guinean *tirailleur*, recounted the fear expressed by many soldiers that they were going to be "sold" as slaves after being transported to France. See Joe Harris Lunn, "Kande Kamara Speaks: An Oral History of the West African Experience in France, 1914–18," in *Africa and the First World War*, ed.

Melvin E. Page (London: Macmillan, 1987), pp. 28–53. On African fears that the soldiers would be sold into slavery, see also, *ANS*: Affaires militaires: 4 D 70.

[82] Curtin, *Economic Change in Precolonial Africa*, p. 333; and Michel, *L'Appel à l'Afrique*, p. 121, and tables, pp. 480–84, 536.

[83] Klein, "The Impact of the Slave Trade," p. 239.

[84] According to Lieutenant Governor Louis Digue, 3,600 Africans were killed during the repression of the revolt in Bobo-Dioulasso, and 593 men were eventually recruited from the *cercle* in 1916. See "Lieutenant gouverneur Haut Sénégal et Niger à gouverneur général, 8 avril 1916," cited in: Michel, *L'appel à l'Afrique*, pp. 104, 113 n.34; and the table "Haut-Sénégal et Niger" [Bobo Dioulasso, 1916], p. 481.

[85] See Curtin, *Economic Change in Precolonial Africa*, table, p. 164. Richardson, "Slave Exports from West and Central Africa, 1700–1810: New Estimates on Volume and Distribution," *Journal of African History* 30 (1989), tables, pp. 13–14; for casualties, see Chapter 5.

[86] Although a comparable number of Senegalese were mobilized by the French army during the Second World War, the methods used to raise them ceased to resemble *la chasse à l'homme* of the 1914–1917 period. By 1939, the colonial bureaucracy was more sophisticated, recruitment had become institutionalized, and flight was less frequent. See Echenberg, *Colonial Conscripts*, pp. 47–70, 87–105.

3

THE WAR TO OBTAIN RIGHTS: CONSCRIPTION IN THE COMMUNES AND THE DIAGNE MISSION OF 1918

In dramatic contrast with the Protectorate, where Senegalese recruitment (prior to 1917) was equated with a "Tax in Blood," in the communes the performance of military duty came to be seen in an entirely different light. Before October 1915, the young men of the communes were exempted from service in the French army. Thereafter, the call-up of soldiers—which was conducted by vastly different means and in entirely different circumstances than that in the Protectorate—became inextricably linked to larger questions of securing communal rights within the colonial system, particularly to their acquisition of French citizenship. In this context, the war early on assumed a novel political significance in the communes that it did not, as yet, have in the rest of the colony. Nevertheless, as the war continued and the French need for soldiers grew ever more dire, the communal precedent became increasingly important. When the conflict eventually became redefined after 1918 by urban African political leaders as a "War to Obtain Rights" in the Protectorate as well, a new and crucial phase ensued that ultimately had long-term and profound implications. To assess this rapid evolution in the meaning of the war for many Senegalese, which was most graphically exemplified in the symbolism of the Diagne Mission of 1918, it is necessary to explore the political ferment in the communes immediately before the war's outbreak and assess how the performance of military duty became interrelated with the quest of the *originaires* to assert their civic rights.

CITIZENSHIP AND MILITARY SERVICE IN THE COMMUNES

The Prewar Civic Status of the *Originaires*

The civic status of the *originaires* was unique in West Africa and represented an historic anomaly. As *habitants* of the communes of St. Louis, Gorée, Rufisque, and Dakar, whose municipal status had been recognized by ardently republican metropolitan governments between 1872 and 1887, they were empowered to vote in local elections and granted access to French legal institutions. The unique status of the *originaires*, who constituted only a tiny fraction of the colony's total population as well as a minority of the communes' African residents, set them apart in significant ways from their kinsmen in the countryside. Unlike the overwhelming majority of their rural counterparts—who were classed as *"sujets"*—they were exempt from the most oppressive features of the colonial regime: corvée labor, the *indigénat*, and (at least until 1912) the head tax. Moreover, in addition to their electoral franchise—which enabled them to vote for municipal councillors, representatives on the *Conseil général* of Senegal, and a deputy in the French Chamber—they were accorded (at least in theory) freedom of speech, rights of assembly and of movement, and legal immunity from colonial "administrative justice," all of which were denied to other Africans.[1]

Nevertheless, until the decade immediately preceding the outbreak of the First World War, the possession of these so-called "privileges" by the *originaires* was of little concern to the municipal ruling elites. Local politics was dominated, as it had been since the communes' inception, by a coalition of French *colons* (who normally supported the business interests of the larger Bordeaux commercial firms) and their Eurafrican ("*métis*") allies. While composing only a fraction of the electorate (never more than about 20 percent of the total), this coalition managed through a combination of ill-kept promises, extensive bribes, and occasional intimidation at election times to secure the support of the African majority of voters in their respective municipalities.[2] Thus, the legal "rights" enjoyed by the *originaires* offered them limited practical advantage. Indeed, far from feeling privileged in their situation, more often than not most African communards felt victimized by French and *métis* domination because they exercised the authority to "do whatever they wanted."[3] Boubacar Gueye, the orphaned son of a petty trader, bitterly recalled: "[In St. Louis] all the government power was held by the *métis*. So they [held] all rights over us. We were considered almost like slaves [because] we had no rights, no justice, nothing at all. Everything was directed and [owned] by the *métis* and the *Tubabs*."[4]

Nevertheless, despite their unchallenged position of supremacy in communal affairs, the Franco-*métis* political elite as well as the colonial administration became increasingly concerned from 1905 onward about the potential impact of the African electorate on their continued control of municipal institutions. This disquieting prospect began to assume tangible form when Galandou Diouf was elected from Rufisque to the *Conseil général* in 1909 as the first truly independent African delegate. The upshot was a concerted effort by the colonial administration aimed at curbing growing African political influence by reducing the number of *originaires* holding the franchise. Thereafter, when this appeared unlikely to achieve the desired result, they attempted to abolish the limited civic rights of the *originaires* altogether and reduce them to a status comparable to that of the *sujets* in the Protectorate.

French countermeasures commenced by seeking to strike Africans from the municipal electoral rolls, and in 1907 the lieutenant governor of Senegal succeeded in having about 30 percent of their number removed from the voting rosters. Thereafter, the anti-republican movement in the communes gained momentum. Between 1910 and 1914, the French administration initiated a series of actions designed to abrogate any rights held by the *originaires* that might be legally construed as conferring citizenship (and hence the right to vote), while denigrating their civic status to that commensurate with *sujets*. These measures included: (1) the denial of voting rights to *originaires* residing outside the communes (which both Frenchmen and *métis* continued to enjoy); (2) the introduction of a head tax in the local municipalities; (3) the abrogation of recourse to legal due process for *originaires* living or traveling in the Protectorate, who thereafter became subject to "native tribunals"; and (4) their exclusion from French schools in the communes.

Moreover, in an action that would soon become a focal point for confrontation, all *originaires* were summarily dismissed from the French army in 1911 and informed that henceforth they would be eligible to serve only among the *tirailleurs*, who were recruited exclusively from among the *sujet* population. This movement culminated in 1913 with a legal challenge in the metropolitan courts by Governor General William Ponty designed to "clarify" the civic status of the African "*habitants*" in the communes. Ponty's case stressed that only those few Africans who rejected Islam and met the administration's stringent criteria for naturalization should be considered citizens. Though unadjudicated before the outbreak of the war, the intent of the colonial authorities was clear: the historic rights of the *originaires* to vote were to be abolished, their claims to French citizenship (which had never been legally recognized) were to be definitively denied, and their other remaining "privileges" were to be curtailed as much as possible.[5]

These systematic efforts by the French administration to undermine the status of the *originaires* aroused a storm of controversy in the communes, especially among the Western-educated Africans. The new ferment was exemplified by the formation of the *Parti Jeunes Sénégalais* in 1912 in St. Louis. As the first urban political action group organized by Africans in Senegal, the party was determined to defend their imperiled rights.[6] Hoping to present their cause directly before the French Chamber, they enlisted the support of other *originaire* leaders in the rest of the communes and resolved to field an African candidate in the election for deputy in June 1914. The odds against success were extremely long. No African had ever stood for this office before, much less been elected to it. And even if locally victorious, there was little likelihood that the deputy's influence in the French Chamber would be sufficient to sway his colleagues to support the claims of the *originaires* in the face of determined opposition from the colonial lobby, the governor general of the Federation, the Minister of Colonies, and, ultimately, the government. Nevertheless, this seemingly unattainable political agenda became realized in only slightly more than two years due to the extraordinary efforts of "a Senegalese from Gorée" and the unexpected confluence of political circumstances unleashed by the Great War.[7]

The Election of 1914

The African who answered the call of the *Jeunes Sénégalais* was Blaise Diagne. Born in 1872 of a nonaristocratic lineage—his father, a Serer, and his mother, a Lebu, worked on Gorée as domestics—he received a French secondary education through the patronage of the wealthy *métis* Adolphe Crespin. Thereafter, Diagne joined the French colonial customs service, in which he worked for the next 22 years. In this capacity he traveled widely throughout the French colonial empire as well as in the metropole. Energetic, intelligent, eloquent, and impetuous, Diagne earned the ire of the local French authorities because of his vociferous and uncompromising commitment to egalitarian ideals. He insisted on being accorded equal treatment with his European colleagues, decried the blatant discrimination and racist policies of the colonial administration, and defended persecuted Africans on a number of occasions. As such, Diagne's behavior was denounced by most of his French superiors, and he was shunted from one colonial assignment to the next before being relegated in 1912 to the absolute bottom of the customs heap—duty in French Guiana.

Nevertheless, Diagne was also politically ambitious and possessed a number of attributes that would serve him well in this capacity. Worldly and extremely well educated by Senegalese standards, he was also physically imposing, a polished and charismatic orator in French, at ease in European forums, and he maintained personal contacts with other deputies representing the "old colonies." Possessing these unique qualifications and realizing that his career in the customs service was forestalled, he returned to Dakar in January 1914 to challenge the old Franco-*métis* political oligarchy for the deputyship.[8]

Arrayed against Diagne were a wide assortment of French and *métis* candidates who initially refused to take his challenge seriously. François Carpot, a *métis* from St. Louis who had been deputy for the past 12 years and enjoyed the tacit support of the colonial administration, was generally conceded a fourth term. Nonetheless, in addition to Diagne, Carpot's reelection was contested by half a dozen other candidates, including Fernand Marsat, the head of the local Dakar political machine, and Henri Heimburger, an Alsacian lawyer supported by the *métis* mayor of St. Louis.

In dramatic contrast to all other candidates, who either opposed or only paid feeble lip service to the issues of voting rights and claims to citizenship of the *originaires*, Diagne made them the centerpiece of his campaign. Recalling the terms in which this appeal was couched, Ndematy Mbaye of Rufisque remembered Diagne's saying:

> I am a Senegalese and I am "black" like you. And my mother is Lebu. And the *métis* for whom you have always voted have never done anything to help you [once] they have gone to France. They have only been there [to serve] themselves. [But] if you vote for me, I am going to get all your rights. You should have been [recognized as] citizens a long time ago, but the deputies—the *métis* deputies—have never asked this right for you. But I'm going to do it. If you vote for me [I will ask for you] to be [made] citizens.[9]

Furthermore, Diagne called for an end to the recently imposed head tax, noncompliance with French efforts to enroll *originaires* as *tirailleurs* in the army, and compensation by the government for the continued alienation of African lands. Finally, Diagne marked himself as an unmistakable foe of the large Bordeaux commercial firms, which he collectively characterized as "a pack of brigands."[10]

These appeals proved compelling, and the results of the first election shocked the Franco-*métis* political elite as well as the colonial administration. Though failing to obtain an outright majority, Diagne gained nearly 40 percent of the total vote and far outdistanced his nearest rivals, Carpot and Heimburger. With the exception of Carpot, who refused to withdraw from the race, most of the other French and *métis* candidates rallied behind Heimburger in a belated effort to stem the rising African tide during the second round of the election.

The last phase of the campaign was extraordinarily vicious. Branding Diagne an agent of racial discord, the opposition also sought to intimidate his potential voters by resorting to a series of ill-disguised threats and breaking up his political rallies. Recounting how the campaign was waged in St. Louis, one young *originaire* remembered: "Whenever Blaise Diagne wanted to hold a public meeting, there were some men sent by the *métis*. [They] threw spoiled potatoes at him and shouted: 'Shame!' 'Dog!' 'Dog!' And they tried to prevent him from [speaking]. But Blaise Diagne was strong enough

M. DIAGNE, Député du Sénégal,
Commissaire général des Effectifs coloniaux.

Blaise Diagne, Senegalese Deputy from the Four Communes and Commissioner for the
Republic on Mission, 1918. From *Annuaire de l'A.O.F., 1917–1921.*

to resist [them], [and he continued to hold his meetings] in spite of these
incidents."[11]

Such underhanded tactics ultimately proved futile. Realizing their worst
fears, Diagne's African coalition—which included the *Jeunes Sénégalais,*

disgruntled Lebu notables in Cape Vert, and influential Muslim marabouts in the communes as well as the countryside—provided just enough votes to sweep him into office.[12] The Wolof song that was sung to celebrate his victory succinctly summarized the new political situation in the communes: "The black sheep [has beaten] the white sheep."[13]

Yet despite the euphoria among his followers, Diagne's triumph settled none of the questions on which he had based his appeal. These would have to be resolved in the French Chamber, where, as one opposition newspaper observed, not without cause: "It is absurd to imagine that a 'native' deputy could have the slightest influence in Parliament."[14]

The Diagne Laws of 1915 and 1916

Diagne's initial reception in the Chamber of Deputies was clouded by controversy. After recovering from the disagreeable outcome of the election, both the colonial administration as well as Diagne's former political opponents challenged his right to be seated as a deputy. Diagne thwarted the efforts of his adversaries to have his victory annulled, however, and aligned himself with the Socialists (who, combined with the other parties of the Left, constituted a majority in the new Chamber) and commenced his duties. Less than six weeks later, the First World War broke out.[15]

Diagne, whose commitment to the egalitarian precepts of French republicanism was sincere, seized the opportunity created by the onset of hostilities to offer the government the services in the French army of the *originaires*. This remained a thorny question for the authorities because it entailed the tacit concession—explicitly repudiated only three years earlier—that in terms of their military status the standing of the *originaires* was identical to that of French citizens.

Indeed, having foreseen the possible legal complications arising from this issue, General Charles Mangin had specifically excluded the Senegalese communards from his earlier proposals to create a *force noire* in West Africa.[16] After some initial equivocation, the Ministries of War and Colonies firmly reasserted their opposition to incorporating the *originaires* in the metropolitan forces. Undeterred, Diagne remained equally intransigent. He cabled his lieutenants in Dakar to discourage enlistment in the communes unless the concessions he demanded were forthcoming.[17]

Forestalled at the highest levels of French officialdom, Diagne moved to have the issue resolved in the Chamber, which held ultimate power to decide all such questions. In April 1915, during the course of debate over the conscription bill then pending, Diagne proposed an amendment that would also include enrolling in the French army *originaires* in the classes from 1899 to 1916. Countering the arguments of the Minister of War Alexandre Millerand, who considered the motion inappropriate, Diagne rose and declared in his maiden speech before the body: "If we can come here to legislate, we are French citizens; and if we are, we demand the right to serve [in the army] as all French citizens do."[18]

Diagne's rhetoric elicited an enthusiastic response, and though his amendment was tabled for the time being, his proposal was referred to committee for further study. The bill came to the floor three months later. During the course of the ensuing debate, Henri Labouse, deputy from the Gironde and a spokesman for the Bordeaux colonial business interests, led the opposition. He was no match for Diagne. The deputy from Senegal humiliated Labouse with his skill at parliamentary repartee and through his forthright declaration of the egalitarian precepts of French republicanism and the patriotism of the *originaires* gained the sympathy of the Chamber.[19] In the face of Diagne's eloquence and sensing the mood of the deputies, the government's representatives, who had prepared an alternative proposal of their own, capitulated. Bowing to the inevitable, they withdrew their motion and opted to support the wording of Diagne's bill. As a result, his measure carried by a voice vote, and the law, which was subsequently approved by the Senate and promulgated on 19 October 1915, was unequivocal in defining the military status of the communards: "The *originaires* of the *communes de plein exercice* of Senegal are liable to military service according to the conditions set [forth in the conscription laws of 1905 and 1913]. They are to be incorporated in French units and subject to the same obligations and advantages."[20]

Granting the eligibility of *originaires* to serve in the French army, the *"loi Diagne"* of 1915 still did not resolve the question of whether they were citizens. Diagne pressed the attack, explicitly linking the performance of military duty with the acquisition of civic rights. In February 1916, Diagne introduced new legislation, ostensibly intended to clarify the provisions of the 1915 law, by making the children of *originaires* born outside the communes subject to military conscription as well. The wording of the statute, however, carried more far-ranging implications. Its crucial phrase read: "The natives of the *communes de plein exercice* of Senegal and their descendants are and remain French citizens subject to the military obligations imposed by the Law of October 19, 1915."[21]

Diagne's bill was passed by voice vote and without discussion in the Chamber on 13 July.[22] In so doing, the action of the deputies clarified once and for all the civic status of the *originaires*. Henceforth, by the Law of 29 September 1916, they were and would remain French citizens.[23]

Diagne's legislative achievements since his arrival in Paris were little short of astonishing. In scarcely more than two years, an unknown African deputy from Senegal had succeeded in confounding a series of powerful political opponents and gained for his constituency parliamentary recognition of the rights to which he so fervently believed they were entitled. Yet, as he well knew, this would have been impossible but for the unprecedented circumstances created by the war. In the aftermath of his successes in the Chamber, his attention turned increasingly to facilitating the conscription of soldiers in the communes and to making the rights he had secured for them seem worth fighting, and indeed worth dying, for.

MILITARY CONSCRIPTION IN THE COMMUNES, 1915–1918

The Administration of Conscription

The methods employed to mobilize soldiers in the communes differed dramatically from those used by the French in the Protectorate. Instead of relying on the threat or use of coercion to round up the requisite numbers of young men, the procedures followed were identical (at least in theory) to those employed in metropolitan France. According to the Diagne law of 19 October 1915, the *originaires* were made liable to obligatory military conscription (as opposed to "recruitment") for a period of three years; they were to be called up by "class" according to their years of birth; and they were expected to report voluntarily to their induction centers on specified days when notified to do so.

In practice, the application of these procedures presented major problems for the colonial administration because, unlike in France, the bureaucratic apparatus necessary for their implementation was deficient. The major stumbling block faced by the local authorities was the absence of accurate census data on which to base the mobilization of recruits. The municipal records of the *état civil* of *originaires* in each of the four communes were ill kept and wholly inadequate for this purpose.[24]

As a result, the colonial administration was compelled to resort to a series of other expedients (illegal in France) to determine who was eligible for military service. To supplement the municipal records of the communal residents, they relied on a list of Senegalese holding election cards in 1914. Moreover, on the recommendation of Diagne, special provisions were also made for those claiming *originaire* status who wished to volunteer but for whom no documentary proof of their identity or place and date of birth existed. This last test—the so-called *jugements supplétifs* based on the corroborating oral testimony of two or more witnesses and adjudicated on an individual basis—posed a major dilemma for the administration. Not only was it comparatively time consuming and costly to administer, but in the eyes of the French authorities it presented a daunting political problem as well. Though generally anxious to enlist soldiers in behalf of *la patrie*, many officials were concerned that granting *originaire* status to yet more potential Senegalese voters could only redound to their subsequent disadvantage in communal elections.[25]

Nevertheless, despite the faulty state of the municipal records and the reservations aroused by the extensive use of *jugements supplétifs*, these methods provided the basis for compiling conscription lists in the communes that were largely completed by the end of November 1915. Thereafter, as in France, these were publicly posted and announced by town criers in each of the communes. Duly notified of their call-up, the *originaires* were expected to report to their respective town halls on specified days (which corresponded to their presumed age groups or military "classes") and present themselves before their local recruiting boards for examination. Failure to comply resulted in arrest warrants being issued by the boards to bring in draft evaders by compulsion.[26]

Three draft boards had been created at the end of November to oversee the enlistment of the *originaires* in Senegal. Though their circumscriptions were subsequently altered several times, eventually one recruiting board was established for Dakar and Gorée, a second for Rufisque, and a third in St. Louis. Consisting of a president, who was a senior administrative official, and several other members, including two or three civilian advisors and a military officer, these draft boards held ultimate authority for determining who should be enlisted in the army.[27] As in the metropole, potential Senegalese recruits were divided into four groups: (1) those liable for service in the *Armée active* (comprising the classes 1917–1913 who were 18 to 22 years of age in 1915); (2) those assigned to the *Réserve de l'armée active* (23 to 33 years old); (3) those in the *Armée territoriale* (between 34 and 39); and, finally, (4) those in the *Réserve de l'armée territoriale* (40 to 46 years of age).

Although it was often difficult—owing to the absence of birth certificates—to determine exactly which categories the potential recruits belonged to, all those in the first two groups as well as the classes 1900–1901 in the third (i.e., all those roughly between the ages of 18 and 35) were deemed fit for duty overseas.[28] After administering their physical examinations—which determined who was fit for service—and entertaining requests for exemptions, the boards inducted the new recruits into the French army. Thereafter, they were assigned to the *Bataillon de l'A.O.F.* to begin their training.[29]

The Response of the *Originaires*

The apprehensions of the administrators that conscription would provoke widespread resistance among the *originaires* proved groundless. Indeed, the reverse was more frequently the case. In this respect, the enthusiasm for military service exhibited by many communards resembled the general patriotic response of the metropolitan French levies at the outbreak of hostilities in August 1914.[30] Moreover, this unexpected eagerness to enlist in the army was stimulated in no small measure by Diagne and his ability to link the performance of military duty in the minds of the *originaires* with the confirmation of their rights as French citizens.

Returning to Senegal in mid-December 1915 after the passage of his con-scription law in October, Diagne toured the communes and sought to explain its implications to his constituents. Although admitting that they were "not yet citizens" (because the "*loi des communes*" of 1916 still awaited passage), he was effective in persuading the *originaires* that military service would soon provide the means for becoming so.[31] The thrust of his program—which foiled administrative efforts to redefine the military status of *originaires* and inevitably consolidated the recent political gains made in the election of 1914—was, as Boubacar Gueye explained, obvious to most: "The *métis* and the *Tubabs* wanted to recruit us into the army as *tirailleurs*. And Blaise Diagne created the [conscription] law [so that we could] become citizens, [and] not be considered as *tirailleurs*. And the law was adopted and [later] all the 'black' Senegalese from the Four Communes became citizens. And from that mo-ment, the *métis* lost all their power; the domination they used to have over all the Senegalese was finished."[32]

Aside from affording a solution to long-harbored grievances, Diagne also sought to define the meaning of the war and the communards' participation in terms of affinity with the French cause. Making a forthright appeal to their sense of honor, he explained to the potential recruits how the new law would be implemented and what was expected of them. Ndematy Mbaye recounted:

> He told us that France had entered a war with the Germans. And he said that: "You are friends of the Frenchmen. So, when you are friends with someone—when someone has troubles—you have to help them. So, the Frenchmen have asked [me] to come [and ask you] to help them in the war. So, right now you must [collect] your papers [in order] for them to know your age and so on. And afterwards, we'll call you to take the [medi-cal] examination to see if you are fit or not. If you are fit, you [will] enter the army; if not, you [will] stay here."[33]

In stark contrast with the terror elicited by the French recruitment drives being conducted simultaneously in the Protectorate, Diagne's appeal to patriotic self-interest proved convincing.

Diagne was also abetted in his efforts to rally support for conscription by the actions of many of his younger political followers, who set an example for other communards. These activists—including Galandou Diouf, Papa Mar Diop, Demba Diallo, and Doudou Saar, among others—all volunteered to enlist in the army before being called. Primarily from St. Louis and Western educated (nearly all were, or had been, teachers), their enthusiasm proved infectious. Indeed, although there were some exceptions to the rule, the vast majority of *originaires* eventually called by the French not only complied

Senegalese *originaires* in Thessalonike, 1916. Ousmane Diagne, aged 19, seated far right.
Courtesy of the Ousmane Diagne family.

with their convocation orders but were enthusiastic about doing so.[34] Frequently describing their feelings in euphoric terms—how "glad" they were
to serve, how "happy" they were to fight, how "proud" they felt to be in the
army[35]—the emotional tenor of the moment was perhaps best conveyed by a
recruit from Dakar, Ousmane Diagne: "I was very young and strong. I was
about 20 years old and I was very proud to get into the army. [And] all of my
friends were very proud and pleased to go and enter the army [as well]. [And
after we had been inducted and were taken to the training camp], we were
jumping and bragging and jumping and shouting—we were very pleased to
be there."[36]

The reasons for this extraordinary response were both general and particular. In addition to the powerful incentive of securing French citizenship—
which was by far the most pervasive reason for wishing to enlist in the army—
conscription in the communes was universal and all able-bodied men called
up were obliged to serve.[37] As a result, avoidance of the draft—"even for the
sons of rich men"—was virtually impossible.[38] Furthermore, though ultimately
having "no [more] choice" about being inducted than many of their rural
counterparts, pressure within the Senegalese communities to comply with
the conscription law was much stronger.[39] Because entire age groups, and
sometimes numerous sons within the same family, were being mobilized, the
sense of obligation to perform the same duties expected of their friends and

brothers was intense.[40] Indeed, even among those few who were reluctant to join, aversion to not enlisting like "all the other young men" made noncompliance something that was literally "never [even] considered."[41]

In contrast with the Protectorate, the prospect of performing military service in the communes was also considerably less daunting. Most *originaires* were in comparatively close contact with the French, spoke their language, and, as a result, had a more sophisticated awareness of what to expect from them in the army and understanding of the reasons for the wartime mobilization of soldiers.[42] Moreover, unlike recruitment in rural Senegal, which was often viewed as a "death sentence," the *originaires* were generally less fearful about what awaited them overseas, and some even felt that they had "a good chance to return."[43] Also, most were aware that the material conditions of service in the French army were much better than among the *tirailleurs*.[44] And this foreknowledge—coupled with the suspicions of some that refusal to fulfill their military obligations as citizens would lead to their being "taken as *tirailleurs*"—provided an added inducement for enlisting.[45]

Finally, many *originaires* were also motivated by other, more personal, considerations. Chief among these was a desire to prove their worth as men: to demonstrate their own courage and to "show [others] that 'black' people were not afraid."[46] Some were also excited at the prospect of being able "to travel and to see other things."[47] Though laudable in intent, such sentiments, especially in light of their subsequent experience, also exemplified the youthful naiveté that was pervasive among the recruits.[48] Recalling his ill-considered enthusiasm at the time of his induction, Demba Mboup, who was subsequently disabled by shrapnel, reflected: "I was very happy because I didn't know what the war was really like. So it was a kind of curiosity [for me]—to know what the war was about, and about being a soldier. . . . So I was happy [thinking] I was going to discover new [things and have new] experiences. I didn't know [what would happen to me]."[49] Nevertheless, despite their youth (or perhaps because of it), most of these men entertained hopes for a better future, and they were willing to make the sacrifices required to bring them about. In this regard, the war and their participation in it often carried a personal significance that ranged far beyond the outcome on European battlefields.

Such sentiments, however, were seldom shared by the parents and loved ones of the recruits. As in the rest of Senegal, the prospect of military service overseas aroused the gravest anxiety. Though very few suggested noncompliance, many feared that they "would not come back," while others—especially those old enough to recall the conquest—were outraged by the enthusiasm the recruits showed for serving on behalf of France.[50] Remembering the furious reaction of his grandfather, Ousmane Diagne recalled being told: "'You know what the French did to Lat Dior and all the *Damels* of Kayor. And you want to go and enter *their* army? If you want to do that, [then] go!'

[And my grandfather was very angry because] the French had done many bad things in Senegal. So, he didn't want to see his little grandson go and enter the French army."[51]

Though often distrustful of the French and seldom "understanding the war" or the reasons why their young men were called to fight in it, the opposition of the elder generation was overcome because they recognized that they had "no choice" about sending them.[52] Under such circumstances, their reactions were predictable, and they mirrored those that occurred in the Protectorate. Fathers prayed, entrusting the fate of their offspring to the beneficence of Allah's grace, presented protective charms to their sons, and performed ancient rituals in the hope of sparing their lives.[53] And as parents wept openly, their sons departed for the army and began training to face the dangers that would soon await them in the trenches overseas.[54]

The Results of Conscription in the Communes

Affirming Mamadou Djigo's recollection that "we were as numerous as the leaves on the trees when we left," the scale of the communards' wartime military contribution to France was substantial.[55] By mid-April 1916, or less than six months after the promulgation of the *loi Diagne*, over 5,800 *originaires* had enlisted in the army.[56] By the end of hostilities in November 1918, a minimum of 7,200 soldiers had been conscripted, and of these, more than 5,700 served as combatants in Europe.[57]

Although the colonial administration later sought to minimize the magnitude of the communards' wartime effort, gauged against any objective standards it was considerable.[58] As a percentage of the total population of the communes in 1914, about 13 percent of all inhabitants were conscripted into the French army, and over 10 percent fought overseas.[59] Moreover, these figures do not include over 1,000 *sujets* living in the communes who were recruited between 1916 and 1918 as *tirailleurs*.[60] If these are added to the numbers of *originaires* enlisted, about 15 percent of all communards were obliged to perform military service. This mobilization of men—which was virtually all the able-bodied *originaires* between the ages of 18 and 35—was far more intense than anywhere else in the colony, and by Senegalese standards it was unprecedented.[61] Furthermore, because military service was performed by such a large segment of the population and was directly tied to the question of acquiring French citizenship, the war resulted in a greater degree of politicization in the communes than anywhere else in Senegal.

While much criticism was voiced at the time about the disparity in both the civic status and conditions of service that existed between *originaires* and *tirailleurs*, the negative implications of this line of argument are debatable. Diagne was certainly sensitive to this issue, and on returning from France in late 1915, he sought to ameliorate the potential grievances among rural

Senegalese by advocating the extension of the political rights enjoyed in the communes throughout the Protectorate. His proposals were thwarted by the French authorities, who, though complaining vociferously about the conscription law creating artificial divisions between urban and rural Senegalese, had no intention of resolving them by granting civic rights in the countryside.[62] Moreover, though some *tirailleurs* resented the comparative privileges accorded the *originaires*, others, aware of the scale of the demands made on them, believed that recruitment in the Protectorate was preferable to conscription in the communes.[63] This latter viewpoint, at least in one respect, is compelling. Though the proportion of casualties suffered by the *originaires* was slightly less than that incurred by their rural counterparts, the impact of the war on them—reckoned in deaths per family—was much greater.[64] In this regard, the price paid by the *originaires* for their French citizenship was very high indeed.

Yet, as their enthusiasm indicates, Diagne's appeal for an amelioration of past injustices through the performance of military duty struck a responsive cord with African communards. Moreover, as the French war effort reached crisis point in 1918 and their need for more soldiers grew even more dire, Diagne attempted to extend the political principle invoked in the communes throughout the rest of A.O.F. In this context, he became the chief recruiting agent of the French government, but he also sought to redefine the meaning of military service in West Africa from a senseless sacrifice into a "war to obtain rights" there as well.[65]

THE DIAGNE MISSION OF 1918

Clemenceau's Decisions

The suspension of military recruitment in West Africa in October 1917 proved brief. One month later, the prosecution of the war reached a defining moment in France. For seven months there had been an uninterrupted series of disasters: the debacle at the Chemin des Dames in April, the outbreak of mutinies in the French army beginning in May, the rout of their Italian allies at Caporetto in October, and the collapse of the Russian front in the autumn followed by the Bolshevik seizure of power on 7 November and their overtures to the Germans for an immediate and separate armistice. These developments, coupled with growing war weariness at home and calls from the extreme Left for a negotiated peace settlement, conspired to bring Georges Clemenceau to power on 16 November 1917.

The situation Clemenceau inherited was grave. In addition to the rapidly deteriorating state of the French army and a projected shortfall of 200,000 "effectives" for the next year, the new premier also faced the unnerving prospect of upwards of 70 German divisions being released from Russia for ser-

Charles Mangin (far left) and Georges Clemenceau (center) conferring near the Front, 1918. Courtesy of Bibliothèque nationale de France, Paris: Collection Mangin (G 136815). Reprinted with permission.

---

vice on the western front before France's new American allies could make their added weight felt. Under such circumstances, Clemenceau authorized a series of extreme measures calculated to stifle domestic dissent and strengthen the army, while once again looking to West Africa for additional troops.[66]

Soliciting the advice of Charles Mangin, Clemenceau requested a study of the feasibility of undertaking further recruitment in the colonies. The general responded affirmatively in a detailed report of 8 December. Nine days later, Clemenceau informed the High Command of his decision to augment French forces with more African troops. Governor General Joost Van Vollenhoven was notified the next day that another extensive drive—comparable in scale to the one conducted in 1915 to 1916—would be carried out in A.O.F. Dismissing administrative forebodings about the threat such an initiative might pose to French control in the colonies, Clemenceau tersely responded: "Better to run the risks [of insurrections] in Africa, than [to suffer defeat] at the Front."[67]

Having resolved to resume recruitment in West Africa, Clemenceau faced the question of how best to implement it. Recognizing that excessive reliance on coercion had precipitated uprisings in the past, he was unimpressed by the feasibility reports submitted by the colonial administration. These anticipated widespread resistance and called for additional troops and weapons (including war planes, machine guns, and grenades) to carry out the policy.[68] Mangin, who had warned him about the administrative opposition he would encounter, had long recommended dispatching special *"commissaires"* of the Republic (which would be high-ranking military officers) to circumvent the civilian authorities and stimulate recruitment.[69] Though accepting Mangin's advice in principal, Clemenceau (whose distrust of the military was notorious) opted for a different means of achieving it, turning instead to the deputy from Senegal for assistance.

This was a shrewd decision. Diagne, although consistently assuming a patriotic stance, had long been a severe critic of both the recruitment methods employed in the colonies as well as the callous misuse of West African troops by the High Command. Moreover, aside from the obvious symbolism involved, as an acknowledged spokesman for African interests, Diagne's support in Parliament would serve to facilitate the implementation of the premier's program. Finally, having been instrumental in precipitating the downfall of the Painlevé government on 13 November, which brought Clemenceau to power, Diagne was perceived by the premier as a dependable political ally.[70]

Diagne, who did not solicit responsibility for the new role envisioned for him by Clemenceau, set conditions for his services. In return for heading the projected recruitment drive as Commissioner for the Republic in West Africa, he demanded powers equal to those of the governor general as well as the right to correspond directly with the Minister of Colonies. Furthermore, he was granted authority to summarily dismiss incompetent officials who impeded the recruitment effort. Finally, consistent with his campaign platform in 1914 and his public pronouncements thereafter, he obtained an "ensemble of reforms" designed to extend the impetus for change throughout the Federation and thereby present the meaning of the war for Africans in a new light.

These concessions—the first ever exacted by West Africans from a French government—were intended to ameliorate the most odious obligations of prewar colonial servitude, to secure tangible benefits for the soldiers after the war, and, hence, offer positive incentives to Africans for performing military service. Specifically, they called for exemption for recruits from the *indigénat* as well as from corvée labor and the head tax for both them and their families. Moreover, veterans were to be accorded preferred status for jobs in the public sector on their return and, provided they were decorated for bravery, to become eligible for French citizenship. An *école de médecine* was to be founded in Dakar to train African medical assistants, as was a school of agriculture (including a veterinary section) to improve farming techniques. Finally, in a more ominous provision (but one that had never been considered), sanatoriums of 200 beds were to be built in each of the colonies to care for ill and wounded veterans. These measures, along with the designation of

Diagne as Commissioner for the Republic, were signed by Clemenceau and promulgated by government decree on 14 January 1918.[71]

Clemenceau's appointment of Diagne to head the new recruitment drive in West Africa aroused a storm of controversy.[72] Despite vociferous opposition to his nomination from a wide array of colonial interest groups and their persistent forecasts that his mission was doomed to failure, Diagne embarked on his new duties with enthusiasm. Departing for Senegal in February 1918, he was determined to convince rural Africans that the reforms he had secured were worth fighting for and that, symbolized in the person of himself, they prefigured a fundamental redefinition in the relations that had previously existed in the colonies between Africans and Europeans.

Diagne's Recruiting Mission

Diagne arrived in Dakar on 12 February 1918. His mission, which toured the Federation during the next six months, was conceived primarily as a propaganda exercise. It was designed to dispel African fears about the fate of the recruits, offer positive incentives for enlisting, and prepare the way for the mobilization of men, which would only ensue after the commission had completed its task in each colony and Diagne had given the order to commence. As such, it placed a premium on persuasion as a means of obtaining recruits, and coercion was explicitly forbidden except as a last resort, and only then in cases of noncompliance or resistance.[73]

The mission was accordingly organized with meticulous care and intended to carry maximum psychological impact. Diagne had prearranged for the furlough of 400 *tirailleurs* (75 of whom were from Senegal), whose dispatch to their colonies of origin coincided with the arrival of his mission there and who sometimes accompanied it. Since soldiers had never before returned from France (except as invalids), these "agents of propaganda" were intended to physically impress on the population that service in the army was not necessarily synonymous with a sentence of death.[74] Moreover, throughout his tour Diagne was accompanied by an extensive entourage. In addition to several French administrators and army officers, it also contained a large group of highly decorated African officers and N.C.O.s, who were intended to demonstrate the enhanced status that might be acquired through military service. Finally, to exemplify the changing tenor of colonial society, its African members were accorded privileges commensurate with Europeans. They rode first-class on trains (which had previously been reserved exclusively for French passengers), and they were housed in official residences when on tour, which had never before been condoned.[75]

The Commissioner for the Republic also sought to demonstrate that the previous contempt exhibited toward Africans would no longer be tolerated and that even French officials were not immune from accountability for their actions. Diagne insisted on, and generally received, public deference from the local authorities, all of whom he outranked, in each of the colonies he visited. In a series of actions charged with symbolic meaning in the colonial mind, he intervened on several occasions to correct misuses of authority and exercised his power to dismiss French officials. No less than three administrators—including two *commandants de cercle*, one of whom had sanctioned the premature "use of armed force" to recruit soldiers—were summarily relieved of their duties by him.[76] Such authority wielded by an African over Europeans was unprecedented, and though it outraged numerous *colons*, it provided a much needed psychological tonic to the downtrodden subjects.[77]

Diagne not only assuaged long-harbored African resentment over their maltreatment by the French but he also displayed a much more sophisticated awareness of internal African power structures than the colonial authorities ever had. He was also much more adroit than they at persuading the rural African elites to comply with recruitment demands. On his arrival in Senegal, for example, he convened a meeting of provincial and cantonal chiefs to explain the aims of his mission and thereafter assiduously courted their assistance. Diagne informed them that during the upcoming recruitment drive, emphasis would be placed on enlisting their remaining sons. In return for setting an example by volunteering, these *fils de chef* would be accorded preferred status in the army and made eligible for immediate promotion.[78] This proved persuasive because, in addition to conforming to their ancient roles as hereditary military leaders, it would also consolidate the position of their families in the postwar political order.[79]

Aside from enlisting the support of the "great" chiefs, the commissioner also sought approbation for his mission from the Muslim elite. Journeying to Diourbel, he met with Amadu Bamba (whom he had befriended as a customs official in Gabon during Bamba's exile there) and received his blessing. He also obtained the active assistance of several other Mouride leaders, including Ibra Fall and Anta Mbacke, as well as that of Malik Sy, the head of the Tidjaniya order.[80] As such, Diagne's overtures resulted in a coalition for the purpose of recruitment between the emerging Senegalese elite based in the communes and the older ones in the Protectorate. Not only was this alliance among African interest groups unprecedented, but it also provided the basis for pursuing still more thoroughgoing reforms in the rural French administration after the war was concluded.[81]

Only after having secured the support of the rural elites did Diagne proceed to convey his message directly to the masses. In Senegal as elsewhere in West Africa where he toured, this was accomplished by means of public gatherings (*palabres*), where Diagne, accompanied by his official entourage and introduced by local notables, addressed huge crowds. These gatherings were conducted throughout Senegal (except along the Fleuve, where the plague epidemic prevented safe passage) between mid-February and mid-

March before the commission traveled to the remaining colonies in A.O.F. Emphasizing the enhanced prestige Africans had acquired through service in the army as well as the concessions he had obtained from the French—which, he maintained, heralded a "new policy" toward Africans by the government— Diagne asserted the egalitarian implications of performing military duty in unmistakable terms: "Those who fall under fire fall neither as whites nor as blacks. They fall as Frenchmen and for the same flag."[82] These sentiments were echoed by his principal lieutenant on the mission, Galandou Diouf, who publicly avowed four months earlier: "We want rights to follow duty. . . . We want equality in society as in the trenches before death."[83] This approach represented nothing less than a forthright appeal to African aspirations for an end to their servile status and a more just and equitable colonial order. Having presented the significance of the war in this context, the recruitment drives, which were otherwise conducted using induction procedures similar to those employed in the past, commenced in Senegal on 17 March 1918.

The African Response

Diagne's appeal proved effective. In Senegal as in the rest of A.O.F., Africans responded to the renewed calls for soldiers in a fashion that belied the expectations of his critics and made the recruitment drive of 1918 the most successful of the war. Moreover, though the degree of enthusiasm exhibited by the recruits varied, this drive seldom inspired the terror elicited by previous ones and, by contrast, aroused comparatively little active resistance. This dramatic transformation in African attitudes toward recruitment was due, in the opinion of nearly all who enlisted, to Diagne's personal prestige and his ability to assuage African fears while presenting military service as a duty to be performed in exchange for acquiring enhanced status and securing more extensive rights in the future.[84] Offering a vivid insight into the psychological dynamics of the Diagne mission—with its careful attention to egalitarian symbolism, its reliance on the influence of local elites, and the aspirations for the future it appealed to—Abdoulaye Diaw remembered:

> I was in Bamako [on leave] when Blaise Diagne and Galandou Diouf came to recruit soldiers. [And my friend and I] attended the meeting he called for recruitment. [And] Blaise Diagne's propaganda [at] this meeting [was very effective]. Because, before he came, he had made the son of the *chef de quartier* in Bamako a lieutenant. [So] almost all the town was there, because the chief had called everybody, and there were a lot, a lot, a lot of people! The fact that Blaise Diagne had made his son a lieutenant was a very important thing for him personally, because . . . for the Bambara becoming an officer in the army was a very great honor. [And Diagne came] with many, many people—August Brunet [the lieutenant governor of Haut-

Blaise Diagne (center, with pointing finger) on his 1918 recruiting mission speaking before a crowd in Bamako. Document preserved at the Centre historique des Archives nationales, Paris: Papiers Galandou Diouf (110/AP/2, 8). Reprinted with permission.

Sénégal et Niger] and [other] French administrators. [And] he was [accompanied by] some Bambara soldiers too. But they were not simple soldiers; all of them had *"grades."* [And after speeches by Galandou Diouf, the *chef de quartier*, and his son, Diagne spoke.] [And although] I have forgotten almost all his speech, I remember that he told them that he was sent by the President of the Republic of France who needed [more] soldiers to go on fighting. And after [he finished], he introduced the son of the *chef de quartier* to [all] the other parents that were at the meeting. [And he told them:] "I want some other soldiers to enter the army, so perhaps they too can become lieutenants." So as soon as he said that, everybody gave him the name of his son. And the secretary was writing down their names. [And] that's why he succeeded with his recruitment mission [among the Bambara]—[because] everybody was expecting his son to become an officer one day.[85]

Some ascribed the success of the mission to other factors than hopes for acquiring a hitherto inconceivable rank in the army. Recalling its significance in the context of the previous servile relationship that had existed between all Africans and Europeans, one Senegalese recruit, Amar Seck, emphasized that "when Blaise Diagne came [here] more respect was given to 'black' people [by the French]."[86] Others, informed that "the Germans were about to win the war," were persuaded to "volunteer" for the army with the expectation that afterwards their services would be "rewarded" by a grateful metropolitan government.[87] In several Lebu villages along the *Petite-Côte*, the residents, aware of the Diagne Laws of 1915 and 1916, demanded similar rights as the communards in exchange for their services. These *sujets*, much to the dismay of the French administration, wanted nothing less than to become citizens. As Momar Cisse of Bargny explained:

> The French wanted to consider us as *tirailleurs*. But we didn't want to be *tirailleurs*; we wanted to be citizens like those in Dakar, Rufisque—the Four Communes. And there were many problems [with the French *commandant*] about this, and [the elders] wrote to Blaise Diagne [to ask him] to arrange the situation [for us]—to make us become citizens. [And Daigne wrote back and] told us that: "you have to enter the army as *tirailleurs*. But later, after you are in the army, I'll change the law and you will become citizens."[88]

In addition to offering compelling incentives for enlisting, the mission also dispelled long-standing misgivings about the fate that awaited recruits. In contrast with the past, when many Africans believed that "all the soldiers sent to France died there," most of those enlisting in 1918 felt they had a reasonable chance of surviving.[89]

This expectation also helps to explain why resistance to the recruitment demands was much less frequent in 1918 than before. Flight ceased to be a major problem. Even though external emigration persisted in several more remote parts of the colony, it appears to have been on a much reduced scale and, with the exception of Basse Casamance, occurred only in areas the commission did not visit.[90] Armed resistance by entire villages also ended, and compliance was obtained with a minimal amount of coercion. Although *navetanes* continued to be seized in several *cercles* and isolated groups of refugees sometimes sought to resist capture, resort to the more brutal recruitment methods of the past—including the wholesale roundup of hostages, the burning of crops and villages, and the forcible suppression of armed resistance—appears to have ceased.[91]

As a result of the altered psychological environment created by Diagne's mission, Senegalese recruits in 1918 were more readily forthcoming than ever before. "Volunteers," which had previously been virtually "nonexistent," were officially reckoned at nearly a quarter of all recruits.[92] The proportion of potential recruits deemed fit for service by the medical examiners, which

had previously amounted to only about one-quarter to one-third of those presented, also appears to have risen substantially.[93] This indicates that compliance with the recruitment regulations was more strictly adhered to by the
chiefs and that their earlier practice of attempting to shield some members of
their communities through the presentation of the physically infirm and the
very young was less frequent.[94]

Furthermore, though ultimately having "no choice" about enlisting, most
recruits willingly complied when called.[95] Like many of their counterparts in
the communes and a few of their predecessors in the Protectorate, these men
were also motivated by a series of personal considerations: by their youthful
naiveté and their ignorance of "what war was like," by their masculine pride,
or by their sense of obligation to their families or their faith.[96] Even among
those who were reluctant to enter the army, their sense of duty to perform the
obligations expected of others ensured that few considered evasion.[97] Even
though most village chiefs continued with the practice of requiring only one
son per family to be presented before the French commissions, now younger
siblings were not the only ones sent. Eldest sons figured among the 1918
recruits, as did married men.[98]

The nature of this response astonished French officials, and the number of
soldiers eventually raised surpassed all expectations. Originally required to
furnish 7,000 men, the colony provided some 7,916 recruits in less than eleven
weeks between the middle of March and the beginning of June.[99] Moreover,
the pattern evidenced in Senegal was not exceptional but was repeated
throughout the West African Federation. Initial projections in January were
for 47,000 recruits; by August some 63,276 had been enrolled.[100] As the scale
of this success indicates, Diagne was perceived in the eyes of Africans not
only as the representative of the communes but of "all of Senegal" and, indeed, "of all the 'black' colonies."[101] As such, the magnetism of his appeal
for a redefinition of the prewar colonial order through military service not
only proved compelling; it also represented a far more extensive politicization
of the meaning of the war among the *sujet* population than had ever occurred.
As their sheer numbers and the nature of their response attests, Diagne symbolized aspirations for the future that not only the Senegalese but all West
Africans were willing to make in order to achieve substantial aims.

Wartime Recruitment in Senegal: A Summation

The recruitment drive of 1918 as well as the implementation of conscription in the communes raised an additional 15,500 men for the French army.
Combined with those enlisted in the Protectorate between 1914 and 1917,
the total number of Senegalese recruited as a direct consequence of the First
World War can be estimated at approximately 29,000 soldiers. The distribution of this burden—which amounted to nearly 2.4 percent of the colony's

Table 3.1 Intensity of Recruitment in Senegal, 1914–1918

	Population	Recruits		Total Recruits	Percentage of Population
	1921	1914–1917	1918		
Communes:					
Originaires	22,771	5,862	1,749	7,611	>33.42
Sujets	35,807	992	56	1,048	2.93
Total	58,578	6,854	1,805	8,659	14.78
Central Senegal:					
"District for the Defense of the Fortress of Dakar"					
Sine-Saloum	189,053	3,179	1,603	4,782	2.53
Tivaouane	109,920	1,339	1,067	2,406	2.19
Thiès	100,434	765	1,117	1,882	1.87
Diourbel	159,922	1,438	1,515	2,953	1.85
Total	559,329	6,721	5,302	12,023	2.15
Northern, Eastern, and Southern Senegal:					
"Military and Territorial Subdivision of Senegal"					
Niani Ouli	47,086	282	176	458	1.35
Haute Gambie	—	114	66	180	1.35
Matam	65,665	550	330	880	1.34
Podor	74,263	500	427	927	1.25
Casamance	196,406	1,050	1,051	2,101	1.07
Bakel	36,515	240	144	384	1.05
Saldé	36,258	223	143	366	1.01
Louga	94,520	757	165	922	0.98
Dagana	41,748	260	92	352	0.84
Total	592,461	3,976	2,594	6,570	1.11
Other *Tirailleurs***:**					
Origins Unrecorded	1,650				
Totals:					
Communes	58,578	6,854	1,805	8,659	14.78
Protectorate	1,151,790	12,347	7,896	20,243	1.65
Total	1,210,368	19,201	9,701	28,902	2.39

Sources: Population: *Annuaire du Governement Général de l'A.O.F., 1922*, pp. 66, 368–405. Recruitment: Archives nationales du Sénégal: Affaires militaire: 4 D 19, 4 D 49, 4 D 54, 4 D 55, 4 D 65, 4 D 68, 4 D 69, 4 D 73, 4 D 76; and Affaires politiques: 17 G 241-108.

total population—is broken down in Table 3.1 by geographic areas, years of enlistment, and comparative intensity.

As these figures indicate, the salient characteristic of wartime recruitment in Senegal was its regional disparity. Less than 5 percent of the colony's population—that residing in the communes—provided over a quarter of all recruits (29.96 percent). When combined with those enlisted in the Protectorate's heartland (the four *cercles* in the District for the Defense of the Fortress of Dakar), these two areas, which accounted for only slightly more than half the population (51.05 percent), furnished slightly over three-quarters (75.89 percent) of all soldiers whose origins are known. By contrast, the more peripheral and less densely populated regions of the colony—the Fleuve, eastern Senegal, and the Casamance—though containing a roughly equal number of the colony's inhabitants, were much less touched by the demands for men and furnished less than one-quarter of all recruits (24.11 percent of those whose origins are known). Though reflecting the comparative degree of French control in particular areas of the colony, this disparity also offers a rough index—corresponding to the intensity of the demands made on them—of the political, economic, and social impact of the war within specific regions.[102]

Despite the incontestable brutality of the recruitment methods employed by the French between 1914 and 1917, it is ironic that Diagne—and especially the role he played in the drive of 1918—has long been the focus of perhaps the most intense controversy. Condemned by French *colons* at the time as a political opportunist compared with Van Vollenhoven, or alternatively as a dangerous threat to the French colonial order, Diagne was also subsequently vilified by generations of African nationalists, who viewed him as a willing agent of French imperialism who needlessly sacrificed the lives of Senegalese soldiers.[103] These judgments are erroneous in the first instance and excessively harsh in the second.

Once Clemenceau came to power, a resumption of recruitment in West Africa was inevitable. Diagne recognized this fact and could not have prevented it any more than Van Vollenhoven could (who, despite his former criticism of the policy, stressed his own willingness to implement it). By becoming Commissioner for the Republic, Diagne did, however, have a major influence on how the policy was conducted. In exchange for his active participation, he obtained significant concessions from the French government, ensured that the harsh and incompetent methods that had created so much suffering in the past were not duplicated, and sought not only to redefine the meaning of the war for Africans but also the nature of the preexisting colonial order. Furthermore, although over 63,000 West Africans were eventually recruited in the spring and summer of 1918, very few of these soldiers actually served as combatants in France before the armistice.

Diagne's stance during this period was consistent with both his avowed Republicanism as well as his life long hatred of racism.[104] As such, his policy was consistently defined within a colonial context, but with the proviso that enhanced rights for Africans were forthcoming as a result. He sought, in short, to strive for increasing egalitarianism in an inherently inegalitarian order. This was the reason behind the success of his appeals, but also eventually the source of disillusionment, after the exaggerated expectations he gave rise to proved at odds with reality.

Irrespective of the rectitude of his actions, Diagne nevertheless continued to pursue these goals not only as commissioner for recruitment in the colonies and in his postwar political activities, but also in the context of overseeing the soldiers' treatment by the French once they were in the army. It is to this later aspect of the Senegalese wartime experience—the fate that awaited the combatants overseas and its impact on the lives of those who survived—that we now turn.

NOTES

[1] Michael Crowder, *Senegal: A Study of French Assimilation Policy*, 2d rev. ed. (London: Methuen, 1967); and G. Wesley Johnson, Jr., *The Emergence of Black Politics in Senegal: The Struggle for Power in the Four Communes, 1900–1920* (Stanford: Stanford University Press, 1971), pp. 3–89.

[2] On the social composition of the communes, see: G. Wesley Johnson, Jr., "The Senegalese Urban Elite, 1900–1945," in *Africa and the West: Intellectual Responses to European Culture*, ed. Philip D. Curtin (Madison: University of Wisconsin Press, 1972), pp. 139–187. On local politics, see: James F. Searing, "Accommodation and Resistance: Chiefs, Muslim Leaders, and Politicians in Colonial Senegal, 1890–1934" (Ph.D. Diss.: Princeton University, 1985), pp. 360–400; and François Zuccarilli, *La Vie politique Sénégalaise (1789–1940)* (Paris: CHEAM, 1987), pp. 25–98.

[3] Abdoulaye Pierre Diaw: 2A.

[4] Boubacar Gueye: 2A.

[5] On French countermeasures against the *originaires*, see: Johnson, *The Emergence of Black Politics*, pp. 93–153; and Searing, "Accommodation and Resistance," pp. 360–400.

[6] On the formation of the *Jeunes Sénégalais*, see: Lamine Gueye, *Itinéraire Africain* (Paris: Présence Africain, 1966).

[7] Boubacar Gueye: 1B.

[8] On Diagne's background, see: ANS: Affaires politiques: 17 G 233 (108) and 17 G 234 (108); Johnson, *The Emergence of Black Politics*, pp. 154–59; Amody Aly Dieng, *Blaise Diagne: Député noire de l'Afrique* (Paris: Editions Choka, 1990), pp. 51–79; and Charles Cros, *La parole est à M. Blaise Diagne* (Paris: Aubenas, 1961).

[9] Ndematy Mbaye: 2A and 2B.

[10] *La Démocratie du Sénégal*, 23 mai 1914.

[11] Boubacar Gueye: 1B.

[12] The final results were: Diagne, 2,424; Heimburger, 2,249; and Carpot, 472. On the election of 1914, see: *ANS:* Affaires politiques: 17 G 15 and 17 G 234 (108); *ANOM:* 14

MI 1091; Johnson, *The Emergence of Black Politics*, pp. 154–77; and Searing, "Accommodation and Resistance," pp. 360–400.

[13] Aminata Ngom: 1A.

[14] *L'A.O.F.*, 2 mai 1914.

[15] Johnson, *The Emergence of Black Politics*, pp. 172–77.

[16] Charles Mangin à Gouverneur Général, *ANS*: Affaires militaires: 4 D 31.

[17] On the changing prewar military status of the *originaires*, see: *ANS*: Affaires militaires: 4 D 19. For discussions of the political impasse between Diagne and the French authorities, see: Marc Michel, "Citoyenneté et service militaire dans les quatre communes du Sénégal au cours de la Première Guerre mondiale," in *Perspectives nouvelles sur le passé de l'Afrique noire et de Madagascar: Mélanges offerts à Hubert Deschamps* (Paris: Editions de la Sorbonne, 1974), pp. 299–314.

[18] *Chambre des Députés*, Débats, 1915, pp. 1072–76.

[19] For a transcript of the debate, see: *Chambre des Députés, Débats*, 1915, pp. 986–91.

[20] *Chambre des Députés*, Débats, 1915, pp. 1072–76.

[21] *Chambre des Députés*, Débats, September 1916.

[22] *Chambre des Députés*, Débats, September 1916.

[23] On the Diagne Laws of 1915 and 1916, see also: Johnson, *The Emergence of Black Politics*, pp. 183–91; Searing, "Accommodation and Resistance," pp. 416–33; Michel, "Citoyenneté et service," pp. 299–304; and Uyisenga Charles, "La Participation de la Colonie du Sénégal à 'l'effort de guerre,' 1914–1918" (Mémoire de Mâitrise: University of Dakar, 1978), pp. 63–69.

[24] For difficulties encountered by relying on the *état civil* of the communards to create conscription lists, see the report of Lieutenant Governor Antonetti: *ANS:* Affaires militaires: 4 D 24.

[25] Such objections were voiced by Lieutenant Governor Antonetti as well as by numerous *colons* and *métis*. For the correspondence pertaining to the use of the *jugements supplétifs,* see: *ANS*: Affairres militaires: 4D25.

[26] For detailed descriptions of notification procedures and penalties for noncompliance, see: Ousmane Diagne: 2A and 2B; Mbaye Khary Diagne: 1B and 2A; Boubacar Gueye: 2B; Abdoulaye Gueye: 1B; Aliou Diakhate: 1B; and Demba Mboup: 3B and 4A.

[27] *ANS:* Affaires militaires: 4 D 19.

[28] *ANS:* Affaires militaires: 4 D 19. *Originaires* in the classes 1892–1889 (42 to 46 years old) were never called. On the difficulty of determining the ages of some recruits, see: *ANS:* Affaires militaires: 4 D 24.

[29] On the medical examinations and induction procedures, see: *ANS:* Affaires militaires: 4 D 25. See also: Mamadou Djigo: 2A; and Demba Mboup: 4A. For discussions of the application of the *loi Diagne* and conscription methods in the communes, see also: Charles, "La Participation de la Colonie du Sénégal," pp. 69–93; and Michel, "Citoyenneté et service," pp. 304–14.

[30] On the initial French response to the war, see Jean-Jacques Becker, *The Great War and the French People* (Leamington Spa/Heidelberg/Dover, NH: Berg, 1993), pp. 9–102.

[31] Abdoulaye Ndiaye: 2A.

[32] Boubacar Gueye: 1B. On the correlation between military service, citizenship, and the end of creole and French domination in the communes, see also: Abdoulaye Diaw: 1B.

[33] Ndematy Mbaye: 2A. On the theme of providing "help" to the French (in the context of either being or becoming French citizens), see also: Ndiaga Niang: 2B; Thiecouta Diallo: 2A and 2B; and Demba Mboup: 12A.

[34] The example set by these men was referred to by one-third of all *originaires* interviewed. See especially: Ousmane Diagne: 2A and 2B; Mbaye Khary Diagne: 1A and 5A; Abdoulaye Diaw: 2A; and Abdoulaye Ndiaye: 2B. Among the 15 *originaires* interviewed, nearly all expressed genuine excitement about entering the army. Exceptions were Aliou Diakhate (2A), who was "not happy to go," and possibly Ndiaga Niang (2B).

[35] See: Thiecouta Diallo: 2B; Abdoulaye Gueye: 1B; and Mbaye Khary Diagne: 1B.

[36] Ousmane Diagne: 2B.

[37] Fully two-thirds of all *originaires* interviewed either mentioned their status as citizens or their desire to become such as decisive considerations influencing their response.

[38] Ndiaga Niang: 2B. Flight to avoid military service—a common occurrence in parts of rural Senegal—was impracticable because of the concomitant recruitment drives conducted there between November 1915 and January 1916.

[39] Abdoulaye Ndiaye: 1B.

[40] Ndiaga Niang (2B), for example, was but one of five sons conscripted in his family. This practice contrasted with the recruitment procedures followed in the Protectorate, where normally only one son was taken from each compound per year. On the influence of peers on the recruits' response, see also: Abdoulaye Gueye: 1B; and Abdoulaye Diaw: 2A.

[41] Aliou Diakhate: 1B and 2A. On the inconceivability of not enlisting, see also: Abdoulaye Gueye: 1B.

[42] At least two-thirds of the *originaires* interviewed were fluent in French at the time of their induction, and over half had attended a French primary school.

[43] Thiecouta Diallo: 2B.

[44] Boubacar Gueye: 1B.

[45] Abdoulaye Diaw: 2A. See also Boubacar Gueye: 1B.

[46] Giribul Diallo: 1A. See also: Mamadou Djigo: 2A; Thiecouta Diallo: 2B; and Aliou Diakhate: 1B.

[47] Giribul Diallo: 1A.

[48] Over one-third of the veterans interviewed explicitly referred to their youth as a factor in shaping their outlook.

[49] Demba Mboup: 4A.

[50] Parental admonitions for noncompliance are referred to only by Mamadou Djigo (2A), whose father had been imprisoned by the French for ten years. On fears that certain death awaited the recruits, see: Aliou Diakhate: 2A; and Mamadou Djigo: 2A.

[51] Ousmane Diagne: 2B.

[52] Ousmane Diagne: 2B; and Aliou Diakhate: 2A. On the absence of parental choice, see also: Abdoulaye Ndiaye: 2B; and Thiecouta Diallo: 2B.

[53] For prayers, see: Demba Mboup: 4A; Thiecouta Diallo: 2B; and Aliou Diakhate: 2A. The use of protective charms may have been less pervasive among the *originaires* than among the *tirailleurs*. For references to being presented with charms before they departed (as well as to the performance of other Wolof rituals by their parents), see: Abdoulaye Ndiaye: 5B; Thiecouta Diallo: 2B; and Demba Mboup: 4A. Those implying they were sent without protective charms include: Abdoulaye Gueye: 1B; and Aliou Diakhate: 2A.

[54] On the weeping of their parents, see: Mamadou Djigo: 2A; Mbaye Khary Diagne: 1B; Ndiaga Niang: 2B; and Demba Mboup: 4A.

[55] Mamadou Djigo: 3B.

[56] The figure was 5,862 according to Governor General Clozel. See *ANS:* Affaires militaires: 4 D 19.

[57] Official and semiofficial estimates of the total number of *originaires* conscripted range from 7,183 to 7,804. The figure of 7,611, which was the estimate submitted by the governor general in a special report immediately after the Armistice, appears most probable. See *ANOM*: 14 MI 2356. Different estimates also exist for the number of *originaires* sent to France. According to transport records, which seem most authentic, 5,732 soldiers were embarked from Senegal during the war. See the report of the Commandent Supérieur, Général Goullet, 18 July 1918, *ANOM:* 14 MI 323. As with the recruitment figures for the *tirailleurs*, it should also be stressed that all such estimates must remain approximations.

[58] On the acrimonious postwar debate between Diagne and the Commandant Supérieur des Troupes de l'A.O.F., Général François Bonnier, over the numbers of *originaire* draft-evaders and combat deaths, see: *AG*: EMA: 7 N 2121. See also Michel, "Citoyenneté et service," pp. 304–08.

[59] Though estimates vary slightly, the African population of the communes was not more than 58,500. Hence, 13 percent were conscripted and 9.7 percent served overseas (see Table 3.1).

[60] According to the archival records, the number was 1,048. *ANS:* Affaires militaires: 4 D 65.

[61] Because of gross inaccuracies contained in the *état civil* in the communes, controversy lingers about the proportion of *originaires* conscripted compared with those who evaded the draft. See, for example, Michel, "Citoyenneté et service," pp. 304–08. Though some evasion may have occurred, it was comparatively insignificant. According to the electoral rolls of 1914, there were some 8,000 electors, of whom about 80 percent were adult African males. Assuming that a substantial percentage of these were over 35 years of age, and taking into account the 2,300 who were declared *originaires* by means of *jugements supplétifs* in 1916, this suggests that the 7,200 Senegalese conscripted during the war represented a near total mobilization of those of military age. This conclusion is also corroborated by the oral histories (see Abdoulaye Gueye: 1B; and Aliou Diakhate: 2A). For the number of African electors and *jugements supplétifs*, see, respectively: *ANOM*: 14 MI 2877 and 14 MI 2356.

[62] On Diagne's proposals for the Protectorate and French objections to the artificial distinction between *originaires* and *sujets*, see Lieutenant Governor Antonetti's report on the implementation of the conscription law, in: *ANS:* Affaires militaires: 4 D 24.

[63] Abdou Karim Gaye: 3A and 6A; Soudou Laye: 2A.

[64] See Chapter 5 for casualty estimates.

[65] Niaki Gueye: 1B. See also Daour Gueye: 2A.

[66] Jean-Baptiste Duroselle, *Clemenceau* (Paris: Fayard, 1988), pp. 610–82.

[67] Clemenceau's remark is cited in: Charles-Robert Ageron, "Clemenceau et la question coloniale," in *Clemenceau et la Justice* (Paris: Publications de la Sorbonne, 1983), p. 80. On Clemenceau's decision to undertake further recruitment in Africa, see: *AN*: Commission de l'Armée, C 7499, 18, 1917–18, p. 229. Mangin's report and his relationship with Clemenceau, see: Archives de la Guerre [hereafter *AG*]: État-Major de l'Armée: 7 N 440; and *AN*: 149 AP 116 (Papiers Mangin); and Charles

Mangin, *Lettres de guerre à sa femme, 1914–1918*, ed. Antoinette Cavaignac Mangin (Paris: Fayard, 1950), pp. 224–34. On administrative reservations about renewing recruitment, see: *ANS:* Affaires militaires: 4 D 74. On the origins of the 1918 recruitment policy and its execution by Blaise Diagne, see also Werner Glinga, "Ein Koloniales Paradoxon—Blaise Diagne und die Rekrutierungsmission 1918," in *Tirailleurs Sénégalais: Zur Bildlichen und Literarischen Darstellung Afrikanischer Soldaten im Dienst Frankreichs. Présentations littéraires et figuratives de soldats Africains au service de la France*, ed. Janos Riesz and Joachim Schultz (Frankfurt am Main: Verlag Peter Lang, 1989), pp. 21–37; Marc Michel, "La genèse du recrutement de 1918 en Afrique noire Française," *Revue Française d'Histoire d'Outre-Mer* 58 (1971), pp. 433–50; and Michael Crowder, "Blaise Diagne and the Recruitment of African Troops for the 1914–1918 War" (1967), in *Colonial West Africa: Collected Essays* (London: Frank Cass, 1978), pp. 104–21.

[68] *ANS:* Affaires militaires: 4 D 73 and 4 D 74.

[69] *AN:* 149 AP 11-6 (Papiers Mangin), and Mangin, *Lettres de guerre*, p. 62.

[70] On Diagne's parliamentary record, including his condemnation of the use of the Senegalese during the attacks on the Chemin des Dames as "human material to be massacred" and his caustic criticism of Painlevé's government, see: *Journal Officiel de la République Française, Chambre des Députés, Comités Secrets*, 29 juin 1917, p. 324; and *Journal Officiel de la République Française, Chambre des Députés*, 13 novembre 1917.

[71] For the text of these decrees and the powers granted to Diagne, see: *Journal Officiel de la République Française*, 17 janvier 1918, pp. 677–81.

[72] See, for example, *ANS:* Affaires militaires: 4 D 74; Mangin, *Lettres de guerre*, p. 234; *AN:* 149 AP 11-6 (Papiers Mangin); and *Union coloniale, Bulletin de la Section A.O.F.* (1918), pp. 10–11.

[73] *ANS:* Affaires militaires: 4 D 74.

[74] *ANS:* Affaires militaires: 4 D 82.

[75] *ANS:* Affaires politiques: 17 G 15.

[76] *ANS:* Affaires militaires: 4 D 74. By contrast, only five administrators had been dismissed from the colonial service in the whole of the French Empire between 1887 and 1910. See William B. Cohen, *Rulers of Empire: The French Colonial Service in Africa* (Stanford: Hoover Institution Press, 1971), p. 81.

[77] An appreciation of the fury that Diagne's mission aroused among some *colons* is evident in the cartoon ridiculing it in *Le Midi Colonial*, 14 mars 1918 (*Institut de France, Bibliothèque* [hereafter *IF*]: MS 5925 (516)).

[78] On Diagne's meetings with the chiefs and their favorable response to his overtures, see: *ANOM:* Affaires politiques: 3036/11, and *ANS:* Affaires politiques: 17 G 15. On the enlistment of *fils de chef* and their preferential treatment in the army (including immediate promotion to the rank of corporal or sergeant), see: *ANS:* Affaires militaires: 4 D 81 and 4 D 87.

[79] On the chiefs' apprehensions about eventually being supplanted by their social inferiors if their sons refused to enlist, see: *ANS:* Affaires militaires: 4 D 82.

[80] On Diagne's overtures to the Muslim elite, and especially to his relations with Bamba, see: *ANS:* Affaires militaires: 4 D 83. For a Senegalese account of Diagne's overtures to Bamba and, significantly, the fact that two of Ibra Fall's sons also enlisted, see: Ibrahima Thiam: 1B.

[81] See Chapter 7.

[82] Speech of 19 February 1918 in Dakar, reported in *L'homme libre*, 24 janvier (cited in: "Le Gouvernement de l'Ouest Africain Français," *L'Afrique française*, 28 (janvier–mars 1918), pp. 26–27).

[83] *L'Indépendant sénégalais*, no. 1, 27 septembre 1917.

[84] This interpretation differs from Marc Michel's, who downplays the significance of Diagne's mission and cites increased administrative efficiency and allied cooperation as important factors contributing to the success of the 1918 recruitment drive (*L'Appel à l'Afrique*, pp. 239–60). In my opinion, however, these factors were of negligible consequence.

[85] Abdoulaye Diaw: 2B and 3A. Prior to 1918, the highest rank normally obtainable for African *tirailleurs* was sergeant-major. Diaw's characterization of the Bambaras' response also subtly conveys Wolof prejudices about their alleged gullibility.

[86] Amar Seck: 4B.

[87] Abdoulaye Gassama: 1A.

[88] Momar Cisse: 1A. For French accounts of the "incidents" in Bargny and their "fears" that if citizenship was granted there, similar demands would be made elsewhere in the Protectorate, see: *ANS:* Affaires militaires: 4 D 77. Diagne kept his promise: the inhabitants of Bargny were incorporated into the communal boundaries in 1919 and became citizens.

[89] Samba Diop: 2A. Among the 1918 veterans interviewed, none viewed military service as a suicidal endeavor. Though aware of the "risks" involved, all who recounted their feelings at the time believed they either "would" or "might return." These sentiments were not, however, always shared by their relatives, some of whom still harbored dire apprehensions. See, for example: Momar Cisse: 1A.

[90] Flight continued in several *cercles* along the Fleuve, including Dagana, Podor, and Matam, as well as in Lower Casamance. The numbers, however, were reckoned by the French administration in scores or a few hundred instead of in the tens of thousands. See: *ANS:* Affaires militaires: 4 D 76. For instances of flight in Matam that are not mentioned in the French records, see: Seydou Amadou Thiam: 1A.

[91] None of the 1918 veterans interviewed referred to the use of any of these methods of coercion. On the seizure of "strangers" in Louga, Thiès, and Diourbel, see: *ANS:* Affaires militaires: 4 D 80. On the resistance of refugees, which occurred only in the *cercle* of Dagana, see: *ANS:* Affaires militaires: 4 D 77.

[92] Some 1,783 soldiers, or 23 percent of the total engaged, were classed as volunteers. *ANS:* Affaires militaires: 4 D 77. By comparison, volunteers during the drives before 1918 were reckoned at between 5 and 8 percent of all recruits. Among those interviewed, 3 out of 9 veterans maintained that they had volunteered. Abdoulaye Gassama certainly did so, but Momar Cisse and Ibrahima Camara were influenced by other personal considerations that effectively left them little choice about enlisting.

[93] In the more densely populated *cercles* of central Senegal such as Tivaouane and Louga, well over 50 percent of those presented were inducted. In more sparsely populated areas of eastern Senegal, such as Niani-Ouli and Haute Gambie, the percentage was a little less than 40 percent.

[94] Although physical specifications for the recruits were also reduced slightly in 1918, this factor alone is not significant enough to explain the difference.

[95] Five out of nine of the 1918 recruits interviewed either volunteered or were "pleased" or "happy" to go. See, Momar Cisse: 1A; Ibrahima Thiam: 1B; Seydou Amadou Thiam: 1A; Abdoulaye Gassala: 2B; and Ibrahima Camara: 1A.

[96] See, respectively: Seydou Amadou Thiam: 1A; Ibrahima Camara: 1A; and Ibrahima Thiam: 1B.

[97] Reluctant recruits include: Amar Seck: 1B; Samba Diop: 3A; Moussa Leye: 1A; and Mody Sow: 1B. None of the 1918 veterans interviewed considered any form of non-compliance, nor were they advised to do so by their parents.

[98] Exceptions included: Samba Diop, Ibrahima Thiam, and possibly Abdoulaye Gassala. In general, however, the rule of primogeniture was adhered to: six of the 1918 recruits were younger sons whose elder brothers were not sent.

[99] *ANS:* Affaires militaires: 4 D 76 and 4 D 82.

[100] *ANS:* Affaires militaires: 4 D 82.

[101] Moussa Leye: 1B; and Ibrahima Camara (who was Guinean): 2A.

[102] See Chapter 7.

[103] For the debate over the respective roles played in 1918 by Van Vollenhoven and Diagne, see: Michael Crowder, "West Africa and the 1914–1918 War," *Bulletin de l'Institut Fondamental d'Afrique Noire*, Série B, 30 (1968), pp. 227–47. For criticism of Diagne's complicity with the French, see: Abdoulaye Ly, *Les Mercenaires noirs: Notes sur une forme de l'exploitation des Africains* (Paris: Editions Présence Africaine, 1957).

[104] See John Gaffar La Guerre, *Enemies of Empire* (St. Augustine, Trinidad: College Press, 1984), pp. 33–45; and Johnson, *The Emergence of Black Politics*.

4

"THE LONG JOURNEY": FROM KAYOR TO THE CÔTE D'AZUR

Regardless of the various means by which the Senegalese entered the French army, their introduction to military life represented a novel experience for all. For most soldiers, but especially for *tirailleurs*, induction into the Colonial Army led to their first sustained contacts with Europeans and their institutions. Encounters with *Tubabs* were no longer restricted to brief and infrequent dealings with *commandants* or *commerçants* in the countryside; instead, the soldiers became exposed to Frenchmen on a daily basis and on far more personalized terms than ever before. Although the character of this military interaction remained constrained, it nevertheless afforded an unprecedented opportunity for the Africans to become more familiar with Europeans—their customs, institutions, and variations in individual behavior.

Before the war, most recruits had never traveled more than a few miles from their homes. Their journey to the coastal training camps in Senegal, and their subsequent oceanic voyage to France, represented a distance that was often literally inconceivable to them. Nor was the mental gulf they were compelled to bridge merely to be reckoned in geographic terms. It also entailed a psychological leap of the first magnitude, as the soldiers were exposed to new ideas, attitudes, sensations, and experiences that were theretofore beyond the bounds of their knowledge.

In this respect, the dramatic contrasts between civilian and military life—which all conscripts in European armies experienced during the First World War—were perhaps most pronounced for the Senegalese. Moreover, because military institutions were explicitly designed to transcend the confines of normal social reality, their sojourn in the army represented an "extrasocial experience" of the highest order.[1] Indeed, it was only within this military context that the subsequent redefinition of self within the colonial environment, which often took place directly as a result of the war, was possible. This gradual transformation also grew out of the soldiers' experience in combat as well as their enhanced wartime contacts with the French metropolitan population, but it nevertheless began with their entry into the army. It is thus within the milieu of the training camps—first in Senegal, then in France—and on the voyage to Europe that the soldiers' views of themselves, other Africans, and the French first began to change. Paradoxically, it was also within this military context that metropolitan financial outlays to extend the "benefits" of French civilization to the colonies assumed their greatest dimensions.

INTRODUCTION TO FRENCH MILITARY SOCIETY

The Administration of the Training Camps in Senegal

The unprecedented scale of the recruitment drives in Senegal from late 1915 onward presented daunting logistical difficulties for the understaffed and ill-prepared French colonial authorities. The massive levy of soldiers in the Protectorate and the communes between November 1915 and April 1916—which amounted to drafting some 14,000 men—witnessed a fourfold increase in the number of recruits that had been raised in Senegal during the previous fifteen months of the war.[2] Moreover, in addition to these troops, the local administration was called on to accommodate the influx of still larger numbers of other soldiers from Haut-Sénégal et Niger who were trained in Senegal as well. This entailed elaborate preparations—including the organization of transport for the soldiers within the colonies; the construction of new facilities to house and train the recruits; the requisitioning of food, uniforms, weapons, and other military equipment; and the expansion of preexisting European cadres to oversee the troops' instruction—all of which far outstripped previous requirements.

Metropolitan subsidies to facilitate this massive mobilization of men were appropriated on a lavish scale. Notwithstanding the vast sums expended by the Ministry of War on maintenance allowances (which amounted to 2,500 francs per year per *originaire* and 1,000 francs per *tirailleur*), the Chamber of Deputies appropriated 46,000,000 francs in October 1915 to cover the additional costs of recruitment over the next six months alone.[3] This sum was more than twice the amount of the entire federal budget for West Africa (which was raised from local revenues) during the same year.[4] In Senegal, 1,000,000 francs of this fund was earmarked exclusively for the construction of new training camps.[5] This sum, which was spent in only a few weeks, was equivalent to nearly 20 percent of the total budget for the Protectorate the last year before the war.[6]

Similar appropriations were also approved during subsequent recruitment drives, and, when combined with the amounts spent on the upkeep of the soldiers and other separately itemized expenses, this expenditure reached astonishing proportions by prewar colonial standards.[7] Indeed, during the next five years the metropolitan government probably spent at least 1,000,000,000 francs raising and maintaining African troops.[8] As a result, by 1918, metropolitan subsidies directly related to recruiting and sustaining African soldiers throughout the war probably surpassed all other French expenditures in A.O.F. during the previous quarter-century of colonial rule combined.[9]

Despite such unprecedented largesse from Paris, in the colonies virtually everything required by the military authorities was in short supply and improvisation was frequently the order of the day. In more remote areas unconnected to the rail network or navigable waterways, recruits were marched hundreds of kilometers overland before connecting roads could be built and lorry transport arranged.[10] In 1915, with many of the new training camps unfinished, soldiers were often housed in tents until permanent barracks were constructed.[11] Moreover, even after they were completed, the haste in which the camps were built, the overcrowding that sometimes occurred in them, and the absence of sanitary precautions created disease-ridden environments in which mortality rates were often exceptionally high. In 1918, for instance, among the 54,844 recruits raised in A.O.F., 872 (1.59 percent) died in the camps, while 728 (1.33 percent) were too ill to be sent overseas when the troopships departed.[12] Frequently, even the most basic sorts of military equipment were scarce. Some soldiers were not issued regulation uniforms or rifles before their arrival in France, and even in 1918, when the recruitment system was much better organized, 30,000 uniforms requested by the Ministry of Colonies were late in arriving.[13]

Shortages were not restricted to logistical concerns: French personnel to staff the new African formations were also lacking in the colonies. In 1915 alone, nearly 4,000 officers and men were requested to serve in A.O.F. as cadres for the *tirailleur* units. Not only did they fail to arrive in the designated numbers, but those who did were frequently of very poor quality. (Indeed, the motivation of gaining temporary escape from service at the front was alleged to be a major factor in their decision.) These French troops also suffered inordinately from disease, and the hardships of their existence overseas led to madness and suicide among some.[14] *Originaires*, on the other hand, were often trained by *colons* who had previously been drafted into the Colonial Army, and relations between them and their European N.C.O.s were often fractious.[15] Extra medical personnel also had to be imported, and, in addition to arriving in insufficient numbers and lacking basic pharmaceutical supplies, they too were frequently incompetent.[16]

Senegal. - DAKAR. - Le Camp des Tirailleurs

Collection Nouvelle Mad Boucher, Editeur

Army barracks at the *tirailleur* training camp at Ouakam, 1908. Courtesy of Centre des Archives d'outre-mer, Aix-en-Provence (Archives nationales. France) (5 Fi 3417). Reprinted with permission.

Nevertheless, despite these handicaps, the successive mobilizations of men in 1915 to 1916, the spring of 1917, and again in 1918 proceeded apace. In Senegal, the new recruits were differentiated between *originaires* and *tirailleurs*. The former, whose conditions of service were ostensibly identical to those of metropolitan troops, were sent to separate compounds to commence their training. These included the older camps of the Colonial Army in Dakar and St. Louis, as well as separate sections of the newer ones in Thiès and Rufisque. Alternatively, the *tirailleurs* were sent to the much larger camps that had been expanded to accommodate them in Thiès and Rufisque as well as in Ouakam and Tiaroye.[17] Notwithstanding the significant distinctions that existed between these two groups in pay, promotion, quarters, and rations, it was in these camps that all Senegalese first became acquainted with the dictates of military life.[18]

Army Regimen

After their induction into the army, Senegalese recruits were taken to one of the half-dozen training camps in the colony to commence their instruction. There they remained for a period varying between a few weeks to six or seven months, undergoing basic training before being shipped overseas.[19]

Although *originaires* and *tirailleurs* were separated, regardless of their official designation the men were initially organized into exclusively African units. In the former instance, communards were formed into companies of the *Bataillon de l'A.O.F.*, the composition of which was determined by the soldier's comparative degree of fluency in French. Communication was also a factor among the *tirailleurs*; although the ethnic composition of companies varied, smaller units such as squads and sections were composed of men speaking the same language. In the case of *tirailleurs*, considerable attention was also devoted to instruction in understanding basic French commands, which, though rudimentary, could be conveyed to all.[20]

Irrespective of the type of unit the Senegalese served in, the daily regimen of camp life was similar. Soldiers were normally awakened at dawn and assembled for *"l'appel,"* when roll was taken. After being dismissed, they were usually formed into sections and, under the supervision of their French officers and N.C.O.s, conducted morning exercises and received drill instruction. Following lunch and a brief midday rest, they were reassembled and resumed similar activities in the afternoon. They ate again in the early evening and thereafter were permitted a brief period of leisure—when they danced, wrestled, played games, or visited with friends—before going to bed at 9:00 P.M.[21]

Instruction in the camps, which was frequently made more difficult by the linguistic barriers between the French cadres and the troops, emphasized basic military procedures. Soldiers were taught by their N.C.O.s to march in lines

to the uniform rhythm of *"une, deux, trois, quatre."* In addition to drill instruction and frequent long marches, the troops were also trained for combat
to the extent that the available military equipment permitted. Most soldiers
learned to care for rifles and were shown how to use them during target practice. The recruits were also taught how to fight at close quarters with bayonets and rifle butts, as well as with fists and feet.[22]

Discipline was harsh. Failure to comprehend or execute orders resulted in
beatings by N.C.O.s that were sometimes so severe that soldiers had to be
hospitalized. More serious infractions—such as the failure to salute French
officers or altercations among the men—led to arrest and incarceration in the
poste de police. Relations with the European cadres—some of whom insulted
and denigrated the recruits by calling them "slaves" or "niggers"—were often abysmal. Such verbal and physical abuse frequently provoked fights between French N.C.O.s and the Senegalese. Indeed, death threats were occasionally issued by the soldiers to the worst malefactors. Nevertheless, the
recruits learned that physical confrontations in the army were not always
prompted by racial antagonisms. African soldiers also witnessed the novel
spectacle of fights between Europeans, especially when they were drunk.[23]

The Senegalese camps were designed to ensure maximum internal secu-
rity. They were surrounded by barbed wire, and the gates were heavily guarded
at all times. Nevertheless, some soldiers—especially if they lived nearby and
were deemed trustworthy by their officers—were permitted to leave for brief
periods in the evening. They usually visited their relatives or frequented the
bordellos, liquor stalls, and other shops that sprang up around the camps.
Other recruits, however—particularly *tirailleurs* who had been taken by
force—were never permitted leave for fear of desertion.[24] Though hazardous
and difficult to accomplish, desertion was in fact not uncommon among *sujets*
from the Protectorate. Indeed, despite the threat of severe reprisals against
them if they were captured, or against their families if they were not, many
soldiers accepted the risks entailed as a preferable alternative to the fate that
awaited them if they remained in the army.[25]

Most recruits, however, especially *originaires*, eschewed attempting to
escape. Out of over 7,000 *originaires* mobilized by July 1917, only four
deserted.[26] Despite the rigor of the regimen and the frequent abuse they were
subjected to in the camps, most Senegalese also interpreted their experience
there as an introduction to a novel, and often previously inconceivable, way
of life.

Military Society

During their sojourn in the Senegalese camps, the soldiers were continually exposed to new ways of thinking and acting. These changes were both
subtle and dramatic. Identical uniforms, denoting the rough equality of the

recruits, were frequently issued to the Senegalese on their induction. Aside from donning a common apparel, coupled with the fact that many soldiers had never before worn trousers, differences from civilian life were evidenced in other ways. Complying with French custom, many soldiers learned to eat with knives and forks for the first time. Moreover, because of their enlistment bounties and salaries, they became men of comparative wealth. As such, they often acquired new habits, such as smoking cigarettes and drinking lemonade—luxuries that few could have afforded before.[27]

The general social leveling that took place among the soldiers in the army, however, was manifested in more fundamental ways. This was most obvious in three respects: in the absence of age grades as a mark of distinction, in the common treatment accorded to all irrespective of their precolonial social standing, and in the ways that previous ethnic antagonisms were ameliorated.

Though eldest sons among the Senegalese *sujet* population seldom entered the army, this was not the case with *originaires*. Moreover, among *tirailleurs* it was not uncommon for several younger brothers of differing ages to be enlisted during successive recruitment drives. As a result, sons of senior status sometimes encountered siblings who, though under normal circumstances had to show them deference, were not necessarily compelled to do so in the army. Indeed, as one younger brother observed, the reverse might sometimes be the case. Recalling an accidental meeting with his elder brother, Abdou Karim Gaye, a former corporal gleefully remembered telling his sibling: "'We are not civilians any more. We are in the army and there are no age [distinctions]. You are no longer my elder brother; I'm your superior.' [So] I said to my brother: 'I'm a corporal and you [don't have any stripes] because you are a simple soldier. So give me a salute, or I'll put you in prison.' [laughter]"[28]

The absence of the recognition of social distinctions—which ranged from aristocrats at one extreme to domestic slaves at the other—struck many soldiers as still more remarkable. Indeed, the experience in the camps often rectified misconceptions about the servile status of members of other ethnic groups, for the French seldom made distinctions between those families who owned slaves and those who had previously served them.[29] Explaining the reasons for this transformation in outlook, Demba Mboup, a *griot*, emphasized:

> We all joined the same army—the French army. . . . So we did not think about our [previous] way of living, our behavior, our [former] kingdoms. We were bound to follow the French regulations and their way of thinking about all these things. [And although] little arguments sometimes [occurred] between soldiers from the same country, [the status of a man's family] wasn't stressed. . . . There wasn't any [social] differentiation [with regard

to slaves] because we were following another system—another [way of] life—which was the French one.[30]

Long-standing ethnic rivalries among the soldiers were also ameliorated as a result of closer contacts within the camps. Initially, however, misunderstandings arising from linguistic differences as well as pejorative stereotypes were common, and they frequently led to altercations. Recalling the circumstances that prompted one such brawl in the camp at Tiaroye, the Wolof recruit Gaye remembered:

> One day, at the lunch hour, I came with my bowl—my *gamelle*—to get my ration. And I saw some flies in the cooking pot. So I kicked it and the whole meal spilled all over [everywhere]. And the guy who was serving [the food] was a Bambara. So he went to the *adjudant* and told him that Abdou Karim Gaye had kicked over the cooking pot. And the *adjudant* came and asked me why I had kicked the cooking pot. And I said that, "We—the Wolof—we do not eat flies!" [And the Bambara became very angry and] wanted to beat me, so I turned and punched him. And there was a very big fight.[31]

Nevertheless, despite such provocations, the Senegalese eventually became "very friendly with the Bambara, the Mossi, and [the other African recruits]." Indeed, in time a new consciousness became discernible among many soldiers, as ethnic particularisms were gradually superseded by the recognition that they were "all Africans."[32]

The sense of rough equality born of the shared experience in the Senegalese training camps was succinctly summarized by one *originaire*, who stated: "When you are a soldier, all soldiers are the same."[33] This was a mentality that was alien not only to prewar Senegalese society but also to the stratified world of the French colonial regime as well. Nevertheless, as the recruits prepared to embark on their long journey overseas, it was an impulse that many felt for the first time. It was, importantly enough, only a short mental leap between the notion that all African soldiers were equal to a recognition that Europeans were no different from them.

VOYAGE BEYOND THE BOUNDS OF KNOWLEDGE

The Logistics of Transport Overseas

No less than the mobilization of men in the colonies, the shipment of thousands of recruits from West Africa to the metropole presented major logistical difficulties for the French authorities. The French merchant fleet, which was already overtaxed due to the enhanced demands made on it by the war

Senegalese *tirailleurs* boarding ship in Dakar for France, 1916. From *Annuaire de l'A.O.F., 1917–1921.*

and shipping losses to the Germans, was ill prepared to satisfy additional requirements.[34] Moreover, aside from a chronic shortage of available shipping space and the problems of organizing armed escorts for the transports, the colonial administration also lacked adequate European personnel—especially doctors—to accompany the soldiers on their voyage to France.

Nevertheless, these obstacles were surmounted through recourse to a series of expedients. Local merchant ships engaged in the West African trade were temporarily requisitioned to transport soldiers. Comprising some 20 vessels in 1916 and again in 1918, these ships varied considerably in cargo capacity. Accommodating between 400 and 2,200 soldiers, they carried on average about 1,200 men apiece. In some instances, their human cargo was also supplemented by other commodities that the metropole sorely needed, including foodstuffs, palm products for lubricants, and timber.[35]

The scale of these operations, which were conducted within a comparatively limited time span, were frequently made possible by doubling the cargo capacity, at least for passengers, aboard the ships. Until the practice was forbidden due to the intervention of Blaise Diagne in 1918, this was accomplished by packing men both below and on top of the deck.[36] Although health conditions varied, all too often the consequences of such overcrowding for sanitation were predictable. The recruits were prone to illness of all kinds, but especially to seasickness, which led to

dehydration, and deaths from this cause as well as from contagious diseases were not uncommon.[37] Moreover, doctors aboard ship were frequently alleged to be inadequately trained. Under such circumstances, it
was acknowledged even in government circles that the conditions under
which the recruits sailed were often "deplorable."[38]

The Senegalese were usually shipped from Dakar to one of the nodal points
of the French West African trade in Bordeaux or Marseilles for disembarka-
tion. Their voyage generally lasted between eight and ten days, although it
might be prolonged depending on the prevailing weather or detours prompted
by apprehensions about German submarines. Eventually some 180,000 Africans were transported overseas by the French between 1914 and 1918.[39] Aside
from coping with cramped conditions, illness, and fears of being intercepted,
the recruits were also prey to other concerns. Some of these—such as their
homesickness and anxiety about being killed in combat—were common to
all soldiers in similar situations; but others—including the unsettling prospect of life in an alien land and apprehensions about the fate that had befallen other Africans when shipped overseas—were unique to their particular situation.

The Soldiers' Impressions of the Voyage

For nearly all Senegalese, the voyage to France represented a journey
beyond the bounds of previous knowledge. Virtually none of the soldiers had
ever had any direct contact with the metropole.[40] Indeed, most of the recruits
had never been on a ship before, and many had never seen the ocean. Moreover, the natural apprehensions that such a journey inspired in the minds of
most soldiers were compounded for some—especially for those from more
remote regions—by the historical memory of the trans-Atlantic slave trade.
European ships had carried Africans overseas for centuries, but, as these men
well knew, the precedents for their kinsmen ever returning were virtually
nonexistent. As a result, the fear of sailing abroad—particularly for those
who "didn't know where they were going"—often carried connotations that
were even more foreboding than the more commonplace concerns that most
soldiers harbored about their prospects of survival in combat.[41]

Nevertheless, the reactions of the men to their voyage varied considerably. Though all were apprehensive about the fate that awaited them in France,
some soldiers recalled their passage as being comparatively free of hardship.
It was often seen as a welcome break from the demanding regimen of camp
life: the soldiers were allowed to occupy themselves in more leisurely pur-
suits such as "sleeping, eating, and playing cards." Favorable impressions of
the voyage, however, were usually influenced by a series of objective factors: their passage was usually swift, the sea remained calm, and there was
little cause for concern about the ship sinking. They were also often com-

paratively free to move about the boat, and, although men became ill, there were few if any deaths among their comrades.[42]

These men were fortunate, and they also represented a distinct minority among the African recruits.[43] Indeed, most Senegalese characterized their journey as having been an arduous and sometimes terrifying ordeal. After departing from their training camps, the soldiers were assembled along the wharves in Dakar (or, more rarely, in St. Louis) for shipment to France. Sometimes they, like the rest of the cargo, were literally lowered by cranes into the holds of awaiting ships, and the conditions to which they were subjected during their voyage were frequently appalling.[44] Irrespective of whether recruits were consigned exclusively to the various levels below deck or also ensconced above it, overcrowding was commonplace. Indeed, soldiers in the hold were often packed so tightly together that movement was severely restricted. Recruits wrapped themselves in blankets and remained huddled in their allotted spaces, individuals were assigned to collect food for those in their immediate vicinity, and movement on deck was often prohibited altogether. As one soldier grimly recalled, "you were in the boat and you could do nothing except to sit there and wait until you arrived [in France]."[45]

For men unused to sailing, the cramped conditions aboard ship were usually made even more miserable by seasickness. Most soldiers became ill during the voyage and were afflicted with vomiting and diarrhea. Though most eventually became acclimated to their surroundings, failure to do so carried dire consequences.[46] Daba Dembele related: "[Because of] the movement of the boat [and] the smell of the sea and the engines, some men couldn't eat or drink anything [without vomiting]. . . . So they became very ill and some of them died from starving."[47] Deaths attributable to dehydration as a result of seasickness, as well as to other diseases, were an everyday occurrence aboard some ships. When the men died, their bodies were unceremoniously carried on deck and dumped into the sea; their corpses were often devoured by the "great fish" that followed in the wake of the transports.[48]

Most soldiers were also prey to more immediate concerns about their self-preservation. When storms broke in the Atlantic, "the waves, which lifted up the boat [and then] let it down," terrified the recruits on board, who feared their ship "was going to sink."[49] Although these apprehensions were usually allayed in due course by the crew, the soldiers' dread of being torpedoed by German submarines was less easily dispelled. Despite being accompanied by armed escorts and knowing that some precautionary measures had been taken to evacuate the transports if they were hit, most soldiers were acutely aware that other troopships had been sunk with extensive loss of life. When the men, many of whom could not swim, actually felt their ship shudder from an explosion beneath the waterline, they reacted with terror.[50] As one *tirailleur*, Samba Diop, recalled:

On the seventh day [after leaving Dakar], we were [torpedoed by a subma-
rine]. . . . We felt the impact when [it] hit [the ship, and we heard] the
sirens begin to wail—"oooh, oooh!" . . . And they gave us the life jackets,
[and I ran] above deck with my life jacket near the small boats. If the ship
sank, I wanted to be one of the first ones to get into a boat [because] I was
thinking about saving my life.

I was not alone near the boats because everybody was trying to get near
them. . . . There were [only] about 10 boats and [everyone] could not fit
into them. Everybody was standing near the boats with his knife to cut the
ropes. And if the ship had sunk . . . there would have been a very, very big
fight. [For] if you were unwilling to fight, you would never have gotten
into [one of] the boats. But the ship did not sink. . . . The hole was below
deck—near the keel—and [they] put something [into it] to stop the water
from running in. And later, the men came with some pumps, and they began to pump the water out of this place. [And] our captain cabled another
ship to have some help [because the rudder on our ship was damaged and]
we were sailing without direction. [And] that's how we continued to go to
France.[51]

Under such conditions, the soldiers coped with their situation during the
voyage as best they could. When they were not talking to their comrades,
many recited verses or asked Allah (or Rog in the case of some Serer) to
spare them during their journey and in the coming fighting. Other soldiers—especially those who were fishermen—also entrusted their fate to
protective charms intended to prevent drowning at sea.[52] In moments of
extreme despair when death threatened, men cried out to whomever they
believed in—"to Allah . . . to Seriny Touba . . . to Malik Sy"—to grant
them "mercy."[53]

Oppressive though the voyage was under normal circumstances for most
recruits, it was sometimes made even more difficult by the malicious actions
of their officers. Some Frenchmen delighted in tormenting the Senegalese,
who were often confined to the sweltering holds of their steamers and occasionally chained to their places.[54] Remembering one such malicious man, an
originaire, Ousmane Diagne, stated:

We [sailed from Dakar] on a boat called *l'Afrique* on May 9, 1916. There
was a French officer with us—[a lieutenant called Oeuvre]—[who] was a
very very bad man. We spent [the first] three days [being allowed to go on
deck] in the boat . . . and we had a good journey. [But] when we arrived at
a place called "the Gulf" [Golfe de Gascogne] . . . this French officer said
that all the soldiers had to go downstairs—deep inside the ship. And he put
[a guard] at the door [to prevent] any of us from going out. . . . And we
[were confined for] the [next] six days in the bottom [of the boat near] the
keel. [And] we suffered a lot in the bottom of the ship because there was

no air. From time to time they opened the [portholes] to let some air [in, but] after that they closed them [again]. And even during meals, we were eating in the bottom of the ship. And it was very hot [there] and it was very tight.[55]

Yet much to their amazement, some Senegalese also discovered that such wanton disregard for their welfare did not always go unpunished. Describing what happened when *l'Afrique* docked in France, the same soldier continued:

When we arrived in Bordeaux, [Blaise Diagne] came with two *commandants* [to greet us]. And [he] asked [us]: "How are you? How was your voyage?" [And one of the soldiers told him] the conditions under which we had traveled, [saying:] "This Frenchman called Oeuvre closed us in the hold of the ship during [most] of the journey, so we had a very, very bad [voyage]." So Diagne said: "Call Oeuvre here!" And they called Oeuvre, and [Diagne took him] down in the bottom of the ship. And [he] told the others to close the door [and keep] Oeuvre in the bottom of the ship for 15 minutes. And after that, [when] they opened the door and he came out, he was covered with sweat. So Diagne said to him: "You have only been in the bottom of the ship for a quarter of an hour, and these men have spent six days [there]. [Now] you know what [it feels like]." And [then] Diagne said to the *commandant*: "Put this man [under arrest]!"[56]

The dispensing of such justice by an African, which the Senegalese who observed it had literally never seen before, provided a much needed tonic for the men.[57] It was, however, but a foretaste of similar scenes that many soldiers would eventually witness in France as they disembarked from their ships and commenced their final training before being sent into combat.

THE TRAINING CAMPS IN FRANCE

The Land of the *"Tubabs"*

The elation and relief that most Senegalese felt when their transports finally docked in France was soon replaced by a sense of disorientation. For all soldiers the metropole provided a dramatic contrast with their homeland, and their initial impressions of it, as they made their way to their nearby training camps, was of a place where "everything was new and strange."[58] Regardless of whether the recruits disembarked in Bordeaux, Marseilles, or, occasionally, smaller ports, their immediate response to their new surroundings focused on three dramatic differences with their previous environment:

the character of the French cities, the fertility of the countryside, and the disconcerting sight of the local inhabitants.

The sheer size of the French cities, which were much larger than any of the towns in Senegal, amazed the soldiers. Indeed, in a city such as Marseilles, it was possible to "go for about 15 kilometers and still be in the same town." The urban landscape also stood out from what they had previously known. The recruits had "never" seen such tall buildings before, which rose "seven," "nine," or "twelve" stories in the air.[59] City streets, which were generally "very wide" and paved with "stones," as well as church bells ringing from nearby steeples and public fountains for collecting water, also filled them with "astonishment."[60] So too did French houses, which were decidedly different from those in Africa but "very nice." On the whole, most soldiers felt that the cities in France were even more "beautiful" than those in Senegal, which many, and especially *originaires* from the communes, had not expected.[61]

The countryside made no less striking an impression. Peasant recruits noted that the "land was very good" and that "everything grew very well [there]." In addition to an abundance of cereal crops, such as wheat and oats, the soldiers also noticed that the trees in France, compared to those in Senegal, were "very large." The troops were also impressed by the amount of livestock they saw, particularly pigs, which were rare in their homeland, as well as by the ways that domesticated animals, including horses, donkeys, and dogs, were used to assist in farm work.[62]

Though effusive about the sights they witnessed in the French cities and countryside, the soldiers' initial feelings about the inhabitants they encountered were much more reserved. All were immediately aware that they "were no longer in [a] 'black' peoples' country," and that the "*Tubabs*" they saw on the streets were far more numerous than they were in Senegal. Moreover their comparative proximity to Europeans—as in the case of one soldier, who recalled that he had never been so close to a "young *Tubab* [woman]" before—often inspired fear at first. Although this reserve, frequently shared by the French as well, eventually abated in time, when the soldiers were first marched to their new barracks, it was the predominant feeling among most African recruits.[63]

The French Camps

The Senegalese, on their arrival in France, were sent to one of two separate types of training camps: either to those reserved exclusively for *tirailleurs* or, alternatively, to those that accommodated *originaires* as well as other French citizens serving in the Colonial Army.[64] Prior to the spring of 1916, when the number of *tirailleurs* in the metropole was still small and none of the conscripts from the communes had yet arrived, most African troops were

KEY

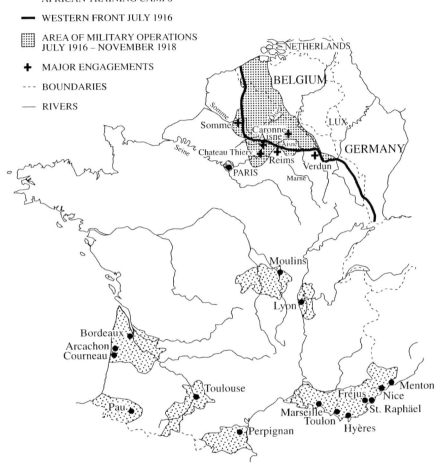

Map 4.1   France, 1916–1918: Areas of Most Extensive Senegalese Presence

garrisoned in the camp at Fréjus, which had been built after 1900 as a center for non-European personnel.[65] Thereafter, with the massive influx of West Africans resulting from the recruitment and conscription drives in the Federation, a period of improvisation ensued in an attempt to accommodate the new soldiers. The network of facilities on the Côte d'Azur, including the older camp at Fréjus and other training centers near St. Raphäel, was expanded, and a second major complex at Courneau, on the Atlantic coast near Bordeaux, was constructed early in 1916. During 1917 and 1918, additional camps for *tirailleurs* were also built at Vernet and Sendets near Pau.[66]

Originaires, on the other hand, were usually transported to Lyon, where their homogeneous formations were eventually broken up and integrated into separate units of the colonial army. There they continued their military instruction before being dispatched to separate fronts, which, in 1916, included Thessaloniki, Verdun, and the Somme. Thereafter, when they, like the *tirailleurs*, were withdrawn from the fighting during the winter, the *originaires* were sent to a series of other camps, including Hyères on the Côte d'Azur and Perpignan and Espira de l'Agly near the Pyrenees.[67]

Conditions within these camps varied. Although all were designed along similar lines—they contained barracks (which were usually prefabricated and housed between 65 and 80 men), mess halls, infirmaries, and guard houses as well as extensive training grounds—the sanitary state of these complexes differed considerably. Because of the rapid expansion of the *tirailleur* camps after 1916, as well as the lack of forethought devoted to medical considerations about their locations, disease and mortality rates were often exceptionally high. This was especially true of the camp at Courneau, constructed near a swamp, where deaths from illness frequently exceeded 1 percent of the African occupants per month.[68] Mortality rates in the other *tirailleur* camps—which often averaged 25 percent higher than those of the French— were also excessive. As late as 1918, when health measures had been greatly improved, deaths still amounted each month to 6.8 per 1,000 of the African complement garrisoned in the complex at Fréjus/St. Raphäel.[69]

A much more obvious distinction between the two types of French camps came in the comparative proximity of Senegalese troops to European and other colonial soldiers. Though the *tirailleur* formations included French cadres, these men were housed in separate barracks and ate in different mess halls. Hence, except when they trained together, intercourse between French and the African recruits was circumscribed.[70] Although the *tirailleur* camps also frequently contained soldiers from North Africa and laborers from Indo-China, these men too were confined to different compounds. Furthermore, contacts with other West Africans were also restricted. Because of the French emphasis on amalgamating African units based on an appropriate mix of "warrior races" (see Chapter 5), the Senegalese often had little opportunity for sustained interaction with less "martial" recruits drawn from elsewhere in the Federation, who usually served in labor battalions (*bataillon d'étapes*) instead of the "line" infantry.[71]

The comparative seclusion of the *tirailleurs* in their camps was in marked contrast with the experience of the *originaires*. After their dispersal to separate units in the Colonial Army, they were usually integrated with French soldiers into heterogeneous squads and sections. These formations also normally included a melange of conscripts drawn from the older French colonies, including Martinique, Guadeloupe, and Réunion, as well as some North Africans. Although ratios varied, French soldiers usually predominated in these units. As a result, the *originaires*, who slept, ate, and trained with European and other colonial comrades, had much greater sustained contact with them than did the *tirailleurs*.[72]

Significant contrasts also existed in the conditions of service and treatment accorded to *tirailleurs* and *originaires* in the French camps. The two groups were issued distinctive uniforms and articles of equipment, and discrepancies also existed in the soldiers' basic rates of pay as well as in the type of food they were generally served.[73] Furthermore, French policy regarding the quality of language instruction and leave from the camps differed. Unless they received specialized training to become N.C.O.s, *tirailleurs* were only taught "pidgin" French sufficient for them to comprehend and execute basic commands. Conversely, *originaires* who did not already speak French were sent to classes to enable them to become fluent in the language. Although leave was seldom granted to the recruits when they first arrived in the metropole, on those rare occasions when it was permitted, the policy was much more liberal for *originaires* than for *tirailleurs*.[74]

Despite these fundamental differences, the Senegalese experience in the French camps also bore striking similarities. On their arrival, all recruits invariably resumed their training. The regimen they underwent overseas, however, differed significantly from their previous instruction. As in Africa, the soldiers continued to be drilled in basics: they were trained to execute the commands of their officers, parade in close order, and march long distances with field packs on their backs. But in addition to these more rudimentary exercises, the focus of attention in the French camps centered on preparing the men for combat. Recruits who had not been issued rifles now received them, and the soldiers were also introduced to an array of new weapons—including grenades, machine guns, and artillery.[75] Aside from spending long hours being instructed in the use of this weaponry, the soldiers were also trained to deal with many of the tactical situations they would encounter at the front. They were taught fire discipline and how to disperse and seek cover when advancing; how to move in conjunction with supporting machine gun and artillery fire; and how to storm enemy positions with grenades, rifles, and bayonets once they arrived there. The quality of this instruction also varied. Some units were well prepared for the combat situations they would encounter, but others—especially those whose officers were deemed substandard by their colleagues—received inadequate training.[76]

Discipline among those who were about to be sent into combat was enforced through coercion. In both the *tirailleur* and *originaire* camps, soldiers continued to be insulted, slapped, and beaten by some of their French N.C.O.s and officers for failing to execute orders properly. Although such abusive behavior was officially disavowed, because of the racial prejudice of some of the French cadres it nevertheless remained commonplace and often provoked fights. Other comparatively minor infractions, such as negligence in saluting superiors and occasional drunkenness among non-Muslims, were reprimanded with fatigue duty, deductions in pay, or detention in the guardhouse.[77] More serious offenses, however, were dealt with by the *Conseil de guerre*. Usually composed of a panel of French officers headed by a president and assisted by lawyers, stenographers, and interpreters, the councils were empowered to impose punishments for a wide variety of transgressions and crimes.[78] These infractions included: theft, assault, absence without leave, manslaughter, murder, desertion, and acts of "collective indiscipline" (or strikes). Sentences imposed on those found guilty ranged from brief periods of incarceration for lesser offenses to the death penalty for violent crimes or serious breaches of military discipline.[79] Though in certain specific instances the penalties imposed on the Senegalese may have been more lenient than those meted out to the French, the soldiers nevertheless dreaded being brought before the councils. Except in unusual circumstances, fear of facing the council was normally sufficient to exact compliance.[80]

The recruits, however, were not motivated exclusively by compulsion; they were also offered the prospect of receiving a promotion if they performed well. Although only *originaires* were normally permitted to hold ranks higher than sergeant, in practice Senegalese officers were so rare that such official distinctions seldom affected the men. Instead, most aspired to become N.C.O.s, and courses lasting several months were conducted in the camps to train African corporals and sergeants. The soldiers selected to participate in these *stages* received additional language and weapons instruction, and they were taught how to deploy their squads or sections in specific combat situations. Promotion was eagerly sought by most Senegalese: in addition to enhanced responsibility, it also brought prestige and an increased salary.[81] A further consideration was that it also permitted them to exercise authority over European soldiers as well as lower-ranking French N.C.O.s.

Senegalese Impressions of the Metropolitan Camps

Life in the French camps made a profound impression on the Senegalese. Irrespective of the types of units they served in, the daily existence of all soldiers was fraught with uncertainties about their future as well as a sense of detachment from their past. Communication with their homeland was infrequent at best. The French initially prohibited the sending of letters from the metropole lest they adversely affect recruitment in the colonies. And even after this policy was reversed in the interest of boosting morale, the content of the soldiers' communications was censored.[82] Nevertheless, despite these constraints, as well as the all too frequent loss of mail en route, the recruits' links with their loved ones were not always completely severed.[83] The frequency of their mutual communication, however, varied. Some families literally received no word throughout the war from those who had departed. Other soldiers managed to send only very brief but poignant messages: "If you see me again; it will be good; if not, know that I am dead."[84] Yet most recruits, whether they were literate or not, strove to maintain tenuous contacts. Relying on camp scribes and readers in some cases, but also corresponding directly in French or Arabic (which confused the censors), they usually sought to assuage the fears of their families by informing them that they were alive and in good health and, if they were Muslims, that they had tended to their prayers.[85]

Far from home, and repeatedly subjected to novel experiences in an alien land, most soldiers looked to their comrades for solace and support. This often fostered an enhanced sense of shared identity among the men of their being Senegalese. Despite the deliberate separation of *tirailleurs* from *originaires*, contact between the two groups was not eliminated altogether.[86] Moreover, despite the discrepancies in their treatment, the military distinctions drawn between the Senegalese were viewed as arbitrary and comparatively superficial by most soldiers. Although this occasionally caused resentment among the less favored *tirailleurs*, discontent was primarily directed against the French rather than toward their counterparts from the communes, who were regarded as being "the same people."[87] For their part, most *originaires* thought such artificial distinctions were "a very great injustice," and though serving alongside Frenchmen and other colonials, they felt much more affinity for their "relatives" among the *tirailleurs* from "Djolof, Kayor, [and the Futa]," as well as for other West African soldiers, than they did for their new comrades.[88] This outlook, which often superseded older ethnic allegiances, was also reinforced, at least for Muslims, by the common bonds of religious affiliation. Regardless of their status as *sujets* or citizens, or the particular orders they belonged to in Senegal, collective prayers and other religious observances were organized in their respective camps to express their shared faith.[89]

This new sense of self-consciousness of being Senegalese was also fostered in other ways. Despite the astonishing size of the metropolitan camps (Fréjus, for example, was nearly twice as populous as any town in Senegal), as well as the novel training they received in them, the soldiers' most lasting impression of the distinction between their previous and present circumstances focused on a single consideration: the recruits were "treated better" in French camps than they had been in the African ones.[90] This was manifested in a variety of ways: the food they received overseas was usually better than in Senegal; the soldiers felt much less constrained—indeed "freer"—in the metropolitan compounds; and, notwithstanding the physical abuse to which they were occasionally subjected in France, in general their N.C.O.s and officers were less brutal than they had formerly experienced. Indeed, the "greater consideration" shown for the soldiers in the metropole was consistently remarked on by the Senegalese precisely because it represented such a dramatic contrast with their experience in the colonies.[91]

The improved treatment accorded to the Senegalese abroad was not, however, exclusively attributable to differences between *colon* and mainland French mentalities. It was also prompted by the direct personal intervention of Diagne. In his capacity as Deputy, as Commissioner for the Republic after January 1918, and as *Commissaire Général aux Effectifs coloniaux* from October 1918, Diagne continually toured both *originaire* and *tirailleur* camps inquiring about the soldiers' grievances and insisting on equitable treatment for Africans. Complaints encompassed a wide array of concerns, including poor medical attention, bad or inadequate food, unhealthy accommodations, physical abuse by French N.C.O.s, as well as lack of respect accorded to African non-coms by European enlisted men. In addition, Diagne also intervened to ensure that Senegalese *originaires*, like their counterparts among the *tirailleurs*, were withdrawn from the front during the winter and that the rights of Muslim soldiers to practice their religion were respected.[92] In instances of negligence or persistent maltreatment by French officers, his retribution was swift. Recounting Diagne's visit to his camp, one soldier recalled:

> When we went [to the camps in France,] Diagne joined us [there] to see about our conditions. Whenever you had problems, he came and solved them. Sometimes the food was bad or insufficient, for example. [So] when Diagne came, if we said the food was not good, he called the officers together and asked [them] why. He said, "I brought soldiers to fight for you and to help you. And I don't see why you treat them like this!" So he would tear off the ranks [of insignia] of the officers and put them on the table.[93]

No less than for those who had witnessed similar scenes when their ships first docked in France, the sight of such authority being wielded by an African had an electrifying impact on the men in the camps.

Yet, while the assertion of enhanced African prestige found its most vigorous expression in the actions of Diagne, it was also tangible in other ways. Indeed, as Africans became promoted during the war, the soldiers became accustomed on a daily basis to seeing their compatriots exercise power over Europeans. As one corporal, Galaye Gueye, proudly explained: "I was ranked . . . among the 'white' men. I was even giving orders to some 'white' men [in France]."[94] Furthermore, though this reversal of customary roles often led to confrontations between Senegalese N.C.O.s and Europeans disdainful of their rank, French officers usually intervened to punish those who disregarded the commands of their African superiors. Under such circumstances, the desire of the Senegalese to attain promotion, and thereby distinguish themselves as "chiefs" not only in their own society but also within the French military system, was very real. As Diagne informed many soldiers on their arrival, the prerogatives to which they might aspire in the army were but an initial step toward securing similar rights in all aspects of colonial life once they returned to Senegal.[95]

Although seldom minimizing the gross injustices and overt discrimination they were continually subjected to in the French army, the recruits were also often impressed by the comparative fairness of the treatment they received. Indeed, even in disputes involving African and French enlisted men, most Senegalese were amazed to learn that Europeans were punished if they were deemed to be at fault.[96] Such evenhandedness on the part of many of their *Tubab* officers was at odds with the previous experience of nearly all African soldiers, and it graphically underscored the dramatic contrast between military and civilian life.

Despite the inescapable fears harbored by many recruits that they were destined to "die [in France]—[that they would] never return to Senegal"— the long journey across the ocean nevertheless represented a turning point in the lives of most soldiers.[97] Their enhanced awareness of the wider world, their increased exposure to the French and their institutions, and the comparative sense of social equality they experienced in the army helped to transform the attitudes and expectations of many. Moreover, this last feature affected not only the previous character of relationships between Africans but also influenced the soldiers' outlook toward the French as well. As Doudou Ndao, a *tirailleur* emphasized: "We were in the same army . . . so we were all equal; we were all the same."[98] This indeed was a substantial leap from the mentality of fear and abject servitude toward the French that pervaded prewar colonial society. In this respect, the soldiers' introduction to military life was paradoxical. Although their social relations within the army were profoundly hierarchical in nature, the Africans who served as soldiers were also exposed to a more egalitarian vision of human relationships than was conceivable in any other context. Yet, in addition to consciously fostering a spirit of common identity among the soldiers, the military as an institution was also designed to train men to dispense, as well as to accept, death. It is to this more horrifying aspect of the soldiers' experience in the army that we now turn, when, with their training in the French camps at an end, the Senegalese departed for the front.

NOTES

[1] On the "extra-social" nature of European armies during the First World War, and particularly the social leveling that occurred there in contrast to civilian life, see: Eric J.

Leed, *No Man's Land: Combat and Identity in World War I* (Cambridge: Cambridge University Press, 1981).

[2] For precise numbers, see Tables 2.2 and 3.1.

[3] On maintenance allowances, see: *ANS*: Affaires militaires: 4 D 24. On appropriations by the Chamber to facilitate recruitment in 1915, see: *Journal Officiel de la République Française*, 19 octobre 1915, pp. 7519–20.

[4] The federal budget for 1915 was 22,673,016 francs. See: Raymond Leslie Buell, *The Native Problem in Africa*, 2 vols. (New York: Macmillan, 1928), vol. 1, pp. 934–45.

[5] *ANS*: Affaires militaires: 4 D 65.

[6] Expenditures in the Protectorate in 1913 amounted to 5,892,326 francs. See: James F. Searing, "Accommodation and Resistance: Chiefs, Muslim Leaders, and Politicians in Colonial Senegal, 1890–1934" (Ph.D. Diss.: Princeton University, 1985), p. 304.

[7] The Chamber authorized 20,600,000 francs, for example, to expand the existing African training camps in France in 1918 alone. See: *AG*: Etat-Major de l'Armée (hereafter EMA): 7 N 1991.

[8] French expenditures (both direct and indirect) on West African soldiers were divided among several ministries (the Ministries of War, Armaments, Navy, Colonies, Public Works and Transport, etc.), which in turn were subdivided into various budgetary categories that often included both African and non-African disbursements. In the case of the Ministry of War, for example, these included such outlays as the soldiers' salaries, family allocations, food, camps, and recruitment. As a result, an accurate assessment of total metropolitan outlays during the war is difficult to make. In the case of the Senegalese (who were not differentiated from other African troops), it is indeed impossible. Nevertheless, fragmentary evidence suggests that by prewar colonial standards, metropolitan wartime expenditures were enormous, amounting to over 30,000,000,000 francs in the 1917 budget, for example.

Since precise breakdowns are unavailable, indirect evidence offers an insight into the magnitude of the sums being spent on African soldiers. By 1915, maintenance allowances alone amounted to 1,000 francs per year per *tirailleur* and 2,500 francs for *originaires*. Using the government's recruitment and casualty figures as a standard, and assuming a minimum term of service of three years for those surviving the war and one year for those who did not, the cost of maintaining the African troops raised between 1914 and 1918 can be reckoned at approximately 475,000,000 francs. This estimate—which does not include the annual allowances for 31,000 *tirailleurs* recruited before 1914 (who also participated in the war) and omits a wide range of other substantial but separately itemized expenses (i.e., for recruitment, transport, hospitalization, pensions, etc.)—should be revised upward to give an approximate idea of the scale of French wartime subsidies. A conservative estimate (which may be much too low) would place the total at perhaps 1,000,000,000 francs, or about double the amount of maintenance costs.

For wartime budgets, including ministerial allocations, internal categories, and outlays, see "Administration des finances pendant l'année 1917: dépenses publique," Ministère de l'Économie et des finances. For maintenance costs, numbers recruited and killed, subsidies, and loans, see respectively: *ANS*: Affaires militaires: 4 D 24 (68); Marc Michel, *L'Appel à l'Afrique: Contributions et Réactions à l'Effort de Guerre en A.O.F.* (Paris: Publications de la Sorbonne, 1982), pp. 42, 407–08, 483.

[9] The estimate of 1,000,000,000 francs spent during the war can be compared to metropolitan subsidies that averaged under 10,000,000 francs per year throughout the period of the Sudanese conquest (1879–1899) and, after the passage of the "Fi-

nance Law" in 1900—which was intended to eliminate metropolitan subsidies to the colonies altogether by requiring them to become financially self-sufficient—were usually considerably less. It may also be contrasted with the annual budgets for A.O.F. (derived exclusively from African revenues), which, prior to 1914, never amounted to more than 31,600,000 francs. Finally, the magnitude of wartime expenditures can be compared to the size of prewar French loans to the Federation, which, unlike subsidies, had to be repaid. After its founding, four loans totaling 346,000,000 francs were made to the Federation between 1903 and 1913, or perhaps about one-third of what was spent directly by the French government on African soldiers during the war. For wartime expenditures, see note 8; for subsidies and loans, see A. S. Kanya-Forstner, "French Expansion in Africa: The Mythical Theory," in *Studies in the Theory of Imperialism*, eds. R. Owen and B. Sutcliffe (London: Longman, 1972), pp. 277–94; and Henri Brunschwig, *French Colonialism, 1871–1914: Myths and Realities*, trans. William Glanville Brown (London: Pall Mall Press, 1966), pp. 135–38. Postwar inflation rates, which saw the value of the franc decline fivefold by 1926, were not yet a factor that would alter the validity of this comparison as of 1918. See Buell, *The Native Problem in Africa*, vol. 1, pp. 934–37.

[10] This was especially the case with recruits from the Sudan. Many Senegalese recruits, however, were also marched considerable distances to their camps. See: Malal Gassala: 1A; Mamadou Bokar: 1A; and Souleye Samba Ndiaye: 1A.

[11] This was the case in St. Louis. See: *ANS*: Affaires militaires: 4 D 65.

[12] On the sanitary state of the camps at Ouakam, Thiès, and Rufisque in 1918, as well as the numbers of ill soldiers who remained in West Africa, see: *ANS*: Affaires militaires: 4 D 81 and 4 D 82.

[13] See, respectively: Yoro Diaw: 1B, and Souleye Sambu Ndiaye: 1B; and *ANS*: Affaires militaires: 4 D 82.

[14] *ANOM*: Affaires politiques: 3035/1. On madness and suicide, see: *ANS*: Affaires militaires: 4 D 139.

[15] *ANOM*: 14 MI 346.

[16] *ANS*: Affaires militaires: 4 D 81.

[17] On the construction of new camps and the movement of troops to them in 1915, see: *ANS*: Affaires militaires: 4 D 65. On conditions in these camps in 1918, see: *ANS*: Affaires militaires: 4 D 81 and 4 D 82.

[18] While garrisoned in A.O.F., the differences in the conditions of service between *originaires* and *tirailleurs* in 1915, respectively, were as follows: *Pay*: 1.5 versus 0.75 francs per day. *Food*: European food with an allowance of 3.76 francs per ration versus African food with an allowance of 1.68 francs per ration. *Quarters*: barracks with beds versus no provision for beds but with blankets issued. *Promotion*: could become officers in regular army versus no promotion beyond rank of N.C.O. and with authority over African troops only. *ANS*: Affaires politiques: 17 G 241 (108) (cited in: G. Wesley Johnson, Jr., *The Emergence of Black Politics in Senegal: The Struggle for Power in the Four Communes, 1900–1920* (Stanford: Stanford University Press, 1971), p. 190).

[19] The duration of the soldiers' stay in the Senegalese camps varied according to a series of interrelated factors, including the date they were recruited, the dictates of the military situation in France, and the availability of shipping space.

[20] On fluency, see: Ousmane Diagne: 3A. See also: Mbaye Khary Diagne: 1B. On ethnic composition, see: Nar Diouf: 3A and 3B. On French instruction, see: Souleye Samba Ndiaye: 1B; Abdou Karim Gaye: 4A; Malal Gassala: 1B; Moussa Leye: 2A; and

Nouma Ndiaye: 2B. On the shortcomings of language instruction among the *tirailleurs*, see also *AG*: Unités: 22 N 2468.

[21] The most comprehensive description of the soldiers' daily routine is that of Niaki Gueye (1B, 2A, and 2B), who was trained at Rufisque. On leisure activities, see also: Nar Diouf: 4A and 4B.

[22] Souleye Samba Ndiaye: 1B. Lattyr Ndoye: 2B; Nar Diouf: 2B; and Abdou Karim Gaye: 5B. Ousmane Diagne: 3A; and Abdou Karim Gaye: 3B. Ishmale Mbange: 2B.

[23] On beatings, see: Sera Ndiaye: 4B; Souleye Samba Ndiaye: 1B; and Nar Diouf: 2B. See also *ANOM*: 14 MI 346. Abdou Karim Gaye: 3B and 5B. Sera Ndiaye: 4B; Mamadou Djigo: 5B. On friction between Africans and the European cadres assigned to their units, see also: *AG*: Grand Quartier Général (hereafter GQG): 16 N 196 and 16 N 2094. On death threats and fights, see respectively: Sera Ndiaye: 4B; Niaki Gueye: 2B; and Doudou Ndao: 1B.

[24] Niaki Gueye: 2B; Abdou Karim Gaye: 4A; and Nar Diouf 2A. On leave and the shanty towns that arose to cater to the soldiers' needs, see: Niaki Gueye: 2A and 2B; and *ANS*: Affaires militaires: 4 D 71. Amar Seck: 3A.

[25] Prior to 1918, desertion rates among *tirailleurs* were slightly higher in Senegal and Guinea than elsewhere in A.O.F. Among those recruited between October 1915 and April 1916, desertions averaged about 8 percent throughout the Federation. In 1918, however, these dropped to only slightly more than 2 percent of all recruits. See: *ANS*: Affaires militaires: 4D 88 and 4 D 82; and Michel, *L'Appel à l'Afrique*, pp. 85–86. On penalties for desertion in the colonies, see: Amar Seck: 3A; for France, where they were much more severe, and the role of the *Conseil de guerre*, see below.

[26] Recourse to such action was considered "shameful" among the *originaires*; see: Abdoulaye Gueye: 1B. For numbers, also see: *ANOM*: 14 MI 323.

[27] Yoro Diaw: 1A; and Abdoulaye Ndiaye: 2B. In the Senegalese training camps, the use of knives and forks was a mark of distinction between *originaires* and *tirailleurs*. See: Niaki Gueye: 1B. Later, in the French camps, *tirailleurs* were forced to eat with European cutlery or they were not fed. See: Sera Ndiaye: 4B. On French concerns about the adverse local effects of the ways in which the soldiers spent their money, see: *ANS*: Affaires militaires: 4 D 71. On cigarettes, tobacco rations (which were sometimes issued in Senegal as well as in France), and lemonade, see: Niaki Gueye: 2B; Mbaye Khary Diagne: 2A; Samba Diop: 1B; and Demba Mboup: 11A and 11B.

[28] Abdou Karim Gaye: 5B.

[29] On misconceptions that arose from the erroneous belief that facial markings among the Bambara and Mossi inevitably implied servile status, see: Abdou Karim Gaye: 3B. Though not making social distinctions within the army between aristocrats and slaves, the French, at the urging of Blaise Diagne in 1918, did accord the former preferential consideration for promotion.

[30] Demba Mboup: 8B. On the absence of social discrimination toward slaves in the army, see also: Niaki Gueye: 1B; and Daba Dembele: 2A. In point of fact, some French commanders advised against promoting men of servile origins to the rank of N.C.O. in the army. See the report of the *Chef de bataillon* of the 44e *tirailleurs Sénégalais*, 17 September 1918, in *AG*: GQG: 16 N 2094.

[31] Abdou Karim Gaye: 3B. Senegalese prejudices against the Bambara—who were deemed to be ethnically and culturally alien, as well as non-Muslims—were often keen. For other such references, see: Masserigne Soumare: 3A; Abdoulaye Gueye: 5B; Mody Sow: 4B; and Abdoulaye Gassama: 1B.

[32] Abdou Karim Gaye: 3B. Abdoulaye Diaw: 1B.

[33] Mamadou Djigo: 4A.

[34] On shipping shortages, see: *AG*: EMA: 7 N 2120.

[35] For the names of the ships and their respective capacities in 1918, see: *ANS*: Affaires militaires: 4 D 81 and 4 D 82.

[36] On the dispute between the local military authorities and Diagne (and ultimately the Ministry of Colonies) over this issue, see: *ANS*: Affaires militaires: 4 D 81 and 4 D 89.

[37] Disease and death rates varied considerably. On the *Venezuela*, for example, which carried Diagne as a passenger on his return voyage to France in 1918, no fatalities occurred among 850 men. This, however, was very exceptional. Overall, fragmentary evidence from 1918 suggests that mortality rates during the short voyage averaged about one percent. See: *ANS*: Affaires militaires: 4 D 89.

[38] This condemnation, voiced during a session of the *Conseil Général du Sénégal*, was that of M. G. Dupil. See: *Procès verbaux des déliberations du Conseil Général* (Paris: Imprimerie national, 1919), p. 97.

[39] On the length of transit for particular ships in 1918, see: *ANS*: Affaires militaires: 4 D 82. This figure includes some 45,000 West African recruited in 1918, who, though shipped overseas, seldom served as combatants before the end of hostilities.

[40] A handful of Senegalese, like the husband of Coumba Niane, who was a medical student before enlisting in the army, had been to France before the war; see: Coumba Niane: 1A.

[41] For examples, see: Mamadou Djigo: 2A; Abdoulaye Ndiaye: 3A; Daba Dembele: 1B; Malal Gassala: 1B; Souleye Samba Ndiaye: 1A; Abdou Karim Gaye: 4A; and Nouma Ndiaye: 2A. The quotation is from Daba Dembele: 1B. See also: Diouli Missine (2A), who witnessed Bambara soldiers jumping overboard to their deaths as they lost sight of the African coast.

[42] The quotation is from: Lattyr Ndoye: 2B. See also: Nar Diouf: 2B; Mbaye Khary Diagne: 2A; Niaki Gueye: 1A; and Souleye Samba Ndiaye: 1A.

[43] Of the soldiers interviewed, 31 offered their impressions of the voyage to France. Near two-thirds of these (20 of 31) described the journey in exclusively negative terms, while only one-third viewed it as tolerable or comparatively favorably.

[44] St. Louis was seldom used as a port of embarkation, but some soldiers did depart there. See: Nar Diouf: 2B. On the use of cranes to load Africans and gangplanks for Europeans, see: Daba Dembele: 2B.

[45] Daba Dembele: 1B. See also: Amar Seck: 3A; Moussa Leye: 1B; Biram Mbodji Tine: 2B; and Diouli Missine: 2A.

[46] Diouli Missine: 2A; Mandiaye Ndiaye: 1B; Abdoulaye Ndiaye: 3A; and Biram Mbodji Time: 2B. On acclimation, see: Malal Gassala: 1B; and Giribul Diallo: 1B.

[47] Daba Dembele: 1B and 2B. On deaths resulting from seasickness, see also: Alassane Kane: 3B; Mbaye Khary Diagne: 2B; Sera Ndiaye: 2A; and Yoro Diaw: 1B.

[48] On other diseases aboard ship, see: Ibrahima Camara: 1B; Alassane Kane: 3B; and Demba Mboup: 4B. Yoro Diaw: 1B; Daba Dembele: 2B; and Sera Ndiaye: 2A. Samba Diop: 1B.

[49] Mamadou Djigo: 2B. See also: Ishmale Mbange: 1B; and Aliou Diakhate: 2A.

[50] On sailors assuaging the soldiers' fears, see: Ishmale Mbange: 1B. For the crew's perspective on these voyages, see: Jacques Joseph William (1A and 1B), who served in the marines on convoy duty from Dakar to the Cameroons and to France. Senegalese

anxieties about submarine attacks were a recurring theme among the soldiers interviewed. See, for example: Lattyr Ndoye: 2B; Diouli Missine: 2A; Mody Sow: 1A; and Abdou Karim Gaye: 4A. On precautionary measures, see: Mbaye Khary Diagne: 2A; Amar Seck: 3A; Nouma Ndiaye: 2A; Demba Mboup: 4B; and Mody Sow: 1A. On the sinking of other vessels, see: Ndiaga Niang: 1A; Daour Gueye: 2B; Alassane Kane: 3B; Mody Sow: 1A; and Abdoulaye Ndiaye: 3A. On the sinking of *l'Athos*, which was torpedoed on 17 February 1917 with a loss of 124 African and 22 European lives, see *AG*: Unités: 26 N 871. On the inability of many soldiers to swim, see: Mody Sow: 1A.

[51] Samba Diop: 1A and 1B.

[52] Sera Ndiaye: 2A; Abdoulaye Gueye: 1B; Mamadou Djigo: 2B; and Biram Mbodji Tine: 2B. Rog was the creator of the universe in Serer cosmology. Mody Sow: 1A.

[53] Samba Diop: 1B; and Mamadou Djigo: 2B.

[54] On chains, see: Abdoulaye Ndiaye: 3A.

[55] Ousmane Diagne 3A and 3B. For similar accounts of being confined below deck by their officers, see: Abdoulaye Ndiaye: 3A; and Alassane Kane: 3B.

[56] Ousmane Diagne: 3A and 3B. See also: Abdoulaye Ndiaye: 3A. For other examples of Diagne's intervention to secure the dismissal of French N.C.O.s and officers accused of maltreating the Senegalese, see *ANOM*: 14 MI 346.

[57] Abdoulaye Ndiaye: 3A.

[58] Lattyr Ndoye: 2B. See also: Abdoulaye Gueye: 2A.

[59] On Marseilles, see: Nar Diouf: 2B. See, respectively: Ishamale Mbange: 1B; Bara Seck: 1A; Nar Diouf: 2B; and Nouma Ndiaye: 3A.

[60] See: Ishamale Mbange: 1B; Ndiaga Niang: 1B; Nouma Ndiaye: 3A; and Mamadou Djigo: 2B.

[61] Giribul Diallo: 1B. Mamadou Djigo: 2B.

[62] Abdoulaye Gassama: 2A and 2B. Ishamle Mbange: 1B; Abdoulaye Gassama: 2A and 2B; and Niaki Gueye: 3B. Abdoulaye Gassama: 2A and 2B.

[63] See, respectively: Nar Diouf: 2B. Masserigne Soumare: 5B; and Daba Dembele: 3A. On the gradual breakdown of initial reservations among both African soldiers and metropolitan inhabitants, see Chapter 6.

[64] The possession of French citizenship was not the sole criterion for this division. Because of the more favorable terms of service accorded to *originaires*, the French authorities sought to limit their contact with *tirailleurs* lest this have adverse effects on their morale. On restriction on interaction between the two groups, see: Abdoulaye Gueye: 1B.

[65] Anthony Clayton, *France, Soldiers and Africa* (London: Brassey's Defence Publishers, 1988), p. 16.

[66] The Fréjus/St. Raphäel complex eventually housed some 50,000 *tirailleurs* by 1918, while Courneau was intended to accommodate 27,000 when it was built. Other Senegalese formations were also shipped to camps in North Africa when there was not enough space available in the metropole. On the construction of new training camps for the *tirailleurs* in France, see: *AG*: EMA: 7 N 1990 and 7 N 1991.

[67] Ousmane Diagne: 3B and 4B; Abdoulaye Ndiaye: 4A; and Boubacar Gueye: 2B. *AG*: EMA: 7 N 144, 7 N 2120—21.

[68] On the physical layout of the camp at Courneau, see: Sera Ndiaye: 2B; and Biram Mbodji Tine: 2B. On the lamentable sanitary state of the *tirailleur* camps in France, see: "Rapports du contrôleur des troupes sénégalaises Logeay," in: *ANS*: Affaires militaires: 4 D 81 and 4 D 89. For comparative mortality rates among the Senegalese at Corneau

and Fréjus—which in May 1917 ranged as high as 13.7 fatalities per 1,000 troops—see the chart "Mortalité des sénégalais": *AG*: EMA: 7 N 1990.

[69] *AG*: EMA: 7 N 1990. On excessive morbidity and mortality rates among the Senegalese compared to the French, see also the report of the director of the health service for the 17th region (Toulouse), 4 February 1918: *AG*: EMA: 7 N 1990. On deaths from disease in the camps during winter, see: *AG*: EMA: 7 N 440. On comparative French and Senegalese disease rates among postwar occupation troops on the Rhine, also see Dr. Lasnet, "Notice concernant l'État sanitaire des divers contingents Européens et Indigènes de l'Armée du Rhin," *Annales de Médecine et de Pharmacie coloniale* 20 (1922), pp. 273–89. For some illnesses such as tuberculosis, disease rates were over eight times as high for West Africans as for Europeans.

[70] Aside from N.C.O.s, the French cadres also trained in separate sections unless these were machine gun sections, which were integrated. See: Nar Diouf: 4A. See also: *AG*: EMA: 7 N 1990. On the parameters, extent, and character of the interaction between the *tirailleurs* and their French cadres, see Chapter 6.

[71] Daba Dembele: 2A; and Nar Diouf: 2B. On the mixing of "warrior" races by section, see: Masserigne Soumare: 3A. On the racial preconceptions of the French and the organization of African units based on their "warlike"—or alternatively their lack of warlike—propensities, see: *AG*: Unités: 26 N 870. See also Joe Lunn, "'Les races guerrières': Racial Preconceptions in the French Military about West African Soldiers during the First World War," *Journal of Contemporary History* 34, 4 (1999).

[72] On the ethnic composition and ratios of Frenchmen to Senegalese (and other colonials) in these units, as well as the character of the interaction between these men, see: Boubacar Gueye: 1B; Mamadou Djigo: 4A; Abdoulaye Ndiaye: 4B; Abdoulaye Diaw: 1A; Thiecouta Diallo: 1A; Abdoulaye Gueye: 1A; and Mbaye Khary Diagne: 1A and 2B. See also Chapters 5 and 6.

[73] *Tirailleurs* wore the distinctive *cheka*—a red cap resembling a *tarboosh*—and they were issued *coupes-coupes* (long knives similar to machetes) for hand-to-hand fighting. On discrepancies in salary and food, see Section 1 and note 18. Food served in the *tirailleur* camps, as well as in combat, was often identical to that served to the French. See: Doudou Ndao: 3A; and Sera Ndiaye: 4B.

[74] On pidgin French, see: Malal Gassala: 1B. See also: *AG*: Unités: 22 N 2468, and *Le Français tel que le parlent nos tirailleurs* (Paris: Imprimerie Libraire Militaire Universelle L. Tournier, 1916), which was used as an instructional guide by French officers teaching "*tirailleurs français*." On language courses for N.C.O.s among *tirailleurs*, see: Nar Diouf: 2B. On French lessons for *originaires*, see: Mamadou Djigo: 3A. On leave, see Chapter 6.

[75] Souleye Samba Ndiaye: 1B; Nar Diouf: 2B; and Mamadou Djigo: 3A. On combat preparation, see: Yoro Diaw: 1B; Souleye Samba Ndiaye: 1B; Daour Gueye: 2B; Biram Mbodji Tine: 2B; and Ishmale Mbange: 2A.

[76] On tactics, see: Ishmale Mbange: 2A; and Biram Mbodji Tine: 2B. On the poor quality of officers in some units—the best officers were seldom assigned to serve with foreign troops—as well as inadequate training between 1916 and 1918, see: *AG*: GQG: 16 N 2094; *AG*: EMA: 7 N 1990; and *AG*: Unités: 22 N 2468 and 22 N 2481.

[77] Nar Diouf: 2B; Souleye Samba Ndiaye: 1A; and Mamadou Djigo: 5B. See also: *ANOM*: 14 MI 346. Nar Diouf: 2B; and Mamadou Djigo: 5A. Doudou Ndao: 1B; and Abdou Karim Gaye: 5B. On prejudice among French cadres see also: *AG*: GQG: 16 N 196.

[78] On the composition of the councils and the nature of their deliberations, see: Masserigne Soumare (2B and 3A), who for three months served as an interpreter for one. See also Guy Pedroncini, *Les Mutineries de 1917* (Paris: Presses Universitaires de France, 1967), pp. 13–20.

[79] For cases involving these offenses, see: Masserigne Soumare: 2B and 3A; Demba Mboup: 10B, 11A, 11B and 12B; Nar Diouf: 3A; Abdou Karim Gaye: 4A; and Mody Sow 4A. The theft of a shirt, for example, resulted in four days' confinement (which was subsequently suspended), while a Senegalese enlisted man was punished with two months' imprisonment for fighting with an African corporal. Murder and especially desertion and strikes (which occurred later in the war and were considered "mutinies") were dealt with very harshly. Penalties included 15 years of imprisonment at hard labor, relegation to the front line during assaults (which amounted to a virtual sentence of death), or execution by firing squad. See, respectively: Masserigne Soumare: 2B and 3A; Demba Mboup: 11A; Nar Diouf: 3A; and Abdou Karim Gaye: 4A.

[80] Masserigne Soumare (2B and 3A) suggests that this may have been the case in charges involving being A.W.O.L., when a plea of being "lost" was sufficient to gain acquittal. Such a defense would have been likely to appeal to French preconceptions about the "child like" character of Africans. For further discussion of this theme, see Chapter 6. Fear of being brought before the councils for fighting, for example, was a significant factor in reducing confrontations between French and Senegalese soldiers in the camps. See: Abdoulaye Ndiaye: 4B.

[81] Only a few Senegalese received commissions as officers during the war. See Michel, *L'Appel à l'Afrique*, p. 325. On the criteria for selection and the nature of the instruction in these courses, see: Nar Diouf: 2B and 4A; Antoine Diouf: 1B; Thiecouta Diallo: 1A; and Ousmane Diagne: 5A. On other French criteria, which, in addition to two years' active service and fluency in French, included a "developed intelligence," see: *AG*: GQG: 16 N 2094. On promotion, see: Nar Diouf: 2A.

[82] Nouma Ndiaye: 2B. Antoine Diouf: 1B. On French policy regarding the soldiers' letters, including prohibition of writing, concerns about morale, censorship, and apprehensions about the spread of "libertarian ideas" to the colonies, see also: *ANS*: Affaires militaires: 4 D 70.

[83] On the loss of mail en route, see: Momar Candji: 2B; and Galaye Gueye: 2A and 2B. See also: *ANS*: Affaires militaires: 4 D 70; and *AG*: Fonds Clemenceau: 6 N 97.

[84] Daba Dembele: 4B. See also: Nouma Ndiaye: 2B.

[85] On literate soldiers serving as scribes for their comrades, see: Mamadou Djigo: 6A; Ousmane Diagne: 5A; and Ishmale Mbange: 3A. On letters in Arabic, see: Alassane Kane: 2B; and Momar Candji: 2B. On the content of the soldiers' letters, see: Ousmane Diagne: 5A; Samba Laga Diouf: 1B; Antoine Diouf: 1B; Sambou Ndiaye: 1B; Nar Diouf: 6A; Yoro Diaw: 2B; and Makhoudia Ndiaye: 2A. For French assessments of the contents of the soldiers' letters, see also: *ANS*: Affaires militaires: 4 D 81.

[86] Though infrequent, encounters between *tirailleurs* and *originaires* did occur during the winter *hivernage*, when soldiers visited friends in nearby camps; in hospitals, when the wounded were convalescing; and sometimes during combat. For examples, see: Nar Diouf: 4A, 4B; Aliou Diakhate: 1B; and Ndiaga Niang: 2B.

[87] Abdou Karim Gaye: 5A; and Amar Seck: 3A.

[88] Thiecouta Diallo: 1A and 1B. Abdoulaye Diaw: 1B. For additional examples of the attitudes of *originaires* toward the *tirailleurs*, see also: Ndiaga Niang: 2B; and Boubacar Gueye: 1B and 2B.

[89] Ishmale Mbange: 2B; and Abdoulaye Gueye: 1A. On French concerns about the propagation of Islam in the camps, see: *ANOM*: Affaires politiques: 3036/3.

[90] On the contrast in size between the camps in Senegal and in France, see: Sera Ndiaye: 2B; and Abdou Karim Gaye: 4B. On better treatment, see: Biram Mbodji Tine: 2B; Sera Ndiaye: 4B; Mamadou Djigo: 3A; and Aliou Diakhate: 2A.

[91] Biram Mbodji Tine: 2B; Doudou Ndao: 1B; and Mamadou Djigo: 3A. Amar Seck: 4B.

[92] See, respectively: Ishmale Mbange: 3A and 3B; Masserigne Soumare: 3A; Momar Candji: 3A; and Abdoulaye Gueye: 2A. See also: *ANOM*: 14 MI 346; and *AG*: Fonds Clemenceau: 6 N 97. On Diagne, see: Demba Mboup: 13 A; and Abdoulaye Gueye: 1A. On the debate over *hivernage* for *originaires*, see also: *AG*: EMA: 7 N 440.

[93] Momar Candji: 3A. On Diagne's visits to the training camps, the apprehensions his presence aroused among the French, and his demotion or transfer of offending officers to other units, see also: Masserigne Soumare: 3A; and Ishmale Mbange: 3A and 3B. On Diagne's breaking of French officers for mistreating their men (or, alternatively, blocking their appointment to command of Senegalese units), see also: *ANOM*: 14 MI 346; and *AG*: Fonds Clemenceau: 16 N 2094.

[94] Galaye Gueye: 1A.

[95] Failure to salute a Senegalese N.C.O., for example, resulted in six days of imprisonment. See: Abdou Karim Gaye: 5B. See also: Nar Diouf: 4A; and *AG*: GQG: 16 N 2094. On promotion, see: Nar Diouf: 2A. Aristocratic apprehensions about the threat to their status this situation posed were also successfully exploited by Diagne during his recruiting mission in 1918. See: *ANS*: Affaires militaires: 4 D 87 and Chapter 3. On rights, see: Mandaw Mbaye: 2A.

[96] Antoine Diouf: 1A. For an especially vociferous denunciation of injustice in the training camps, which recounts an incident in Bordeaux where many Senegalese were killed by the French, see: Boubacar Gueye: 2A.

[97] Mamadou Djigo: 5A.

[98] Doudou Ndao: 3A.

5

"To Meet Death Far Away": The Senegalese in the Trenches

Nearly 140,000 West Africans served as combatants in Europe during the First World War. Their presence on the western front, as well as their purported conduct in the fighting, aroused intense controversy at the time, while the use made of them by French generals has been the subject of ongoing debate ever since.

The ferocious image of the Senegalese *tirailleur* brandishing his *coupe-coupe* and beheading Germans in behalf of *la patrie* was widely disseminated by the French in an effort to terrify their adversaries and boost the morale of metropolitan forces. The Germans, for their part, eagerly repeated allegations of African brutality.[1] It was also frequently asserted that French officers regarded the Senegalese primarily as "cannon fodder" and systematically employed them as assault troops with the deliberate intention of sacrificing their lives in order to spare French ones.[2] This charge was denied by the government. Rather, they portrayed their willingness to use African soldiers as an example of the nonracist character of French society that was consistent with the egalitarian principles of French Republicanism.[3]

In addition to the myths and controversy surrounding Senegalese participation in the fighting, the nature of the soldiers' experience in the trenches has also remained enigmatic. The combat experience of the Senegalese in Europe can be assessed by examining how African troops were deployed at the front and exploring their interpretations of their ordeal and motivations for fighting. With respect to their use, a new interpretation of the evidence will show that during the last two and a half years of the war, the casualties suffered by Africans were indeed significantly higher than those incurred by the French. Moreover, it is maintained that this was not accidental but rather the product of a calculated policy concerning their use on the part of many French commanders. Senegalese recollections of the Great War thus paint a compelling picture of the nature of their combat experience from their particular vantage point in the frontlines.

"LES TROUPES DE CHOC"

The Use of the Senegalese at the Front

The use that the French made of the Senegalese in combat between 1914 and 1918 fell into three distinct phases. During the first year and a half of the war, the French High Command, imbued with the erroneous belief that the conflict would be brief and often skeptical about the military value of the Senegalese, generally opted to use them as garrison troops to release French units in North Africa or in secondary operations outside of France, notably at the Dardanelles and later in Thessaloniki.[4] In the wake of the disasters suffered during the first year of the fighting, French policy toward the Senegalese was revised in late 1915. In light of the inescapable evidence that the war would be both bloody and protracted, massive recruitment was authorized in West Africa, and the new formations raised there were combined with preexisting units and deployed in large numbers on the western front. In this capacity, over 30,000 West Africans were engaged on the Somme between July and October 1916 and also at Verdun, where a "tactical group" composed in large measure of *tirailleurs* and *originaires* participated in perhaps the most celebrated French military action of the war, the "retaking" of Fort Douaumont.[5] French policy thus crystallized, and thereafter Senegalese troops were extensively used in France.

With the near collapse of the French army a year later after the debacle on the Aisne, the use of the Senegalese (who had suffered extensive losses in the fighting there) entered its final phase. From mid-1917 onward, Africans were dispersed along the front to serve as the tactical spearheads for larger French units.[6] In this role, Africans served in the frontlines—notably in the counterattacks at Reims and in the assaults against Villers-Cotteret and St. Mihiel—until the armistice.[7]

Organizational Principles

Just as the use of African troops went through distinct phases, so too did the principles governing the organization of Senegalese formations in combat undergo continual modification between 1914 and 1918. The French High Command was presented with two main options regarding the organization of African troops: they might be grouped with European and other colonial soldiers within squads to form fully integrated units in the *Armée coloniale*, or they could be segregated in separate battalions or regiments composed (with the exception of their French cadres) exclusively of Senegalese. In addition, they entertained a third possibility, which was to retain the principle of segregation of the Africans except in combat. When fighting, African units of various sizes—companies, battalions, or regiments—might be temporarily "amalgamated" (*amalgamée*) or "juxtaposed" (*accolant*) with other similar sized formations in the Colonial Army to create larger units, either in "variegated" (*panaché*) or mixed (*mixte*) units of battalions, regiments, or brigades.[8]

With the exception of the Senegalese *originaires*, who were usually integrated at a company level with French soldiers in the Colonial Army, the first option was never considered by the military authorities.[9] Instead, the *Tirailleurs sénégalais*—which accounted for over 96 percent of the African combatants in Europe—were systematically "isolated" in units behind the lines and, frequently, during combat.[10] The third option was, nevertheless, also employed by the army. Never formally systematized by the High Command, which, depending on particular situations, left the tactical organization of combat formations largely to the discretion of unit commanders, the range of African-European alignments utilized during the fighting varied in the extreme.

Though occasionally formed into regiments composed entirely of Senegalese troops, the prevailing practice during the first two years of the war was to combine two African battalions with a third battalion of French (or other colonial) soldiers to form a mixed regiment of colonial infantry.[11] The guiding organizational principle throughout this period was that the Senegalese battalion—including its small French cadre, which amounted to about 11 percent of its complement[12]—should remain inviolate.

The decision to utilize large numbers of Senegalese troops on the western front in 1916 initiated a period of ongoing experimentation that continued throughout the war. During 1916, African units were deployed by the Colonial Army in one of three types of combat formations: in regiments composed entirely of Senegalese battalions; in regiments consisting of both Senegalese and European battalions; and, much more rarely, in battalions or "tactical groups" that interspersed African companies among other companies of colonial infantry.[13] Regardless of how they were deployed, all African combat units used during 1916 also contained a very high percentage of soldiers recruited from "warrior races."[14]

After General Charles Mangin's rise to a position on the High Command in 1917, Senegalese units were concentrated in order to maximize their "shock" power. Two organizational patterns predominated. Senegalese battalions were temporarily assigned to *régiments "blancs"* to create a fourth battalion for assault, or they were grouped into exclusively African regiments.[15] Limited experimentation was also conducted with the *panaché* of units, whereby Senegalese and European battalions placed in line next to each other exchanged one company apiece.[16] These measures, however, failed to achieve the desired result.

In the aftermath of the mutinies that erupted in May 1917 following the disastrous attacks on the Aisne, the High Command's general policy concerning the deployment of Senegalese troops was again revised. Though still assigned primarily to the Colonial Army, African battalions were also dispersed among metropolitan formations for the first time. During the last year and a half of the war, these latter units were temporarily "loaned" to French infantry divisions as "tactical groups" of two or three battalions whenever a "determined" attack (or counterattack) was planned.[17] Their cadres had been increased to about one-fifth of their complement by this time, and the variegation of Senegalese and French battalions was often (though not exclusively) practiced by divisional and corps commanders.[18]

French Tactical Doctrine

French tactical doctrine about how best to use the Senegalese in combat, no less than military opinions about their value, was sharply divided at the beginning of the war. This internal dispute represented a continuation of earlier disagreements within the army about the efficacy of undertaking expanded recruitment in West Africa in 1912, and it remained largely unresolved during the first two years of the war. Thereafter, when it was decided to deploy the Senegalese in large numbers on the western front, controversy continued over the question of their qualities as soldiers, while the tactical principles concerning their employment were subject to ongoing experimentation and revision. Nevertheless, military doctrine governing their use was conditioned throughout by French racial preconceptions about Africans.[19]

Early advocates of the policy of deploying the Senegalese as combatants in Europe stressed their hereditary qualities as "warriors." Ranking the comparative martial prowess of West Africans according to "race," they sought—by means of apportioning appropriate combinations of these groups within infantry formations—to exploit their "natural" combativeness to maximum advantage. Though conceding their alleged intellectual inferiority to Europeans, this faction argued that several of the more "advanced" races were capable of providing the requisite number of N.C.O.s for their units and that the remainder, if they were provided with proper French leadership, made excellent soldiers. Moreover, their comparative lack of "nervousness" made them ideal for use as "shock troops." Their tactical role was thus envisioned from the outset as primarily an offensive one.[20]

While those who advocated using Senegalese troops emphasized their innate fighting qualities, detractors laid stress on their "limited intellectual faculties."[21] Because of the perceived "simplicity" of their languages, preventing their comprehension of complex instructions in French, it was sug-

Quelques types des principales Races de l'Afrique Occidentale d'où proviennent les Tirailleurs Sénégalais combattant en France.

1. — **Wolof.** — Tirailleur BAKARI DIAGNE, né en 1879, à Tivaouane (Sénégal).

2. — **Wolof**, de Dakar. — Soldat MAMADOU SOW, né à Dakar, incorporé au 5e régiment colonial comme originaire de l'une des Quatre Communes du Sénégal.

3. — **Wolof**, fils de chef. — Caporal ALIOURI GUEYE, fils de Daligué Bodi, ancien chef de canton de N'guel Salaw, Cercle de Diourbel (Sénégal).

4. — **Wolof** fils de chef. — Caporal SAGGNGO DIENG, fils de Lassa Bavi, ancien teigne (roi) du Baol (Sénégal).

5. — **Wolof-Lébou.** — Tirailleur OUSMAN NIA, né à Rufisque (Sénégal), âgé de 52 ans.

6. — **Sérère.** — Tirailleur AMADY BAROUFE, né à Gandiole, Cercle de Kaolack (Sénégal).

7. — **Sérère.** — Sergent MALIK KOR DIOLF, né en 1891, à N'dilène (Sénégal), cousin du Bour Sine chef de la province de Sine; et fils de Baum Bara Diouf, chef du canton de Ngayo Klem Sine Saloum, au Sénégal; s'est engagé pour servir d'exemple aux administrés de son cousin.

8. — **Toucouleur**, fils de chef. — Caporal MAMADOU SALI, fils de Lambara Mamadou Mbaba, ancien chef du Fouta Toro et neveu du chef actuel, né à Podor (Sénégal), en 1896.

8 bis. — **Toucouleur.** — Caporal DEMBA NDIAYE, né au village de Dioum, Cercle de Podor (Sénégal), en 1890; blessé à la bataille de la Somme.

9. — **Diola**, de Casamance Fogny. — Tirailleur BOUBAMA FATIE, né au village de Maude Guen, près Bignona (Fogny, Sénégal), âgé de 20 ans.

10. — **Saharien.** — Tirailleur SIDI HAIDARRA, né à l'oasis de Oualata (Haut-Sénégal-Niger), âgé de 25 ans environ.

11. — **Maure**, de Mauritanie. — Tirailleur MOUHAMED BABEN, né au village de Diorbivol, près Cascas (Sénégal), âgé de 23 ans.

12. — **Peulh.** — Tirailleur MAMADOU SIDIBE, né au village de Baru, Cercle de Dédougou (Haut-Sénégal-Niger), âgé de 23 ans; engagé en 1910.

13. — **Peulh**, du Kaarta. — Tirailleur OUMARU DIALLO, né à Segou (Haut-Sénégal-Niger), âgé de 25 ans.

14. — **Bambara.** — Sergent MAMADOU DIARRA, né en 1879, à Nyamina (Haut-Sénégal-Niger); ancien caravanier en dioula; engagé en 1901 à Conakry; 3 années de service en Guinée française; vient au Maroc en 1907; blessé devant l'ennemi en 1908, à Kenifra; nommé caporal, puis décoré de la médaille militaire; fait, en 1914, la campagne de France, et en 1916 la Somme; grièvement blessé; a deux fils écoliers à Saint-Louis. A obtenu la belle citation reproduite plus haut.

★ ★ ★ ★

NE PAS COUPER

"Warrior Races" from Senegal—Wolof, Serer, Toucouleur, and Bambara. From *La Dépêche coloniale Illustrée*, January 1916.

gested that communication with the Senegalese was perforce restricted and command thereby made more difficult. In addition to their being unable to conduct sophisticated maneuvers, they were also stigmatized as being poor marksmen. Africans, it was argued, were also excessively dependent on their European officers, and if these were killed or otherwise disabled in action, their formations quickly lost cohesion. Worst of all, in such circumstances they were prone to rout. These inherent deficiencies were impossible for the Africans to overcome, and they were accordingly disparaged as unreliable troops who were incapable of mastering the intricacies of "modern" warfare.[22]

Nevertheless, these dramatically opposing views about Senegalese "aptitudes" in combat gradually became reconciled in French military doctrine. In light of their inconsistent performance on the western front in 1916 and 1917, principles governing their tactical use were codified in the *Notice sur les Sénégalais et leur emploi au combat* issued during the last year of the war. Distributed to French officers commanding African units, this directive provided a policy that represented a synthesis of earlier preconceptions.[23]

Accepting the martial ranking of African races as a basic premise, the "notice" enumerated the specific military attributes and shortcomings of each group. It further espoused the view that the vocabularies of most African "dialects" were only sufficient to convey "very simple ideas." Under such circumstances, officers were counseled to be patient, to demonstrate their basic commands visually, and to rely on African N.C.O.s as interpreters.

The most "basic" element of the Senegalese infantry battalion was the company, and these were to be composed of races whose dialects permitted intercommunication and whose natural fighting qualities complemented each other. Units composed of Wolofs, Serers, "Tukulors," and Bambaras, for example, were considered to be among the very "best" combat formations. And regardless of how the Senegalese battalions were deployed at the front, under no circumstance was the internal organization of the African companies to be touched.

Senegalese combat characteristics were discussed in detail in the *Notice*, and a series of tactical recommendations concerning their use were made. Though possessing "[highly] developed warrior instincts," they also suffered from serious shortcomings. While there were exceptions to this rule, defensive operations frequently posed difficulties for Africans because of their "unskillful" use of terrain. Offensive actions were, however, a different matter, provided certain necessary precautions were taken.

"Brave" and "impetuous" in attack, the Senegalese were said to pursue assaults to the very "limit of their endurance" if these developed favorably. If they were "checked," however, they became easily confused and unreliable. In such situations, their "sole idea" was to escape from

Figure 5.1 Tactical Deployment of Senegalese Troops during Assaults: *Panaché* and *Accoler* of Units.

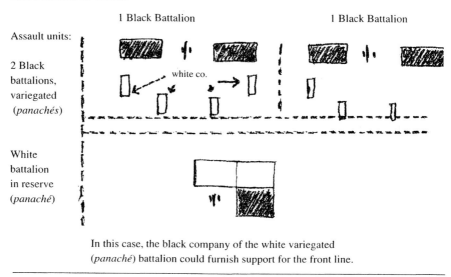

1 Black Battalion   1 Black Battalion

Assault units:

2 Black
battalions,
variegated
(*panachés*)

white co.

White
battalion
in reserve
(*panaché*)

In this case, the black company of the white variegated
(*panaché*) battalion could furnish support for the front line.

The schemes below represent diverse combinations—all possible—
without which it would be necessary to disrupt the command at the
last moment.

    A. Brigade by Regiments placed side by side (*accoler*)
      and surrounded (*encadres*)

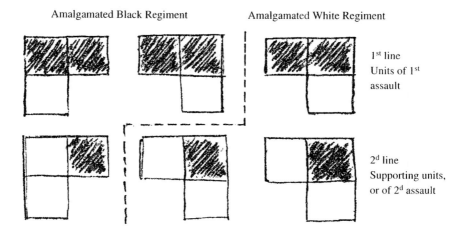

Amalgamated Black Regiment   Amalgamated White Regiment

1st line
Units of 1st
assault

2d line
Supporting units,
or of 2d assault

Source: Archives de la Guerre: Fonds Clemenceau, 6 N 96: "Note au sujet de l'organisation d'unités offensives mixtes Sénégalaises," Chef de bataillon Arnaud, Commandant de 64e bataillon de Tirailleurs Sénégalaises, 12 février 1917.

the "hot spots" where their officers had led them and to seek safety in "flight without stopping."

Because the French cadres within African battalions were insufficient to prevent such a situation from occurring, it was "indispensable to provide [additional] support" for Senegalese units in combat. The means of doing so was made explicit: "*behind* black battalions one always ought to have a French unit to sustain [them]" and to "stay their movement if necessary." The recommended method for making such troops available was to variegate Senegalese and French battalions in the lines (*panaché*), which would permit the temporary exchange of one company from each unit during combat. The French company "loaned" to the Senegalese would thus provide the requisite "support" in their rear, while the extra African company would thereby be freed to participate in operations with the European battalion (see Figure 5.1). As these instructions indicate, French tactical doctrine by 1918 embraced the notion that the Senegalese were useful primarily as assault troops, but that they required European formations both behind them and at their sides to fulfill this role properly.

Even though the principles governing the use of the Senegalese changed during the war, the frontline experience of the vast majority of African combatants was nonetheless remarkably similar. Almost always segregated from French troops except at the front, they were usually used in hazardous operations and especially as shock troops. In the face of callous treatment by their commanders and their unenviable role in fighting, their experience is of particular interest in revealing how they reacted to the terrifying combat situations they faced.

SOLDIERS' MEMORIES OF COMBAT

Senegalese impressions of their experience at the front varied considerably depending on individual circumstances. These factors included: their date of entry into the army, and hence their duration of service; their legal classification as French *sujets* or citizens; and, perhaps most significant, the units to which they were assigned. Among *originaires* there was a significant difference in the views of those who served in the *Infanterie coloniale du Maroc* and in other French regiments of the Colonial Army, while among the *tirailleurs* the primary distinction was between the infantry and (much more rarely) the artillery units.[24] Nevertheless, in general the reactions of the Senegalese to their ordeal as combatants were strikingly similar, no doubt because they exemplified a shared cultural heritage. Recalling their experience, veterans invariably addressed common themes: impressions of the front, memories of combat, ways they sought to cope with their ordeal, and motivations for fighting.

Impressions of the Front

Alien though the troglodite world of the trenches was to most European soldiers, it was even more bewildering for the Senegalese. Possessing "no idea of war" and frequently unfamiliar with many of the sights, sounds, and physical sensations to which their French counterparts were accustomed, the Africans' impressions of the front convey a mixture of awe and dread.[25]

The landscape was desolate. Most buildings and houses near the front lines were "destroyed" and the terrain was as barren as the "bush" in Senegal. Soldiers "dug holes to hide in" or were conveyed to deeper redoubts, where they "hid underground before attacks." The trench system was "built in a curved way instead of a straight line" to minimize losses; it was protected by "iron thread with barbs" to prevent encroachments by the enemy; and it was illuminated at night by flares—"white, red, and ones with many colors"—that made their surroundings "as clear as day." "Sentinels" stood guard at the *petit poste* in No Man's Land to warn of unexpected attack, where passwords—such as "Dakar"—were whispered to identify friend from foe.[26]

Agents of death came in many forms. Artillery fire, which "sounded like thunder," sent shells "exploding and flashing overhead." On impact these made "deep holes in the ground," "buried men [alive]," and covered those they missed in "powder and smoke." In addition to the roar of the cannons—which made their heads "ring" and "deafened" and "burned" those near to them—the lethal but distinctive "tat, tat, tat, tat" of machine guns was also "continuously" audible. "Strange metallic birds" with "men inside" inspired wonder and fear among soldiers who had never seen such sights. They shot and bombed terrified soldiers, and fell to earth in flames. "Balloons attached with cords to the ground" directed the fire of French field guns; these were also attacked by the Germans and "burned with men inside them." And amid this visual spectacle and deafening inferno—many "never heard louder noise than at the front"—death also came imperceptibly. Gas blinded or killed those whose masks were defective, and its corrosive effect on lungs lingered decades after the battles ceased.[27]

The soldiers were not alone at the front. Dogs, whose scent and hearing were keener than men's, forewarned them of impending attacks. Pigeons carried written messages to distant places and hence became targets whenever they were spotted. Horses pulled guns and other heavy equipment, and their corpses were usually the first sign that death was close at hand when the soldiers moved up to the front. In addition to the presence of other creatures, the soldier's dead comrades were also constant companions. References to them were ubiquitous, though descriptions of their appearance varied in detail: "the ground was covered with dark uniforms"; corpses were "everywhere"; and the dead were "like flies."[28]

Though such sights provided a graphic reminder of the fate that might soon await the soldiers, life among those who survived was one of constant physical hardship. Whenever they were at the front, the men were "always tired, always hungry, and always thirsty." Fatigue was caused by the constant exertions demanded of the soldiers, and in some cases this was so intense that men died of exhaustion. Food was provided irregularly and was often of poor quality. Because of their inability to make "fires or smoke in the trenches" lest they alert the enemy of their whereabouts, the soldiers were unable to cook and subsisted on rations of "cold meals in tins." Moreover, even when deprived of food for extensive periods, such as during prolonged attacks, soldiers seldom felt "like eating [after battle] because [many of] the men they had been with during the day were dead."[29]

The harshness of the European climate was extremely difficult for the soldiers to endure, perhaps even more so than battle itself. Indeed, veterans referred to this more frequently than any other single aspect of their daily experience in the trenches. Rain lasted for days on end, filling the trenches with water and forcing the soldiers to wade waist deep in mire. If the weather then turned cold, even worse consequences followed. None of the Senegalese had ever seen snow before and many were entranced by its sight, describing it as "a kind of ice that fell from the sky [looking] like cotton; [it] stays on the ground but when the sun comes out becomes water and begins to run." But the consequences of its appearance were dire for sub-Saharan Africans. The cold was often so intense that soldiers "couldn't button [their] uniforms" or "handle [their] rifles," and the "water in [their] canteens became blocks of ice," causing many of them to become so dehydrated that they "couldn't piss." Prolonged exposure to the cold led to frostbite. For some, their "feet became so swollen that they couldn't keep their shoes [on]; they had to be cut off with a knife and they took a pullover and put it around their feet."[30] Recounting how frostbite was contracted, Ndiaga Niang remembered:

[One] morning the shells were falling near the trenches, [and] it was very, very cold. And when we got out of the trenches [after the German bombardment, we] were walking to get back [to the rear]. I was walking, but my hands began to get paralyzed because of the cold. I had my rifle in my hand, but I couldn't let go of it because my fingers were completely bent. But I was still walking. After a while my toes began to be[come] paralyzed too, and I realized that I had frostbite and I fell down. One of my friends told me: "Come on, come on, we have to [go]." And I wanted to come, but I couldn't walk any more. Some officers came and said to me: "What's this; who is this guy? Get up and walk like everybody else!" And I said to the officers: "I can't walk anymore—my feet are frozen." And one came and looked at my feet and he told five soldiers to [carry] me on their rifles [like] a stretcher. I was taken to the infirmary to get healed.

The next day I was taken to the hospital in Salonique [Thessaloniki], where all of the soldiers had their feet frozen. When the sun [became] hot enough, our feet were hurting so badly that everybody was shouting and crying in the hospital. And the doctor came and told me that he had to cut [off] my feet. [But on] the day he [had] fixed to cut [them off], when he arrived he found that I was sitting [up in bed]. So he told me "you are very lucky . . . you are going to get better. I have no need to [amputate] your feet [now, because] I can heal them."[31]

Others were less fortunate. Many Africans died of exposure in the trenches, while the sight of amputees missing hands and feet, which was commonplace in postwar Senegal, was often attributable to the frostbite the veterans contracted at the front.[32]

Memories of Combat

Miserable though the soldiers' experience usually was in the trenches, it paled in comparison with the horrors they were subjected to during combat. Indeed, as one soldier succinctly expressed it, "Nothing in life is worse."[33]

Despite their differing views about where (or when) the hazards they faced were most perilous, the soldiers' impressions of combat bore striking similarities. For nearly all the experience was extremely disorienting. Senses of time and direction frequently became confused. Often guided only by the position of the "sun" or "stars"—which sometimes appeared to come from "different directions," the soldiers frequently had little idea of where they were. They also lost count of the number of days—and sometimes hours— they spent at the front, which were often reckoned simply as "long" or "short" periods. And despite their preparatory training and the commands issued by their officers, in the midst of combat, with "soldiers falling all around you," the men seldom had "time to think [about] what to do."[34]

Not surprisingly, the experience of the soldiers at the front was not uniform but depended on the various types of operations they had to perform. These fell into several different categories; though all of them were hazardous under adverse circumstances, they differed in significant respects. Sectors of the trench network (at least until the summer of 1918, when the fighting became more open) might be occupied in the normal rotation of units. This entailed the upkeep of the position, wariness against sniper fire, and defense against unexpected attack. Night patrols into No Man's Land, on which the soldiers strung barbed wire and gathered reconnaissance information, also figured prominently in the soldier's routine. Though entailing risk— especially if the patrols were spotted in the open and subjected to artillery or machine-gun fire—this type of duty was usually less dangerous than other assignments.[35]

Alternatively, the Senegalese might be used for *coups de main*—brief surprise attacks by companies or battalions—intended to probe the strength of enemy defenses and dull their preparedness before major attacks. Usually conducted at night by units brought to the front especially for this purpose, these attacks frequently had disastrous results for those involved if the enemy was forewarned or encountered in unexpected strength.[36]

Finally, the soldiers might also be used in major offensives intended to carry the German positions. Assault troops were normally divided into "three waves," and the soldiers were instructed to advance in lines if they faced artillery fire but to disperse and lie down if they encountered machine guns. They were also taught to advance (or retreat) as well as to fire only on the commands of their officers, who "the Germans always tried to shoot first."[37]

This last type of operation was regarded as a Senegalese specialty by the French High Command, and it was the one most frequently referred to by the soldiers. Though placing their lives at maximum risk, their experience during the assaults differed depending on the circumstances surrounding them, and they exemplify the range of conditions to which combatants might be exposed. Recounting the ill-fated diversionary attack on the Dardanelles, Daba Dembele vividly described the effects of high explosives on attacking troops:

> The first thing we saw when we [disembarked from the ships] were boots just coming out of the ground—they were dead soldiers that had been buried by the shells. . . . And we saw many coins of money everywhere because the soldiers had been bombed by the shells. And most of them [had been] buried without their "change"—only their boots were out. Both the French and the Germans were bombing everywhere when we arrived. I was in the crowd and was advancing. [And a shell] dropped near my legs, and I was blown up about 20 meters [in the air] from where the cannon ball fell. I was not wounded, but I had a stomach full of air . . . because of the impact of the [explosion]. And I was lying there for . . . hours [because] I could not move.[38]

After literally "walking over the bodies of the dead" during their advance, assault troops getting closer to enemy entrenchment confronted additional obstacles.[39] Describing an all too common experience among First World War soldiers, a veteran of the fighting at Thessaloniki remembered:

> The general told us that in the morning—the next morning—we would make an attack. [And the next day] he ordered the attack. And the artillery began to shoot the cannons, and after the bombing of the artillery we started to advance toward the Germans. And when we arrived near their trenches, we found that the threads—the barbed wire—were not cut. And that's where many soldiers died because they could not go [any] further. And the Ger-

mans were shooting at us [with their machine guns], and we lost almost all of our soldiers there. . . . The dead bodies were lying on the ground like leaves under a tree.[40]

Even if they reached the enemy lines, the soldiers still had to take them. Though defenders sometimes fled before onrushing troops, if they continued to resist, the actual seizure of the enemy trenches often produced the most ferocious form of combat.[41] This type of experience was recalled by Sera Ndiaye:

> In Champagne we were shooting [our] rifles [as we advanced], and [the next] moment we were so close to the Germans that [our] officers told us to stop shooting and to take out our *coupe-coupe*. And we were as near to the Germans as you and I—so close that we were obliged to fight [them] with knives. And from time to time, I saw a soldier who was fighting with a German and another German came from behind him and shot him or stabbed him with a knife. . . I thought I was going to die. I never [considered that I would be] wounded; I thought I was going to be killed.[42]

Even if such attacks proved successful, the soldiers inevitably paid a fearful price for them. After each assault, when the Senegalese were withdrawn from the front, "replacements were very numerous," and when the troops were sent to the camps in the Midi for the winter, their units were frequently disbanded altogether or had to be reconstituted.[43]

Coping with Combat

The psychological distress caused by combat was extreme. Coping with fear was an omnipresent concern among the soldiers, and though thresholds of anxiety fluctuated according to particular situations and individual temperaments, the "terror" engendered by the fighting was pervasive. Under duress, men often "wept like women," soldiers "cried [out] for their mothers," and the wounded said "very strange things before dying." Witnessing their "comrades [being] killed daily, or by the moment," the survivors were preoccupied with "thought[s] about death." Indeed, many soldiers experienced the most dire forebodings. They were convinced that the "war would never end"; that they would "never return [to Senegal]"; or that they "would never escape death."[44]

French efforts to overcome Senegalese apprehensions and bolster their fighting spirit usually proved ineffectual. Customary palliatives, such as alcohol, which were offered before attacks so that the soldiers "would not be conscious of what they were doing," were usually eschewed by most of the troops, who were Muslim. And martial music, which was played to reduce fears and instill "courage" in the face of the enemy, seldom made an impression. Indeed, far from reassuring the soldiers, the obvious futility of the sacrifices demanded by some French commanders had exactly the opposite effect. Seeking to explain the murderous fate that all too often befell them, many Senegalese attributed it to the "treason[ous]" behavior of particular generals intent on "massacr[ing]" them.[45]

Most Senegalese coped with their emotional ordeal by drawing on a fund of cultural assumptions and beliefs. In this regard, the arbitrary distinctions between *sujets* and *originaires* were reduced to insignificance; in moments of extreme personal crisis most Senegalese sought to fortify themselves in similar ways. And like the responses of their European counterparts, those of the Senegalese exemplify many of the deeper psychological yearnings common to most combatants as they confronted the prospect of their eminent deaths.

Such efforts on the part of the soldiers were not always successful. The stress of battle drove some men "mad," while others—and especially amputees convalescing in hospitals—also frequently "lost their minds." In addition to insanity, despair compelled others to commit suicide. Particularly common among wounded men who were subsequently judged fit to return to the front, acts of suicide also occurred in times of repose, when soldiers had the opportunity to reflect on their fate. Still others sought to enlist help to end their lives: when the pain from wounds became extreme, men begged for death.[46]

Most soldiers, however, managed to persevere through recourse to a variety of psychological supports. Above the din of battle, the will of the men was fortified by the incantations of their comrades. Some of these evoked pride in their ethnic heritage, especially those that derived from their pre-Islamic past. As Souleye Samba Ndiaye recalled, "When fighting was very hard and men were dying, the *ceddo* used to sing the *Goumbala* to encourage Tukulors."[47] Alternatively, Muslim soldiers, and especially Mourides, recited *Khassidas* to dispel fear in the face of death. The song *Mawahibou*, for example, reminded soldiers as they fought of the promise of paradise that awaited them:

> If you are going to Paradise,
> these are the steps of Mawahibou.
> The steps that take you from this world to eternity,
> these are the steps of Mawahibou.
> And the steps from eternity to paradise,
> these are the steps of Mawahibou.[48]

Like most soldiers, the Senegalese also sought to distance themselves from the specter of death by clinging to the illusion of their personal invulnerability. Nearly all Africans wore protective charms to shield them from the hazards of battle, although the faith they instilled in them varied. For some, and especially those who were never wounded or who descended from families with a precolonial martial heritage, their survival was interpreted as proof of the potency of their charms. Other soldiers—including those who were grievously wounded, had had brothers killed, or who were particularly devout Muslims—were more skeptical about their efficacy. Their attitudes resembled those of most European soldiers, who yearned to believe in their "lucky charms" but harbored doubts about their ultimate effectiveness. Though hedging their bets, most of these men believed that "charms were ineffective compared to the [power of the] Almighty."[49]

Indeed, like their European counterparts, the soldiers' entreaties for divine intercession on their behalf—and faith in the ultimate rectitude of His eternal design if this were not forthcoming—usually provided a far more compelling source of solace. Regardless of their various religious predilections, the Senegalese were generally sustained in combat by their faith in an Almighty Spirit. This was, however, especially evident among Muslims. In the midst of battle, soldiers—knowing that "only Allah can protect you from death"—"cried [out] to God [to bless them] and continued to go forward." Moreover, because many believed that "the destiny of men in war is predetermined by Allah," even if a person were fated to die, "it [was] good."[50]

Most soldiers, however, sought clues about what awaited them. The tension between the fears they experienced in combat and their hopes of salvation were exemplified in their dreams, which many sought to interpret. Recalling the symbolism in a dream the day before he was wounded, the Fulbe *griot* Demba Mboup believed it to be a premonition:

> I dreamed about this event the night before it happened. I dreamed that I was attacked by two lions, but I saw Seriny Touba [Amadu Bamba] in my dreams. And when the two lions came, [he] put me in a basket and raised [me] up like this [away from harm]. But one of the lions scratched my left leg [while I was being lifted up, which was] where I was wounded the next day. So [Seriny Touba] protected me.[51]

Despite the range of psychological and spiritual devices the soldiers used to sustain themselves at the front, prolonged exposure to death eventually rendered these of limited utility. In time, the normal distinctions between "life and death" became blurred as their friends perished, and men "acquired the idea that [they] made no difference." In such situations the soldiers progressively lost the will to survive; indeed they frequently "became indifferent to whether [they] lived or died."[52]

And death did come to many. Once all further hopes of survival were extinguished, the soldiers' thoughts in extremis convey how they reconciled themselves to the fate that befell them and their own mortality. Those who were fortunate enough to make a final plea to their comrades, or who falsely believed themselves to be on the point of death, were preoccupied with two concerns. Their thoughts turned to the loved ones they would leave behind and their hopes of an afterlife. Most young soldiers spoke of their mothers or fathers and beseeched their friends to ease the pain of their passing by "explain[ing] to their families, how they had been shot and how they died."[53] Others distanced themselves from the suffering of their temporal existence and contemplated eternity. Aliou Diakhate recalled his feelings at such a moment:

> I was going to die. . . . And I was thinking about God and his Prophet. . . . And when you wish to pray you have to stand up—to stand and bend down on your knees, and put your forehead on the ground. But I could not do that [because I was wounded so badly]. So I took some earth in my hand and I put it to my forehead. And I prayed to God [to bless me] in that way.[54]

Such sentiments offer a fitting epitaph of how the Senegalese coped with their experiences as combatants in Europe. Indeed, even among those who eventually returned to their homeland and were distanced by a lifetime from their ordeal, their interpretations of why they survived harkened back to the same points of reference. As Diouli Missine, who had once nearly been killed by a bullet that tore off his epaulet, explained: "[I escaped] death only by the Grace of Allah and the prayers of my mother and father."[55]

Motivations for Fighting

Unlike most French conscripts, who were aware of the ostensible causes of the war and believed that they were defending their nation against unprovoked German aggression, the Senegalese harbored only the vaguest notions about what had precipitated the conflict or their participation in it. Most frankly acknowledged that they had no idea why the French were fighting the Germans: "The men who took us to France to fight knew the reasons they were fighting, but we only knew that we had to fight for them. That was the only thing I knew. Personally I was never told reasons [for the war]."[56]

Moreover, although some possessed a general awareness of the various European rivalries that precipitated the war, more often than not these were interpreted in the context of precolonial Senegambian struggles between kingdoms and ruling lineages.[57] Nevertheless, despite their lack of comprehension of the origins of the conflict, the Senegalese were inculcated with compelling motivations for why they should fight. These help to explain why they were willing to risk death.

Though their "officers never explained the reasons for the war [to them]," they did endeavor to stimulate African antipathy toward Germans. The *"boche"* were characterized as "very wicked" people, for whose defeat the French required Senegalese "help." In addition to being enemies of the French, however, the Germans also were said to despise "'black' people" (whom they regarded as "cannibals" and whose fighting qualities they disdained). Moreover, they were told that it was in their self-interest to defeat the Germans. If Germany won the war, the soldiers would never be repatriated to their homeland but imprisoned instead. In this event, Senegal would become a German colony and the people there would have "a very bad time." This propaganda appears to have had only a marginal impact, for many of the Senegalese veterans felt no animosity toward the Germans, whom they regarded as "human beings like us."[58] Nevertheless, French efforts to arouse African hostility toward Germans ultimately proved unnecessary: the grim realities that the soldiers confronted in combat offered ample and compelling inducements to fight.

The threat of French reprisals should they not do so, moreover, virtually convinced the Senegalese that they had no alternative but to fight. Daba Dembele remembered that desertion in the face of the enemy was dealt with summarily: "We were [at] the Front [and the fighting] was all around [us]. And one of my friends was telling me: 'Daba, let's try and run away.' But I said: 'No, I prefer to stay and fight.' And my friend tried to flee, [but] a *Tubab* saw him running and he was caught and shot."[59]

Despite the fearful penalties imposed for desertion, many Senegalese did contemplate it, especially in the aftermath of debacles such as occurred on the Aisne. They were dissuaded from making such attempts, however, by a second consideration. Unlike their French counterparts, who might find sanctuary if they escaped, the Senegalese literally had "no place to run to." Under these circumstances, most accepted their fate and complied with their "officers' orders," in even the most dire situations.[60]

In addition to fearing execution by the French if they abandoned their positions, the Senegalese were also motivated in combat by anxiety about being captured by the Germans. The enemy's willingness to take Africans as prisoners—as well as the subsequent treatment accorded to them as P.O.W.s—varied considerably depending on particular circumstances. Nevertheless, most Senegalese—like their counterparts across No Man's Land—gave credence to the more exaggerated rumors about enemy atrocities. Indeed, most soldiers believed that the Germans "killed 'black' people if they caught them," which in at least some instances was true.[61]

Surrounded by agents of death at both their front and their rear, most Senegalese realized that they had "no choice" except to "kill or be killed." Under such circumstances, nearly all opted for self-preservation. When confronting their enemies at close quarters, they were obliged to "shoot first" to save their lives.[62]

In addition to responding to the mortal fears prompted by their hostile and coercive environment, some Senegalese were motivated to fight for more positive reasons. Though constituting a minority among the soldiers, and far more frequently drawn from among *originaires* than *tirailleurs*, these men viewed the war as an opportunity to assert their dignity as Africans in a variety of ways.

For many *originaires*, the "rights" conferred on them by their acquisition of French citizenship offered a convincing rationale for fighting. Some identified with the French cause and adopted it as their own; others took a more self-interested view of the implicit bargain struck by Blaise Diagne with the government. In their eyes, "We were not fighting for the French; we were fighting for ourselves [to become] French citizens."[63]

Paradoxically, other soldiers were motivated in battle by a desire to kill particular French officers. Men who repeatedly "insulted, beat, and harassed" the troops were singled out for reprisals during combat, which frequently ended in their deaths. Such actions, which were inconceivable in a colonial context, signaled the refusal by some Africans to continue being abused as "dirty niggers."[64]

Finally, despite their travails, a few soldiers were motivated by a desire to prove their worth in combat and gain indisputable recognition from the French for their deeds of valor. Recalling his feelings after he participated in the *repris de Douaumont*, Masserigne Soumare stated:

> We felt very proud after the attack because the French had tried many times to retake the fort, but finally, we [were the ones] that took it. . . . And when we were leaving the fort, our officers told us not to wash our uniforms even though they were very dirty and covered with mud. But we were told: "Don't wash your uniforms. Cross the country as you are so that everyone who meets you will know that you made the attack on Fort Douaumont." And we took the train [and traveled] for three days between Douaumont and St. Raphäel. And in every town we crossed, the French were clapping their hands and shouting: "*Vive les tirailleurs sénégalais!*" . . . And afterwards, whenever we were walking in the country—everywhere we used to go—if we told people that we made the attack on Fort Douaumont, the French were looking at us with much admiration.[65]

"TO SPARE A FRENCHMAN'S LIFE"

The number of casualties suffered by the Senegalese during the First World War, as well as their proportion in comparison to those of French

Senegalese "shock troops" marching through a French village, 1917. Courtesy of Bibliothèque nationale de France, Paris: Collection Poincaré (G 136624). Reprinted with permission.

soldiers, have long been a subject of debate. This lingering controversy is explored here through pursuing three lines of inquiry: (1) examining the attitudes of French commanders toward their Senegalese troops and gauging whether the Africans were used in combat with the conscious intention of sacrificing their lives to save French ones; (2) surveying recent scholarly opinion on this question; and (3) providing a new analysis of African wartime casualties in general, and losses among the soldiers from Senegal in particular, and comparing these figures with those for their ill-fated French counterparts.

French Commanders and the Senegalese

Despite the initial reservations of some about deploying the Senegalese on the western front, there is compelling evidence that from 1916 onward (when this issue ceased to be in question) many French commanders readily sacrificed African troops in an effort to spare the lives of French soldiers. Indeed, this attitude was so widespread that it was expressed at all levels of the French command structure. Although these views were frequently expressed within the context of the ongoing military debate between 1916 and 1918—specifically, whether to deploy the Senegalese in larger or smaller combat formations and whether they should fight on their own or be variegated with French units—the arguments were invariably predicated on two assumptions: that the Senegalese were especially effective as shock troops and that placing them in the first wave (*première ligne*) of assaults would husband French lives.

During the offensive on the Somme in 1916, the largest number of Senegalese battalions used in the fighting was assigned to the 1st Corps of the Colonial Army commanded by General Pierre Berdoulat. Berdoulat later assessed the performance of his African troops during the battle and speculated about how best to deploy them in the future. Stressing the "limited intellectual faculties" of Africans, which diminished their effectiveness in combat, they were, in his judgment, primarily useful "for sparing a certain number of European lives at the moment of assaults."[66]

Similar sentiments were echoed by General Robert Nivelle, the commander of the French army, during the preparations for the offensive on the Aisne in February 1917. Insisting on the maximum deployment of Senegalese troops during the impending attack, he presented the following argument to the Ministry of War: "It is imperative that the number of [African] units put at my disposition should be increased as much as possible. [This will] increase the power of our projected strength and permit the sparing—to the extent possible—of French blood."[67]

Even among officers most directly responsible for the welfare of the Senegalese troops, such attitudes were not absent. In April 1917, Lieutenant Colonel Debieuvre, commander of the 58ᵉ *Regiment d'Infanterie colonial* (composed exclusively of Senegalese battalions), expressed his views about how best to deploy African soldiers: "[The Senegalese *tirailleurs*] are finally and above all superb attack troops permitting the saving of the lives of whites, who *behind them* exploit their success and organize the positions they conquer."[68]

Similar considerations were also voiced the same year by the commander of the 64ᵉ *Bataillon de tirailleurs Sénégalais*. A strong advocate of variegating African and French battalions in combat, he contended that such a tactical scheme would "better utilize [*la force noire*] in order to save, in future offensive actions, the blood—more and more precious—of our [French] soldiers."[69]

Less than a year later, in January 1918, the commander of the Senegalese training camp at Fréjus, Colonel Eugene Petitdemange, set forth his views to General Philippe Petain about how his African charges could best serve "the interest of the country" in the spring: "My aim is to seek the increasing use of the Senegalese . . . in order to spare the blood of French servicemen, France having already paid a heavy tribute during this war. It is essential to try by all means possible to diminish their future losses through the enhanced use of our brave Senegalese."[70]

Petitdemange was also anxious to prevent the proposed transfer of Senegalese battalions to metropolitan units in 1918 as well as to minimize the practice of variegating them in combat with French troops. Alluding to "the combative spirit of men born to make war," he asserted: "The Senegalese have been recruited to replace the French, to be used as cannon fodder (*chair à canon*) to spare the whites. It is essential then to use them in an intensive fashion and not in small groups (*petits paquets*)."[71]

Though there were exceptions to this pattern, such attitudes were nevertheless pervasive.[72] The fine line between callous indifference to the suffering of the troops (which existed among all European officer corps), and the calculated disregard for the lives of particular groups, was crossed by many French commanders in the case of African soldiers. Indeed, irrespective of their opinions about the merits of the Senegalese as combatants, they frequently sought to use them at the front in ways intentionally designed to husband the lives of French *poilus*.

Nor was this outlook restricted to military commanders. Citing the benefits of the "civilization" that France had brought to Africa (which might now be paid for) and lamenting the loss of three million men during the war, Georges Clemenceau defended his resumption of military recruitment in West Africa before a group of senators on 18 February 1918 in the following terms: "Although I have infinite respect for these brave blacks, I would much prefer to have ten blacks killed than a single Frenchman, because I think that enough Frenchmen have been killed and that it is necessary to sacrifice them as little as possible."[73]

The Debate over African Casualties

The question remains whether this deliberate practice by many French commanders led to disproportionately high casualties among the Africans. Many contemporaries thought so—including Blaise Diagne, Charles Mangin, and the former *tirailleur* and early Senegalese nationalist, Lamine Senghor, among others—and herein lies the origin of the current debate among historians.[74]

The current opinion among recent investigations of this question, however, remains divided. Several eminent scholars have flatly disputed the claim of higher African casualties. Marc Michel, who has undertaken the most exhaustive inquiry, holds such a position. Arguing that the French were less racist than other Europeans of the era, and pointing to the tactical amalgamation of African and French troops in combat, which ostensibly exposed all soldiers to equal peril, Michel has concluded that

Table 5.1   Postwar Estimates of Senegalese Casualties

Year	Categorization	Dead	Missing	Total
	Tirailleurs			
1919	Formations indigènes	17,826	7,112	24,938
1919	Indigènes coloniaux	24,000	7,300	31,300[a]
1920	Indigènes coloniaux	26,700	7,500	34,200
1920	Sénégalais	—	—	29,224
1923/ 1924	Indigènes des colonies: A.O.F.	24,762		—
	All colonies	—	6,393	30,196[b]
1931	Sénégalais	—	—	29,520[c]
	Originaires			
1919		423	45	468
1919		—	—	790
1923		709	59	768

[a] Does not include deaths from disease, which in Charbonneau's estimation increased overall losses by about one-third, or approximately 45,000 men.

[b] Although "dead" in these publications is differentiated between those from A.O.F. and other colonies, "missing" is not. Senegalese losses amounted to 85.4 percent of the total dead from all colonies; this percentage has been used to estimate the approximate number of missing, and hence the total number of fatalities.

[c] Identical to the 1920 figure (cited in *L'Afrique Française*) except that it adds 296 combat deaths in Togo and the Cameroons to those incurred in Europe and explicitly does not include either those dying "from sickness in the army" or from "later exhaustion attributable to the war."

Sources: Yearly figures, respectively, derived from: *Archives de la Guerre*: État-Major de l'Armée: 7 N 2121: "État numérique faisant ressortir la situation des militaires indigènes au Dépôt Commun des Formations Indigènes d'infantrie et d'Artillerie Coloniale à la date du 1er janvier 1919" [no date]; "Rapport du Général Bonnier, Commandant Supérieur des Troupes d'A.O.F., au Direction des Troupes coloniale," 24 May 1919; and "Le Commissaire aux Effectifs Coloniaux [Blaise Diagne] au Président du Conseil," 7 October 1919, p. 12; Charbonneau 1931, pp. 21–22; "Rapport Marin," *Journal Officiel de la République Française, Documents Parlementaires,* Chambre, 1920, t. 2, annex 633, p. 44; "L'Armée Coloniale pendant la Guerre," *L'Afrique Française,* 1920, Suppl., p. 155; Sarraut 1923, p. 44; *Histoire militaire de l'A.O.F.* 1931, p. 826.

Senegalese casualties were equivalent to those incurred throughout the war by the French infantry.[75]

Michel's contention is supported by Charles Balesi, who emphasizes many of the same cultural and organizational considerations. Though his study of the question is less extensive, Balesi concludes that African and French losses—even on the Aisne—were roughly equivalent.[76] These general findings are also endorsed by Myron Echenberg. While stressing the "cultural and racial" stereotypes held by French military planners about Africans, Echenberg suggests that instead of being higher than French losses, Senegalese casualties were actually proportionately lower.[77]

One exception to these recent assessments about casualty rates is that provided by Anthony Clayton. Also emphasizing "the extraordinarily racialist views" held by many French commanders, Clayton contends that the casualties sustained by Senegalese units were "slightly higher" than the French ones.[78]

These seemingly irreconcilable conclusions are prompted by the nature of the available evidence employed to support them, and by using differing indexes to gauge the results. It is therefore appropriate to examine these findings more closely and, utilizing different modes of analysis, indicate what the figures presented signified for the soldiers involved.

The total African casualties during the war, based on the most consistent and generally accepted official estimates, can be reckoned at approximately 31,000 soldiers.[79] (On the variation in postwar French estimates, see Table 5.1.) Although almost certainly an underestimate because incidental deaths—including those from disease—were probably not included, this figure nonetheless affords a means for a comparative inquiry about the dimensions of the sacrifice of the Senegalese and their particular use in combat.[80]

Conclusions about African and Senegalese Casualties

African casualties can be contrasted with those suffered by the French using a variety of standards. As a percentage of all the soldiers mobilized during the war, Senegalese losses were slightly less than those incurred by the French: roughly 15.5 percent were killed in the former group compared to 16.5 percent in the latter.[81] The picture changes significantly, however, when only combatants are considered. Using this criterion, Senegalese losses were nearly 20 percent higher than those sustained by their French counterparts.[82] Unlike European combatants, however, Africans seldom served in cavalry, artillery, engineering, and aviation units, where casualties were substantially lower than in infantry formations. If only infantry fatalities are considered, the pattern changes again. Using this standard, French and African losses between 1914 and 1918 were virtually identical: they amounted to slightly over 22 percent in both cases.[83] This last gauge is the one cited by Marc Michel and other historians who contend that the deaths suffered by African and French combat troops were comparable and offer these figures as evidence against the

Table 5.2   Senegalese and French Casualties: Numbers by Year and Percentage of Total Wartime Losses[a]

Year	Categorization	Casualties	Percentage
1914	French[b]	491,000	27.05
	Senegalese[c]	850	2.84
1915	French	439,000	24.19
	Senegalese	1,615	5.40
1916	French	361,000	19.89
	Senegalese	5,440	18.18
1917	French	184,000	10.14
	Senegalese	8,118	27.13
1918	French	311,000	17.30
	Senegalese	11,688	39.06
1919	French	29,000	1.60
	Senegalese	2,210	7.39

[a] The numbers of French and Senegalese combatants fluctuated by year, but this does not significantly affect the overall trend indicated by the table. In the case of French combatants, numbers fluctuated between 2,215,000 and 1,688,000 during the period from May 1915 to October 1918; Senegalese combat battalions varied between 39 and 45 between July 1916 and November 1918.

[b] French losses include prisoners (which was the practice in reporting the diminution in a unit's effective strength in the French army).

[c] Senegalese casualty rates have been adjusted from those presented in the "Rapport Marin." They have been calculated at 85% (29,750) of those listed for "Indigènes coloniaux" (35,200). This adjustment omits *originaire* losses, all of which were sustained after June 1916.

Source: "Rapport Marin," *Journal Officiel de la République Française. Documents Parlementaires*, Chambre, 1920, t. 2, annexe 633, pp. 65, 74, 76.

charge of the systematic misuse of the Senegalese by their commanders.[84]

This interpretation is valid insofar as it goes. It neglects, however, to consider a series of other compelling factors that should be taken into account. The most important one is of a temporal nature. The Senegalese were not employed in significant numbers as combatants in Europe, where 98 percent of all casualties were incurred, before July 1916.[85] Prior to this time, African losses accounted for less than 10 percent of their eventual wartime total, and these were born primarily by the as yet small prewar army.[86] Conversely, French combat deaths during this same period amounted to over 60 percent of all fatalities that occurred between

Figure 5.2 Senegalese and French Casualties: Percentage of Total Wartime Losses by Year.

Percent

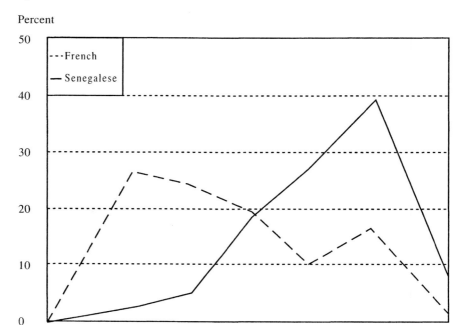

Source: "Rapport Marin," *Journal Officiel de la République Française. Documents Parlementaires,* Chambre, 1920, t. 2, annexe 633, pp. 65, 74, 76.

August 1914 and November 1918.[87] Indeed, it was precisely because of the staggering dimensions of French losses during the first 22 months of the war—and the general recognition that these were likely to continue— that earlier resistance to the massive recruitment of West Africans and their deployment on the western front was overcome. If this factor is taken into consideration, a very different picture begins to emerge. During the last two and a half years of the war, Senegalese casualties in Europe were approximately twice as high as those suffered by French infantry combatants.[88] Moreover, Senegalese losses continued to rise throughout the conflict and, even though roughly equivalent numbers of troops were engaged from 1916 onward, only reached their apogee in 1918, when about 40 percent of all fatalities occurred. Conversely, the percentage of French losses steadily declined throughout this period, with the exception of 1918, when it rose as the war reached crisis point (see Table 5.2 and Figure 5.2).

A second consideration is the comparative probability of death faced by foot soldiers when they were in the trenches. Under the policy known as *"hivernage,"* Africans were removed from the front for five months (between November and March) each year. During these periods, about 18 percent of all the post-July 1916 French losses occurred. As a result, when Africans were deployed in combat during the late spring, summer, and early autumn (the time when all the major offensives took place), their likelihood of being killed was nearly two and a half times as great as that of their French counterparts.[89]

A final factor that gives an indication of both absolute casualties as well as life expectancy at the front was the ethnicity of the African soldiers. Those recruited from "races" deemed by the French to have special "military aptitudes" were prominent in the assault battalions that bore the heaviest casualties.[90] These "warrior races" constituted about two-thirds of the African complement used in major attacks in 1916 and 1917 and perhaps constituted a majority thereafter.[91] Well over 90 percent of the Senegalese recruited during the war, however, were classed as "warriors." Although ethnic breakdowns of casualties are lacking, it is highly probable that the Senegalese were overrepresented in those formations where the loss of life was the greatest and, hence, that the proportion of their fatalities was significantly higher than among other West African groups. In terms of what this portended for the soldiers, it is probable that a Wolof, a "Tukulor," or a Serer recruited as a *tirailleur* between 1915 and 1917 was about three times as likely to die in combat as his French counterpart, while absolute losses were on the order of two-and-a-half to one.[92]

As these proportions indicate, Africans paid a very dear price indeed for their prominence in the fighting forces during the last two and a half years of the war, but those from the so-called "warrior races" were most victimized. Moreover, by 1916, very few generals or foot soldiers harbored any illusions about the fate awaiting assault troops attempting to cross No Man's Land to storm entrenched positions. Indeed, by 1918, when French combat losses were a concern to all, the Senegalese were disseminated more widely to French units and used more frequently than ever. Earlier disputes over their relative military merits notwithstanding, Africans were used in this capacity precisely because of this foreknowledge and with the expectation that employing them in this fashion would lessen French losses.

In this regard, the arguments by historians that stress the tactical "mixing" of African and European formations in combat (and, by inference, the equality of danger faced by all) are no more convincing than their conclusions about comparative casualty rates. Although the French experimented with various organizational schemes throughout the war, all of these were intended to "steady" African formations in combat, and thereby maximize their "shock" potential, rather than to ensure that Senegalese and French infantry faced the same perils. Furthermore, the mixing of battalions or companies, which was never adopted as a systematic policy, was far from pervasive. Regiments composed entirely of Senegalese battalions continued to be deployed as "heavy" units in assaults from 1916 until the armistice. Moreover, because of French tactical doctrine governing offensive operations, the temporary amalgamation, juxtaposition, or variegation of battalions (and, much less frequently, of companies) does not indicate that the African probability of death was lessened. One battalion from each regiment usually formed the first wave in attacks, with the other two (or three) following in support (see Figure 5.1). In mixed regiments, this role almost invariably fell to the Senegalese and, as the distribution of African wartime casualties suggests, the increasing variegation (*panaché*) of units at the end of the conflict proved to be even more lethal than had the earlier tactical doctrine of "massive" deployment. Hence, far from strengthening the contention that there was no discrimination in the army, the temporary mixing of units—particularly the loaning of African battalions to metropolitan formations after the summer of 1917—tends to support exactly the opposite conclusion. Indeed, the tactical function of French and African units in variegated formations was made explicit by the commander of the 44ᵉ *Bataillon de tirailleurs Sénégalais* in September 1918: "It is useful to have a unit of whites in support [of the African formation], not only to urge them on, but for the most rational exploitation of success . . . once the great blow is delivered [by them]."[93] Finally, even among the Europeans serving in Senegalese battalions (as officers, N.C.O.s, machine gunners, gunners, etc.), the casualties appear to have been less. Although the evidence is fragmentary, it suggests that African losses in combat were about 25 percent higher than those of their French cadres.[94]

These conclusions are not intended to impugn the courage exhibited by French combatants, or to minimize the scale of their sacrifices, which were horrific. Indeed, as one Senegalese veteran, Mbaye Khary Diagne, succinctly expressed it, "The French were not afraid to die."[95] Moreover, even though their overall losses were less than the Senegalese, those *poilus* in close proximity to them during assaults probably suffered much more heavily than others defending quieter sectors of the front. Nevertheless, as the nature of their tactical deployment and the proportion of their resulting casualties indicate, the Senegalese were systematically misused by many commanders. This practice of deliberately sacrificing "others" in combat was nothing new, nor was it restricted to the French. Indeed, it is probably as old as warfare itself. It was commonly practiced by other belligerents during the First World War and persists to this day.[96] Thus, despite the efforts of government officials and subsequent historians to deny these claims, the accusations first raised by Diagne in 1917 are not a myth: they are all too true.

The human toll exacted among the soldiers from Senegal in Europe is impossible to estimate with precision. Nevertheless, a rough approximation of their casualties can be given. Among *originaires*, at least 768 were killed in combat. Fatalities among *tirailleurs* (who were not differentiated by colony) can only be surmised. If casualties are assumed to have been distributed evenly among these troops, approximately 3,835 *tirailleurs* from Senegal (or 13 percent of the total fatalities among African combatants) may be presumed to have lost their lives.[97] This, however, was almost certainly not the case. Among the 31,000 men in the prewar army whose casualties are included in this total, the vast majority were recruited in either Senegal or Haut-Sénégal et Niger. Furthermore, as previously indicated, nearly all Senegalese were considered warriors, and as such they were probably overrepresented among those troops that incurred the most severe losses. As a result, the proportion of casualties sustained by the *tirailleurs* from Senegal was significantly higher than that among their counterparts from other colonies in the Federation. Exactly how much higher is open to speculation, but it seems likely that at least 5,000 to 6,000 were killed, and perhaps more. When combined with the fatalities estimated among the *originaires*, it may be assumed that, at a minimum, between 6,000 and 7,000 Senegalese soldiers perished while fighting in Europe.[98]

Although the Senegalese paid an awesome price for their prominence in the fighting lines, the wartime experience in France influenced the lives of those who survived their ordeal in the trenches in other ways. It enhanced the soldiers' knowledge of the world beyond their homelands and often transformed their image of themselves and of Europeans. It is to the increasing contacts between the African troops and French soldiers and civilians occasioned by the war, and the influence this exerted on changing the previous perceptions of the Senegalese of Europeans, that we turn in the next chapter.

NOTES

[1] On images of the Senegalese in combat, see Myron Echenberg, *Colonial Conscripts: The "Tirailleurs Sénégalais" in French West Africa, 1857–1960* (Portsmouth, NH: Heinemann/London: James Currey, 1991), pp. 32–38. On the evolution of French and German stereotypes, see Hans-Jürgen Lüsebrink, "'Tirailleurs Sénégalais' und 'Schwarze Schande': Verlaufsformen und Konsequenzen einer deutsch-französischen Auseinandersetzung (1910–1926)," in *"Tirailleurs Sénégalais": Zur Bildlichen und Literarischen Darstellung Afrikanischer Soldaten im Dienste Frankreichs—Présentations*

Littéraires et Figuratives de Soldats Africains au Service de la France, ed. János Riesz and Joachim Schultz (Frankfurt am Main: Peter Lang, 1989), pp. 57–73, and Keith L. Nelson, "The 'Black Horror on the Rhine': Race as a Factor in Post-World War I Diplomacy," *Journal of Modern History*, 42 (1970): 606–27.

[2] The use of this term to describe the manner in which the Senegalese were employed in the fighting is ubiquitous; references to it range from French officers to postwar African nationalists. See, for example, the comments of Colonel Eugene Petitdemange, Commandant of the Senegalese troops at Fréjus in 1918: *AG*: Grand Quartier General (hereafter GQG): 16 N 100.

[3] This interpretation was also endorsed by some Americans of African descent, such as Richard Wright and W. E. B. Du Bois. See Tyler Stovall, *Paris Noir: African Americans in the City of Light* (Boston: Houghton Mifflin, 1996), and Shelby T. McCloy, *The Negro in France* (Lexington: University of Kentucky Press, 1961).

[4] For Senegalese battalion and regimental histories for 1914, including their participation in the fighting along the Ijzer, see: *AG*: Unités: *Journaux de marche et d'opérations* (hereafter JMO): 26 N 869, and Léon Bocquet and Ernest Hosten, *Un fragment de l'Epopée sénégalaise: Les Tirailleurs noirs sur l'Yser* (Brussels and Paris: G. Van Oest, 1918). The attempt to seize the Dardanelles was a British scheme in which the French High Command was reluctant to participate because they regarded it as a diversion of strength from the more crucial theater of operations in northwest France. This outlook helps to explain why Senegalese battalions were prominent in the French Expeditionary Corps. On the failure of this attack, see especially: Maurice Dutreb, *Nos Sénégalais pendant la Grande Guerre* (Metz: R. Ferry, 1922), and the Senegalese JMOs for 1915: *AG*: Unités: 26 N 869. See also: *Les Troupes coloniales pendant la Guerre 1914–1918* (Paris: Imprimerie national, 1931).

[5] Many troops used on the Somme were composed of recruits raised in West Africa in 1915 and early 1916. Their movement to France enabled the High Command to create the 2nd Corps of the Colonial Army in 1915. The significance of Douaumont's recapture for the French is perhaps best conveyed in Jean Renoir's classic film, *La Grande Illusion*.

[6] On the decision of the High Command, see: *AG:* GQG: 6 N 100. On the re-evaluation of tactical methods in 1917, see *AG*: Fonds Clemenceau: 6 N 96 and *AG*: Unités: 22 N 2481.

[7] *AG*: Unités (JMOs): 26 N 869–871, and *Les Troupes coloniales pendant la Guerre*, pp. 187–205, 223–30.

[8] African units, and their theoretical complement of soldiers, were composed as follows: a squad (9 men), two squads comprised a demi-section (18), two demi-sections a section (40), 4 sections a company (160), 4 or more companies (including one of machine gunners) a battalion (ranging between 800 and 1,200 men), 3 or more battalions a regiment, and 2 regiments (sometimes with additional battalions) a brigade. Although the use of brigades fell into disuse during the war, two of them, or alternatively three regiments, comprised divisions, with two to four divisions composing an army corps. On unit organization and tactical alignments between 1914 and 1918, see especially: *AG*: État-Major de l'Armée: 7 N 441; *AG*: Fonds Clemenceau: 6 N 96; and the JMOs of the 28th, 54th, and 68th battalions of Senegalese *tirailleurs*: *AG*: Unités: 26 N 869 and 26 N 871.

[9] The *originaires* were initially formed into distinct battalions in Senegal. Upon their arrival in France, they were assigned to different battalions in the Colonial Army,

which might be designated as either "non-white" or "white" units. See: *AG*: État-Major de l'Armée (hereafter EMA), pp. 7 N 144, 7 N 440, and 7 N 2120. See also: Anthony Clayton, *France, Soldiers, and Africa* (London: Brassey's Defence Publishers, 1988), p. 343.

[10] This was the term used to designate the status of the Senegalese training camps, and it is repeatedly cited by French policy makers to characterize their intentions regarding contacts by the soldiers with the metropolitan population. See, for example, *AG*: EMA: 7 N 440. See also Chapter 6.

[11] This practice, which derived from the French Revolutionary tradition of juxtaposing units of "volunteers" with *ancien régime* infantry in a two-to-one ratio, was intended to steady the former in combat while infecting the latter with their offensive ardor. On organizational principles, which varied throughout the war, as well as the role of the Senegalese in combat, see especially the JMO entries for the Senegalese units: *AG*: Unités: 26 N 869–871; and *AG*: GQG: 16 N 196. Also see the following official publications: *Histoire des Troupes Coloniales pendant la Guerre, 1915–1918: Fronts extérieurs* (Paris: Imprimerie national, 1931); *Les Troupes Coloniales pendant la Guerre 1914–1918* (Paris: Imprimerie national, 1931); *Histoire militaire de l'A.O.F.* (Paris: Imprimerie national, 1931); and *Les Armées Françaises d'Outre-Mer* (Paris: Imprimerie national, 1931–1932).

[12] *AG*: EMA: 7 N 444.

[13] The first two types of alignments were used by the 1st and 2nd Corps of the Colonial Army on the Somme. In general, the 1st Corps of the Colonial Army tended to deploy a higher proportion of its Senegalese troops in larger units (i.e., regiments composed exclusively of "African" battalions) than did the 2nd Corps, which experimented with amalgamation of African and European companies. On types of combat formations, see especially the JMOs of the Senegalese regiments and battalions: *AG*: Unités: 26 N 869–871. For differences between the 1st and 2nd Colonial Army Corps' patterns of combat organization, see *AG*: GQG: 16 N 196 and *AG*: Unités: 22 N 2468.

[14] On the instructions of General Joseph Joffre, Senegalese assault battalions on the Somme were to be constituted from among those races possessing special military aptitudes: *AG*: EMA: 7 N 1990. In the event, troops from "warrior races" constituted at least a majority and often upwards of two-thirds of the soldiers in the African battalions engaged: *AG*: GQG: 16 N 196 and *AG*: Unités: 22 N 2481.

[15] Nine of the 21 Senegalese battalions deployed on the Aisne were grouped in African regiments; the remaining 12 were either added as a fourth battalion to other Colonial Infantry Regiments or formed into "mixed tactical groups," in which the Senegalese predominated by ratios ranging from two-to-one to three-to-one. See *AG*: GQG: 16 N 100 and *AG*: Unités: 22 N 2468.

[16] Four of the 21 Senegalese battalions engaged on the Aisne were variegated (*panaché*) with European battalions: *AG*: Fonds Clemenceau: 6 N 96.

[17] Of the 44 Senegalese battalions engaged in France in 1918, 22 were assigned to the 1st or 2nd Corps of the Colonial Army, while the remainder were loaned to metropolitan formations. On the decision in 1918 to loan Senegalese battalions to metropolitan units, see *AG*: GQG: 16 N 100. On their use as tactical groups for "determined" attacks, see: Jean Charbonneau, *Les contingents coloniaux: du Soleil et de la Gloire* (Paris: Imprimerie national, 1931), p. 62.

[18] By 1918, French cadres amounted to 22 to 24 percent of the complement of Senegalese battalions: *AG*: Unités (JMOs): 26 N 869–871.

[19] See Joe Lunn, "'Les Races guerrières': Racial Preconceptions in the French Military about West African Soldiers during the First World War," *Journal of Contemporary History* 34, 4 (1999).

[20] These principles concerning the use of Senegalese troops were codified during the immediate prewar period. See: *Centre militaire d'information et de documentation: Outre-Mer* [hereafter *CMIDOM*]: A.O.F.-INT-C III-27-B, "Manuel tactique pour le Groupe de l'A.O.F.: Notions générales" (1910).

[21] The quotation is that of General Pierre Berdoulat, commander of the 1st Colonial Army Corps during the attacks on the Somme in 1916: *AG*: GQG: 16 N 196: 9. For the results of surveys conducted by the High Command among officers commanding Senegalese troops about the soldiers' combat performance on the Somme in 1916 and on the Aisne in 1917, see *AG*: GQG: 16 N 196 and *AG*: Unités: 22 N 2481.

[22] These arguments, voiced by "detractors" opposing the use of Senegalese, appear to have represented a minority viewpoint within the Colonial Army by 1916 and certainly by 1917. For a sampling of these opinions, see: *AG*: GQG: 16 N 196 and *AG*: Unités: 22 N 2481.

[23] *CMIDOM*: Publications, "Notice sur les Sénégalais et leur emploi au combat" (no date, but definitely written between May 1917 and September 1918, and most probably either in late 1917 or early 1918 while the Senegalese were in winter quarters). For reactions to the "Notice" by French officers commanding Senegalese combat units in 1918 (all of which were appreciative), see: *AG*: GQG: 16 N 2094. The description below is drawn from this document.

[24] On these distinctions, see: Mamadou Djigo: 4A; Abdoulaye Ndiaye 2B and 4B; Ndiaga Niang: 1B; Boubacar Gueye: 1A; and Ndiaga Niang: 1B.

[25] Nar Diouf 3A. Citations from the veterans' oral histories are hereafter grouped together at the end of paragraphs in the order of quotation.

[26] Daba Dembele: 4B; Abdoulaye Gassala: 2B; Momar Khary Niang: 1B. Yoro Diaw: 2A; Sera Ndiaye: 2B. Nar Diouf: 3B; Alassane Kane: 1A; Mamadou Djigo: 5A; and Doudou Ndao: 2B. Alassane Kane: 1B.

[27] Sera Ndiaye: 2B; Ndiaga Niang: 1A. Mamadou Djigo: 3A; Biram Mbodji Tine: 2B; Ndiaga Niang: 2A and 1A. Demba Mboup: 12B; Doudou Ndao: 2B; Niaki Gueye: 3B and 4A. Momar Khary Niang: 1B. Niaki Gueye 3B; Daba Dembele 4A. Alassane Kane: 4B. Mamadou Djigo: 3A and 4A. Biram Mbodji Tine 2B; Nar Diouf: 3A. Ishmale Mbange: 2A. Alassane Kane 2B; Ishmale Mbange 2A. Alassane Kane: 4B. Alassane Kane 2B; Mbaye Khary Diagne: 5A.

[28] Doudou Ndao: 2B. Mamadou Djigo: 3A and 4A; and Doudou Ndao: 2B. Ishmale Mbange 2A. Daba Dembele: 4B and 3B. See also Ndiaga Niang: 1B.

[29] Abdoulaye Diaw 3B. Malal Gassala: 3A; Ibrahima Camara: 2B. Alassane Kane: 1B. Abdoulaye Diaw: 1A.

[30] Ndiaga Niang: 1B. Alassane Kane 1B; see also: Mamadou Djigo: 3A; Demba Mboup: 13A. Sickh Yero Sy: 1A; Masserigne Soumare: 1B; Abdoulaye Diaw: 2A and 2B. Alassane Kane: 1B.

[31] Ndiaga Niang: 2A.

[32] Abdoulaye Gueye: 2A; Thiecouta Diallo: 2A and 2B. On French concerns over the propensity of the Senegalese to contract frostbite, see: *AG*: Unités: 22 N 2481, 26 N 869, and 26 N 871.

[33] Sera Ndiaye 4A.

[34] Ibrahima Camara: 2B; and Masserigne Soumare: 2A. Nouma Ndiaye: 1A. Giribul Diallo: 1B.

³⁵ Nar Diouf: 5A; and Masserigne Soumare: 1B. On unit rotation, see: Momar Khary Niang: 1B; Abdoulaye Gueye: 2A; and Nouma Ndiaye: 1A. On snipers, see: Daba Dembele: 3B. Nouma Ndiaye: 1A; and Makhoudia Ndiaye: 1A. On casualties incurred during sector occupation compared to attacks in the 45th *Bataillon de Tirailleurs Sénégalais* (hereafter BTS), see also *AG*: Unités: 26 N 870.

³⁶ On *coups de main*, see, Masserigne Soumare: 1A; and Ndiaga Niang: 1A. For officers' descriptions of them, see the JMOs: *AG*: Unités: 26 N 869–871.

³⁷ On assault tactics, see: Sickh Yero Sy: 1A and 1B; Antoine Diouf: 1A; Masserigne Soumare: 3B. For especially detailed French descriptions of assault tactics, see also: *AG*: Unités: 24 N 3027 and the JMOs of the 28e, the 54e, and the 61e BTS: *AG*: Unités: 26 N 869 and 26 N 871. Ndiaga Niang: 2A; see also: Momar Khary Niang: 1A; Sambou Ndiaye: 1B; and Sickh Yero Sy: 1A.

³⁸ Daba Dembele: 3B. On the effects of high explosives (including the inadvertent but "very frequent" shelling of friendly troops by their own artillery), see also: Ndiaga Niang: 2A; Momar Khary Niang: 1A; Demba Mboup: 5A and 10A; Malal Gassala: 2B; and Nar Diouf: 3A.

³⁹ Diouli Missine 1A. See also: Demba Mboup: 12A.

⁴⁰ Ndiaga Niang: 1B. See also: Abdoulaye Diaw: 1A and 1B.

⁴¹ On flight, see: Nar Diouf: 4B and 5A; Mamadou Djigo: 3A and 4B; and Abdoulaye Ndiaye: 4A.

⁴² Sera Ndiaye: 3B. For other descriptions of storming the trenches, including the use of grenades and bayonets in hand-to-hand fighting, see: Malal Gassala: 2B; Sera Ndiaye: 3B; Momar Khary Niang: 1B; and Mamadou Djigo: 3A.

⁴³ Nar Diouf: 3A. Mbaye Khary Diagne: 3A. On the disbanding and reconstitution of units, also see the JMOs: *AG*: Unités: 26 N 869–871.

⁴⁴ Biram Mbodji Tine: 2B. On differing levels of anxiety, including indiscriminate seizures of fear by recent recruits and veterans alike, distinctions between the anxiety experienced during attacks and when being subjected to them, as well as that undergone while waiting in depots as opposed to being at the Front, see respectively: Mbaye Khary Diagne: 5A; Giribul Diallo: 1B; and Alassane Kane: 4B. Sera Ndiaye: 3B; and Mamadou Djigo: 5B. Diouli Missine: 1A. Momar Khary Niang: 1B; Souleye Samba Ndiaye: 1B; Sera Ndiaye: 2B. European troops also suspected that the war might never end. See Paul Fussel, *The Great War and Modern Memory* (Oxford: Oxford University Press, 1975).

⁴⁵ Mamadou Djigo: 5B. Sera Ndiaye: 3A; and Antoine Diouf: 1B. Ndiaga Niang: 1A. Bara Seck: 1A; Abdoulaye Ndiaye: 5A. These references are to disasters occurring at Verdun and Monastir (in Thessaloniki). See also: Mamadou Djigo: 4A.

⁴⁶ Mbaye Khary Diagne: 1B. See also: Mamadou Djigo: 4A; and Sera Ndiaye: 3B. Bara Seck: 1A. Sera Ndiaye: 4B; Daba Dembele: 5A; and Abdoulaye Gassama: 2A. See also *AG*: Unités: 26 N 869–871.

⁴⁷ Souleye Samba Ndiaye: 1A. The *Goumbala* was traditionally sung before blood was about to be shed, and particularly before battles. It was also normally sung by *griots*. Bara Seck: 2B.

⁴⁸ Ishmale Mbange: 2B.

⁴⁹ On the wide variety of charms and the particular perils they were intended to protect against, see: Mody Sow: 1B; Yoro Diaw: 1B; and Abdoulaye Ndiaye: 5B. Momar Candji: 2B. Many European wartime memoirs—including those of Erich Maria Remarque, Siegfried Sassoon, and Robert Graves—attest to soldiers' widespread use of charms. For a discussion of the subject among English soldiers, see: Fussel, *The Great War and Modern Memory*, p. 124.

[50] For European religious beliefs and the soldiers' perceptions of the relationship between God and their experience in combat, see: Fussel, *The Great War and Modern Memory*. For thoughts of Rog during combat, see: Biram Mbodji Tine: 1B. Malal Gassala: 2A and 2B; Ishmale Mbange: 2B. Abdoulaye Diaw: 1B; Mbaye Khary Diagne: 3A.

[51] Demba Mboup: 5B. For other references to the soldiers' interpretation of dreams, see: Demba Mboup: 9A; and Masserigne Soumare: 3B.

[52] Nar Diouf: 4B. Sera Ndiaye: 3B. On the progressive deterioration of the psychological mechanisms for coping with combat, based on studies conducted by the United States Army of their troops' performance in the Pacific theater during the Second World War, see: John Keegan, *The Face of Battle: A Study of Agincourt, Waterloo and the Somme* (Harmondsworth: Penguin Books, 1976), pp. 290–343.

[53] Sera Ndiaye: 3B. See also: Mamadou Djigo: 5B.

[54] Aliou Diakhate: 1B.

[55] Diouli Missine: 2B.

[56] Nouma Ndiaye: 2A and 2B.

[57] For a sample of such statements, which equated the fighting between France and Germany with that between "Kayor and Jolof" (and reconstructed the German ruling lineage from "William II" through his son "the Crown Prince," or alternatively, his other son, "Hitler"), see: Doudou Ndao: 1A; Demba Mboup: 9B; and Momar Candji: 1A and 1B.

[58] Aliou Diakhate: 2A. Samba Laga Diouf: 1B. Ndiaga Niang: 3A; and Samba Laga Diouf: 1B. This acknowledgment by the French of their need for African help was remembered by many; see: Nar Diouf: 3A; Sickh Yero Sy: 2A; Yoro Diaw: 1B; and Mamadou Bokar: 1B. Mamadou Djigo: 6A; Giribul Diallo: 2A; Mbaye Khary Diagne: 5A. The particular reference to disparaging African fighting qualities is to the purported vow of a German general to defeat the Senegalese at Verdun and then "drink his coffee in Paris" (see Masserigne Soumare: 1B), which is identical to the story recounted in the memoir of a Guinean veteran. See Joe Harris Lunn, "Kande Kamara Speaks: An Oral History of the West African Experience in France, 1914–1918," in *Africa and the First World War*, ed. Melvin E. Page (London: Macmillan, 1987). Samba Laga Diouf: 1B. Ndiaga Niang: 3A. Sambou Ndiaye: 1B.

[59] Daba Dembele: 3B. On incidents of flight during combat and subsequent executions, see also: Mamadou Djigo: 4A; Sera Ndiaye: 3B; and Demba Mboup: 11A.

[60] Nar Diouf: 4B. Similar thoughts occurred to other soldiers after the attacks on the Somme; see: Yoro Diaw: 1B. Yoro Diaw: 1B; see also: Daba Dembele: 3B; and Nar Diouf: 4B. Mbaye Khary Diagne: 3A. On rare incidents of Senegalese desertion in Europe, see also *AG*: Unités: 26 N 870–871.

[61] German willingness to take Senegalese prisoners was influenced by whether they were wounded (those hurt severely were often killed) and by the reciprocal treatment accorded by Africans to German comrades in their sector; see: Demba Mboup: 5A; and Masserigne Soumare: 2A. African P.O.W.s were treated well in some instances, but were compelled to perform hard labor and were poorly fed in others; see, respectively: Mamadou Bakar (who was a P.O.W.): 1B and 1B; Masserigne Soumare: 2A; and Momar Candji (who recounted stories told to them by other P.O.W.s): 1B. Mbaye Khary Diagne: 5A. On German aversion to taking Senegalese prisoners, see also: Samba Laga Diouf: 1B; and Mamadou Djigo: 6A. On being captured by Germans, see: Thiecouta Diallo: 2A.

[62] Yoro Diaw: 1B; Nouma Ndiaye: 1A; and Biram Mbodj Tine: 2B; Ishmale Mbange: 2A.

[63] On identifying with the French cause, see: Kamadou Mbaye: 1A. Giribul Diallo: 2A. See also: Mandow Mbaye: 2A.

[64] Mamadou Djigo: 5B. See also: Sera Ndiaye: 4B. For French inquiries into such incidents, see: *AG*: EMA: 7 N 440. For instructions to French officers to avoid using the term "niggers" in addressing Africans, see: *Notice sur les Sénégalais et leur emploi au combat*, p. 4.

[65] Masserigne Soumare: 1B.

[66] *AG*: GQG: 16 N 196/9.

[67] *AG*: GQG: 16 N 85.

[68] Rapport du Lt-Colonel Debieuvre, 30 April 1917, *AG*: Unités: 22 N 2481.

[69] See: Chef de Bataillon Arnaud, "Note au sujet de l'organisation d'unités offensive mixte sénégalaises," 12 February 1917, *AG*: Fonds Clemenceau: 6 N 96. On the deliberate sacrifice of African troops instead of French ones, also see the summary by the commander of the 28e Senegalese battalion, who described his unit's role in the fighting at Reims between 28 July and 2 August 1918: "This position had to be held at any price, and it was judged preferable, with good reason, to sacrifice a black battalion instead of Europeans." The 28e BTS lost over half its soldiers during the fighting: Chef de Bataillon Cros, "Monographie du Bataillon": *AG*: Unités: 26 N 869.

[70] Colonel Petitdemange, Commandant la subdivision de Fréjus, à Monsieur Général Petain, Commandant en Chef les Armées du Nord et du Nord-Est, 5 January 1918, *AG*: GQG: 16 N 100.

[71] Colonel Petitdemange, "Note sur l'utilisation des Sénégalais," 5 January 1918, *AG*: GQG: 16 N 100.

[72] This was also true of commanders who opposed using the Senegalese. General Maurice Sarrail, commander of the French expeditionary force at Thessaloniki, as well as several of his subordinates, who vociferously objected to being assigned African troops, reportedly perpetrated intentional "massacres" of them. Ousmane Diagne: 4A; Abdoulaye Ndiaye: 5A; and Abdoulaye Diaw: 1B.

[73] Clemenceau's remarks are cited in Charles-Robert Ageron, "Clemenceau et la question coloniale," in *Clemenceau et la Justice* (Actes du Colloque de décembre 1979 organisé pour le cinquantenaire de la mort de G. Clemenceau) (Paris: Publications de la Sorbonne, 1983), p. 80.

[74] On the history of the debate over Senegalese casualties, beginning with the charges leveled by Diagne against Mangin in June 1917, see: Joe Lunn, "Memoirs of the Maelstrom: A Senegalese Oral History of the First World War" (Ph.D. Diss.: University of Wisconsin–Madison, 1993), pp. 299–302.

[75] Marc Michel, *L'Appel à l'Afrique: Contributions et réactions à l'effort de guerre en A.O.F. (1914–1919)* (Paris: Publications de la Sorbonne, 1982), pp. 403–08.

[76] Charles Balesi, *From Adversaries to Comrades-in-Arms: West Africa and the French Military, 1885–1918* (Waltham, MA: Crossroads Press, 1979), pp. 101–02.

[77] Echenberg, *Colonial Conscripts*, p. 46. It should be emphasized that the respective interpretations offered by Michel, Balesi, and Echenberg differ in fundamental respects. Michel and Balesi focus on casualty rates and offer these as evidence of the absence of malicious intent on the part of French commanders in particular and the comparatively nonracist character of French society in general. Echenberg, on the other hand, is well aware of the impact French race theory had on military calculations and popular perceptions of Africans, which he consistently emphasizes in his work.

[78] Clayton, *France, Soldiers and Africa*, p. 338.

[79] This figure is cited by Michel, *L'Appel à l'Afrique*, pp. 407–08, and also by Echenberg, *Colonial Conscripts*, p. 46 (excluding the losses of *originaires*). It accords with the most reliable estimates for combat fatalities (see Table 5.1).

[80] On the omission of incidental deaths, including those from disease, see Table 5.1.

[81] The precise figures are 15.56 percent to 16.56 percent. The total number of West Africans mobilized during the war (including 31,000 in the prewar army, 161,000 *tirailleurs*, and 7,200 *originaires* subsequently recruited or conscripted between 1914 and 1918) was approximately 199,200. Of these at least 31,000 died during the war. French figures are based on the "Rapport Marin," which was submitted to the French Chamber in 1920 as the definitive assessment of this question. The total number of Frenchmen mobilized during the war was 7,740,000, of whom 1,281,979 perished. See "Rapport Marin," *Journaux Officiel de la République Française. Documents Parlementaires*, 1920, t. 2, annexe 633, p. 44.

[82] Approximately 140,000 West Africans, including *originaires*, served as combatants, of whom 31,000 were killed, representing 22.14 percent of the total. By contrast, 6,987,000 Frenchmen served as combatants, of whom 1,255,766 are reckoned to have died, or 17.97 percent of the total. Hence, African fatalities were 18.84 percent higher than those among French combatants. "Rapport Marin," *Journaux Officiel*, p. 44.

[83] Among French infantrymen, 5,056,900 were mobilized and 1,158,000, or 22.9 percent, were killed: "Rapport Marin," *Journaux Officiel*, p. 66. Although not all West Africans served in the infantry, very few were assigned to "other services" such as the artillery. Since there are no records of the numbers in this latter group, the figures cited for the proportion of losses among all West African combatants (22.14 percent) have been retained. Though representing a small underestimate of the percentage of Senegalese infantry casualties, the discrepancy is slight.

[84] For examples, see Michel, *L'Appel à l'Afrique*, pp. 337, 405–08, 423–24; and Balesi, *From Adversaries to Comrades-In-Arms*, pp. 101–02.

[85] According to the *Histoire militaire de l'A.O.F.*, p. 826, out of a total of 29,520 combatant fatalities, 29,224 (or 98 percent) occurred during the fighting in Europe.

[86] In 1914 and 1915, losses among all *indigènes coloniaux* amounted to 2,900 men. Senegalese losses during the war constituted about 85 percent of this category. If these are distributed proportionally by year, Senegalese losses in 1914 and 1915 amounted to less than 8 percent of their total wartime casualties (2,465 men or 7.95 percent). See "Rapport Marin," *Journal Officiel*, p. 76; see also Table 5.2. Fragmentary contemporary evidence supports this conclusion. Among the approximately 5,000 men who fought in France in 1914, 3,728 were available for active duty at the end of the year. Hence, their losses (including ill and wounded as well as dead) did not exceed a maximum of 1,572 men: *AG*: EMA: 7 N 444.

[87] French losses (including dead, missing, and prisoners) between August 1914 and the end of June 1916 amounted to 62.26 percent of the eventual wartime total. See "Rapport Marin," *Journaux Officiel*, p. 74.

[88] Assuming that at a minimum 90 percent of all West African casualties were sustained after June 1916, some 27,900 men out of 140,000 combatants (or 199 per 1,000 engaged) were killed during the final 29 months of the war. By contrast, estimating French infantry losses for this period at not more than 40 percent of their wartime total, approximately 532,000 casualties were sustained among 5,057,000 combattants, or 105 per 1,000. Hence, African losses were 89.45 percent higher than those incurred by the French infantry after June 1916, or nearly twice those of their European counterparts. On West

African losses, see "Rapport Marin," *Journaux Officiel*, p. 76, which reckoned losses among "indigènes coloniaux" from 1916 onward at 91.75 percent of the wartime total; on French losses, see pp. 44, 66, 74.

[89] Approximately 18 percent of post-June 1916 French losses were incurred during the periods of *hivernage* between November and March in 1917 and 1918. Hence, the fatalities among French infantry when the Senegalese were deployed in combat from 1916 to 1918 can be reckoned at 436,240, or 8.63 percent of the total engaged. West African losses during this period amounted to 19.93 percent of all combatants. As a result, the probability of their death at the Front was almost two-and-a-half times as great (i.e., 2.31 percent).

[90] On the use of "military aptitudes" of particular "races" as a basic organizational principle among Senegalese combat units, see General-in-Chief Joseph Joffre's letter of January 1916 to the Minister of War, *AG*: EMA: 7 N 1990.

[91] West Africans recruited from "warrior races" constituted about two-thirds of the "line" infantry used during the attacks on the Somme and Aisne in 1916 and 1917, while soldiers recruited from "nonwarrior races" were generally sent to communication battalions (*bataillons d'étapes*). Races with special "military aptitudes" probably composed at least one-half of the compliment of "line" infantry during 1918. Some battalions, however, were also composed exclusively of "warriors," while the arrival of reinforcements frequently led to the culling of "nonwarriors" from units in order to replace them with men from ethnic groups deemed warlike. On unit ethnic compositions and proportions, see: for 1916: *AG*: GQG: 16 N 196 and *AG*: Unités: 26 N 872; for 1917: *AG*: EMA: 7 N 2990 and *AG*: Unités: 24 N 3027; for 1918, *AG:* Fonds Clemenceau: 6 N 94 and *AG*: EMA: 7 N 440. On the ethnic composition of particular units at different times, as well as the culling of non-warriors from units to replace them with warriors, see the JMOs: *AG*: Unités: 26 N 869–872.

[92] Overall, about 60 percent of the West African formations that were most prominent in the fighting from 1916 to 1918 were drawn from those groups regarded as especially warlike by the French. In Senegal, however, at least 90 percent of all recruits probably belonged to these "races." As a result, it is extremely likely that they were overrepresented—and probably on the order of about one-third again as much—in those units that sustained the heaviest casualties. Although ethnic breakdowns for casualties are lacking, it seems probable that in absolute terms their losses may be reckoned at approximately two-and-a-half times greater (2.46 calculated at 30 percent more) than those of the French infantry during the last 29 months of the war, while their probability of death when at the Front was about three times as great (3.00 calculated at 30 percent more) during this same period.

[93] Rapport du Chef de Bataillon Bertault, Commandant le 44ᵉ BTS, 17 September 1918, *AG*: GQG: 16 N 2094. For similar explanations of these tactical alignments by other battalion and corps commanders, see also *AG*: Unités: 22 N 2468 and 22 N 2481.

[94] Senegalese losses appear to have been at least 25 percent higher than those suffered by their French cadres in 1918 during the fighting at Reims and the offensive of the 10th Army between July and August. In the former engagement, among battalions where such breakdowns were recorded, West African fatalities were 26.2 percent greater than those of the French; in the latter, they were 27.0 percent higher. These calculations are derived from figures given in the JMOs: *AG*: Unités: 26 N 869–872. On Senegalese losses being higher than those of their cadres, see also *AG*: Unités: 22 N 2481.

[95] Mbaye Khary Diagne: 1B.

[96] The deliberate sacrificing of "others"—irrespective of whether such distinctions were defined along racial, ethnic, social, religious, or national lines—is a very old practice indeed. It dates from at least the Punic Wars (when Hannibal deployed Spaniards against the Roman center at Cannae to spare Carthaginians) and was practiced by French, British, and Swedish commanders (among others) during the Napoleonic Wars. During the First World War, the British misused Indian troops (whose proportion of casualties was even higher than those of French West Africans over a shorter period of time), as well as the troops of the Australian and New Zealand Army Corps (ANZAC), most notably at Gallipoli. Such practices continued during the Second World War, when Canadian troops were selected by British commanders to test the German continental defenses at Dieppe in 1943.

[97] The percentage of these soldiers that came from Senegal was 12.89; the colony also furnished a larger proportion of *tirailleurs*—1.73 percent of the total population—than any other colony in A.O.F.

[98] As a percentage of total recruits, this estimate suggests that between 20 and 25 percent of those enlisting during the war did not return.

6

"Bons Soldats" and "Sales Nègres": Senegalese Contacts with the French

Despite the terror of the trenches, the wartime experience in Europe also transformed many soldiers' perceptions of themselves and of the French. Closer contacts with the French metropolitan population helped to break down long-standing stereotypes, and although this was true among both the Senegalese and the French, it was especially apparent among the Africans.[1] Contact was much more likely to happen behind the lines, where opportunities for interaction between the Senegalese and French soldiers and civilians were greatest, although it did sometimes occur during the course of brief encounters at the front. To explore this transformation, we will examine the nature of the Senegalese experience during the time they were garrisoned among the French population. Controlled in large measure by French policy concerning the deployment of African troops in the metropole, the parameters of interaction between Senegalese soldiers and the French public were circumscribed. Nonetheless, it is clear that as a result of the wartime encounter, along with the wide dissemination of more favorable public images of Africans, reciprocal images of the Senegalese of the French and the French of the Senegalese—both derived from a colonial context—were substantially altered.

THE FRENCH CONUNDRUM

Paradoxes of French Policy

The terrifying wartime image of the Senegalese in combat cut both ways. It not only aroused dread among German soldiers but also unnerved French

citizens as well. Having imported tens of thousands of Africans to help drive
"*le boche*" from their homeland, the French authorities faced the dilemma of
how to assuage popular apprehensions aroused by the soldiers' presence when
they were not fighting at the front.

Despite the enthusiasm often exhibited by the French public for the
Senegalese on their arrival, their anxieties were genuine and widespread.
French fears derived from the racist preconceptions of the era and were exacerbated by the blood-curdling image of Africans that had been propagated
in the metropole during the two decades since the colonial conquest. That
image portrayed Africans not only as biologically inferior to Europeans, but
also stressed how their "savage" nature, which was the hallmark of their "re-
tarded" development, offended all "civilized" conventions. Inherently "warlike" and "ferocious" in combat, Africans were said to have scant regard for
their own lives and to be merciless toward defeated enemies. Driven by "bes-
tial" or "animal-like" impulses, which called into question their very humanity, they were regarded as sexually depraved and morally repellent. In addition to holding women in low esteem and practicing polygamy, the catalogue
of sins attributed to them extended to human sacrifice and cannibalism.[2]

Although early proponents of raising African troops for service in Europe
sought to modify this image by emphasizing a set of more congenial alternative stereotypes about the soldiers, their efforts appear to have had little effect on the popular imagination.[3] Indeed, long after African soldiers made
their initial appearance in Europe, most metropolitans persisted in regarding
the Senegalese as "savages," if not worse.[4] As Doudou Ndao, among other
African soldiers, recalled, "The French thought we were cannibals, [even
though] we never ate anybody."[5]

Faced with the paradoxical side affects of their wartime initiative, the
French authorities responded to the dilemma they confronted in two ways.
Publicly, they sought to placate popular misgivings. Embracing the paternalistic imagery espoused by advocates of African recruitment in the colonial
army, the metropolitan authorities issued a flood of pro-Senegalese propaganda for domestic consumption. At the same time they also systematically
strove to restrict the contacts of Africans with French citizens as much as
possible, at least to the extent that military priorities permitted.

Public Images

With the arrival of tens of thousands of African troops in France at the
beginning of 1916, official and semiofficial characterizations of the Senegalese
began to change. Though still incorporating many of the racist preconceptions of the past, the new image of Africans that was propagated nevertheless
stressed positive attributes. These were intended to present the soldiers in a
more favorable light and thereby make their presence more palatable to the

large sectors of French society that inevitably came into contact with them. This transformation in public parlance was evidenced in all manner of discourse: in official pronouncements by government and military leaders; in propaganda disseminated by such agencies as the *Comité d'assistance aux troupes noires* and the French press; and in popular wartime literature.

The Senegalese were repeatedly praised by French leaders for their exemplary valor, their disciplined behavior, and their devotion to France in its hour of need. Exemplifying this trend, the president of the republic, Raymond Poincaré, spoke in November 1916 of "[our] brave Senegalese," emphasizing that all who "knew them" recognized their "brilliant courage" as well as their "wholesome cheerfulness."[6] Similar edifying remarks were also voiced by other members of the government. A month later, in December 1916, Gaston Doumergue, the minister of colonies, lauded the Senegalese for their military qualities—for their "heroism" and "loyalty" as well as "their bravery and their spirit of discipline." He also stressed their "love [of France]," the "generosity" with which "they shed their blood in order to defend [it]," and the invaluable "contribution" to ultimate "victory" they were making against "the unjust and brutal aggression of the 'true barbarians.'"[7] Nor were such testimonials restricted to political figures. By 1918 General Ferdinand Foch, newly appointed leader of the allied armies, publicly declared his admiration for the Senegalese; he praised them for "their marvelous courage, their indomitable tenacity, their impetuosity of spirit," as well as for "their loyalty and their absolute devotion" to the French cause.[8]

This official image of African soldiers was embellished in a wide range of French publications. Not restricting their comments exclusively to the customary litany about Senegalese bravery and devotion, many of these accounts endeavored to present to their readers a fuller awareness of the African character. In some instances, such as the ongoing series of articles published after January 1916 under the auspices of the *Comité d'assistance aux troupes noires* in *La Dépêche Coloniale Illustrée*, distinguished colonial "experts" were called on to correct popular misconceptions about Africans. Eulogistic in tone, their contributions described the history of West Africa, the discernible social "evolution" of the populations (calculated to make them increasingly "respectable" in French eyes), and the "loyalty" of the inhabitants to *la patrie*.[9] The popular press adopted a similar line. For example, the national weekly *l'Illustration* ran a series of articles in 1916 and 1917 about the Senegalese, which, though stressing the soldiers' military contribution to the national defense, also depicted them in more reassuring moments of repose: fishing, washing laundry, and listening to the gramophone. In February 1916, *Le Petit Var*, whose readers were in close proximity to the Senegalese training camps on the Côte d'Azur, described the soldiers in similar ways. Not only were they "brave men," but they were also "gentle, warm hearted, and thankful" for any assistance the local inhabitants might offer them.[10]

This shift in the imagery of Africans, however, was most fully developed in French literary treatments of the Senegalese published during the war and immediately thereafter. The characterizations of some writers such as Pierre Mille were superficial. Applauding the Senegalese for their "discipline," Mille stressed that "no soldier is braver and possesses greater confidence in his chiefs than the black."[11] Others based their accounts on firsthand experience and sought to assess the mentality of the soldiers in greater detail. Wartime memoirs included the works of Léon Gaillet, a "metropolitan" lieutenant serving in an African battalion, and those of Léon Bocquet and Alphonse Séché. Gaillet's two books, *Coulibaly: Les Sénégalais sur la terre de France* and *Deux ans avec les Sénégalais*, appeared in 1917 and 1918, respectively. In them, Gaillet recounts his initial repugnance on meeting the soldiers, deploring their "savagery," their "animality," and their physical resemblance to "great monkeys." Gradually, he begins to distinguish between different African "races" (which are alternatively judged to be "brave," "loyal," or "intelligent") and eventually even between individuals. He speaks of some of the men having adopted "white manners," although the true qualities of their "heart" derived from the "good nature of the primitive."[12] Eventually he concludes that Africans are "great children," but because of their "sacrifices" in behalf of France—their "godmother"—the "infants" will one day become "men."[13]

Léon Bocquet and Alphonse Séché stress similar themes. Like Gaillet, they embrace the metaphor of Africans as "*grands enfants.*" For Bocquet this state is a result of the "primitive humanity" of Africans, which, by turns, makes them "passionate," "gentle," and "severe." Possessing a "generous spontaneity," they were also "loyal" and "trustworthy" and implacable foes of the *boches.*[14] For Séché, whose work did not appear until after the armistice in 1919, the soldiers' "childishness" exemplified the "characteristics of youth: naiveté, astonishing ignorance, generosity, enthusiasm of spirit."[15] Also "proud" and "easily offended" but "brave to the point of folly," the essence of their character derived from the "simplicity of spirit" of the "primitive," who was incapable of "analysis" and reacted instead by "instinct" or "impulse." "Loyal" to France and absolutely devoted to their officers, these *grands enfants* required "benevolent paternalism" to guide them.[16]

Collectively, these public images of the Senegalese disseminated during the war represented a dramatic departure from those that had prevailed since the conquest.[17] The earlier visions were intended to underscore the moral rectitude of French colonization in Africa and extol the courage of the French army during its campaigns of conquest against "savage" hordes. The new image drew on the older myths to the extent that Africans continued to be perceived as racially inferior to Europeans and inherently warlike, but it also integrated some novel elements. The Senegalese were not only brave, but their recently acquired "loyalty" to France, their selfless contribution to the war effort against Germany, and their unswerving obedience and devotion to their officers represented incontestably positive attributes. Moreover, the "paternalistic" stereotype of the "child-like" character of the soldiers (which itself was an embellishment of the older eighteenth-century notion of the "noble savage") represented a significant departure from the immediate past. Though pejorative, it stressed the humane qualities of Africans. As such, it was intended to assuage domestic fears by presenting the Senegalese in an altogether more sympathetic light. This image of the congenial *grand enfant* fighting on behalf of *la patrie* was, in short, designed to reassure the French public that apprehensions about the soldiers' presence in their midst were ill founded. Though having a discernible effect on metropolitan opinion, these public pronouncements were also at marked variance with official policy regarding the deployment of the Senegalese in France.

Official Policy

In addition to introducing an alternative and more congenial image of African soldiers, the metropolitan authorities sought to limit domestic outcry arising from their presence by keeping contacts between the Senegalese and the French people at a minimum. In the case of the comparatively small number of *originaires*, who had obtained French citizenship and won the right to serve in predominantly European units of the Colonial Army, these efforts were least effective. For the vast majority of *tirailleurs*, however, the restrictions imposed by the military and civilian authorities were far more thoroughgoing. Indeed, they amounted to a systematic attempt to segregate the *tirailleurs* as much as possible from both French soldiers and civilians.

The constraints imposed on "interracial" contacts were exemplified in a wide variety of ways. At the front, the encounters of the *tirailleurs* with the French rank-and-file soldiers were highly circumscribed. Although sometimes "mixed" with other French battalions or companies during combat, such contacts with the *poilus* were invariably brief, often occurred only immediately before attacks, and were normally restricted to chance encounters. This policy was never practiced systematically, and, in any event, the soldiers were always reformed into segregated battalions or regiments as soon as they were withdrawn from the fighting. Otherwise, the contacts of *tirailleurs* with French soldiers were confined to their officers or to the cadres within their units. The former generally retained their distance, while the latter—even when they were training in camp—were customarily separated from the African troops.[18]

Care was also taken to restrict intercourse between the Senegalese and French civilians behind the lines. African training camps in the Midi and the Gironde were invariably "isolated" (the army's official designation for them), and considerable forethought was devoted to their location.

Though usually placed in the south of France, where the weather was warmest, climate was not the only factor that entered into play. Contemplating the influx of African recruits in 1918, Georges Clemenceau underscored the concerns of the government and issued instructions to the regional military commanders that the "places selected for the [new] camps must provide for the installation of the natives in housing as removed as possible from the civilian population."[19]

Similar considerations also factored into the treatment of Africans in French hospitals. In March 1916, the Military Health Service recommended the creation of segregated hospitals for the Senegalese, purged of all civilian personnel and run exclusively by the army.[20] Although this practice proved difficult to apply in all cases, the example of the "isolated" hospital at Menton, which was supported through the aid of the *Comité d'assistance aux troupes noires*, illustrates the concerns and intent of the authorities. Menton was designed to correct the ostensibly "deplorable influence" that care by civilian staffs in other hospitals—especially by the nurses of the Red Cross—had had on convalescing African soldiers. The prescription at Menton was accordingly both "medical and moral." In the latter case, the "deformed mentality" arising from contacts with civilian personnel was to be cured by a process of "re-Senegalization," which would prepare the soldiers for their return to the colonies after the war.[21]

Communication between the soldiers and French inhabitants was also inhibited by linguistic barriers. Few *tirailleurs* spoke fluent French when they entered the army, and the quality of the instruction they received in the camps was intended to ensure that—aside from understanding military commands—things remained that way. The *tirailleurs* were taught only pidgin French, or *"petit nègre,"* which rendered communication outside the confines of the military difficult.[22] Moreover, when such exchanges did occur, the speech the soldiers were taught reinforced the popular image of African intellectual inferiority.[23]

African opportunities for interchanges with French civilians were, in any event, extremely limited and usually tightly regulated by military authorities. Although the policy regarding "leave" from the Senegalese camps occasionally varied depending on locale and circumstances, commandants were directed that it be kept to a minimum.[24] Normally soldiers were permitted to leave their camps and visit local towns only for a few hours each week, on Sunday afternoons.

Encounters between soldiers and civilians increased when the former were wounded. During convalescence, those who were ambulatory were often permitted to leave their hospitals for brief walks among the local people. Hospital policy, however, was left to the discretion of medical directors, and such practices were much more common when they were under civilian rather than military control.[25]

Opportunities for more prolonged contacts with French inhabitants occurred during the course of "permissions" or furloughs (which granted leave
from the army for periods of several weeks), but these were seldom given to
Africans. *Originaires*, like all other French servicemen, did receive them,
but before the final months of 1917 they were usually sequestered in
"casernes" run by the Colonial Army and thereafter sent back to Senegal.
The *tirailleurs*, on the other hand, were not allowed permissions until 1918,
when concerns among military officials about their "morale" enforced a re-
laxation of official restrictions. Even then, however, they were usually only
excused from duty within the camps if they submitted a "written" request for
a *certificat d'hébergement* to the military authorities.[26]

Finally, French apprehensions about Africans were underscored by a variety of other concerns. Undue attention was devoted to preventing "drunkenness" among the troops, which was a fiction insofar as most Muslim soldiers
were concerned.[27] Similar cares were also expressed about the diffusion of
"Muslim propaganda" within the army and the prospect of increased conversion to Islam among nonbelieving soldiers.[28]

Official anxieties, however, were most acute over the possible "depravity
of French women" that might occur as a result of chance encounters with
Africans.[29] Although the authorities were little concerned about women of
"ill repute" (and indeed they sanctioned the access of Africans to brothels
supervised by the army), contact with girls from "good families" was an
entirely different matter.[30] Female nurses were expelled from Senegalese
hospitals, not only because of their adverse effects on the soldiers "morale"
but also to spare them the undue attentions of the men.[31] Identical concerns
also applied to *"marraines de guerre,"* who were warned of the African "contempt for women" and advised to avoid becoming too close to those they
befriended.[32]

Yet despite the lengths to which the authorities went to restrict contacts
between Africans and the French population, these could not be prevented
altogether. It is therefore appropriate to explore the parameters within which
such contacts occurred, their character, and their variation in intensity. In so
doing, it will be possible to appreciate how the combination of altered public
imagery and closer interpersonal relations affected African and French perceptions of each other.

SENEGALESE CONTACTS WITH THE FRENCH

Extent of Encounters

As the contradictions between public rhetoric and official policy make
clear, it was not feasible to isolate tens of thousands of African troops from
the French population completely. Although the Senegalese were never bil-

Figure 6.1   Senegalese Contacts with the French

Most frequent		
	With French soldiers	**With French civilians**
Originaires	Integrated Units	Furloughs
(citizens)		Hospitals
		Leave
Tirailleurs	Segregated Units	Hospitals
(subjects)	(except cadres)	Leave
		Least frequent

leted in many provinces of France, in those areas where they were concentrated—the southwest, the Pyrenees, the Côte d'Azur, and (when they were sent to the front) the northeast—encounters were unavoidable (see Map 4.1).[33] Moreover, although contacts between African soldiers and French citizens remained highly circumscribed—even in those regions where they were most likely to occur—they exhibited a wide variation. The extent of this variation, which differed depending on the individual circumstances of each of the soldiers recruited in A.O.F., was most pronounced among the troops raised in Senegal, composed of both *tirailleurs* and *originaires*. Their experiences thereby best exemplify the range of encounters that occurred between Africans and Europeans during the war, as well as the circumstances under which such contacts took place. Broadly speaking, the interaction of the Senegalese with the French can be differentiated according to whether they occurred with military personnel or with civilians, while the quality of their interaction depended in large measure on whether they were recruited as colonial *sujets* or conscripted as French citizens (see Figure 6.1).

All Senegalese soldiers had some contact with French military personnel. Opportunities for interchanges between African and European soldiers were, however, most restricted among the *tirailleurs*. Systematically "segregated" from French formations behind the lines, they were seldom exposed to metropolitan soldiers "except during attacks," and these encounters were perforce brief and distorted. The *tirailleurs* did, however, have more extensive contacts with French officers, N.C.O.s, and the cadres assigned to their units. Although they were separated from the cadres in the training camps (and frequently during combat), interchanges between them, and especially with the N.C.O.s responsible for overseeing the execution of their duties, were unavoidable.[34]

The character of these associations varied greatly. Friction often developed between the Senegalese and the European contingents in their units, especially when the men were initially brought together. French enlisted men sometimes refused to salute African N.C.O.s,[35] while the soldiers were also physically abused by some of their French N.C.O.s. Such provocative behavior by the French cadres was held in check, however, by two considerations. Officers intervened to stop fights between the men before they escalated, while persistently abusive behavior by individual Frenchmen also led to murderous reprisals against them in combat by those they had tormented.[36]

In time, however, some *tirailleurs* became better acquainted with Frenchmen in their battalions. The soldiers occasionally "played games" together in the camps when off duty or accompanied each other into nearby towns when permitted leave. In combat, personal attachments sometimes became more intense. One grateful *tirailleur*, Momar Khary Niang, never forgot his "friend" Michel, a *"Tubab* sergeant" who saved his life by carrying him to the casualty clearing station when he was wounded. On the whole, however, close attachments with Europeans in Senegalese units were the exception rather than the rule, and relations usually remained ephemeral, correct, and superficial. Yet despite periodic harassment and the maintenance of social distance among the men, few soldiers felt uniformly maltreated by the French. Indeed, some were favorably disposed toward their European comrades, while most, citing obvious exceptions among them, believed that the way they were treated depended on the personality of the individual.[37]

The situation of the *originaires* within their units was much different. Though initially formed into African battalions in Senegal, the men were eventually integrated into various regiments of the Colonial Army. Like the *tirailleurs*, they too were withdrawn to camps in the rear during the winter, but they usually served the rest of the year in formations where Frenchmen predominated.[38] As a result, their contacts with European soldiers were much greater than among their rural counterparts from Senegal.

Like the *tirailleurs*, the *originaires* were also subjected to insults by some of their French comrades. Usually "racist" in character—"dirty nigger" or "dirty race" being the preferred slurs—the prejudices such verbal onslaughts exemplified were often intensified by the claims of the *originaires* to French citizenship. The inevitable fights that resulted occasionally ended in deaths, but more often these were broken up by French officers before this occurred.[39] Paradoxically, such confrontations also sometimes led to closer ties among the men. Describing one such incident, Ndiaga Niang from St. Louis recalled:

One day I was in the [mess hall] in the camp [where] we used to eat. And often after eating, we used to drink coffee in cups. But before drinking it, we used to make "cheers" with the other soldiers. So on this day, I took my cup and I wanted to make "cheers" with a French soldier who was sitting next to me. So I made the "cheers," [but] the soldier said to me, "don't touch my cup, you are too dirty!" And [this made] me very angry. [So] I punched him and we began to fight. And when they went to get the captain, the captain told me that I was right, and he told the French soldier that he would be punished. But afterwards, I became very friendly with this same soldier.[40]

Aside from allowing them to stand up for themselves, persistent abuse of *originaires* in these units was also curtailed through the intervention of Blaise Diagne. And while friction between Africans and Europeans (as well as between other "colonials" serving with them) was unavoidable, on the whole prolonged association usually led to the development of closer personal relationships.[41] This growing spirit of "camaraderie" was exemplified in a variety of ways: by the exchange of "nicknames" among the soldiers, by hospital visits when wounded comrades were convalescing, and by offers of assistance by some Frenchmen in the face of provocations from others.[42] Indeed, in contrast with most *tirailleurs*, nearly all *originaires* eventually counted several French soldiers among their "friends." Enhanced familiarity with Europeans did not, however, appreciably affect the perceptions the *originaires* formed of how they were collectively treated as Africans in the army. Like the *tirailleurs*, the majority of Senegalese communards keenly appreciated that, although they were accorded respect by some individuals and might become friends with them, the reverse was also often the case.[43]

In addition to encountering Europeans in their units, the Senegalese also had contacts with French civilians away from the fields of battle. These exchanges—like their comparative proximity to French soldiers—depended in large measure, however, on whether they served as *tirailleurs* or *originaires*. *Tirailleurs*, whose opportunities were most circumscribed, were exposed to the metropolitan population under a variety of circumstances. When moving between their training camps and the front, they met Frenchmen in railway stations, on march, and when they were billeted near French villages behind the lines.[44] Less frequently, they also encountered French citizens, if they were wounded, in those hospitals where civilian personnel were permitted and in factories, where some *tirailleurs* were assigned to work during the *hivernage*.[45] The soldiers also came into contact with civilians when they were on leave from their camps, during promenades while convalescing in hospital, and in exceptional cases when they were granted "permissions" late in the war.[46]

The occasions for interaction by *originaires* with civilians were similar to those of the *tirailleurs*, but they were considerably less restricted. In addition to meeting Frenchmen during transit to and from the front and occasionally in factories, encounters also frequently occurred in hospitals to which they were sent, which invariably included civilian staff members to minister to the wounded along with European soldiers who were injured.[47] Moreover, aside from a generally more liberal policy of leave from their camps and greater freedom during convalescence, the *originaires* were also consistently permitted extended furloughs, which more than any other policy increased their opportunities for contact with civilians.[48] Although this preferred treatment afforded the *originaires* greater opportunities for contact with French civilians than the *tirailleurs* had, the range, intensity, and character of the encounters that occurred during the war were also influenced by a series of other, less obvious factors.

The Character of the Contacts with French Civilians

The range of the soldiers' contacts with French civilians varied in the extreme. Aside from brief glimpses or occasional superficial encounters, some Senegalese literally "never had any contact" with the metropolitan population.[49] On the other hand, many had extensive opportunities for interaction, and some developed personal relationships with Frenchmen. Furthermore, the character of these exchanges naturally differed from those occurring in the army. Unfettered by the strictures of military life—which was hierarchical, disciplined, and exclusively male—the soldiers were usually much freer to express themselves and learn about the French and the broader aspects of their society in return. As a result, the soldiers' contacts with civilians were frequently a crucial element in changing their preconceptions about Europeans, just as they often were in altering metropolitan assumptions about Africans.

Aside from the fundamental differences in the treatment accorded to *tirailleurs* and *originaires* in the army, which affected the parameters of their contact with the metropolitan population, the quality of the encounters between the Senegalese and French civilians were influenced by a series of more subtle considerations. Chief among these were their comparative facility with the French language; whether they were wounded or not and, if so, how severely; and the image of individual soldiers in French eyes.

Notwithstanding discrepancies in the regulations regarding leave from the camps and permissions, perhaps the single most important factor governing African interaction with them was the individual's ability to communicate in French. This, of course, varied greatly. Some Senegalese barely spoke French at all; others could comprehend it but had difficulty making themselves understood; still others could speak with a restricted vocabulary (but often only in *petit nègre*); and some were not only fluent but also literate, with a few able to mimic the different regional accents of metropolitans as well.[50] The intensity of personal contacts varied accordingly and were usually directly proportional to the soldiers' command of the civilians' mother tongue.

Figure 6.2   Character of Senegalese Contacts with French Civilians:
Personal Factors

Originaires versus *Tirailleurs*

Acculturation	• Facility with the French language ("intelligence")
	• Military rank (N.C.O.s versus soldiers)
Bravery	• Noted combats (e.g., Douaumont)
	• Wounds (and severity)
	• Decorations (*croix de guerre, médaille militaire*)

Wounds also entered into play. An astonishingly high proportion of
Senegalese—particularly *tirailleurs*—were wounded in combat. Furthermore, a substantial number of these required prolonged treatment in French
hospitals before either being discharged to Senegal or returned to their
units for further duty.[51] Although there were notable exceptions to the
rule, periods of extended convalescence, aside from permissions, were
usually the times when contacts with French civilians—including both
hospital staff and local inhabitants—were most likely to occur. Moreover,
because of their obvious physical infirmities, these soldiers usually elicited sympathy instead of guarded apprehension, and they were therefore
often treated more tolerantly than they would have been under ordinary
circumstances.

Finally, the character of Senegalese encounters with the French was influenced by the citizens' perceptions of individual servicemen. Two factors were
accorded primacy among metropolitans: the soldiers' comparative degree of
acculturation (often misinterpreted as "intelligence") and their bravery (see
Figure 6.2). Fluency in French was an obvious indication of the former, while
wounds received in battle ostensibly offered proof of the latter. An African's
rank was another consideration, and the generally more favorable treatment
accorded to high-ranking N.C.O.s was one reason for many soldiers' urge to
acquire "stripes." Participation in noted "combats" (especially if their outcome was "victorious") also impressed French opinion. Decorations received
for courage under fire epitomized this outlook. Soldiers bemedaled with the
médaille militaire and the *croix de guerre* on their chests were generally not
only well received by civilians but honored.[52]

Despite their wide range, and notwithstanding the diversity of factors
that influenced both the likelihood and nature of their encounters, a rough
typology of the collective character of Senegalese contacts with French
civilians emerges.[53] This scheme of social interaction is depicted in Figure 6.3.

Figure 6.3   Character of Senegalese Contacts with French Civilians: Space and Group Considerations

---

Most personal

	Private Spaces	**Public Spaces**
As Individuals	• With *marraines de guerre*	
	• French homes	
	• Hospitals	• Public entertainment
		• Commercial establishments
		• Public buildings
	Indoors:	• Factories
		• Brothels
In Groups		• Railway stations
		• Markets
	Outdoors:	• Parks
		• Country roads

                                                                      Least personal

---

Whether *tirailleur* or *originaire*, most Senegalese encountered European civilians in public spaces. Outdoors the soldiers chanced on French men, women, and children in a variety of places. These included country roads and municipal streets, civic parks, open-air stalls and village markets, and railway platforms.[54] Usually venturing forth in French society in small groups, where one soldier (especially in the case of *tirailleurs*) usually acted as a spokesman for the rest, such exchanges with local citizens were usually perfunctory. They entailed customary "greetings" and exchanges of "good will" and occasionally small commercial transactions. More rarely, and especially at train stations, they also sometimes provided opportunities to make plans for a future rendezvous elsewhere.[55]

The range of indoor public spaces to which the soldiers had access was vast, and they varied according to function. Brothels were regulated by the army, and many soldiers visited them on designated evenings or looked for them surreptitiously when favorable opportunities arose. Nearly always going in groups, Senegalese encounters with French prostitutes were usually brief and restricted to "business." Though the soldiers were not racially discriminated against, the womens' attentions were usually lavished on those with the most money. This seldom included the *tirailleurs*, and, after 1917, when Africans and Frenchmen alike were supplanted by the comparatively wealthy American soldiers, this often created resentment that led to brawls.[56]

During the *hivernage*, *tirailleurs* and *originaires* were sometimes employed in French factories, particularly munitions plants, which were exceptionally dangerous work environments. They were used in the production lines or, alternatively, as guards to oversee the workforce. Always sent in large groups, which were subject to military discipline, a few Senegalese became acquainted with their co-workers; still, these contacts were exceptional. Indeed, more often their presence (and the coercive threat it sometimes represented) was resented.

Soldiers also sought out places that provided public entertainment, including theaters, casinos, cabarets (which were sometimes adjoining the gambling halls), and cinemas. Going either in small groups or individually (depending—with the notable exception of the silent cinema—on the extent of their French), the Senegalese appear to have been generally well received. Like their European counterparts, they were also particularly thrilled by the "moving pictures."[57]

The soldiers' reception in places intended to stimulate sociability, however, was not always equable. Usually welcome in bars, bistros, cafés, and restaurants, their presence nevertheless sometimes provoked indignant protests from French clients. One African recalled, for example: "We were in a café, and a *Tubab* said [to the owner], 'We will never return to this café [if you continue] to allow 'black' soldiers to come into it!'" Although fights occasionally broke out—especially in bars—when racial insults were hurled at the soldiers, on the whole the presence of Africans was tolerated if not well received, and some became well acquainted with the proprietors. Many Senegalese remembered with special fondness the apparent generosity of café and restaurant owners when the armistice was announced and they were allowed to eat and drink (usually lemonade) their fill without charge.[58]

Some Senegalese were admitted to public buildings officially designated as such. These included brief stays in *hôtels de ville* (where some African troops were billeted immediately after the armistice), as well as the French Chamber of Deputies in Paris. Only *originaires* seeking to meet Blaise Diagne attempted to visit the Chamber, but his personal intervention was usually sufficient for them to gain entry.[59]

Hospitals generally represented areas intermediate between "public" and "private" space. Though the sole criterion for admission (notwithstanding "race" in some cases among *tirailleurs*) was being wounded or ill, visitation by outsiders was usually restricted, but medical care—even in the midst of huge wards—was personalized. Although most soldiers characterized their treatment in hospitals as being "very good," there were exceptions to the

Mamadou Djigo, exemplar of those characteristics that earned Africans honor in French eyes, circa 1917. An *originaire* from Dakar and literate in French, Djigo was a sergeant in the *Regiment d'Infantrie coloniale de Maroc* and lost his left arm during the retaking of Douaumont, for which he was decorated with the *croix de guerre* and the *médaille militaire*. During his lengthy convalescence, he was accepted into some French homes on terms very near to social equality. Courtesy of the Mamadou Djigo family.

rule. A few doctors were overtly prejudiced against Africans and systematically maltreated them.[60]

In hospitals that retained their civilian staffs, the soldiers often developed personal relationships with precisely those members whom the authorities were most anxious to prevent contacts with—female nurses. Most of the wounded regarded these women, who often acted as intermediaries between soldiers and the doctors, with fondness.[61] In nonsegregated hospitals, some Senegalese also formed friendships with their French ward mates and were introduced to other civilians who visited their friends. Not infrequently, they were invited to call on them when they became well enough to venture outside the hospitals, which they gratefully accepted.[62]

Access to private spaces, such as French homes, was much more restricted. Though some *tirailleurs* were occasionally invited to visit, such courtesies were more commonly extended to *originaires*, and even in their case this was an infrequent occurrence. Moreover, the circumstances governing the character of these contacts varied considerably. In some instances, the visits were so formal as to border on semipublic rituals. Soldiers were invited in groups to the homes of wealthy (and celebrated) French patrons, where they dined and recipients of the *médaille militaire* were sometimes presented with gifts such as watches. Though appreciated, such encounters were brief, constricted, and sometimes represented little more than elegant versions of the interaction that took place in mess halls.[63]

Nevertheless, some Senegalese were welcomed into metropolitan homes on terms resembling social equality. Occasionally invited by chance acquaintances, but more often by French soldiers with whom they had become familiar and especially by their *marraines de guerre*, such encounters, which might be prolonged, offered the best opportunities for becoming more acquainted with French life through close personal interaction.[64] Describing the nature of his relationship with a French comrade, Mamadou Djigo, a decorated sergeant, recalled the reception accorded him by the man's family when he visited his home.

> I had a very good [French] friend—his name was Perout—[and we] were in the same unit. . . . I was his only African friend, [but] we spent a lot of time together. [And] I often went to his house [when on leave]. He invited me [there] for lunch, or dinner, and sometimes I spent the night. . . . And when his [family] came to visit him, they kissed me before they kissed him—his father, his mother, and his sisters.[65]

Relationships with *marraines de guerre* were often still more private affairs and constitute a special category. Though *marraines* facilitated access to French homes, relations with them generally were the most intimate dev ˙ ᴣd by the soldiers with French civilians during the war and transcended purely spatial considerations. Both *tirailleurs* and *originaires* often had French "girlfriends." Mbaye Khary Diagne explained how these relationships were formed and what they signified.

> *"Marraine de guerre"* . . . was the term used by the soldiers to say "my girlfriend;" instead of saying "my girlfriend," they said "my *marraine de guerre*." [And] the African soldiers in France had their *marraines de guerre* too. They were not prostitutes. They were girls of good families who saw us and knew that we were [far from] our countries. [And they realized] we needed some affection and some money . . . to buy cigarettes with, to go to the movies, and so on.
>
> [And we met them] on the street or in cafés. A French girl saw you and felt very pleased by [your appearance]. And she said to you that she wanted to take you to her house to present you to her parents. And you got [an adopted] French family in that way. [But] it wasn't necessary to have love affairs [with them]. From time to time some *marraines de guerre* fell in love with the soldiers they invited home. But generally, they were only friendly relations.[66]

Regardless of the comparative degree of emotional attachment involved in such associations—and some soldiers, as the requests by their *marraines* to marry them attest to, did develop deep personal relationships with them— they afforded the best opportunity for Africans to become more aware of French society.[67] Furthermore, among all their contacts with metropolitan civilians, these were the ones that almost invariably left the most favorable impression on the soldiers.

Though difficult to gauge in quantitative terms, all Senegalese experienced some contact with French soldiers and civilians during the war. The intensity of these encounters, and especially with private citizens, however, varied widely. At one extreme, some Africans remained virtually "isolated" from civilians, and their fleeting impressions of them were often formed only through intermediaries who spoke fragments of their language. At the other, some Senegalese formed intense and lasting personal relationships with individuals they met. Collectively, contacts were generally most frequent and more extensively developed among the *originaires*. These were followed by some *tirailleurs*, especially those who were N.C.O.s or decorated for bravery. Ordinary *tirailleurs* came last, and social intercourse with the French among recent recruits, or those who could not communicate directly with them, was usually the most marginal.[68] Nevertheless, despite the limits of these encounters, they were much more extensive than any that had ever occurred before. These contacts were also substantial enough to contribute toward altering both French and Senegalese prewar perceptions of each other.

RECIPROCAL IMAGES

The French Image of the Senegalese

The metropolitan image of Africans was appreciably altered as a result of the war. In part this was due to more favorable public representations of the soldiers, which assuaged domestic concerns about the Senegalese by casting them in a more acceptable light. But it was also attributable to closer and more sustained contacts with Africans than had ever occurred before in France. Although it is possible to exaggerate both the extent of this change and the influence of personal interaction in facilitating it, the emergence after 1916 of novel attitudes toward Africans is nevertheless discernible.

Prior to the war, most metropolitans, according to Senegalese veterans, had "never seen 'black' people before." Steeped in older myths about African "savagery," initial encounters with the troops usually aroused considerable apprehension. Indeed, as one soldier recalled, at first "the French were [very] afraid of us" and "only eyed [us] from a distance."[69]

The obvious differences in physical appearance between Africans and Europeans nevertheless stimulated intense curiosity. After overcoming their initial reservations, the first impulse, on meeting the Senegalese, of most French men, women, and children was usually identical: they "used to rub [the soldiers'] skin" to see whether the pigmentation was permanent or, beneath a veneer of "dirt" or "paint," their bodies were "white."[70] Indeed, French curiosity about Africans was so pervasive that it was sometimes exploited commercially by the cadres within the Senegalese units. Recalling the carnival atmosphere in which one such early encounter took place, Sera Ndiaye remembered:

> Some of the French who had never seen a "black" man used to pay to come and see us. [And the European soldiers] were making money selling tickets. [They] used to take us to a hidden place and told us: "Stay here. We are going to bring some Frenchmen who have never seen 'black' people before." [But] we didn't know they were making money in that way.
>
> [And after they] got the money, they used to bring the *Tubabs* to look at us. And [they] said: "This one is a Senegalese, this one is a Somalian, [and so forth]." And the *Tubabs* were touching us, and peeking, creeping very close to us because we [looked so different].[71]

After initial fear and curiosity about the Senegalese subsided, the subsequent reactions of the French to the soldiers they met varied. Among a minority of the metropolitan population, earlier racial prejudices apparently persisted unabated and hostility toward the troops was the norm. Africans continued to be denigrated by many as "inferior" beings, and all contact between them and Europeans—especially with French women—was deeply resented. The persistence of these attitudes often led to attempts to intimidate the men: soldiers were publicly humiliated, verbally insulted, and physically provoked. Characterizing this mentality, one decorated and disabled *originaire* bitterly remembered: "For some Frenchmen, the 'nigger' was nothing—nothing!"[72]

Nor were such attitudes manifested only during encounters between individuals. The undiluted racism of the pre-1914 vintage was also frequently exhibited in the actions of many civic officials and military commanders throughout the war. Indeed, even after the armistice, many French municipal councils, though publicly lauding the Senegalese for their contribution to the war effort, refused to countenance the presence of African troops in their communities to undertake public works projects.[73]

Among most metropolitans, however, the more virulent prejudices of the immediate past were ameliorated as a result of the wartime encounter. While this did not necessarily imply acceptance on terms of equality, it did exemplify an enhanced knowledge of Africans and the emergence of more tolerant attitudes toward them. The influence of the more congenial public image of the Senegalese was reflected in the selective response of many metropolitans toward the soldiers, which differentiated among them according to their perceived degree of acculturation or bravery. But beyond these general stereotypes, changing metropolitan attitudes toward Africans were also manifested in other, more direct ways.

Official declamations aside, most ordinary French citizens were genuinely "grateful" to the Senegalese for their contribution to the nation's defense. This was evidenced in the heartfelt cheers of *"bravo les soldats"* and *"vive les tirailleurs sénégalais,"* which accompanied the troops to and from the front.[74] It was also apparent in the warmth of the reception they were frequently accorded when they were on leave from their camps or during convalescence, and after the armistice.

Moreover, in contrast with the immediate prewar period, Africans frequently came to be perceived (and were often treated) as sympathetic figures in the metropole. This was generally apparent in the more charitable literary characterizations of the soldiers that were presented for public consumption after the war, but it was also evidenced in the behavior of many French individuals.[75] It was perhaps most tangible in the expressions of concern for the soldiers' welfare that were offered by *marraines de guerre*, nurses, and other French citizens, who, through their personalized demonstrations of compassion, exemplified a sense of shared humanity that transcended previous racial boundaries.

Finally, among those metropolitans who developed the most intimate relationships with the soldiers, social acceptance on terms of equality was sometimes granted. This was comparatively rare. Nevertheless, some Senegalese formed lasting friendships with their French comrades based on mutual respect, and their relationships were often maintained long after the war ended. The acknowledgment of social equality was, however, most strikingly apparent in the desires to marry that some French women expressed to Senegalese after the armistice. Such plans usually required the approval of their parents, who extended or denied their permission depending on "the character of their [families]." Although some parents and most soldiers were reluctant to give their consent, such overtures illustrate a degree of acceptance that would have been unimaginable before the war.[76]

Despite lingering racial hostility and the superficiality of the alternative stereotypes about the soldiers that was publicly propagated by the government, the wartime encounter nevertheless initiated a discernible shift in French popular perceptions of the Senegalese. This was most pronounced in those areas where maximum contact with the soldiers occurred, but it was also apparent throughout the metropole. No longer abstract figures inspiring horror, the Senegalese now took on discernibly humane qualities. Although French attitudes toward the Africans were still highly pejorative—only in the rarest of circumstances were individuals prepared to accept their basic equality as persons—this gradual transformation was nevertheless a step toward the eventual adoption of an egalitarian viewpoint.

The Senegalese Image of the French

The image that the Senegalese had of the French was also influenced by older preconceptions that derived in large measure from their collective experience in the colonies in the aftermath of the European conquest. Indeed, the soldiers' impressions of the metropolitans they encountered during the war were almost invariably framed within this context. But like their European counterparts—at least after their initial fears of the *Tubabs*, whom some still regarded as "devils," were overcome—closer personal contacts often engendered new attitudes among the soldiers that were dramatically different from their previous perceptions.[77]

Senegalese images of the French were as varied as those of the metropolitans whom they met. Broadly speaking, however, some believed that their experience in France demonstrated a continuity with their treatment in the colonies, and their views of Europeans accordingly remained largely unaltered. Alternatively, others, stressing that "the French had much more consideration for [us] in France than in Senegal," came to see Frenchmen in a significantly different light.[78]

Those espousing the opinion that their perceptions had not been altered probably comprised about one-half of the soldiers recruited or conscripted in Senegal.[79] Composed predominantly of ordinary *tirailleurs*, this group usually had comparatively little contact with local inhabitants, and their impressions of the French were largely circumscribed by their experience in the army. Allowing for individual exceptions among their officers, under such circumstances most felt that there was little appreciable difference in their general treatment by the Europeans overseas as opposed to those they encountered in the colonies. Succinctly summarizing this outlook, the *tirailleur* Malal Gassala explained: "We had no contact with French civilians during the war. . . . The only French we knew fairly well were our officers. . . . Some [were] good, [but] others were very bad; [they] didn't like Africans [and they treated us accordingly]."[80]

The experience of many soldiers, however, often provided a striking contrast to what they had known before the war in Senegal. This group, which included most *originaires* as well as those *tirailleurs* who generally experienced the most intense contacts with metropolitans, obtained a much more sophisticated understanding of Europeans, and this experience, in turn, transformed their earlier image of their colonial overlords. Moreover, although they, like the most isolated *tirailleurs*, drew distinctions between individuals—"there were good and bad people [in the army], just as in life"—they also exhibited a broad consensus about the factors that were most likely to contribute to this differentiation.[81] These soldiers, in short, developed a hierarchical ranking of the French that was founded on the nature of their experiences with those they encountered.

Africans who believed their prewar perceptions had been altered were generally the ones who were exposed to virtually all strata of French society. Aside from soldiers in the army, they encountered peasants, factory and dock workers, members of the petty bourgeoisie (including shopkeepers, bakers, restaurateurs, and hotel concierges), professionals (including bankers, doctors, and lawyers), and the very wealthy. Though frequently aware of these internal social distinctions among the French, the Senegalese did not regard them as especially significant and generally felt well treated by most of the French population, irrespective of their class origins. Nevertheless, they were surprised to learn that social distinctions appeared to be more pronounced in the metropole than in the colonies, and many were especially astonished to discover that some Frenchmen were illiterate.[82]

Although social status appears to have been a comparatively unimportant consideration, notable variation nevertheless existed in the French response to the soldiers. The most fundamental distinction was between the treatment that military personnel and civilians accorded to them. As one *tirailleur* recalled: "We had no problems with the French civilians; [we only] had problems sometimes with French soldiers . . . when they pretended they were superior to [us]."[83]

Gender and the regional origins of the French also entered into play. Overall, the Senegalese were much more favorably disposed toward French women than men. Though this no doubt was due in part to the closer relationships some developed with their *marraines de guerre*, the soldiers generally felt more sympathetically treated—and accepted as individuals—by the women they encountered.[84] Moreover, this assessment stands in marked contrast with their experience in the colonies. There women were few in number and were almost invariably the most racist element among the French *colon* population.[85]

Many of these soldiers also noted regional distinctions among the French. Differences were observed between those from the south and the north; the former were generally more accustomed to seeing Africans, while the latter were often disconcerted by their appearance. Parisians, at least among the *originaires*, were also judged to be more forthcoming and easier to become familiar with than their counterparts from elsewhere in the country. Exceptions to the normal treatment accorded to the soldiers were, however, conspicuous in two instances. Frenchmen from Alsace-Lorraine were considered to have been unusually hostile toward Africans. Their behavior, nevertheless, paled in comparison with that of the "malevolent" Corsicans, who were uniformly regarded as the "most racist" and malicious of the French.[86] Describing the antipathy that developed between them and the Senegalese, as well as lengths to which this might be pursued, Demba Mboup recalled:

A *Tubab* and an African soldier named Ngoue had a very rude discussion [when the Frenchman tried to make him fetch his soup]. And afterwards they fought. And the *Tubab* was a Corsican. [When it was over, he] said to Ngoue, "I'm going to [kill] you."

After [the incident], we went to a restaurant to eat. [And] there was a girl [there]—[she] had a water [bucket] in front of her and she was standing near the restaurant. And the Corsican was very angry because he had been beaten by the African soldier. So he took a rifle and put some bullets in it. [He followed us to the restaurant] and tried to shoot [Ngoue]. But [when he fired] he missed, and instead of hitting the soldier he shot the girl in her chest . . . and she died when they were taking her to the hospital.

The nine soldiers of our squad jumped all over him and tied him up with a rope. And after that, an officer [came] and told [the Corsican] that he would be brought before the *conseil de guerre*.[87]

Despite these conspicuous exceptions, most of these Senegalese felt that they were accorded a greater degree of respect in France than they had ever known in the colonial environment. Though sometimes subjected to personal abuse, they also learned that overt expressions of racism, in contrast with their previous experience, no longer had to be tolerated. Indeed, by the end of the war, the Frenchman who called an African a "dirty nigger" risked a physical beating for his insult. While some Europeans continued to denigrate Africans, most soldiers believed that, overall, those who treated them with "good will" were "much more numerous." Furthermore, they also recognized that for some Frenchmen "the color of a man's skin was unimportant": they might be accepted as "brothers" because, beneath the superficiality of external appearances their "blood was all the same." Africans, in short, might be treated as "equals with the French."[88] This was a heady realization that carried profound implications.

This enhanced awareness of the French arising from the war contrasted dramatically with the image Europeans had previously inspired in the colonies. No longer viewing the French as fearful abstractions—"spirits" or "kings" who treated Africans like "slaves"—many soldiers could distinguish Frenchmen according to important differences, and they came to recognize that like "all people" French attitudes and behavior varied.[89] This knowledge, combined with a wider awareness of the world and an enhanced sense of self-worth engendered by their participation in the war, also spawned novel attitudes and expectations among many.

Such a change in outlook represented a fundamental departure from the mentality of the prewar colonial order. Hence, though the French image of Africans was altered by the war, the reciprocal Senegalese image of their European overlords was changed even more dramatically by it. This new outlook would become manifest in the immediate postwar political environment in Senegal when, with their service overseas at an end, the soldiers returned to their homeland.

NOTES

[1] On the impact of social contact as a stimulus for changing preexisting stereotypes in a colonial setting, see: Rita Cruise O'Brien, *White Society in Black Africa: The French in Senegal* (London: Faber & Faber, 1972), p. 242.

[2] On the history of French attitudes toward Africans, see William B. Cohen, *The French Encounter with Africans: White Responses to Blacks, 1530–1880* (Bloomington and London: Indiana University Press, 1980), pp. 35–100. On the impact of the colonial conquest on images of Africans, see: William H. Schneider, *An Empire for the Masses: The French Popular Image of Africa, 1870–1900* (Westport, CT, and London: Greenwood Press, 1982), pp. 152–211; Véronique Campion-Vincent, "L'image du Dahomey dans la presse française (1890–1895): Les sacrifices humains," *Cahiers d'Etudes Africaines* 25 (1967), pp. 27–58; William B. Cohen, "Literature and Race: Nineteenth Century French Fiction, Blacks and Africa, 1800–1880," *Race and Class* 16 (1974), pp. 181–205. On the pervasiveness of pseudo-scientific racist assumptions about African biological inferiority to Europeans during the late nineteenth and early twentieth centuries, see: George L. Mosse, *Toward the Final Solution: A History of European Racism* (London: Dent, 1978), pp. 77–94; Seymour Drescher, "The Ending of the Slave Trade and the Evolution of European Scientific Racism," *Social Science History* 14 (1990), pp. 415–50; and Nancy Stepan, *The Idea of Race in Science* (London: Macmillan, 1982).

[3] Joe Lunn, "Memoirs of the Maelstrom: A Senegalese Oral History of the First World War" (Ph.D. Diss.: University of Wisconsin–Madison, 1998), pp. 76–102.

[4] Masserigne Soumare: 4A.

[5] Doudou Ndao: 3B; and Momar Khary Diagne: 5A. See also the cartoon in *L'Illustration*, 25 May 1917, in which a cringing German P.O.W. is confronted by a Senegalese guard, with the caption: "Don't be afraid. My marabout forbids me to eat swine" (*Institut de France: Bibliothèque*, Fonds Auguste Terrier, MS 1519: 279). The image of Senegalese soldiers as cannibals was a long-standing French literary theme. See, for example, Guy de Maupassant, "Tombouctou," in *Contes du jour et de la nuit* (Paris: L'Edition d'art H. Piazza, [1885]).

[6] *Les Idées Noires*, no. 1, novembre 1916, p. 1.

[7] *Les Idées Noires*, no. 2, décembre 1916, p. 1.

[8] Cited in: Maurice Dutreb, *Nos Sénégalais pendant la Grande Guerre* (Metz: R. Ferry, 1922), p. 165.

[9] *La Dépêche Coloniale Illustrée*, special numbers of January 1916 and February 1917. The *Comité d'assistance aux troupes noires* (C.A.T.N.) was created as a philanthropic organization that also represented the views of the colonial lobby. Contributing authors to the January 1916 special issue included Maurice Delafosse, Marie-François Clozel, Émile Maurel, and Joseph Chailley.

[10] See "La Prise de la Maisonnette," *L'Illustration*, 9 septembre 1916, pp. 238–42; and "Nos Troupes noires sur la Côte d'Azur," *L'Illustration*, 22 septembre 1917, pp. 301–05. "Nos Sénégalais," *Le Petit Var*, 9 février 1916, p. 1.

[11] *Les Idées Noires*, no. 1, novembre 1916, p. 1.

[12] Léon Gaillet, *Coulibaly: Les Sénégalais sur la terre de France* (Paris: Jouve, 1917), pp. 15–22.

[13] Léon Gaillet, *Deux ans avec les sénégalais* (Paris: Berger-Levrault, 1918), p. 64.

[14] Léon Bocquet and Ernest Hosten, *Un fragment de l'épopée sénégalaise: Les tirailleurs noirs sur l'Yser* (Brussels and Paris: G. Van Oest, 1918), pp. 5–8.

[15] Alphonse Séché, *Les Noirs: D'après des documents officiels* (Paris: Payot, 1919), p. 50.

[16] Ibid., pp. 37–39, 42, 26–36, 59.

[17] This trend became still more accentuated immediately after the war. Though incorporating many of the wartime literary conventions about African soldiers, the portrayal of the fate of a single *tirailleur* in the novels of the Tharaud brothers was intended to elicit sympathy for his plight. See: Jérôme Tharaud and Jean Tharaud, *La randonnée de Samba Diouf* (Paris: Plon, 1922). For a still more compelling portrait of the soldiers that eschews many of the prevailing stereotypes (and which, significantly, was written by a woman), see: Lucie Cousturier, *Des inconnus chez moi* (Paris: La Suene, 1920).

[18] Nar Diouf: 2B; and Sickh Yero Sy: 1B.

[19] *AG*: État-Major de l'Armée (hereafter EMA): 7 N 441. On other considerations governing the location of the training camps (including rail access, availability of drinking water, etc.), see also: *AG*: EMA: 7 N 440 and 7 N 1990.

[20] *AG*: EMA: 7 N 144.

[21] Séché, *Les Noirs*, pp. 235–56. On the hospital at Menton, see also: Momar Khary Niang: 1A; and Mbaye Khary Diagne: 1A and 6A.

[22] On the connection between race theory and language instruction, see the guide issued by the army to teach the Senegalese French: *Le Français tel que le parlent les tirailleurs sénégalais* (Paris: L. Fournier, 1916).

[23] The practical consequences of instructing the soldiers in "*petit nègre*" are discussed at length in: Cousturier, *Des inconnus chez moi*.

[24] *AG*: EMA: 7 N 440.

[25] Séché, *Les Noirs*, pp. 235–56.

[26] After August 1917, *originaires* were granted furloughs of 25 days to their colony of origin after 18 months of service, while *tirailleurs* obtained 4 months of leave in Africa after 4 years of service only in October 1918: *AG*: Fonds Clemenceau: 6 N 97; *AG*: EMA: 7 N 144 and 7 N 1990. On the permission policy, see also: *AG*: EMA: 7 N 440 and 7 N 2121.

[27] *ANOM*: Affaires politiques: 3036: 2.

[28] *ANOM*: Affaires politiques: 3036: 3; and *ANS*: Affaires militaires: 4 D 71.

[29] *ANOM*: Affaires politiques: 3034: 3.

[30] On the regulation of brothels by the army, see especially: Masserigne Soumare: 3B and 4A. On the authorities' attitudes toward "dissolute" women, see: *AN*: Papiers Mangin: 149 AP 12.

[31] *ANS*: Affaires militaires: 4 D 89. See also: *ANOM*: Affaires politiques: 3034/3; and Séché, *Les Noirs*, pp. 235–56.

[32] *ANOM*: Affaires politiques: 3034: 3. *Marraines de guerre* were encouraged to "adopt" soldiers and sustain their morale with letters, gifts, and visits to their homes when the soldiers were on leave. See also: Charles J. Balesi, *From Adversaries to Comrades in Arms: West Africans and the French Military, 1885–1919* (Waltham, MA: Crossroads Press, 1979), pp. 296–98.

[33] For those departments where the Senegalese presence was most extensive, see Map 4.1.

[34] Sickh Yero Sy: 1B. Nar Diouf: 2B. On the character of junior officers, N.C.O.s, and French cadres assigned to the Senegalese units, who were often deemed to be poor soldiers and changed assignments rapidly, see: *AG*: Grand Quartier Général (hereafter GQG): 16 N 196 and 16 N 2094; *AG*: Unités: 22 N 2481 and 26 N 871.

[35] Yoro Diaw: 2A; see also *AG*: GQG: 16 N 196 and 16 N 2094. On the refusal of some French soldiers to salute Africans, see: Abdou Karim Gaye: 5B.

[36] Antoine Diouf: 1A; Souleye Samba Ndiaye: 1B; Malal Gassala: 2B. Sera Ndiaye: 4A.

[37] Doudou Ndao: 3A; Nar Diouf: 2B; and Sera Ndiaye: 4A. Momar Khary Niang: 1A and 1B. Almost two-thirds of the *tirailleurs* interviewed (19 out of 32) referred to encounters with French soldiers. About one-third of these characterized their relations in a consistently positive light, while two-thirds indicated that the nature of their experience depended on the attitudes of the individuals involved. Only one respondent (Abdoulaye Gassama) described the behavior of the French in exclusively negative terms.

[38] The ratios of *originaires* to Europeans varied considerably depending on the units. For the range of variation and the circumstances that prompted it, see: Abdoulaye Diaw: 1A; Thiecouta Diallo: 1A; and Abdoulaye Gueye: 1A.

[39] Mamadou Djigo: 5B; Mbaye Khary Diagne: 4A; and Ousmane Diagne: 4A. On verbal and physical abuse by French N.C.O.s, see also: *ANOM*: 14 MI 346. On deaths ultimately resulting from insults, see: Mamadou Djigo: 5B; Boubacar Gueye: 2A; and Demba Mboup: 10A and 10B.

[40] Ndiaga Niang: 2A.

[41] Abdoulaye Gueye: 2A; Mbaye Khary Diagne: 4A; Aliou Diakhate: 1A; and Ousmane Diagne: 3B. On Diagne's intervention on behalf of the soldiers, see also: *AG*: Fonds Clemenceau: 6 N 97, *AG*: EMA: 7 N 1990, and *ANOM*: 14 MI 346. On friction caused by contact with other "colonials," and particularly with those from Martinique and

Guadeloupe, who also denigrated the Senegalese, see: Jacques William: 2B; and Aliou Diakhate: 1A.

[42] See, respectively: Abdoulaye Diaw: 1B; Mamadou Djigo: 6A and Abdoulaye Ndiaye: 4B; Mamadou Djigo: 5B; and Mbaye Khary Diagne: 4A.

[43] For especially detailed descriptions of personal friendships, see: Thiecouta Diallo: 1A; Giribul Diallo: 1B; and Mamadou Djigo: 3A. Thirteen of fifteen *originaires* interviewed offered characterizations of the French soldiers they served with. Two-thirds felt that their relations with them depended on the attitude of the individual; one-third described them in a consistently favorable light, and one (Boubacar Gueye) was exclusively negative in his critique of their behavior.

[44] See, respectively: Sickh Yero Sy: 1B and Masserigne Soumare: 1B; Malal Gassala: 2B; and Yoro Diaw: 2A and Nar Diouf 2A.

[45] For descriptions of French hospitals, which ranged from those that were segregated and devoid of civilian staff, those that were segregated but included civilians, to those that were integrated and maintained by civilian personnel, see, respectively: Nouma Ndiaye: 2B, and Momar Khary Niang: 1A; Antoine Diouf: 1A, Makhoudia Ndiaye: 1A and 1B, and Bara Seck: 1A; and Sera Ndiaye: 3A. On factories, see: Doudou Ndao: 3B; Yoro Diaw: 2A; and Abdou Karim Gaye: 4A and 4B. See also: *AG*: EMA: 7 N 441 and *AG*: Unités: 22 N 2468.

[46] On leave, see especially: Doudou Ndao: 3B; Sambou Ndiaye: 1B; Nar Diouf: 2B; Yoro Diaw 2A; Masserigne Soumare: 5B; Souleye Samba Ndiaye: 1B; and Nouma Ndiaye: 2B. On convalescence, see: Sera Ndiaye: 4A; and Nouma Ndiaye: 2B. On permissions, see: Daba Dembele: 5B; Masserigne Soumare: 2B and 3A; and Abdou Karim Gaye (5A), who expressed the bitterness felt by many *tirailleurs* about the favoritism shown to *originaires* with regard to this policy.

[47] On transit, see: Momar Candji: 1B. On factories and work in French harbors, see, respectively: Alassane Kane: 3A, and Ndiaga Niang: 2A. For descriptions of the integrated hospitals in which the *originaires* received care, see: Mamadou Djigo: 5A; Demba Mboup: 5B; Mbaye Khary Diagne: 3B; and Aliou Diakhate: 1B.

[48] On the more liberal leave policies in some camps where *originaires* were garrisoned, see: Ousmane Diagne: 5A. On convalescence, see: Mamadou Djigo: 5A; and Mbaye Khary Diagne: 4A. On French policy regarding "permissions" for *originaires*, see: Ndiaga Niang: 1B; and Giribul Diallo: 2B. See also: *AG*: EMA: 7 N 144.

[49] Samba Laga Diouf: 1B.

[50] Among fifteen *originaires* interviewed, over 85 percent were fluent in French before the war, and the remainder became so in the army. Moreover, about 50 percent of these men were literate. Among 32 *tirailleurs* consulted, 2 (6 percent) were literate; at least 5 (16 percent) were probably fluent; 10 (32 percent) could communicate in French, although their vocabularies were limited; and 3 (9 percent) could not speak the language at all. Also, 14 (44 percent of the total) made no reference to their comprehension of French, and it is likely that their command of the language was either limited or nearly nonexistent. For examples of the range of variation, see especially: Demba Mboup: 10B, Boubacar Gueye: 2A, and Ndiaga Niang: 1B (all of whom could mimic regional accents); Antoine Diouf: 1B; Nar Diouf: 2B; Yoro Diaw: 2B; Nouma Ndiaye: 2B; and Biram Mbodj Tine: 2B.

[51] There are no official records of the numbers of Senegalese wounded. Nevertheless, fragmentary information suggests that the percentage was very high indeed. In 1922, the *Commandant Supérieur de Troupes du Groupe de l'Afrique Occidentale*

Française reported that among the *originaires*, soldiers wounded severely enough to be released from service (e.g., missing limbs) amounted to 86.1 percent of those who died during the war: *ANOM*: 14 MI 2356. Among 26 *tirailleurs* interviewed who served as combatants, 18 mention whether they were wounded or not. Of these, 89 percent were wounded on one or more occasions; 72 percent required hospitalization; and 39 percent were hurt so badly that they were subsequently discharged to Senegal with permanent disabilities. As a percentage of all *tirailleur* combatants, including those who make no reference to wounds, the figures are 62 percent, 50 percent, and 30 percent, respectively. These proportions represent an absolute minimum among these men. Among 15 *originaires*, 60 percent referred to being wounded, at least 40 percent were hospitalized because of their injuries, and 20 percent were permanently disabled.

[52] Abdou Karim Gaye: 5B; and Nar Diouf: 3B. Masserigne Soumare: 1B. Mamadou Djigo: 3A; and Abdoulaye Ndiaye: 5A. This outlook was also institutionalized. Among *originaires*, recipients of the *médaille militaire avec palmes*, which was awarded for conspicuous acts of courage, were granted one week "permission" in Paris and 300 francs (Demba Mboup: 10B). Medals such as the *croix de guerre* (presented for distinguished military service) were also much more rarely awarded to Senegalese than to French troops: *AG*: Fonds Clemenceau: 6 N 97.

[53] This typology derives from W. Scott Haine, *The World of the Paris Cafe: Sociability among the French Working Class, 1789–1914* (Baltimore: Johns Hopkins University Press, 1996).

[54] On encounters of the Senegalese with French children—which was an especially favorite French theme about Africans because it corroborated their image of them as *"grands enfants"*—see: Nar Diouf: 2A; Demba Mboup: 10B, and Jacques William: 2B. For examples, see, respectively: Nouma Ndiaye: 2B; Yoro Diaw: 2A; Mbaye Khary Diagne: 4A; Doudou Ndao 3B; and Niaki Gueye: 3B.

[55] Nar Diouf: 2B. Souleye Samba Ndiaye: 1B; and Ishmale Mbange: 4A. Niaki Gueye: 3B; and Giribul Diallo: 1B.

[56] On brothels and prostitutes, see: Masserigne Soumare: 3B; Alassane Kane: 3A; Ibrahima Camara: 2B; and Giribul Diallo: 1B. On the comparatively high salaries of American troops (which in the case of privates were nearly double that of their French and British counterparts), see "Rapport Marin," *Journal Officiel de la République Française. Documents Parlementaires, Chambre*, 1920, annexe 638, pp. 68–69.

[57] On factories, see: Yoro Diaw: 1B and 2A; Abdou Karim Gaye: 4A and 4B; and Alassane Kane: 3A. See also: *AG*: EMA: 7 N 1990 and 7 N 1991; and Tyler Stovall, "The Color Line behind the Lines: Racial Violence in France during the Great War," *American Historical Review* 103 (1998), pp. 737–69. On places of public entertainment, see: Abdoulaye Gassama: 2A; Mamadou Djigo: 5A and 5B; Niaki Gueye: 1B and 2A; Mbaye Khary Diagne: 4A; and Sera Ndiaye: 4A. On the cinema, see: Sera Ndiaye: 4A; and Mamadou Djigo: 5A.

[58] Boubacar Gueye: 2A. On barroom brawls, see: Masserigne Soumare: 3B and 4A. On relations with proprietors, see: Ousmane Diagne: 5B. Nar Diouf: 6A; Momar Candji: 1B; Ousmane Diagne: 5B; and Abdoulaye Ndiaye: 4B.

[59] On *hôtels de ville*, see: Momar Candji: 1B. Abdoulaye Ndiaye: 5A; and Aliou Diakhate: 1A.

[60] Aliou Diakhate: 1B; Nouma Ndiaye: 2B; Mbaye Khary Diagne: 3B; Antoine Diouf: 1A; Demba Mboup: 5B; Makhoudia Ndiaye: 1B. Demba Mboup: 11A.

Wounded German prisoners were also maltreated by some French doctors (Demba Mboup: 9B). On German wounded in French hospitals, see also: Mbaye Khary Diagne: 6A.

[61] Makhoudia Ndiaye: 1A and 1B; Demba Mboup: 11A, and Antoine Diouf: 1A. This was also true in German hospitals (which were not segregated), where wounded Senegalese were cared for after being taken prisoner. See: Mamadou Bokar: 1A.

[62] Sera Ndiaye: 3A; Masserigne Soumare: 3B; Mamadou Djigo: 5B; Mbaye Khary Diagne: 3B. Mamadou Djigo: 5B; Mbaye Khary Diagne: 3B.

[63] Aliou Diakhate: 1A and 1B; Abdoulaye Ndiaye: 5A; and Sickh Yero Sy: 1B.

[64] On invitations to French homes, see: Giribul Diallo: 1B; Mamadou Djigo: 2B; Mbaye Khary Diagne: 4A and 4B; Ousmane Diagne: 5B; Abdoulaye Ndiaye: 5A; Masserigne Soumare: 4A.

[65] Mamadou Djigo: 3A.

[66] Mbaye Khary Diagne: 4A and 4B. On relationships with marraines de guerre, see also: Ousmane Diagne: 5B; Mamadou Djigo: 6A; Demba Mboup: 10B and 11A; Aliou Diakhate: 1A; and Masserigne Soumare: 3B and 4A.

[67] On marriage proposals by marraines de guerre, see: Masserigne Soumare: 4A; Ousmane Diagne: 5B; Mamadou Djigo: 6A; and Mbaye Khary Diagne: 4A.

[68] Among the originaires interviewed, 12 of 15 mentioned contacts with the French. Three-quarters of these described encounters with military personnel, while all but one referred to meetings with civilians. The comparative intensity of these encounters can best be indicated by the fact that nearly two-thirds of the men in this latter group had marraines de guerre, or French "girlfriends." Among tirailleurs, about two-thirds mention the degree of contact they had with metropolitans; these were divided almost equally between those who interacted with French civilians and those who had little or no contact with them. Among those in the former group, nearly one-half were N.C.O.s, one-half probably spoke French, and three-quarters were hospitalized for wounds. In the latter group, only 1 in 9 was an N.C.O. or spoke French, while only about one-third (which included noncombatant 1918 recruits) were hospitalized for wounds.

[69] Nar Diouf: 2B. Masserigne Soumare: 4A; and Abdoulaye Ndiaye: 5A. On initial contacts, see also: Marc Michel, "Les troupes coloniales arrivent," Histoire, no. 69 (1984), pp. 116–21.

[70] Daba Dembele: 3A; see also Yoro Diaw: 2A. Daba Dembele: 1A and 2B; Sera Ndiaye: 4A; Sambou Ndiaye: 1B; and Jacques William: 2B. Later in the war, and depending on the circumstances, such behavior could be interpreted as insulting, and it sometimes provoked fights. Mbaye Khary Diagne: 4A.

[71] Sera Ndiaye: 4A. On prewar French exhibitions of Africans, which the European soldiers may have used as models for their activities, see: Schneider, An Empire for the Masses.

[72] Masserigne Soumare: 3B; and Boubacar Gueye: 2A. See also: ANOM: Affaires politiques: 3034: 3. Sera Ndiaye: 4A; Ndiaga Niang: 2A; and Mbaye Khary Diagne: 4A. Mamadou Djigo: 5B.

[73] See Chapter 5. On the "racist" paranoia of some French commanders about contacts between Senegalese and European troops, see also: Ousmane Diagne: 4A. On postwar opposition to stationing Senegalese troops in Marseilles, Sète, La Rochelle, Bordeaux, St. Louis du Rhone, and other towns, see: AG: EMA: 7 N 1990. The French aversion to having Africans garrisoned in their towns can be contrasted with German resentment to their use in the occupation of the Rhineland.

[74] Sera Ndiaye: 4A. See also Philippe Dewitte, *Les Mouvements nègres en France, 1919–1939* (Paris: Editions L'Harmattan, 1985), pp. 44–50. Ousmane Diagne: 5B; and Masserigne Soumare: 1B.

[75] For examples of literary characterizations, see: Cousturier, *Des inconnus chez moi*; and Tharaud and Tharaud, *La randonnée de Samba Diouf*. See also: Ada Martinbus-Zemp, *Le Blanc et le Noir: Essai d'une description de la vision du Noir par le Blanc dans la littérature française de l'entre-deux-guerres* (Paris: A-G Nizet, 1975).

[76] Mamadou Djigo: 2B; and Amar Seck: 3A. Mamadou Djigo: 6B. On proposals of marriage, see: Ndiaga Niang: 1B and 3A; Ousmane Diagne: 5B; Mamadou Djigo: 6A; Niaki Gueye: 2A; Demba Mboup 10B and 11A; Mbaye Khary Diagne: 1A and 4A; and Masserigne Soumare: 4A. Significantly, most of these men were *originaires* and all were fluent in French. The social class of the women involved in these love affairs warrants further research. Only two soldiers referred to the origins of the women they considered becoming betrothed to. One was the daughter of a baker in Meurthe et Moselle; the other, whose name was Jeannette Limon, lived in Marseilles. See, respectively: Ndiaga Niang: 1B and 3A; and Ousmane Diagne: 5B. Such marriages, as was well known, faced formidable difficulties. In addition to the racial prejudices harbored by many French people, most African families were strongly opposed to interracial matches on cultural grounds. And although some did occur—notably Lamine Senghor's marriage to his *marraine de guerre*—most soldiers eschewed them for this reason. For a novel exploring the theme of marriage between an African soldier and a French woman, see: André Demaison and Pierre Mille, *Amour d'une blanche pour un noir* (Paris: Editions de France, 1924).

[77] Daba Dembele: 3A. On initial apprehensions about the French, see also: Nar Diouf: 2B.

[78] Abdoulaye Diaw: 3B.

[79] Comparatively few of the Senegalese interviewed expressed an opinion about whether their prewar image of the French was altered as a result of their service overseas. Among *tirailleurs* who did so, two looked on the French more favorably after the war, while four believed there was no appreciable difference. Among *originaires*, however, the corresponding numbers were three to one. If one infers what the soldiers' attitudes would be from other remarks, the estimate for other *tirailleurs* would be four favorable to ten unchanged. For other *originaires*, the estimate would be two favorable and none unchanged. The outlook of the remaining soldiers is either difficult to gauge or unmentioned.

[80] Malal Gassala: 2B.

[81] Lattyr Ndoye: 2B.

[82] See, respectively: Nouma Ndiaye: 2B, and Ndiaga Niang: 1B; Yoro Diaw: 1B and 2A, Abdou Karim Gaye: 4A and 4B, and Ndiaga Niang: 2A; Nar Diouf: 2B, Ndiaga Niang: 1B, Ousmane Diagne: 5A, and Abdoulaye Ndiaye: 5A; Abdoulaye Ndiaye: 5A, Aliou Diakhate: 1B, and Masserigne Soumare: 2B. Thiecouta Diallo: 1A.

[83] Sera Ndiaye: 4A. See also Masserigne Soumare: 3B.

[84] None of the soldiers characterized any of the women they met in France (in contrast to those they encountered in the colonies) in a negative light. For examples of favorable impressions of women in a wide variety of contexts, see: Doudou Ndao: 3B; Momar Candji: 1B; Sickh Yero Sy: 1B; Makhoudia Ndiaye: 1A and 1B; Demba Mboup: 11A; Mamadou Bokar: 1A and 1B; Niaki Gueye: 1A; Aliou Diakhate: 1A; Abdoulaye Gassama: 2A; Ousmane Diagne: 5B; and Mbaye Khary Diagne: 1A.

[85] O'Brien, *White Society in Black Africa*, pp. 237–36, 240–60. See also Chapter 1.

[86] Abdoulaye Ndiaye: 5A. On differences between the views of northerners and southerners, see also: Boubacar Gueye: 2A; and Ousmane Diagne: 5A. Ndiaga Niang: 2A. Malal Gassala: 2B; and Demba Mboup: 11A. On accusations by Blaise Diagne of Alsacian hostility toward the Senegalese, see also: *ANOM*: 14 MI 346. Demba Mboup: 10B; and Boubacar Gueye: 2A. On Corsicans, who, significantly, were overrepresented in the prewar colonial administration, see also: Malal Gassala: 2B; and *AG*: GQG: 16 N 2094.

[87] Demba Mboup: 10A. Some Corsicans also shot African soldiers they saw with French girls (Boubacar Gueye: 2A).

[88] Mbaye Khary Diagne: 4A; and Mamadou Djigo: 5A. Ishmale Mbange: 4A; and Doudou Ndao: 3A. Mamadou Djigo: 5B; Daour Gueye: 4B; and Mbaye Khary Diagne: 2B. Doudou Ndao: 3A.

[89] Mamadou Djigo: 6A. On prewar Senegalese images of the French, see the table of equivalents in Chapter 1.

7

Beneath the Roots of the Baobab:[1] The Repatriation of the Soldiers and the Postwar Colonial Order in Senegal

With the cessation of hostilities in November 1918, French imperatives once again shifted dramatically. No longer concerned with raising unprecedented numbers of African troops to help sustain the metropolitan war effort, the French authorities turned toward reintegrating tens of thousands of returning veterans back into colonial society.

The prospect of this transition aroused dire forebodings among many colonial administrators. Seeking to return to the prewar status quo, most local officials were apprehensive about the changes in the soldiers' attitudes arising from their service overseas, and about the impact their presence would have on the stability of the colonial regime and on Senegalese society.

The *colons* had cause for concern. Most soldiers had indeed acquired a new view of themselves and of the French as a result of their wartime experience, which they soon conveyed in a wide variety of ways to those in their homeland. Exactly how the tensions between the novel attitudes and aspirations aroused among many Africans as a result of the war and the interests of the colonial regime were resolved during the subsequent decade is the theme of this chapter. It explores the veterans' postwar reintegration into colonial society from several perspectives: how they were received by the French authorities as well as by their families when they first returned to Senegal; how the political aspirations engendered by the war, particularly the emphasis on acquiring "rights" articulated by Blaise Diagne between 1915 and 1918, influenced the dynamics of the postwar colonial order; and the extent to which the soldiers' subsequent lives were affected by their wartime service.

THE SOLDIERS' RETURN

Demobilization

The signing of the Armistice on 11 November 1918 was greeted with scenes of ecstatic rejoicing throughout France. In the trenches, the eerie quiet that ensued after the guns finally fell silent was quickly replaced by noisy exultation. The soldiers "beat on boxes," danced at their posts, joked with their comrades, and shouted the unbelievable news: "The war is over! The war is over!" Indeed, within a few hours "it seemed that all the bells in France were ringing together."[2]

Amid the ongoing celebrations that followed during the subsequent weeks, the soldiers' thoughts also turned to more personal concerns. Most longed to see their loved ones and homeland again. As one soldier recalled: "We had had enough of France; [the] only thing in our heads was returning home."[3]

After their battalions were disbanded, the soldiers embarked for Africa either from Marseilles or Bordeaux.[4] The voyage to Senegal was much better than the one to France. The soldiers were freed from most of the apprehensions that had plagued them during their earlier transit, and they contented themselves with the pursuit of leisure activities and by contemplating the reunion with their families and friends. Many of the men also bridled at being treated by outgoing *colons* as they had been before their departure from Senegal. Indeed, the soldiers' insistence on being accorded a new degree of respect from Europeans sometimes led to confrontations with them. Recalling one such incident, a decorated veteran, Demba Mboup, recounted:

> One day [we were on] the ship that brought us back to Senegal from Bordeaux. . . . There were [many] Senegalese soldiers [aboard, and sometimes] they got into arguments with some of the "white" men who treated them like "dirty niggers." . . . And one of these soldiers—a citizen from Goree—was [called] a "*sale nègre*" by a "white" man. . . . I think maybe the [French]man was not well educated, or perhaps he was drunk. [And the soldier hit] him hard . . . and [they] started fighting. [And] we all [joined in] and started to give our friend some help. And we beat [the Frenchman] badly until he asked to be forgiven. He was crying and said that he would never do it again.
>
> So what happened [afterwards]? Nothing! We were within our rights, because discrimination between people [was no longer tolerated] at that

time, [and] we were French citizens like anybody else. [If] the "white" man wanted to start acting like that, we [could retaliate] and nothing happened. [But] if the same thing had happened before the war, [we] would not have done the same thing. Because we had less power then, and [we] were treated badly like this [by the French] all the time.[5]

Other such manifestations of this "new mentality," with its unwelcome implications for the previous tenor of colonial relations and the "prestige of [our] authority," were precisely what the local French authorities were most anxious to avoid when the soldiers returned to Senegal. On their arrival in Dakar, the men were dispatched to one of the training camps of the Colonial Army, where they usually spent several days or even weeks having their discharge papers processed and receiving back pay before being mustered out of the army.[6] Thereafter, the *tirailleurs* were instructed to report to the local *commandants* upon their return to their respective *cercles*. In addition to providing a record of their arrival, however, such visits also often served to impress on the veterans the type of behavior that was expected of them. Mandiaye Ndiaye recalled:

When we came back here, we went to the house of the *commandant*. And he told us: "You have been in the army [and] you were performing a service for the country. But the men and women you left [behind] here were also contributing a service to the country. So don't presume you are better than they are because you have been in France and you have been in the army. You are [all] the same. So you are to act like [you did] before [the war], and if anyone tries to provoke you, don't respond to him. Try to come and tell me [what happened]. I don't want you to have any trouble with [any of] the people here."[7]

The Veterans' Homecoming

For most young veterans, the day they finally returned to their homes and were reunited with their loved ones was "one of the most memorable" of their entire lives. Usually having been absent for three or more years, and sometimes having had no communication with their families, the soldiers were welcomed by relatives who had often given up all hope that they would ever return.[8]

Under such circumstances, the soldiers' sudden reappearance—which often took those whom they had left behind completely by surprise—occasioned the most effusive outpourings of emotion and thanksgiving. Parents embraced their children and wept for joy; friends crowded around, touching them to reassure their disbelieving eyes of their physical presence or paraded them about held aloft on their shoulders; and praises were offered to the Almighty for their safe deliverance. Spontaneous celebrations were also or-

ganized everywhere. Entire communities were often invited to eat and join
in the festivities: people sang and danced until they were weary, the soldiers
presented gifts acquired in France to their families, and everyone extolled
the courage of the veterans.[9] Describing one such scene in the Serer village
of Diakhao, Nouma Ndiaye recalled:

> [When I came walking towards my father's house, everyone] was very
> surprised to see me coming. And they were [all] shouting. And all night
> long, no one went to sleep; everyone was awake. [And] they prepared a lot
> of couscous and killed a lot of goats. [And] everybody was singing, and
> dancing, and eating all night long. And they were beating *tam tams* too.
> [And] there was a specific song [they used to sing] for the soldiers coming
> back from the war. It was different from [all] the other songs. They were
> singing:
>
>> "You have proved your courage during the war.
>> You are very brave.
>> You were wounded [in the war].
>> So that is proof you have been in the fight."
>
> And everyone was singing—even those of noble [birth]. But they [also]
> gave some money to the *griots* after they sang.[10]

The joyous reception accorded to the soldiers was, however, tempered in
some instances by a few unpleasant realizations. Though relieved to see their
sons again, many families were distressed when they returned not as they
had left but as invalids. Some veterans were distressed to learn that their
wives had remarried in their long absence.[11] And, worst of all, many soldiers
simply did not return, and the painful task of informing parents about the
manner of their deaths usually fell to the young men who had survived:

> [The parents of those who had been killed] knew the number of soldiers
> who went to the war together, and they [also] knew the number of soldiers
> who came back. So no one [had to tell] them that their sons were dead;
> they guessed it [on their own]. [But afterward], we told them how they
> died. Those [of us who] knew how their sons had died explained to their
> families [what had happened to them]. . . . [I had to do this once.] . . . A
> son [from my grandfather's family] was lost in Champagne. . . . And [they]
> knew that we went [to the war] together. But when I came back, they didn't
> see him. And after a while, they began to ask me where he was. And I told
> them: "He is dead; you have to make the sacrifices."[12]

Hence, after the celebrations commemorating the safe arrival of returning
soldiers subsided, there followed a period of mourning for those who failed
to come back.

The *Anciens Combattants*

Nearly all of the returning veterans were "tremendously happy to be home [again]." Deeply weary from their exertions during the war, frustrated by the years they had "lost" in the army, and delighted to be "free" from the dictates of military discipline, most of the demobilized soldiers desired nothing more than to resume their former lives.[13] Nevertheless, despite their yearning for a return to "normalcy," the veterans had been changed by their wartime experience, and, as a group, this inevitably set them apart from those they had left behind. Their new outlook was manifested in a series of ways, ranging from subtle alterations in their behavior to more profound changes in their attitudes, which often bespoke an altogether novel mentality. These changes were evidenced in the soldiers' relations with both those in their communities and with the French.

Although some inhabitants were "a little bit afraid" of the veterans when they first reappeared, the reverse was far more often the case. Indeed, most soldiers were treated with exceptional "consideration" by the members of their communities, who recognized that they "had changed" but did their utmost to "make [them] feel at home again." Notwithstanding the heightened "nervous[ness]" exhibited by some former combatants, the most obvious difference in the soldiers' behavior was in their acquisition of "*Tubab* habits." Most veterans returned wearing "European clothes" instead of the traditional *boubou*, many mixed French words with their mother tongues, some smoked tobacco, and nearly all "kept papers."[14] In addition to these new personal idiosyncrasies, the former soldiers' patterns of interaction with others also sometimes deviated from customary social conventions. Describing the transformation in one returning *tirailleur*, his female cousin, Gamou Wade, remembered:

> I felt a change in [Abdoulaye], because he was very kind when he came back. He used to do everything in the house. [For example,] when I wanted to cook something, [and when] the cooking pot was too heavy for me [to lift], [he] used to come and help me. And when I wanted to burn some pieces of wood during the rainy season, [he] used to come and tell me: "Let me do that for you. When I was in France, we used to burn some wet wood, [but] you don't know how to [do it]." And he was showing me how to burn wet wood and some [other] small things like that, [which] he didn't do before going [to the war]. ... And I appreciated very much that Abdoulaye was helping me, [because] none [of the other men] ever thought of helping [the women] in the kitchen.[15]

Though occasionally arousing indignation—especially if customary dress continued to be eschewed or if religious rituals, such as Ramadan, failed to be observed—most veterans eventually modified their peculiar habits to the extent that they became acceptable. Nonetheless, they continued to exert a novel influence on their communities in other ways. Knowledge was ordinarily considered the preserve of elders, while the acquisition of bride wealth usually depended on the patronage of older kinsmen. In both cases, however, the former soldiers frequently presented exceptions to these rules. While most young men gave the money they received in the army to their parents or guardians, some retained it, and they could afford to enter into marriage contracts without assistance. Moreover, the veterans possessed a knowledge of the world beyond their homeland that was ordinarily unattainable through any other means. Despite the comparative youth of the returning soldiers, most members of their communities were eager to learn about their experiences: their lives in the army, what the war was like, and especially their impressions of Europe and the *Tubabs*. Although this attention sometimes aroused the envy of elder kinsmen, their knowledge also proved beneficial, particularly in dealings with the French.[16]

In this regard, the veterans frequently acted as cultural intermediaries for their communities. Fathers of young men about to be drafted eagerly sought their council about what their sons could expect in the army; village chiefs asked those who were fluent in French to act as their interpreters during discussions with *commandants*; and visiting French *commerçants* accorded the former soldiers a degree of "respect" seldom witnessed before.[17] The local impact of the presence of the veterans was also evidenced in the outspoken example they set for others, which contrasted with the ways most Africans were accustomed to being treated by the French. As Aliou Dioama, the son of a former *tirailleur*, remembered with pride:

> When [my father] came back, he had learned many things from the war and [about] the "white" man. . . . He had gained more understanding about the kinds of ways officials should [behave]. So he contributed a lot to the change of many things. Because he said "no" when he was [within his rights] to say "no" and "yes" [only] when he [decided] to say "yes." And he didn't accept any longer this official cheating [of] people or telling [them] something that was not [true].[18]

The Veterans' Associations

The unique status of the former soldiers in Senegalese society was further exemplified by the introduction of a novel institution immediately after the war— the Veterans' Association. By 1919, *Anciens combattants* had founded associations in each of the communes. They were also established in many commercial towns in the interior, even though the local French authorities often sought to prohibit them, a move that was overruled by the Ministry of Colonies in response to formal complaints from the veterans. Soon thereafter, the organization spread to still remoter villages in the countryside. These latter groups were usually small and informal associations of former soldiers. They met periodically to

Review of Senegalese troops, Dakar, 1919. Courtesy of Centre des Archives d'outre-mer, Aix-en-Provence (Archives nationales. France) (5 Fi 2575). Reprinted with permission.

discuss common problems, provided collective financial assistance to members to meet special needs, and organized festivals and other collaborative endeavors in their communities.[19]

The larger associations, which usually numbered several hundred members, in the communes and the principal towns of the Protectorate were organized more formally. Officers were elected, and meetings were held on a regular basis (usually two or three times per month) in the local *maison des anciens combattants*. Different sections existed for *originaires* and *tirailleurs*, as well as sub-sections for *mutilés de guerre* and P.O.W.s. Parades were held on special occasions, including 14 July and 11 November, when bemedaled veterans marched beneath regimental flags to commemorate their service on behalf of France.[20]

In contrast with the smaller rural associations, these larger veterans groups took an active interest in political affairs. Though officially nonpartisan in communal elections, many of their members nevertheless actively campaigned for candidates, and collectively they constituted an influential and important interest group. The associations also included prominent political activists, who, in addition to helping found the veterans' groups, were instrumental, for example, in organizing the first Senegalese labor unions in the colony. The veterans' associations also frequently functioned as formal lobbies, and they periodically convoked assemblies to select spokesmen to "defend [their] rights," both as veterans and as Africans, before the colonial administration.[21]

Such actions were unprecedented in Senegal, and they exemplified a novel mentality on the part of many veterans. This new sense of self-assurance engendered by their wartime service and the absence of fear it bespoke was perhaps best summarized in the observation of Mbaye Khary Diagne, a former soldier from the communes: "Before you know well about life you have to enter the army. [Because once] you have been in the army and [fought in] the war, [compared to that] nothing [else in life] can [ever] give you a problem."[22] This was an outlook that, when combined with the aspirations aroused among other Senegalese between 1914 and 1918, also had profound repercussions on the postwar political life of the colony.

POSTWAR POLITICS IN SENEGAL, 1919–1930

The Communal Elections of 1919

Blaise Diagne's unexpected victory in the communal elections of 1914 represented a stunning, if singular, African political triumph. Diagne's selection as deputy nevertheless had little immediate effect on the complexion of local government in the communes, which continued to be dominated by his French and *métis* political opponents. The communal elections of 1919 represented the first test of Diagne's political appeal since the end of the war, and they served as a local referendum on the reforms and initiatives he had undertaken during the conflict. As such, the elections pitted the representa-

KEY

```
----    CERCLE BOUNDARY
······  RAILWAY
△       COMMUNE
▲       PROPOSED COMMUNE (1919)
○       PRINCIPLE COMMERCIAL CENTER
        IN THE PROTECTORATE (1921)
```

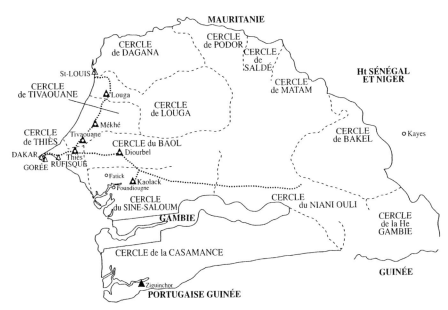

Map 7.1 Senegal in 1919: Communes and Proposed Communes
Source: Archives nationales du Sénégal: 1 G 359. Politique et administration général:
Circonscriptions administratif du Sénégal, 1908–1920.

---

tives of the prewar status quo against the advocates of postwar change symbolized by Diagne. Yet, as both sides knew, the outcome of the elections also carried much larger implications. Gaining control of the elective institutions in the communes was only the first step in Diagne's broader program for securing enhanced political rights for Africans living beyond their confines.

The postwar political climate in Senegal, as well as the comparative strength of the contending factions within the communes, had changed dramatically since 1914. Despite their undisputed control of the communes' municipal councils as well as the *Conseil général*, the Franco-*métis* coalition had seen the local balance of power shifting against them during the intervening war years. Conversely, the African electorate in the communes increased substantially during these years. Due in large measure to the introduction of the *jugement supplétif* as a means of raising *originaire* troops during the war, the number of Senegalese electors increased by over 50 percent, or about 5,000 potential voters.[23] Moreover, Diagne's battle to have the status of *originaires* confirmed as citizens and his subsequent efforts to redefine the meaning of the war for Africans politicized the Senegalese electorate as never before. These communal voters also contained a very high proportion of veterans, who, keenly aware of their wartime sacrifices on behalf of France, were especially outspoken in their demands for enhanced African participation in the political affairs of the colony.

These developments, and the prospect of local Senegalese political supremacy they foreshadowed, horrified the colonial establishment. Despite the fundamental shifts in the composition of the communal electorate, Diagne's opponents were determined to defeat him at the polls. His political foes included the large Bordeaux and Marseilles trading firms, most of the European expatriate community in the colony, and much of the old *métis* oligarchy. Their efforts were also abetted by numerous colonial administrators, who, though technically neutral in elections, were frequently partisan. Galvanized by the threat Diagne presented to their collective interests, they selected François Carpot, the former *métis* deputy who had lost his seat to Diagne in 1914. Slates of candidates were also chosen by the Franco-*métis* coalition to run for each of the communal offices.[24]

Diagne returned to Senegal in mid-November to launch his campaign for reelection. As deputy, former Commissioner for the Republic, *Commissaire général des Effectifs coloniaux*, and recent chairman of the first International Pan-African Congress in Paris, he was at the height of his postwar prestige.[25] Diagne went to work immediately and implemented a series of unprecedented initiatives designed to secure African success in the communal elections and broaden his base of support further afield. He announced the formation of the first permanent political party in Francophone Africa, the Republican-Socialist Party of Senegal. Composed of diverse elements from his African constituency—Western-educated *fonctionnaires*, Lebu and Wolof notables in the communes as well as others in the countryside, Muslim clerics, and many returning veterans—it also included some French *petit colons* and small businessmen, as well as several recently acquired and influential *métis* allies. Financially sustained by donations from diverse sources, including Mouride leaders in the interior, the party put forth slates of candidates for the municipal councils and the *Conseil général*. Composed predominantly of Africans, many of whom were former soldiers, these lists were the first ever advanced by the Senegalese *originaires*. Finally, as an indication of the broader mandate he eventually sought to secure, the name of the pro-Diagnist newspaper *La Démocratie du Sénégal* was changed to *L'Ouest Africain Français*.[26]

The opposition's campaign to discredit Diagne was extraordinarily vicious, and its tenor suggests the near hysteria his demands for reform aroused among the old guard. He was publicly slandered as a coward for failing to perform active military service during the war and "seeking shelter" overseas during the recent epidemics of plague and Spanish flu, which "cruelly decimated" the population of Senegal. Said to be acting only in his "personal interests" and "lining [his] pockets" while others died, Diagne was also accused of having performed poorly as a deputy during the war with disastrous consequences.[27]

Appalling though Diagne's record had been in France, so his foes claimed, the divisive impact of his "ambitious and stupid politics" in Senegal was even worse. Labeled an "agent of discord and hate between the two races," Diagne was further claimed to have a political agenda that amounted to a dangerous "form of Bolshevism," which would end in "destroying" the colony. Though extolling Senegalese "sacrifices" during the war and endorsing an extension of African "rights," the opposition urged voters against undue haste in undertaking such major reforms. In the present circumstances, it was imperative to return Senegal to its previous state of "well being," which would, in time, inaugurate a new "era of prosperity . . . social peace [and] productive work" for all.[28]

Diagne fought fire with fire. Condemning the "reactionary designs" of his adversaries, he focused his attacks on "the sharks of Bordeaux" and their "pitiful" and "dim-witted [local] representatives." Accusing them of being motivated by "base [financial] interests," he denounced their attempts to manipulate the outcome of the elections by means of "money, [false] promises, threats, and blackmail." Diagne also stigmatized his foes as a "handful of [cynical] social malefactors," who "ceaselessly attempted to provoke . . . a race war in order to accuse the African inhabitants (*indigènes*) [of having started it]." Demanding an end to the "politics of exploitation and hypocrisy," he called for "the complete emancipation of the proletariat," "the respect of all rights and all liberties" irrespective of "skin [color]," and a "Senegal free for all."[29]

Diagne's campaign platform explicitly advocated a series of sweeping, comprehensive reforms that would have, had they been implemented, completely transformed the colonial order in Senegal. It called for: (1) changes in the government's fiscal policy (including unification of the separate budgets for the communes and the Protectorate in Senegal and control of the federal budget by a colonial council composed of three elected representatives from each colony); (2) extensive public works projects designed to stimulate the growth of the postwar colonial economy; (3) enhanced opportunities for Africans to receive Western education; and (4) social legislation to protect the rights of workers. Finally, and most ominously in the eyes of his opponents, Diagne's program advocated major political changes in rural Senegal. It envisioned an end to the artificial division between the communes and the Protectorate through the "unification" of the two territories; the creation of *communes de plein exercice* identical to those on the coast, with full voting rights for the inhabitants of "Louga, Mekhe, Tivaouane, Thiès,

Diourbel, Kaolack, Ziguinchor, and other important centers in Senegal"; and the introduction of *justices de paix* with extended jurisdiction in these locales to provide an alternative to administrative justice. Furthermore, he called for citizenship to be granted to all soldiers in French West Africa who had served three or more years in the army during the war.[30]

In public, Diagne sought to unify and expand his diverse coalition by calling for racial fraternity, while striking a loftier note with regard to his opponents. Recalling Diagne's performance at one campaign rally, Abdoulaye Ndiaye, a recently demobilized veteran, remembered his declaring:

> For the second time I come to ask for your votes conscious of the implacable war which has been imposed on us during five years. Citizens, the next 30th of November, you have to choose a deputy. And my opponent might [appear] to be very [well] qualified. [But to represent] you in all the questions of politics and social life, you will have to vote for me because my program is reason and justice for all. Europeans, vote for my wife! Creoles, vote for my children! Senegalese, vote for me![31]

In the face of Diagne's political onslaught, the opposition crumbled. In the balloting for deputy on 30 November 1919, Diagne received over 85 percent of the vote and defeated Carpot by 7,444 to 1,252. Three weeks later, a similar landslide occurred when the Diagnist slate carried every seat on the municipal councils in each of the Four Communes. And on 4 January 1920 the local supremacy of Diagne's party was confirmed when its candidates swept the elections for the *Conseil général.*[32]

Having broken the power of the old Franco-*métis* coalition in the communes, Diagne and his followers embarked on their even more ambitious program of extending political reforms to the Protectorate. In so doing, the former Commissioner for the Republic remained true to his wartime pronouncements, as well as to his subsequent campaign platform. Yet the odds against achieving success were very great indeed. No longer engaged in a straightforward electoral contest, in which his supporters constituted an absolute majority of the voters, Diagne now faced the far more complex, difficult, and protracted task of outmaneuvering the colonial administration, which by and large remained an implacable foe of his designs. More important, his adversaries in A.O.F. were supported by powerful interest groups in the metropole, which recognized full well that the outcome of the struggle in rural Senegal would have far-ranging consequences for the future of the French colonial regime throughout Africa. The hopes of the reformers, as well as the fears of their antagonists, were perhaps best expressed by a former soldier and the newly elected mayor of St. Louis, Amadou Ndiaye Duguay-Cledor. On the eve of their confrontation with colonial officialdom, he declared: "We

Africans, under French guidance, of course, want to control the political destiny of our own country."[33]

The Struggle to Extend Rights to the Protectorate, 1920–1923

Diagne seized the initiative immediately after the communal elections and launched a vigorous campaign to secure political reforms in the Protectorate. His attitude in this larger undertaking, expressed while representing the French government at the presidential inaugural in Liberia in January 1920, echoed Duguay-Cledor's sentiments. "Blacks," he declared before his African hosts, "are as capable as whites of governing themselves, [and of] running their own country."[34]

The focus of the deputy's initial attacks were directed against the unreconstructed "*broussards*" in the rural administration, whom he sought to replace. Relying primarily on local notables, who constituted the backbone of the Republican-Socialist Party in the countryside, as well as on veterans, who had often acquired "[distressingly] libertarian ideas [while] overseas," he organized public demonstrations that agitated for the dismissal of particularly brutal French officials.[35] Recalling one such confrontation, a former soldier, Masserigne Soumare, recounted:

> There was a very wicked *commissaire* [superintendent of police] in Kaolack who used to beat people. ... And when Blaise Diagne came [there] in 1920, people told him that the *commissaire* was very wicked and [that] he used to mistreat them. So Blaise Diagne said: "You are not talking about a governor or an administrator, only a *commissaire*. You will see [what happens to him]."
>
> [And] the next day, he convoked a meeting at the school and [he] told the *commissaire* to come. So when he came, [Diagne] told him: "Go and put on [your] uniform." So the *commissaire* went home where his uniform was and [then he] returned. And he said he wanted to sit down. [But] Blaise Diagne said: "No, no. Stand up!" And [the *commissaire*] was standing up and Blaise Diagne was haranguing him [and humiliating] him [in front of the crowd]. And [finally] he told him: "Tomorrow, you will take the first train to go back home!" And the next day, the *commissaire* took the train and left Kaolack.[36]

Similar protests—notably against the maladministration of M. Siadous, Commandant of Sine-Saloum, which was also led by Diagne—were repeated in the Protectorate during the early months of 1920.[37]

Concomitant with these demonstrations in the countryside, the newly elected *Conseil général*, which first met in March 1920, took up the call for reform. Though their purview was technically restricted to budgetary matters rather than political questions, these restrictions were ignored by the Diagnist councillors. In addition to demanding the replacement of administrators such as Siadous—who was denounced as a "Congolese"—they called for the immediate transformation of the *communes mixte* in the interior into *communes de plein exercice*; the abolition of the *indigénat* and the extension of French law to the entire colony; and reform, as well as extension, of French primary education in Senegal. These measures were seen by the councillors as just recompense for Senegalese sacrifices during the war.[38] Meanwhile, Diagne, who had returned to Paris to resume his duties in the Chamber, publicly advocated an increase in the number of African deputies to include representatives from the other colonies in A.O.F. as well as one each for Afrique Équitoriale Française (A.E.F.) and Madagascar.[39]

These initiatives were denounced by the local French authorities, and particularly by Martial Henri Merlin, who assumed office as governor general in September 1919. A former secretary general of the Federation under Ernest Roume, Merlin was exceptionally familiar with Senegal. He was also militantly opposed to the urban reformers because of the "dangerous challenge they posed to French authority." Belittling their "pretensions" to speak for the Senegalese rural masses, Merlin endorsed the view that it was imperative to confine the current "disease" to the Four Communes and to "prevent, *at any cost*, the extension of the right to vote beyond its actual limits."[40] Looking to the "great chiefs" in the Protectorate as natural administrative allies against the communards, he began compiling detailed police records on the conduct of the African activists and embarked on a systematic purge of the "*négrogogue*" commandants in Senegal, who were deemed to be soft on the Diagnists.[41]

Merlin's countermeasures to stem the reformist tide in Senegal were abetted by powerful supporters in the metropole. Much of the French press, echoing the views of the colonial lobby, undertook a campaign to discredit Diagne in the eyes of the public. "Diagnism"—as the reformist movement was labeled—represented a radical expression of African nationalism (or, alternatively, communism) that would ultimately jeopardize French control in the colonies if it were not stamped out.[42] More specifically, the newly appointed Minister of Colonies, Albert Sarraut, accepted Merlin's recommendation to abolish the *Conseil général* in the wake of the political outbursts by the Diagnists during the March session. Merlin's proposal was made acceptable, however, by the volatile political climate in Senegal. The new *Conseil colonial*, which included a total of 40 members, would be composed of equal numbers of representatives from the communes and the rural areas of the colony. The former were to be elected, but the latter were to be selected by their peers from among the French-appointed chiefs in the countryside. The *Conseil colonial* thus became the only institution in Senegal that contained representatives from the entire colony, and it was through the manipulation of the chiefs that Merlin hoped to provide a local counterweight to the political ambitions of the reformers.

Perhaps surprisingly, Diagne consented to this change. Although the composition of the council differed from the elective body he advocated, he had campaigned in favor of a unification of the colony's separate budgets to streamline its finances. More pragmatically, Diagne also remained confident that he could outmaneuver the governor general. In addition to counting on victory in the upcoming communal elections, he also expected to gain the support of enough chiefs to constitute a working majority on the *Conseil colonial*. Effective veto power over the colony's budget would, in turn, strengthen the reformers' position and provide the means for exacting further concessions from the administration.[43]

The communal elections for the council were held in June 1921. The Diagnist slate again swept all of the contested seats, although by considerably reduced margins in some locales compared to 1919. The opposition lists, while backed by the Bordeaux interests, were composed predominantly of Africans for the first time, and St. Louisian *originaires* were especially incensed by Diagne's support for the abolition of the old *Conseil général*. The twenty chiefs representing the Protectorate were chosen a few weeks later. Their delegation included members from among the most eminent of the precolonial Senegambian ruling lineages as well as representatives whose families had risen to prominence under the patronage of the French.[44]

During the first session of the council in August 1921, the communal politicians bided their time and avoided conflict with the chiefs, some of whom they hoped to convert. The meetings nevertheless turned fractious when Bouna Ndiaye, *Burba Jolof* and an ally of Merlin's, and Mbakhane Diop, son of Lat Dior and a supporter of Diagne's, confronted each other over the issue of the abuse of *prestations* [compulsory labor service] in the Protectorate. In protest against this "political" turn in the discussion, Ndiaye, supported by the French Secretary General, and several other chiefs terminated the session by storming out of the chamber.[45]

Before the council reconvened in 1922, both Diagne and Merlin maneuvered to strengthen their positions. Diagne attempted to have the governor general removed. This hope proved illusionary because when Sarraut arrived, he used the occasion to reassert his personal confidence in Merlin. Meanwhile, the governor general continued his efforts to discredit Diagne in the metropole and to abrogate the laws he had passed during the war. Specifically, legislation was introduced in the Chamber to deny Muslims their citizenship. Merlin also assiduously courted the chiefs. Those considered "loyal" to the administration had their salaries raised, were provided with official residences, and were given additional land (as well as seeds and tools) to increase their incomes through cash-cropping. Moreover, in an ominous forewarning to all, Diagne's main chiefly ally, Mbakhane Diop, was brought up on charges of "corruption" in May 1922 and eventually forced to resign his chieftaincy as well as his position on the *Conseil colonial*.[46]

Under these circumstances, the nascent political alliance between the reformers and some of the chiefs disintegrated when the council met again in November 1922. Already forced on the defensive, the communards' position was rendered more untenable by the new tax proposals submitted by the administration, which placed the burden on commercial transactions and were therefore weighted against urban interests. Faced with defeat on this motion, it was the turn of the communal politicians to walk out of the assembly.[47]

The open split of the *originaires* with the chiefs in 1922 amounted to a repudiation of the *Conseil colonial* as an institution and the inclusion of the chiefs as the sole representatives of the rural population. It also signified the triumph of Merlin's efforts to contain the Diagnists and effectively terminated the most active phase of the postwar reform movement in Senegal. Diagne and his followers had gambled that Senegalese wartime sacrifices on behalf of France could be parlayed into enhanced civic rights for all and, with this, effective African control over the internal political affairs of the colony. This was a concession that neither the colonial administration nor, ultimately, the French government was prepared to countenance in the early 1920s, and once it became evident that they were unified in their determination to prevent it, the initiatives of the reformers were bound to be thwarted.

Elite Co-optation and Expatriate Radicalism, 1923–1930

Recognizing that the prevailing political wind had shifted irrevocably against him, Diagne accommodated himself to these new realities. Confronted by declining popularity in the communes, the possible repeal of his most significant wartime reforms, and the effective control of the *Conseil colonial* by the administration and their chiefly allies, Diagne sought conciliation with his adversaries. The ensuing *Pacte de Bordeaux*, as the arrangement between Diagne and his most implacable foes, the large Bordeaux commercial houses, became known, also signalled his rapprochement with the colonial administration. In exchange for improved relations with them, Diagne not only indicated his willingness to cooperate with Bordeaux but halted his demands for further political reforms in the Federation. Diagne, in short, ceased to be an agent for militant change in 1923 and became instead the primary African spokesman for metropolitan commercial interests in the colonies, as well as their supporters in the administration, whom he had so often decried.[48]

What was Diagne's rationale for this stunning about-face? His *modus vivendi* with the colonial establishment secured his electoral future in the communes while permitting him to retain a degree of influence with the government. In the circumstances of 1923—especially in the absence of the political leverage created by the demands of a major war—Diagne recognized that further efforts at reform were destined to be defeated and struck the best bargain he could. Although the *Pacte de Bordeaux* effectively vitiated much of what he had stood for and was an astonishing act of personal political expediency, it also exemplified the fundamental realities of interwar politics in the colonies. Senegalese representatives would be allowed limited influence over French policy only as long as they collaborated with the regime.[49]

Diagne's dramatic political reversal aroused immediate and intense controversy among Africans, and it has been the subject of ongoing debate ever since.[50] Though initially retaining the allegiance of most of his followers, the deputy was denounced by other communal politicians—notably by Theicouta Diop and Lamine Gueye, who soon constituted his main local opposition. In the legislative elections of 1924, however, their coalition was soundly defeated by the well-oiled Diagnist machine. Nevertheless, within three years the Republican-Socialist Party became factionalized when Galandou Diouf, Diagne's oldest and most important collaborator, disavowed his policies and challenged him for the deputyship. Diouf's program was not new; indeed it was virtually indistinguishable from Diagne's in 1919.[51] As a veteran, however, Diouf was also especially effective in denouncing Diagne's accommodation with the French; he claimed that the deputy had only attained his current position of responsibility by virtue of the wartime sacrifices of thousands of Senegalese. Diouf's indictment proved persuasive, and it was probably only through the machinations of Diagne's administrative allies—who now viewed Diouf as a dangerous radical—that Diagne managed to avoid defeat in 1928.[52]

While these events transpired in Senegal, groups of West African expatriates in France also vociferously condemned Diagne's actions after 1924. Composed in large measure of veterans, who were predominantly Senegalese and *originaires*, they created a series of successive organizations—including the *Ligue universelle de la défense de la Race noire* (L.U.D.R.N.), the *Comité de défense de la Race nègre* (C.D.R.N.), and the *Ligue de défense de la Race nègre* (L.D.R.N.)—that agitated for political change in the colonies during the 1920s.[53] In touch with other expatriates from the Francophone colonies, they also maintained contacts with North American reformers of African descent as well as with colonial activists from the other European empires, notably Indians. Inspired by a diverse range of intellectual influences—Garveyite and Du Boisian Pan-Africanism, Wilsonian national self-determination, and Leninist communism and anti-imperialism—they assailed the "stupid dogmatism of the supremacy of the 'white' race," asserted the unique cultural heritage of Africans, and demanded political equality with Europeans.[54] In their desire to promote these goals, they eventually espoused an even more radical program than Diagne at the height of his militancy, or any of the subsequent political reformers in Senegal, envisioned.

This evolution, however, was gradual. Indeed, the policies advocated by the expatriates in 1924 were not dissimilar to those previously pursued by Diagne. Though condemning the abuses of the French colonial regime, they still called for granting citizenship to the *sujet* population and the abolition of the *indigénat* as the primary means for securing redress for African grievances. Moreover, their demands for political equality, though delivered in more uncompromising tones than by the reformers in Senegal, were still couched in the patriotic context of their wartime service in behalf of *la patrie*. Summarizing their position, as well as the logic that would soon lead many to abandon it, Tovalou Houenou, a former *tirailleur* from Dahomey, stated in an editorial in the L.U.D.R.N.'s journal *Les Continents*: "We have shed our blood for France. . . . Why do we not [now] enjoy the rights of citizenship? We demand to be citizens, whatever the country, and that is why, if France rejects us, we call for autonomy."[55]

Within less than two years, the goal of obtaining citizenship as a means of achieving political equality within a colonial context had been rejected by the most militant expatriates. In collaboration with other leftist Senegalese veterans—including Ibrahima Sow, Ouande Tounkara, and Paul Caminade—Lamine Senghor, an ex-serviceman from Joal and a *mutilé de guerre*, founded the C.D.R.N. in 1926 after the L.U.D.R.N. disbanded.[56] Composed of other disaffected West Africans and West Indians as well as veterans, Senghor's group was radical and its aims revolutionary and direct. Denouncing colonialism in unequivocal terms, the C.D.R.N. sought the "[re]conquest of our independence, like Abyssinia and Liberia." The organization's program to achieve this end called for the expansion of the C.D.R.N.'s membership in France (with particular emphasis on the recruitment of African soldiers and sailors); the formation of local sections of the *Comité* in the colonies; and the dissemination of propaganda via the group's newspaper, *La voix des Nègres*, to educate the rural "masses."[57] By the end of the decade, the L.D.R.N., which succeeded the C.D.R.N. after Senghor's death in 1927, was even more explicit in enunciating its nationalist program. Founded by Senghor's young Sudanese associate, Tiemoko Garan-Kouyate, and composed of West African students and workers as well as veterans and soldiers, its journal *La Race nègre* asserted: "The right to independence is a fundamental right of all peoples, and the thirteen and a half million oppressed Negroes of French West Africa are entitled to raise, in no uncertain terms, the question of their self-determination."[58]

Although largely ignored during the interwar years, the aspirations of the expatriates were eventually realized in the aftermath of the Second World War. Moreover, though the nationalist alternative to colonial rule they proposed represented a fundamental departure from the program of the Senegalese reformers in 1919, there was also a continuum between these two positions. The desire to obtain political equality with Europeans, which both groups bespoke, traced their origins to the hopes first aroused during the "War to Obtain Rights." In this respect, the example set by Diagne between 1914 and 1923, as well as the soldiers' wartime experience in France, ultimately carried far-ranging political implications indeed.[59]

POSTWAR SENEGALESE SOCIETY AND THE LATER LIVES OF THE VETERANS

Social Trends, 1919–1930

Unlike postwar politics, where the repercussions of the war were immediate and dramatic, the social transformations that occurred in Senegal between 1919 and 1930 were more gradual and measured. Indeed, many facets of life were comparatively untouched by the war, and continuity with the past, rather than change, frequently appeared to be the hallmark of everyday existence. This was particularly true in the more peripheral regions of the Protectorate. In contrast with central Senegal, where French recruitment levies were heaviest and economic dislocation was greatest, these areas were less severely affected by wartime demands. Moreover, though the changes taking place in Senegalese society after 1919 were often set in motion by the war, they were also influenced by other factors, notably by the designs of the colonial regime and the return of peace. Nevertheless, postwar African society differed in significant respects from the pre-1914 order. The changes that took place during this period can be broadly differentiated into two distinctive types: those that were prompted by external factors beyond the control of the local inhabitants, and those that were particular to the internal social arrangements of the Senegalese themselves.

Despite the widespread resistance provoked by military recruitment in the Protectorate, the war, paradoxically, facilitated the consolidation of French administrative control in rural areas. Armed insurrections against the French ceased completely after the war, while the added demands for soldiers, as well as for taxes and labor, ultimately led to a tightening of the French administrative grip. Although the number of French officials in the countryside increased slowly during the 1920s, the presence of a much enlarged pool of African auxiliaries—which included many returning veterans—nonetheless enhanced administrative efficiency.[60] This change was perhaps best exemplified after 1926 by the reliance on census data instead of the local chiefs to determine who was liable for military service during the annual call-ups of men.[61]

The gradual expansion of the colony's European infrastructure, which had ground to a virtual halt as a result of the war, was also resumed in the 1920s. Though public works projects were seriously hampered by an absence of metropolitan appropriations, modest initiatives (which were paid for from colonial revenues) were nevertheless undertaken. The number of Western primary schools increased slowly, while the new medical school in Dakar, founded at Diagne's behest in 1918, trained a steady flow of African medical assistants, who helped to improve health care and combat contagious diseases in the colony. The prewar transportation network in Senegal, including rail, road, and port facilities, was also augmented.[62] Spurred by demands from both the public and private sectors, the construction industry, especially for houses, flourished during the 1920s.

This expansion also contributed to the first public manifestations of collective discontent by African wage earners. Strikes for higher pay and better working conditions broke out immediately after the war. Frequently led by ex-servicemen, work stoppages occurred among stevedores, masons and carpenters, and especially railway employees. Although these early efforts to organize African workers were outlawed by the colonial authorities, quickly suppressed, and affected only a tiny minority of the Senegalese urban population, they nevertheless represented a novel social phenomenon in the colonies.[63]

After the severe economic dislocation wrought by the war, the colony's export sector recovered and, despite the recession of the early 1920s, boomed throughout the rest of the decade. Peanut production, which was the mainstay of the export economy, provides an indication of this expansion. After plummeting to an average of 142,000 metric tons per year between 1916 and 1918, prewar production levels were surpassed in 1924 when 319,000 tons were exported, and during the next six years harvests increased by over 60 percent, when a high of 508,000 tons was attained in 1930.[64] As far as the peasantry was concerned, however, increased output was not achieved by means of technological innovation or improved farming techniques. The diffusion of French-controlled *Sociétés de prévoyance* in the countryside notwithstanding, production levels were raised by opening vast new tracts of land to cultivation in eastern Senegal and through the increased labor of farmers.[65]

This last phenomenon, which resulted in ever increasing internal migration within the colony, probably represented the most important external influence on the changing character of postwar Senegalese society. Although the population of the coastal urban centers increased gradually due to African rural (and French metropolitan) emigration, the massive, exponential explosion that would occur after 1945 had scarcely begun.[66] Instead, the major demographic shift during the 1920s was eastward rather than to the west. Following the recently completed Thiès-Kayes rail route, which provided peasant producers in the interior with direct access to the nodal points of overseas commerce on the coast, hundreds of new settlements (or *daras*) were founded in eastern Saloum, Niani Ouli, and eastern Senegal. Indeed, by the late 1920s, eastern Saloum was absorbing Senegalese migrants whose numbers eventually reached some 175,000 by the middle of the next decade, or roughly 15 percent of the colony's total population.[67]

Though often spurred by external factors, these general trends also reflected internal changes within Senegalese society. The period between 1919 and 1930 witnessed the progressive deterioration of the precolonial Senegambian social hierarchy. Declining aristocratic prestige was further undermined by their ongoing collaboration with the French. In some cases this was exacerbated by the aristocracy's wartime role in recruiting soldiers, but such grievances were symptomatic of a broader malaise. Having largely surrendered their former spiritual authority to preserve a vestige of their secular power, the ancient hereditary elites were progressively reduced to cogs in the colonial administrative machinery.[68]

Although this development had only a marginal impact on the free peasantry, it had a profound effect on the lower orders. Casted lineages were deprived of their main source of patronage. Moreover, during the 1920s artisanal craftsmen—including blacksmiths, weavers, and leather workers—began to face increasingly stiff competition from European manufactured goods, which progressively rendered their previous functions anachronistic and eventually drove some to abandon their trades altogether. Even more significant, domestic servitude declined dramatically during this period. Though stimulated by waning aristocratic power and enhanced economic opportunities elsewhere, the manumission of much of the remaining servile population was also a direct consequence of the war. Having survived as combatants overseas, many returning *captifs* refused to resume their former obligations to their masters and migrated with their families elsewhere. Indeed, the founding of many autonomous villages in Saloum composed of slave descendants dates from the early 1920s, while the bulk of the seasonal workers, or *navetaans,* migrating to Senegal from other colonies in the Federation were of servile origin. In this respect, the egalitarian impulse acquired by many soldiers in the army applied not only to the French but to the prewar internal social hierarchies among Africans as well.[69]

The decline of the old order was also exemplified in other ways. The postwar period witnessed the increasing diffusion of Islam throughout Senegal. Conversion continued among the Wolof, but it was especially pronounced among the Serer and significant inroads were also made among the Jola. Although Islam represented a spiritual alternative to the increasingly discredited belief systems of the past (as well as to European-imported Christianity), in many instances submission to the will of Allah also implied something more. Among Mouride *talibes*, for example, it also entailed the substitution of older patronage networks and relations of interdependency for new ones. This was especially evident among the *dara* settlers in eastern Senegal. Recruited primarily from among the lower Wolof orders, these *talibes* in effect replaced their former aristocratic overlords by indenturing themselves to marabouts. In exchange for submitting to their authority and providing them labor, they received not only their spiritual blessing but also the promise of eventually acquiring land for themselves and, hence, enhanced economic independence.[70]

Although the Mourides afford the most obvious example of the changing patterns of social interrelationships among the Senegalese in the 1920s, this phenomenon was by no means restricted to them. Patronage—especially when it concerned intercession with the French—was also dispensed by the urban-based African politicians from 1914 onward, almost none of whom were from aristocratic lineages. Moreover, the growing numbers of Senegalese auxiliaries employed in the French administrative and commercial sectors created a small, but discernibly new, social class. Because their comparative wealth derived from French instead of African sources, the ways in which it was redistributed were not ultimately dependent on reciprocal arrangements within the preexisting social framework.[71] Finally, new collective associations, exemplified by veterans groups and the nascent labor unions, provided alternative sources of support for their members that were unprecedented in Senegalese society.

These broader trends also influenced the internal organization of Senegalese families, particularly among the Wolof. The beginning of the long-term decline in the size of rural residential units dates from the immediate postwar period. Alternative sources of wealth arising from new economic opportunities slowly eroded the dominant social influence of compound heads, as well as status hierarchies within the group based on seniority. Young men became less dependent on elder kinsmen to start them in life. Marriages were contracted at an earlier age, particularly by soldiers returning from the war, and these young men frequently left to form new households of their own. Moreover, this was especially common if their father was dead and an elder brother was the head of the compound. Combined with the departure of other bonded dependents, the net result was a fission of many larger family units, as well as an undermining of the internal hierarchies on which their cohesion was based.[72]

The Postwar Lives of the Veterans

The later lives of the veterans graphically exemplify many of the transformations occurring in Senegalese society after 1919. Both the advent of change, and the persistence of social continuity (as well as the factors influencing them), are embodied in their personal experiences. By examining their subsequent lives from a series of vantage points—including their choice of postwar residence, the means by which they earned their livelihoods, and the personal considerations that entered into their decision making—it will be possible to indicate how the tensions between older Senegalese social norms and the external influences wrought by the imposition of the colonial order were resolved by them.

A fundamental distinction needs to be made between the postwar experiences of *tirailleurs* and *originaires*. By assessing each of these groups in turn, it will be possible to illuminate not only the variation in their responses to the transformations taking place in postwar Senegalese society, but also to show how the interplay between new opportunities created by their wartime service and other personal considerations influenced the choices they made during their later lives.

Perhaps the best indication of the comparative attraction of the prewar social order among *tirailleurs* is whether they wished to be permanently reintegrated into the communities from which they had been recruited. About two-thirds of those who were sent to France returned to their homes, but nearly one-third did not.[73] This decision was influenced by a series of factors. The precolonial social status of the veterans' families was a major consideration. Virtually all of the free peasantry sought to resume their former lives, but a disproportionately high number of ex-soldiers drawn from the aristocracy, casted lineages, or of servile ancestry (including former royal retainers) did not. Ethnic identity (which provides a crude indication of geographic variations) also entered into play. The Wolof (and perhaps the Serahuli) were particularly prone to migrate elsewhere, while the Serer, and especially the Fulbe and the Lebu, generally returned to their places of birth.[74]

The most significant indicator of the veterans' comparative propensity to leave their former homes, however, was their personal family situation. Among *tirailleurs* who moved elsewhere, a very great proportion were missing either one or both of their parents when they came back after the war. Furthermore, their status within the family unit was also a factor: those whose mothers were from later marriages were especially prominent among the departed, while friction arising from rivalry with elder siblings, who had usually not been recruited, sometimes entered into consideration. Indeed, as one deracinated *tirailleur* explained, the obligation to "always follow your elder brother" and to defer to him in public, "even if you know he is lying," was the primary reason he left his village.[75]

A second gauge of the transformations that occurred in rural Senegal, as well as the extent of the role that *tirailleurs* played in them, was the means by which they earned their livelihoods after the war. Most veterans who returned to their prewar residences—which included the vast majority of free peasants, who had access to land—quickly resumed their former agricultural functions. As a Lebu soldier remembered: "When [we first] returned to Senegal, I was eager to see my family and to [be with] them. But, then I started [doing my] daily work as I had done before the war. [I was] farming, fishing, and learning the Koran; these were my [only] occupations."[76]

Although a few of these men supplemented their incomes in alternative ways—by becoming local traders in French goods, for instance—nearly all who returned to their former homes took up their previous ways of making a living. This was even true of some Tukulor veterans from artisanal castes, who refused to forsake their villages.[77] Moreover, although *tirailleurs* were generally less well equipped to obtain jobs in the French sector than their urban counterparts, the comparative lack of such alternative options was not always a limiting factor. Indeed, because of the soldier's apprehensions about offending the members of their communities, the reverse was sometimes the case.

[Although the *commandant* offered me the option of a job in the police force] I didn't want to become a policeman because I didn't want the people of my village to be angry with me. Because they might [have] said that [I did] it because I had been in France and in the the war and that I had kept French habits. So that's why I wanted to come back to my village and to remain a farmer like before.[78]

Ex-*tirailleurs* who distanced themselves from their former lives earned their livings either as before or in new ways. Many returned to cultivating the land or performing artisanal functions, although they were integrated into different patronage networks. This was best exemplified by Mouride veterans, who labored in new settlements founded by their marabouts. Though their decision represented a departure from their previous African existence, it also entailed a repudiation of the alternative presented by the French. As one *talibe*, Bara Seck, put it: "When I came back here, I [only] wanted to follow Seriny Touba's teachings and to be one of his followers. I never wanted to work with the 'white' man."[79]

Many other former soldiers, however, felt differently. After leaving their prewar homes, they entered the French sector of the economy or became middlemen servicing it. In this capacity, they earned a living in a wide variety of ways. Some were employed in the public sector as medical assistants, policemen, or market guards; others worked in the new towns along the rail line as agents for the major European export firms; and still others earned livings as carpenters, lorry drivers, and mechanics. Although these men included a disproportionately high number of former N.C.O.s, rank and comparative familiarity with the French and their language were not the only factors affecting the choice of such careers.[80] Indeed, other personal considerations, which often exemplified an altered mentality arising from the war, also entered into play. As Daba Dembele, a former private, explained:

My mind was changed in France by my experience. [And this] was the will of God. [But] when I came back [to Africa], if I had gone back to my village, I would have talked about my experiences during the war. And the people of the village would not [have] understood the [things] I was explaining to them. They would have thought I was trying to show them that I knew more things than they [did]. So that's why I preferred to stay here [in Thiès and accept a job as a policeman].[81]

Although reflecting many of the same influences that affected the *tirailleurs*, the prevailing patterns of postwar life among most *originaires* were considerably different. A notable exception to this rule, however, was provided by the veterans from the *banlieue* of Dakar. Overwhelmingly Lebu, they were more predisposed to return to their homes and resume their former occupations as farmers and fishermen than any other group in Senegal, including free peasants among the *tirailleurs*.[82] For the rest of the communards, on the other hand, their participation in the war brought significant personal changes. Probably between one-half and two-thirds of them departed from their communities after the war to pursue careers elsewhere. While the precolonial social standing of their families was a comparatively inconsequential consideration among communards, otherwise these veterans exhibited many of the same general characteristics displayed by the other Senegalese soldier-migrants. Ethnically, the Wolof were proportionately overrepresented, although some Fulbe and Lebu also left their homes.[83] Moreover, the vast majority, unlike their counterparts who remained with their families, were missing at least one parent, and frequently both, when they returned from overseas. Soldiers who were the offsprings of subsequent marital unions were also especially prone to depart. Nevertheless, despite these general similarities between their situations and those of the *tirailleurs*, a further distinction between the two groups existed: most of the *originaires* eventually returned in later life to their communities of origin, whereas the departure of the *tirailleurs* usually signified an irrevocable break with their pasts.[84]

Their means of obtaining a livelihood also differed significantly from that of their rural counterparts. Virtually all the veterans leaving the communes for greener economic pastures further afield secured employment in the French sector. Indeed, a few among them returned to live in the metropole itself. There they earned livings as prize-fighters or, in far less lucrative and hazardous ways, as factory workers, lorry drivers, or *gendarmes*.[85] The rest were dispersed throughout the Federation or the colony, where they were employed as *fonctionnaires* by the colonial administration, foremen on the railroads, middlemen for the commercial houses, or carpenters for French construction companies, among other occupations. Furthermore, even among those ex-servicemen who remained behind, only a minority resumed their former dependency on the land. Instead, most of them worked for the French in some capacity too, as government employees, hospital orderlies, railway workers, or mechanics in the Dakar shipyards, for instance.[86] Aside from the absence of social stigma attached to working for Europeans among communards, the key to being able to do so derived in large measure from the conditions of wartime service of the *originaires*—especially the universal use of French in their units— that placed their services at a premium. As Thiecouta Diallo, who had only had chance encounters with Europeans and possessed a very limited French vocabulary before 1914, reflected: "I learned many things in France [and] I got a very great education during the war. [And] the war gave advantages to those who had [become] educated. After the war they had very good jobs and they were considered [almost] like the French consumers. But for those who [had] not [become] educated, there were not many lasting opportunities [arising] from the war."[87]

Although all Senegalese veterans were affected by their experience during the war, the extent of its impact on their subsequent lives varied. The effect of the wartime experience was most apparent among *originaires*, who were the most active agents for European-oriented social change in the colony. Nevertheless, service overseas also altered the lives of many *tirailleurs*. Some—especially former N.C.O.s—joined their counterparts from the communes and used the skills they acquired in the army to obtain jobs in the French sector of the economy. Others—notably those from the lowest orders of prewar society—refused to resume their former positions of servitude and opted for other arrangements. In so doing, all contributed to an alteration of the fabric of prewar Senegalese society. Thus, although many soldiers strove to preserve a continuity with their previous lives, change was nevertheless perceptible. In this regard, the postwar transformations occurring in Senegal were stimulated by the experiences of veterans who had fought in France between 1914 and 1918 and by novel changes directly and indirectly related to the war.

War and Remembrance

Regardless of the broader social or political ramifications of the war, or the ways that it subsequently influenced their later lives, memories of the maelstrom in which the Senegalese were engulfed between 1914 and 1918 lived on in the aged thoughts of all veterans. The power of these reflections, as well as their vividness and resiliency, often surprised even the former soldiers themselves when they recalled them from the vantage point of an extended lifetime. Indeed, irrespective of their personal circumstances in old age, their memories of the war constituted an enduring aspect of their lives. And, as they contemplated the imminence of their own deaths, which most had made peace with, they remembered their youths, when death was all about them and they had been less prepared to meet it.

Ousmane Diagne, age 86, Dakar (compare with photo on page 70). Photograph by the author.

These reflections encompassed an enormous range of feelings. Elderly and usually feeble, most recalled with delight the long-lost vitality of their youths as well as the strength and courage they once had exhibited. Many also emphasized humorous and often self-effacing aspects of their experience in the army: the youthful pranks they played on their friends, the peculiar oddities of outlandish situations they found themselves involved in, and especially their own often woeful naiveté. But the flood of memories also contained harsher images. The frequently long-suppressed horrors of the war often bordered on the overwhelming. Instances of extreme fear, pain, and suffering were recounted in chilling detail. Many soldiers also still grieved for long-dead comrades—friends and loved ones alike—whose unique personalities and distinctive mannerisms were never forgotten. And, amid the expressions of pride many veterans derived from their service overseas—and especially their enhanced feelings of worth as men and dignity as Africans—there was also lingering bitterness. *Mutilés* recounted with anger the permanently debilitating effects of the war on their lives. And most soldiers were outraged by the racial injustice they had usually experienced at the hands of the French, which continued to be manifested in particularly flagrant ways even after many had shed their blood in behalf of *la patrie*.

Reflecting on the course of their lives, many also speculated on whether they would have enlisted in the army if, with hindsight, they were called on by the French to do so again. This amounted to a personal critique of their previous conduct in light of their attitudes toward their wartime experience. Opinions were divided. Perhaps surprisingly, about a quarter of the veterans would have reenlisted in the army (as, indeed, a handful of *originaires*, who were still classed as reservists, were forced to do when Dakar was threatened by the "Free French" during the Second World War).[88] These men cut across all segments of Senegalese society and included *tirailleurs* as well as former soldiers from the communes and the *banlieue*. The rationales they offered for their attitudes, however, differed. Although, a very few would have repeated their experience because of a desire "to help the French," most cited other considerations. These included martial pride in their ethnic (or family) heritage, or a masculine sense of duty to perform the obligations expected of other men.[89]

In light of their subsequent knowledge about the character of the war, the vast majority of veterans would never have enlisted if they could have made a different decision. Indeed, most dismissed the idea of repeating their experience as preposterous: "Even if I was crazy, I would never return [to the war]. Even if they gave me a million francs I would [never enter the army again]!" laughed Ibrahima Camara. And many were explicit about the course of action they would have taken to avoid such a fate. In the mirthful reflections of one *tirailleur*, when the recruiting commissions appeared, "I [would have] run away to the furthermost place possible."[90]

Despite the use of humor to divert attention from the tragic aspects of their ordeal, the veterans' comments convey a fundamental realization shared by all. Irrespective of their attitudes toward their experience between 1914 and 1918 or whether they would have repeated it, all *combattants* were in accord about the nature of the war itself. Repeatedly characterized as "a very, very bad thing" or "the worst thing I ever saw," the war was also keenly perceived by most veterans as having ultimately been futile.[91] In Alassane Kane's words: "War is a very terrible thing. Even if you are the victor you lose [much]. And if you are defeated, you lose everything. So [regardless] of whether you win, or you are beaten, you lose, because war [itself] is evil."[92]

This knowledge, born of harsh personal experience, was also indelibly etched in the memories of the veterans. Their collective conviction that "nothing is better than peace" was also why, when the killing ceased and they returned to Senegal, they "prayed to God to prevent another war."[93]

NOTES

[1] The title is derived from a Wolof story about the origins of the baobab's distinctive appearance. Once the most beautiful tree in the world, the baobab became excessively vain about its looks. This provoked the intercession of the Almighty, who, seeking to teach it humility, plucked it from the Earth and replanted it upside down so that henceforth only its roots would show.

[2] Masserigne Sourmare: 1B; Ousmane Diagne: 5B. Ndiaga Niang: 1B.

[3] Momar Candji: 1B. See also: Masserigne Soumare: 1B; and Demba Mboup: 5B, 6A.

[4] On the disbanding of Senegalese battalions, see the *Journaux de marche et d'opérations* (hereafter JMO): *AG*: Unités: 26 N 869–873.

[5] Demba Mboup: 13A. On instructions circulated within the colonial army prohibiting the use of the term "sale nègre" when addressing African soldiers, see: *AG*: Grand Quartier Général (hereafter GQG): 16 N 2094.

[6] Governor General Merlin, speaking in December 1920, *L'Afrique française*, 1921, p. 97; Governor General Clozel, 26 May 1916, *ANOM*: 3034/3. On the duration of their stay in the camps and discharge procedures, see: Niaki Gueye: 3A; Mandiaye Ndiaye: 2A; Abdoulaye Gueye: 2A; Mamadou Bokar: 1B; Masserigne Soumare: 1A; and Sera Ndiaye: 5A. Also see: *AG*: Fonds Clemenceau: 6 N 97 and *AG*: EMA: 7 N 144.

[7] Mandiaye Ndiaye: 2A. See also: Sera Ndiaye: 5A.

[8] Ishmale Mbange: 4B. For example, Yoro Diaw (2B) and Giribul Diallo (2B) were gone four years before they returned home. On the lack of communication, see: Galaye Gueye: 2B; and Mandiaye Ndiaye: 1B. On assumptions that the young men would never come back, see: Aliou Diakhate: 2A; Mandiaye Ndiaye; 1B; Coumba Ndiaye: 5B; and Souleye Samba Ndiaye: 1B.

[9] See especially: Biram Mbodji Tine: 2B; Nouma Ndiaye: 2B; and Makhoudia Ndiaye: 2A. For examples, see: Demba Mboup: 6A; Abdoulaye Ndiaye: 6A; Souleye Samba Ndiaye: 1B; Ishmale Mbange: 3A; and Ibrahima Thiam: 2A. On the presentation of gifts, which included money, manufactured clothing (usually shirts or trousers), cloth, cooking

utensils, and food, see: Demba Mboup: 6A; Aliou Dioama: 1A; Amar Seck: 4A; and Daour Gueye: 4A.

[10] Nouma Ndiaye: 2B. Specific songs to welcome the soldiers home were also sung among the Tukulor and the Wolof. For examples (as well as lyrics), see: Diouli Missine: 2B; Souleye Samba Ndiaye: 1B; Sickh Yero Sy: 2A; Gamou Wade: 1A; and Samba Diop: 2B.

[11] Thiam Nding: 1A. Samba Diop: 2A. See also: *ANS*: Affaires militaires: 4 D 71.

[12] Nouma Ndiaye: 2B. See also: Samba Diop: 2A; Momar Candji: 2B; and Aminata Ngom: 1A.

[13] Ibrahima Thiam: 2B. Giribul Diallo: 2B; and Momar Candji: 3A. See also: Malal Gassala: 3A; and Sickh Yero Sy: 2A.

[14] Sickh Yero Sy: 2A. Sera Ndiaye: 5B; and Amar Seck: 4A. Coumba Kebe: 2B; and Aminata Ngom: 1A. For examples, see respectively: Sera Ndiaye: 5B; Niaki Gueye: 1A; and Aminata Ngom: 1A.

[15] Gamou Wade: 1A.

[16] For examples of friction that arose because of some soldiers' comportment, see: Daba Dembele: 5A and 5B; Sera Ndiaye: 5B; and Mandiaye Ndiaye: 2A and 2B. Galaye Gueye (2B), for example, received 650 francs in back pay upon his discharge. This was sufficient for him to buy two cows, build a house, and provide the bride wealth necessary for him to marry. On knowledge, see: Niaki Gueye: 1A; Sera Ndiaye: 5B; Amar Seck: 4A; Saer Anta Loum: 1B; Makhoudia Ndiaye: 2A; and Aminata Ngom: 1A. On envy, see: Daba Dembele: 5A.

[17] See, respectively, Amar Seck: 4A; Makhoudia Ndiaye: 2A; Souleye Samba Ndiaye: 2A; Aliou Diakhate: 2A; and Sera Ndiaye: 6A.

[18] Aliou Dioama: 2A. On the veterans' intercession with the French on behalf of their neighbors, see also: Yoro Diaw: 2A; Sambou Ndiaye: 2a; and Nar Diouf: 6A.

[19] On the founding of veterans' associations in Dakar, St. Louis, Thiès, Louga, and Diourbel, see respectively: Ousmane Diagne: 6A; Demba Mboup: 6B; Abdoulaye Ndiaye: 6B; Mandiaye Ndiaye: 2B; Doudou Ndao: 4A; and Bara Seck: 3A. On the opposition of local French administrators to the creation of an association in Louga, see: Abdoulaye Ndiaye: 6B. On the organization of veterans' groups as well as descriptions of their activities in Ouakam, Yoff, Yeumbeul, Bargny, and Koungheul, see respectively: Momar Candji: 2B; Daour Gueye: 4B; Alassane Kane: 4B; Ishmale Mbange: 4B; Niaki Gueye: 1B; Moussa Leye: 2A; Amar Seck: 4A; Momar Cisse: 1A; and Masserigne Soumare: 1A.

[20] In Dakar, about 200 veterans regularly attended meetings; in Louga, the association comprised 400 members. See: Ousmane Diagne: 6A; and Abdoulaye Ndiaye: 6B. On the internal organization and rules of procedure of the associations in Dakar, Louga, and Diourbel, see: Ousmane Diagne: 6A; Abdoulaye Ndiaye: 6B; Bara Seck: 3A. On parades, see: Aminata Ngom: 2B; Moussa Leye: 2A; and Niaki Gueye: 1B. On the symbolism of national holidays in Senegal during the interwar period, see also: Marc Michel, "'Memoire Officiel': Discours et pratique coloniale le 14 juillet et le 11 novembre au Sénégal entre les deux Guerres," *Revue française d'histoire d'outre-mer* 77 (1990), pp. 145–58.

[21] On the official neutrality of the associations during elections, see: Abdoulaye Ndiaye: 6B. On the political initiatives of their members, see: Alassane Kane: 3B, 4A, and 4B. François Gningue, for example, helped to found the Veterans' Association as well as the union of African railway workers in Thiès (Demba Mboup: 6B). See also: Ousmane Diagne: 6A.

[22] Mbaye Khary Diagne: 5A.

[23] *ANS*: Affaires politiques: 20 G 70 (23).

[24] *ANS*: Affaires politiques: 20 G 69 (23) and 20 G 70 (23). See also: G. Wesley Johnson, Jr., *The Emergence of Black Politics in Senegal: The Struggle for Power in the Four Communes, 1900–1920* (Stanford: Stanford University Press, 1971), pp. 196–212.

[25] Diagne was appointed *Commissaire général des Effectifs coloniaux* by decree on 11 October 1918. On his role in the Pan-African Congress in February 1919, see Imanuel Geiss, *The Pan-African Movement*, trans. Ann Keep (London: Methuen & Co., 1974), pp. 229–62, v; and George Shepperson, "Pan-Africanism and 'Pan-Africanism': Some Historical Notes," *Phylon* 23 (1962), pp. 355–56.

[26] *ANS*: Affaires politiques: 20 G 70 (23). See also: Johnson, *The Emergence of Black Politics in Senegal*, pp. 196–212; and James F. Searing, "Accommodation and Resistance: Chiefs, Muslim Leaders, and Politicians in Colonial Senegal, 1890–1934" (Ph.D. Diss.: Princeton University, 1985), pp. 452–543.

[27] See François Carpot, "Profession de foi," in *ANOM*: Affaires politiques: 595: 1; and "Aux Anciens Combattants," *L'A.O.F.*, 20 novembre 1919.

[28] *ANOM*: Affaires politiques: 595: 1; and *L'A.O.F.*, 20 novembre 1919.

[29] See, respectively, Diagne's "Profession de foi," *ANOM*: 595: 1; Michael Crowder, "Blaise Diagne and the Recruitment of African Troops for the 1914–1918 War (1967)," in *Colonial West Africa: Collected Essays* (London: Frank Cass, 1978), p. 104; and Blaise Diagne, "À mes Compatriotes et Concitoyens," in *ANOM*: Affaires politiques: 595: 1.

[30] Diagne, "Profession de foi," *ANOM*: 595: 1; and *AG*: Fonds Clemenceau: 6 N 97.

[31] Abdoulaye Ndiaye: 2A. Ndiaye wrote down Diagne's words at the rally and later committed them to memory.

[32] For legislative election results, see: *ANS*: Affaires politiques: 20 G 70 (23). For municipal election results and lists of candidates, see: *ANS*: Affaires politiques: 20 G 69 (23). On the social backgrounds and occupations of the Diagnist candidates, who included "many . . . veterans just returned from the war," see also: Johnson, *The Emergence of Black Politics in Senegal*, pp. 203–05.

[33] See Pascal Dumont's article in *L'A.O.F.*, 6 novembre 1919. On Duguay-Cledor, see also: Abdoulaye Diaw: 2A.

[34] *ANS*: Affaires politiques: 17 G 234 (108).

[35] *ANS*: Affaires militaires: 4 D 70.

[36] Masserigne Soumare: 4A.

[37] See: Masserigne Soumare: 4A; and *ANS*: Affaires politiques: 17 G 234 (108). On additional demonstrations against the French authorities, notably in Dakar in May and Tivaouane in August 1921, see John Gaffar la Guerre, *Enemies of Empire* (St. Augustine, Trinidad: College Press, 1984), pp. 42–53.

[38] On the meetings of the *conseil général* in March and December 1920, see: Searing, "Accommodation and Resistance," pp. 487–89.

[39] Interview by Georges Joutel, *La Presse coloniale*, 31 décembre 1924. This program reflected the demands made by African *sujets* elsewhere in the Federation—notably in Porto Novo and Conakry—where postwar agitation occurred in favor of making them *communes de plein exercice* and granting them parliamentary representatives. See: John Ballard, "The Porto Novo Incidents of 1923: Politics in the Colonial Era," *Odu: University of Ife Journal of African Studies* 1 (1965), pp. 52–75; and Anne Summers and R. W. Johnson, "World War I Conscription and Social Change in Guinea," *Journal of African History* 19 (1978), pp. 25–38.

[40] *ANS*: Affaires politiques: 17 G 234 (108). The latter quote is from Bouna Ndiaye's correspondence with Merlin; the governor general was, however, in full accord with these views.

[41] "*Négrogogue*" was the disparaging term used by Merlin and his associates to describe these French officials.

[42] On various characterizations of "Diagnism" in the French press, see: *ANS*: Affaires politiques: 17 G 233 (108).

[43] On the creation of the *conseil colonial* and the respective attitudes of Merlin, Sarraut, and Diagne toward this initiative, see: *ANS*: Affaires politiques: 17 G 234 (108). See also: Searing, "Accommodation and Resistance," pp. 489–96; Johnson, *The Emergence of Black Politics*, pp. 211–12; and La Guerre, *Enemies of Empire*, pp. 27–29.

[44] On the communal elections of 1921, see: *ANOM*: 14 MI 2356. On the social backgrounds of the chiefs as well as their political leanings, see: Searing, "Accommodation and Resistance," pp. 499–507; and La Guerre, *Enemies of Empire*, p. 28.

[45] On the 1921 session of the *conseil colonial*, see: Searing, "Accommodation and Resistance," pp. 501–07.

[46] On Sarraut's visit and Diagne's efforts to have Merlin replaced, see: *ANS*: Affaires politiques: 17 G 234 (108). On Merlin's countermeasures against the Diagnists, see: *ANS*: Affaires politiques: 17 G 233 (108) and 17 G 234 (108).

[47] On the 1922 session of the council, see: Searing, "Accommodation and Resistance," pp. 514–15.

[48] On the *Pacte de Bordeaux*, see: *ANS*: Affaires politiques: 17 G 234 (108). See also: Searing, "Accommodation and Resistance," pp. 517–32.

[49] In this guise, Diagne continued to serve as deputy until his death in 1934. For interpretations of Diagne's motives in concluding the *Pacte de Bordeaux*, see: G. Wesley Johnson, "Blaise Diagne: Master Politician of Senegal," *Tarikh* 1 (1966), pp. 51–57; Searing, "Accommodation and Resistance," pp. 517–32; and Amody Aly Dieng, *Blaise Diagne: Député noire de l'Afrique* (Paris: Editions Choka, 1990), pp. 142–48, 167–70.

[50] For a recent Senegalese's interpretation that condemns Diagne's actions as "political treason," see Dieng, *Blaise Diagne*, p. 108. For an elaboration on the veterans' views of Diagne, see, for example, Galaye Gueye (3A), and Masserigne Soumare (4A).

[51] See Diouf, "Aux Electeurs sénégalais," *ANOM*: 14 MI 2880.

[52] On the communal legislative elections of 1924 and 1928, see: *ANOM*: 14 MI 2880. See also: Searing, "Accommodation and Resistance," pp. 532–43; and François Zuccarelli, *La Vie politique Sénégalaise (1789–1940)* (Paris: CHEAM, 1987), pp. 123–38.

[53] On the backgrounds of the members of these organizations, information on which was compiled by police informers, see: *ANS*: Affaires politiques: 21 G 27 (17); 21 G 30 (17); 21 G 38 (17); and 21 G 111 (28). For discussions of the political orientation of these groups as well as the intellectual influences on them, see also: J. Ayo Langley, "Pan-Africanism in Paris, 1924–1936," *Journal of Modern African Studies* 7 (1969), pp. 69–94; James S. Spiegler, "Aspects of Nationalist Thought Among French-Speaking West Africans, 1921–39" (D. Phil. Thesis: Oxford University, 1968); Mar Fall, *Des Tirailleurs Sénégalais aux . . . Blacks: Les Africains noirs en France* (Paris: Editions L'Harmattan, 1986), pp. 19–26; and Philippe Dewitte, *Les Mouvements nègres en France, 1919–1939* (Paris: Editions L'Harmattan, 1985), pp. 74–89, 125–210.

[54] The quote is from *Les Continents*, 1 octobre 1924.

⁵⁵ "L'Esclavagisme colonial: nous ne sommes pas des enfants," *Les Continents*, 1 juillet 1924.

⁵⁶ On Sow, Tounkara, and Caminade and Senghor's relations with them, see: *ANS:* Affaires politiques: 21 G 27 (17). On Senghor's political activities during this period, see: *ANS:* Affaires politiques: 21 G 30 (17). For biographical sketches of him, see also: Robert Cornevin, "Du Sénégal à la Provence: Lamine Senghor (1889–1927) pionnier de la négritude," in Mélanges André Villard, *Provence historique* 25 (1975), pp. 69–77; and Dieng, *Blaise Diagne*, pp. 105–11. See also Masserigne Soumaire (4A).

⁵⁷ *ANS:* Affaires politiques: 21 G 27 (17) and 21 G 38 (17). In October 1926, the French sections of the C.D.R.N. ostensibly numbered 250 in Marseilles, 150 in Bordeaux, 300 in Havre, and 200 in Paris. A section also existed in Dakar, where *La voix des Nègres* was disseminated illegally.

⁵⁸ *La Race nègre*, novembre–décembre 1930.

⁵⁹ This political continuum was also evidenced in other specific ways. Diagne's proposals for increased African representation in Parliament in the early 1920s anticipated the legislative reforms adopted by the Fourth Republic in 1946. See: G. Wesley Johnson, Jr., *The Emergence of Black Politics in Senegal*, pp. 209–10, 216. Léopold S. Senghor, the future president of Senegal, was also influenced by the example of both Diagne, whom Senghor visited in Paris in the late 1920s, and the expatriates in France. His theory of negritude owed much to the earlier writing of René Maran, the West Indian novelist and member of the L.U.D.R.N. Senghor's party, the *Bloc Démocratique Sénégalais*, was based on a political coalition of rural and urban interests that was prefigured by the alliance Diagne attempted to forge with his Republican-Socialist Party in 1919. On Senghor's intellectual and political influences, see: Léopold Senghor, "René Maran, précurseur de la négritude," in *Hommage à René Maran* (Paris: Présence Africaine, 1965), pp. 9–13; William B. Cohen, "French Racism and its African Impact," in G. Wesley Johnson, Jr., ed. *Double Impact: France and West Africa in the Age of Imperialism* (Westport, CT, and London: Greenwood Press, 1985), pp. 305–18; and Janet G. Vaillant, *Black, French, and African: A Life of Léopold Sédar Senghor* (Cambridge and London: Harvard University Press, 1990), pp. 64–86.

⁶⁰ See: *Annuaire du Gouvernement Général de l'Afrique Occidentale Française, 1917– 1921* (Paris: Emile Larose, 1921), pp. 378–81.

⁶¹ Myron Echenberg, *Colonial Conscripts: The "Tirailleurs Sénégalais" in French West Africa, 1857–1960* (Portsmouth, NH: Heinemann/London: James Currey, 1991), p. 51.

⁶² On schools and improved health care due to the training of *médicins indigènes*, see: Catherine Coquery-Vidrovitch, "French Black Africa," in *Cambridge History of Africa*, Vol. 7: *1905 to 1940*, ed. A. D. Roberts (Cambridge: Cambridge University Press, 1986), pp. 329–92. On the expansion of the transportation network, see: Paul E. Pheffer, "The African Influence on French Colonial Railroads in Senegal," in G. Wesley Johnson, Jr., ed., *Double Impact: France and West Africa in the Age of Imperialism* (Westport, CT, and London: Greenwood Press, 1985), pp. 31–49.

⁶³ On postwar labor movements and the prominence of veterans, see: *ANOM:* 14 MI 2356. See also: Uyisenga Charles, "La Participation de la Colonie du Sénégal à 'l'effort de guerre,' 1914–1918" (Mémoire de Maîtrise: University of Dakar, 1978), pp. 162–63; Pheffer, "The African Influence on French Colonial Railroads," pp. 36–38; and Frederick Cooper, *Decolonization and African Society: The Labor Question in French and British*

Africa (Cambridge: Cambridge University Press, 1996), pp. 31–43. See also: Demba Mboup: 6B.

[64] On the volume of peanut exports, see: Xavier Guiraud, *L'Arachide sénégalais: Monographie d'economie coloniale* (Paris: Librairie Technique et Economique, 1937), table, p. 37.

[65] Gellar, *Structural Changes and Colonial Dependency*, pp. 49–67.

[66] For example, the population of Dakar, which far outstripped the growth rate in any of the other communes, increased by less than 25,000 between 1921 and 1932, or from 37,145 to 61,400. On interwar and post-World War II migratory patterns, see: François Manchuelle, *Willing Migrants: Soninke Labor Diasporas, 1848–1969* (Athens: Ohio University Press/London: James Currey, 1997), pp. 146–212.

[67] L. B. Venema, *The Wolof of Saloum: Social Structure and Rural Development in Senegal* (Wageningen: Center for Agricultural Publishing and Documentation, 1978), p. 41.

[68] See Searing, "Accommodation and Resistance," pp. 549–57, and Martin Klein, "Traditional Political Institutions and Colonial Domination," *African Historical Studies* 4 (1971), pp. 659–68.

[69] On the decline of artisanal craftsmanship, see: Klein, "Colonial Rule and Structural Change," pp. 90–93; and Moitt, "Slavery and Emancipation in Senegal's Peanut Basin," p. 46. On the circumstances of postwar manumission, see: Thiam Nding: 3B. For general trends, see also: Venema, *The Wolof of Saloum*, pp. 91–92, 170–77; Martin A. Klein, *Slavery and Colonial Rule in French West Africa* (Cambridge: Cambridge University Press, 1998), pp. 197–251; Klein, "Colonial Rule and Structural Change," pp. 79–83; and Andrew F. Clark, "Slavery and its Demise in the Upper Senegal Valley, West Africa, 1890–1920," *Slavery and Abolition* 15 (1994), pp. 51–71.

[70] On the Mouride settlers, see: Donald B. Cruise O'Brien, *Saints and Politicians: Essays in the Organisation of a Senegalese Peasant Society* (London: Cambridge University Press, 1975), pp. 57–185.

[71] On the social backgrounds of the communal politicians and their function as political patrons, see: Searing, "Accommodation and Resistance," pp. 462–65; and Johnson, "The Senegalese Urban Elite," pp. 143–86.

[72] On the decline in size of rural residential units among the Wolof, see: Venema, *The Wolof of Soloum*, pp. 124–46, 174–83; and Klein, "Colonial Rule and Structural Change," pp. 90–95.

[73] Among the Senegalese veterans interviewed, 9 out of 32 decided to leave their prewar domicile. The proportion increases slightly (11 out of 34) if expatriate *tirailleurs* from Guinea and Mali are included. One respondent did not mention his postwar life.

[74] In the sample interviewed, 14 of 17 free peasants returned to their fields (two were unclear about their later lives, while one emigrated). Conversely, over half of the other orders did not return (i.e., 2 of 2 aristocrats, 2 of 5 from casted lineages, and 3 of 5 among veterans of servile origin). Among the *tirailleurs* interviewed, the distribution of those leaving was: Wolof: 6 of 14; Serer: 1 of 5; Fulbe: 0 of 7; and Lebu: 0 of 5. Among the Serahuli, 2 of 2 also departed. Although the sample is too small to be statistically valid, it is useful (with the possible exception of the Serahuli) as an indication of likely trends.

[75] Of those interviewed who did not return home, 10 out of 11 were missing at least one parent after the war. Two-thirds (4 of 6) of the *tirailleurs* interviewed who were the children of unions with a later wife departed. Daba Dembele: 5A and 5B.

[76] Momar Candji: 2A. See also: Sickh Yero Sy: 2A.

[77] For example, Yoro Diaw (2B), who became a commercial middleman dealing in African peanuts and merchandise obtained from French firms, stayed in his village and eventually became chief. On Tukulors, see: Seydou Amadou Thiam: 1A; and Malal Gassala: 3A.

[78] Saer Anta Loum: 1B. See also: Nar Diouf: 5B.

[79] Bara Seck: 2B. On the persistence of previous modes of labor to earn a livelihood among Mouride *talibes*, see also: Thiam Nding: 4A; and Ibrahima Thiam: 2B.

[80] For examples, see, respectively: Doudou Ndao: 1A and 4A; Daba Dembele: 5B; Abdou Karim Gaye: 5A and 6A; Galaye Gueye: 1A and 2B; Masserigne Soumare: 4A; Antoine Diouf: 1A; Ibrahima Camara: 1B; and Abdoulaye Gassama: 2B. Among *tirailleur* N.C.O.s, 5 of 8 belonged to this group.

[81] Daba Dembele: 6A.

[82] Among veterans from the *banlieue* communities of Yoff and Ouakam interviewed, 6 of 7 returned home after the war and resumed their former occupations. Significantly, all 6 of those returning were Lebu; 5 became farmers again, while 1 alternated between tending crops and working as a petty *commerçant* in Diourbel, just as his father had done before 1914. The sole exception to this pattern was Niaki Gueye (1A), a Wolof, whose family had emigrated from Kayor and who subsequently became a carpenter.

[83] Of 15 *originaires* interviewed, 13 described their postwar lives. Among these, at least 7 of 13 departed their homes after 1919 to pursue jobs elsewhere. Two-thirds (4 of 6) of the Wolof veterans interviewed worked outside of the communes after the war. For similar examples among the Fulbe and Lebu, see, respectively: Mamadou Djigo: 1A; and Mbaye Khary Diagne: 4A, 5A, and 5B.

[84] Among the *originaires* who left their prewar communities, five of seven were missing either one or both their parents when they returned from the war. Two *originaires* fell into this category, and both left their homes. See: Ndiaga Niang: 2B; and Abdoulaye Gueye: 1B. Among departed *originaires*, 4 of 7 eventually returned to their prewar communities, though often only after they retired. The balance remained in the towns where they had worked. Conversely, none of the 11 *tirailleur* migrants returned to live in their pre-1914 residences.

[85] Among the ex-servicemen interviewed, all 7 in this group were employed directly by the French. On prize-fighting in France during the early 1920s, see: Mbaye Khary Diagne: 4B. On factory work, lorry driving, and the offer of a job on the metropolitan police force (declined), see respectively: Mbaye Khary Diagne: 5A and 5B; and Abdoulaye Ndiaye (Z): 2A.

[86] For examples, see respectively: Mamadou Djigo: 1A; Boubacar Gueye: 1A; Thiecouta Diallo: 1B; Ndiaga Niang: 3A; Abdoulaye Gueye: 2A; and Abdoulaye Ndiaye: 6A and 6B. Among the *originaires* interviewed in this group, only 2 of 5 returned to farming (or fishing) as their primary means of earning a livelihood after the war. See: Giribul Diallo: 2B; and Aliou Diakhate: 2A. On working for the French, see: Abdoulaye Diaw: 3A; Demba Mboup: 1A, 2A, and 6A; and Jacques William: 2B.

[87] Thiecouta Diallo: 2A.

[88] Among 57 ex-servicemen interviewed, 36 expressed an opinion about whether they would have reenlisted: 9 would have done so. On the remobilization of some *originaires* during the Second World War, see: Mbaye Khary Diagne: 5B; Abdoulaye Ndiaye: 6B; and Ndiaga Niang: 1B.

[89] The distribution was: 2 of 7 *originaires*; 1 of 3 from the *banlieues*, and 6 of 26 *tirailleurs*. There is no apparent correlation between ethnicity, precolonial status, military rank, or postwar occupations among those expressing these views. On attitude, see: Nouma Ndiaye: 3A; and Thiecouta Diallo: 2B. On pride, see: Mody Sow: 4B; Doudou Ndao: 4A; Galaye Gueye: 2B; and Malal Gassala: 3A.

[90] This was the viewpoint of 27 of the 36 veterans who expressed an opinion on this subject. Ibrahima Camara: 3A. Biram Mbodji Tine: 3A.

[91] Giribul Diallo: 2B; Mbaye Khary Diagne: 6A.

[92] Alassane Kane: 5A.

[93] Saer Anta Loum: 1B; and Samba Diop: 3A.

CONCLUSION: THE LEGACY OF THE FIRST WORLD WAR IN SENEGAL

The European maelstrom in which the Senegalese were engulfed between 1914 and 1918 had a profound and far-ranging impact on the lives of West Africans. The wartime demands made by the French touched Africans more directly than any other previous exactions imposed on them by the colonial regime, and on a scale that was hitherto unprecedented. Any assessment of the legacy of the war must therefore be tempered by an awareness of the transformations that were wrought by it, and also of the human suffering that was endured.

THE DIALECTIC OF MILITARY SERVICE

The recruitment policy in West Africa was designed to serve French, not African, interests. A response to the numerical inferiority of the French army before 1914, and the perilous military situation of *la patrie* thereafter, the policy placed a premium on raising colonial soldiers to satisfy metropolitan needs. In this regard, it represented nothing less than the direct expropriation of African labor and lives (in the guise of military conscripts) by the French state. Nevertheless, although the French initiated the recruitment policy, they did not foresee, nor could they negate, the ideological implications of what they had set in motion. Indeed, the logic of military service on behalf of the state, which in Western and Central Europe had been equated since the mid-nineteenth century with the acquisition of "constitutional" rights by those bearing arms, was extended to the colonies.[1]

First enunciated during the war by Senegalese *originaires* and subsequently echoed by other Africans throughout the Federation, the tangible effects of such appeals remained restricted during the immediate postwar period. Yet the transformation of the war's meaning into an African quest for "rights" offered a compelling counterpoint to the worst injustices of the recent colonial past, and it bespoke a mentality that was a harbinger of things to come. In this respect, the origins of the mentality that brought about an end to alien political domination can be traced to the aspirations first aroused among many Africans as a result of France's wartime recruitment policy.

THE IMPACT OF THE WAR ON SENEGAL

The price Africans paid for this change was very high indeed. Between 1914 and 1918, Senegal provided more soldiers for the French army (as a percentage of its total population) than any other colony in A.O.F. In all, nearly 29,000 men—representing 2.4 percent of the entire population and probably more than one-third of all males of military age—were mobilized. Moreover, in addition to those sent overseas, upwards of 15,000 able-bodied men (according to the most conservative French estimates) fled to seek sanctuary from the recruiters in foreign colonies. When combined with those departing for France, it seems likely that, at a minimum, about 45,000 men were uprooted from Senegal as a direct result of the war. This figure represents 3.6 percent of the prewar population, and in terms of the capacity of preindustrial agrarian societies to sustain themselves in times of war, it exceeds the upward limits of what was historically supportable.[2] It also suggests that between 1914 and 1918, perhaps as many as one-half of all adult males in Senegal between the ages of 20 and 28—constituting the most physically active and productive element of society—were temporarily displaced from their homeland.[3]

Discounting those permanently disabled in the fighting (which may have approximated a quarter of those engaged), combat fatalities among the Senegalese (and especially the *tirailleurs*) were exceptionally high. Though impossible to calculate with accuracy owing to the inexactitude of the French records, these may be reckoned at a minimum of 4,600 men. It is extremely likely, however, that Senegalese casualties were much higher still—perhaps on the order of 7,000 soldiers killed.[4] As a percentage of the prewar population, the scale of these losses approximated, and in some cases exceeded, the suffering experienced by the European belligerents during the war.

THE LEGACY OF THE EXPERIENCE

The legacy of the participation of Senegalese soldiers in the First World War can be assessed from different vantage points. In France, the massive wartime contribution made by African troops to the nation's defense was seen in a positive light, and it had two abiding consequences. At a policy level, it was interpreted as vindicating the ideas advanced by Charles Mangin and other prewar proponents of *la force noire*. As a result, immediately after the conclusion of hostilities in 1919, Clemenceau's government institutionalized annual military recruitment in West Africa, though on a considerably reduced scale. Thereafter, the policy became a mainstay of French military calculations until it was finally abandoned some forty years later on the eve of African decolonization.[5] This policy continued to accord primacy to military considerations—particularly in periods of national crisis—over all other colonial concerns. As such, African soldiers frequently continued to be viewed by the policy makers in Paris as A.O.F.'s most valuable resource long after the First World War had ended.

Among the French populace, official praise and genuine popular gratitude for the soldiers' wartime contribution also led to a discernible change in the prewar image of Africans. Although French society continued to be deeply imbued with racist preconceptions—indeed, the military's hierarchical ranking of African "warrior races" was not abandoned until the 1930s—the earlier harsher images of Africans gradually became softened. In their place, alternative stereotypes emerged—epitomized by the sympathetic figure of the Senegalese *tirailleur*. Though pejorative and paternalistic, this image of Africans differed significantly from the prevailing preconceptions in the aftermath of the conquest. While this change in attitudes was gradual and highly circumscribed, the mental leap between an abstract prewar image of Africans as ferocious savages to an initial appreciation of their shared humanity was vast indeed.

The political legacy of the war for the Senegalese may be viewed from three temporal points of reference. Gauged against the standards of the pre-1914 era, the war represented a dramatic departure from the past. The status quo ante, with its unbridled administrative tyranny and its disregard for outrages committed against Africans, proved impossible to reimpose. Instead, the postwar period witnessed an amelioration of the most flagrant abuses of the earlier era and allowed the Senegalese some latitude for negotiations with the French. This represented a fundamental modification in the previous relations that had existed between the conquerors and the colonized. Irrespective of how it was manifested—in the rights conferred on African citizens, in the ability of veterans who were immune from the *indigénat* to speak their minds, or in the growing official toleration for the Mourides—it derived directly from the war.

Paradoxically, this transformation in the tenor of the colonial order led to a more complete consolidation of French control during the interwar period. Elite co-optation—which entailed only minor concessions but eventually enlisted the support of virtually all important Senegalese interest groups—proved a more effective means of governance than continued reliance on force. Nevertheless, the consolidation of the colonial regime during the interwar years proved ephemeral, and the movement that culminated in Senegalese independence also traces it origins to new political forces set in motion by the war. Indeed, the post-1945 political reforms that led, during the course of the next fifteen years, to complete independence, as well as the coalition between urban and rural Senegalese elites that helped bring independence about, were prefigured by the earlier initiatives undertaken by Diagne and his followers between 1918 and 1923.

Within Senegalese society, the legacy of military service overseas had an abiding effect. In social terms, the war and its immediate aftermath accelerated the breakdown of precolonial social allegiances as older networks of dependency and interdependency were replaced by new ones. This transformation was perhaps best exemplified by the rapid decline of domestic servitude as an institution as well as continued erosion of the prestige of the older African hereditary elites. Nevertheless, these changes, though significant in the long term, occurred gradually and, manumission aside, their effects were seldom perceived by contemporaries. Instead, for most veterans returning to their villages after the war, continuity rather than change was the hallmark of everyday life. Notwithstanding some significant exceptions, most resumed a style of life much as it was before.

If the pace of social transformation stimulated by the war was measured, the change in the Senegalese image of the French arising from the wartime experience was immediate and profound. Indeed, compared to the alteration in the metropolitan image of Africans, the change in Senegalese perceptions of the French was far more dramatic and complete. Among those groups that contributed to this process in Senegal, veterans played a paramount role. Indeed, far from viewing their former conquerors in a forbidding or exalted light, Africans also began to view the French in more humanistic terms because of their encounter overseas. As a result, the myth of universal European racial superiority, which the *colons* had earlier striven to assert and which provided the principal intellectual rationale for prewar colonial domination, was called into serious question.

The altered perceptions both of the French and of themselves inspired in the Senegalese by the veterans signified a mental transformation of cardinal importance. Indeed, it represented nothing less than an essential prerequisite for all subsequent redefinitions in the relationship between Africans and Europeans during the colonial era and thereafter. In this respect, the contemporary belief that Africans and Europeans are united through their common humanity rather than divided by immutable racial differences stems, at least in part, from the encounter in the Great War.

NOTES

[1] John Kegan, *The Second World War* (London: Hutchinson, 1989), pp. 22–25.

[2] The limit of sustained wartime mobilization in agrarian societies is considered by military historians to be about 3 percent of the population. It has only been achieved in

very exceptional circumstances, such as during the Punic Wars. See Gwynne Dyer, *War* (New York: Crown Publishers, 1985), p. 44.

[3] No reliable data on age and sex distributions in Senegal exist for the period 1914 to 1918. This estimate is based on the 1976 census, which was the first in which such information was compiled; it indicates that males between the ages of 20 and 28 constituted about 8 percent of the population. Though the demographic pyramid may have subsequently shifted owing to improved diet and health care as well as declining infant mortality, this figure nevertheless suggests that the proportion of young males dislocated by the war was very high and almost certainly unprecedented. For demographic statistics, see: Moussa Soumah, "Population," in *Atlas du Sénégal*, ed. Paul Pélissier (Paris: Editions Jeune Afrique, 1980), pp. 26–29.

[4] For a discussion of Senegalese casualty figures, see Chapter 5.

[5] See Myron Echenberg, *Colonial Conscripts: The "Tirailleurs Sénégalais" in French West Africa, 1857–1960* (Portsmouth, NH: Heinemann/London: James Currey, 1991).

POSTSCRIPT:
DISCORDANT VOICES:
THE VETERANS SPEAK

To assess the legacy of the Senegalese experience during the First World War, it is appropriate to conclude with the personal interpretations of those who fought in it. Although frequently aware of the broader themes historians have used to shed light on this aspect of the African past, for them the war was not an abstraction but a palpable reality, and their interpretations of its significance were deeply personal. Moreover, though often sharing similar memories and concurring about some facets of their experience, they often profoundly disagreed about its meaning.

This variation in individual interpretations can be seen as having been influenced by a series of objective factors: the prewar social backgrounds of the veterans; the year and conditions under which they entered the army; and the units in which they served, their rank or status, and the nature of their ordeal during the fighting. It was also affected by the wounds they incurred, the extent of physical disability they suffered, or the deaths of brothers or kinsmen in the army or of loved ones at home during their absence. Other influencing factors include the extent of their contacts with metropolitan French and their treatment by them; the range of opportunities (or lack thereof) they were afforded on their return to Senegal; and their mature reflections about the course their lives had taken viewed from the vantage point of eighty-odd years. In some instances, however, a rational explanation for certain attitudes defies the logic of such analytical correlations. For a few, the causal nexus prompting their views ultimately remains subjective, elusive, and inexplicable.

Nevertheless, the divergent outlook of the soldiers offers a poignant and eloquent testament that is essential for the historian to contemplate. The first generation to come of age under the colonial system, the soldiers represented an important transitional group between those whose formative experience and outlook derived from the conquest and those born after the war. Although not unaware of what had transpired earlier, the postwar generation was temporally distanced from these events and generally viewed the movement that culminated in independence as the seminal public event in their lives. As such, the veterans exemplify the painful price that one generation often pays in giving birth to another.

Although many lived long enough to witness these later events, most sought to define the meaning of the war within the context of what had come before rather than after. Whether or not they perceived the war as an agent of change, the prewar era was the ultimate arbiter of its meaning and the way in which they defined its significance.

Despite offering extremely diverse interpretations of the war's significance, the views of the veterans fall into three categories. Some felt that "nothing [of] lasting" significance occurred as a result of the war.[1] Others felt that their participation in the conflict inaugurated a series of important changes, evidenced in a wide variety of tangible ways: in their increased knowledge of the wider world and their feelings about themselves; in changing the structure of Senegalese society, the tenor of the postwar colonial order, and their subsequent relations with the French. Finally, some remained profoundly ambivalent about their experience and retained a philosophical aversion to rendering such judgments.

Broadly speaking, the *tirailleurs* recruited between 1914 and 1917 were most inclined to believe that little was changed as a result of the war or, if changes had occurred, that these were comparatively insignificant and incommensurate with the scale of their sacrifices.[2] This is understandable. These men were frequently coerced into the army against their will, normally secluded from the French as much as possible, and bore a disproportionate share of Senegalese casualties. They were also usually released from the army without having acquired skills that would be of subsequent value to them and frequently resumed their lives much as before. Succinctly summarizing this outlook, Sambu Ndiaye explained: "I didn't feel many [personal] changes [as a result of the war]; I was a farmer before I left, and I was still a farmer after I came back."[3]

Moreover, even though the "knowledge gained" of the world beyond their homeland was most frequently mentioned as a benefit resulting from the war, this was obtained at too high a price for others: "Nothing I saw [overseas] was worth our [sacrifices], and the [loss] of all the people who died during the war."[4] Furthermore, the curbs placed on knowledge acquisition in the army were a source of indignation rather than of personal satisfaction for some. Sera Ndiaye, who had been buried alive by high explosives, angrily recalled:

> We went to France, we fought for France, and the French took us by force
> to fight for them. [But] we learned nothing [there]—[not] even the French
> language. They only taught us some rudimentary [commands], [in order]
> to use us in the war. But they didn't care about teaching us the structure
> and the sound of their language. So [although we] went to the war, [we]
> came back here without any real knowledge of the French language.[5]

Indeed, in addition to stressing the continuity in village life and the absence
of personal change in themselves, the other single most pervasive feeling
among these soldiers about their wartime experience was of having been
exploited by the French.

Although sentiments of exploitation were held to some degree by nearly
all pre-1918 *tirailleurs*, the most bitter denunciations of French bad faith
came, not surprisingly, from those men whose lives had been most distorted
by the war—the Senegalese *mutilés de guerre*.[6] Some were excoriating in
their indictments: "Tiaroye, when they killed many of [the Senegalese prisoners of war returning from Germany at the end of World War II]," was but
one example of the type of recompense that Africans could expect from the
French for their sacrifices.[7] Others like Momar Khary Niang, though no less
indignant, were more explicit in explaining their personal grievances: "I have
nothing. I am poor. And all I had to give them at that time was my blood.
[But after making this kind of] sacrifice [for the French], you didn't receive
anything in compensation. Only this unfair pension."[8]

Indeed, the inequality of pensions symbolized in the most graphic way
possible for *tirailleurs* both their maltreatment during the war as well as the
lingering injustice and ingratitude of the French government thereafter. "What
they pay us as a pension and what they pay the French [veterans] is different.
[But] we all went to the same war and there was no difference [there] because the bullets could not distinguish between a 'white' man and a 'black'
man. They shot everyone. [But] the division [is] not equal between [us], [even
though] we went to the same war and faced the same dangers."[9] Hence, the
legacy of the wartime experience for these men was one of continued misuse
and neglect, perhaps best exemplified by the Wolof saying recalled by one
veteran: "We sacrificed much during the war, but the Frenchmen never com-
pensated us for our efforts."[10]

Yet other Senegalese veterans disagreed with this perspective and considered the war as nothing less than a crucial turning point in their lives. Those
who believed that enduring changes had resulted from their military service
in France roughly fall into three groups: (1) the *originaires* enlisted in the
communes, (2) most soldiers recruited in the Protectorate in 1918, and (3) a
significant minority (about one-quarter of the total) of *tirailleurs* who entered the army during the first three years of the war. With a few notable
exceptions, these men in general offered more positive assessments of the

outcome of the war. Like most pre-1918 *tirailleurs*, their views appear to have been tempered by a series of objective factors.

The mobilization in the communes was far more intense than anywhere else in Senegal, and as a result the war became more highly politicized there than elsewhere in the colony. In addition to receiving a tangible reward—citizenship—for their military service, the *originaires* suffered proportionately fewer casualties than the majority of their rural counterparts. Soldiers recruited in 1918 were also frequently influenced by Diagne's rhetoric; hence, they were inclined to interpret their experience in a considerably different light than did those who had gone to France before them. Moreover, they suffered no direct casualties during the war, apart from the few who were later killed in North Africa or Syria.

Even among those conscripted between 1914 and 1917, however, a few interpreted the legacy of the war in positive terms. Although subjected to the full horrors experienced by the *tirailleurs*, these men too were frequently distinguished from their counterparts in particular ways. They included a high proportion of noncommissioned officers, soldiers who were exceptionally lucky and never seriously wounded in the fighting, and veterans whose prewar status was most dramatically and favorably affected as a result of the war. Although consistently emphasizing the terrible nature of combat in the trenches as well as the harshness of their ordeal, these soldiers nevertheless felt that their service on behalf of France had led to important and lasting changes manifested in virtually all aspects of postwar life.

Like many *tirailleurs*, they too believed that their overseas experience had contributed to an enhanced understanding of the world, but instead of minimizing its significance, they viewed its implications as profound. As Samba Laga Diouf affirmed: "The war brought an awakening among the people, because [we] learned some things that [our] fathers and [our] ancestors had not known."[11] Moreover, the knowledge they acquired in the army often resulted in tangible material benefits afterwards. Having often become fluent in French and been exposed to more prolonged and varied contacts with the metropolitan population, they consequently gained a more sophisticated understanding of European society than most ordinary soldiers. As a result, many of these men obtained (or were offered) jobs in the colony's administrative or commercial sectors after the war.

Aside from enhanced employment opportunities, the contrast with the prewar period also extended, in the opinion of many from rural areas, to the internal dynamics of Senegalese society. Village life, though in many ways unaffected by the war, was nevertheless exposed to new influences as soldiers returned from abroad, others were attracted to nearby towns, and those remaining adopted new modes of existence.[12] Domestic servitude, which had scarcely been affected by French rule before 1914, came to an end after the war. For those manumitted this change was profound, and regardless of the magnitude of the personal sacrifice they were required to make during the war, it was deemed worthwhile. In the words of Thiam Nding, a former slave who lost a leg in the fighting but obtained his freedom: "It is always better to be free, because [then] you can make a life of your own."[13]

In the eyes of these veterans, however, the most dramatic changes occasioned by the war were manifested in new ways "of thinking and behaving."[14] This was evident in the enhanced "prestige" enjoyed by the Senegalese and the "growing respect" accorded them by the French.[15] For those who lacked this prior to 1914, these accomplishments represented nothing less than a basic transformation in the relations that had existed between the colonizers and the colonized since the advent of the conquest. In the communes, the acquisition of citizenship (and hence the opportunity to seek legal redress for grievances) ensured that the previous maltreatment of Africans as "things—as nothing" by many *colons* came to an end. Henceforth, such prewar standards of behavior became "unacceptable," while overt expressions of racist denigration ceased to be tolerated.[16]

Nor were such changes restricted to the communes. In the Protectorate, in addition to the new respect accorded to returning soldiers, the aftermath of the war also led to an amelioration of previous abuses of authority by the French. Explaining the enhanced status enjoyed by veterans and the example they set for those around them, Nar Diouf, a former corporal recruited in 1915, recalled:

I received many lasting things from the war. I demonstrated my dignity and courage, and [I] won the respect of the people and the [colonial] government. And whenever the people of the village had something to contest [with the French]—and they didn't dare do it [themselves] because they were afraid of them—I used to do it for them. And many times when people had problems with the government, I used to go with my decorations and arrange the situation for [them]. Because whenever the *Tubabs* saw your decorations, they knew that they [were dealing with] a very important person. . . . And I gained this ability—of obtaining justice over a *Tubab*— from the war.

[For example], one day a *Tubab* came here [to the village]—he came from the *service de génie* (he was a kind of doctor)—to make an examination of the people. So he came here, and there was a small boy who was blind. And [the boy] was walking, [but] he couldn't see, and he bumped into the *Tubab*. And the *Tubab* turned and pushed the boy [down]. And when I saw that, I came and said to the *Tubab*: "Why have you pushed this boy? [Can't] you see that he is blind?" And the *Tubab* said: "Oh, *pardon, pardon*. I did not know. I will never do it again, excuse me!" [But] before the war, [no matter what they did], it would not have been possible to do that with a *Tubab*.[17]

Though some veterans attributed this transformation in the tenor of colonial society directly to Diagne—who "freed [us] from French slavery"—others were more skeptical about the significance of Diagne's contribution, and a few felt they had been "betrayed" by him.[18] Nevertheless, most believed that the war initiated fundamental changes and many felt that a direct link existed between military service in France and the eventual fruition of the independence movement forty years later. As Ibrahima Thiam, a devout Mouride and a 1918 recruit, commented:

> The war changed many, many things. At first, when we joined the army, when you had an argument or a problem with a "white" man, what happened? You were wrong; you were [always] wrong. But later, those things changed. [Then] they looked into the matter and determined who was wrong or right. [But] before that time, the "black" man didn't mean anything. So that [change] was something [very important]. [And] the respect we gained [from] the war [continued] increasing; it never [diminished]. [And this] respect [continued] increasing day to day—up until [it culminated in] the Independence Day.[19]

From this perspective, the First World War was perceived as the crucial turning point between the degradation following the conquest and the eventual reclamation of Senegalese sovereignty. Indeed, the assertion of African dignity and the altered consciousness that arose as a result of the war were deemed by these individuals as nothing less than an essential prerequisite for all else that followed.[20]

Other veterans were less comfortable making such sweeping judgments and, indeed, were reluctant to render an interpretation about the historical significance of the war at all. Though few in number (and defying systematic categorization), this group remained profoundly ambivalent about the meaning of their experience. One veteran—the son of a *chef de canton*, literate in French, and a former sergeant—looked back on the war from the vantage point of an extended lifetime and sought to assess its impact. Although exceptionally knowledgeable about the events of the period as well as what had transpired in Senegalese public life, he professed uncertainty about the war's ultimate significance. In Masserigne Soumare's eyes, the only indisputable change arising from his wartime experience was an enhanced sense of personal humility: "I prayed [more] after the war [than I had before]."[21]

Several others shared similar sentiments. Though of less exalted ancestry and having had entirely different experiences during the war and in later life, they were no less unequivocal in asserting their feelings of ambiguity. Their outlook was perhaps most aptly expressed by one *tirailleur* who viewed historians' efforts to seek a correlation between

African participation in the war and subsequent change as a non sequitur. The sole survivor among four young men sent from his village, Mahmout Demba declared: "I don't know whether there was anything lasting [that resulted] from the war, but [I do know] that no one can replace a human life."[22]

This interpretation is compelling. Indeed, it is appropriate to recall, as Demba did, some of those who never returned from France—men who often had no choice in the matter of their induction, were compelled to fight in a conflict they did not comprehend, and whose lives were sacrificed in a war that was not theirs. Long since forgotten by the French, who kept incomplete records of their names, their lives were remembered only in the aged thoughts of their youthful comrades.[23] As the *griot*'s drum beaten in their villages to announce their deaths echoes the anguish felt at their loss across the years, remember and do not forget:

"Baidy Ba" from Dioumandou

"a boy called Baba" from Bayenadji

"Salif Beye" from Guia

"Momar Diagne" from Dakar

"Ousmane Diagne" from Ouakam

"Omar Diahatti"

"Momar Diop" from Kabrousse

"Papa Mar Diop" from St. Louis

"Samba Gueye" from Pout

"Ibrahim . . . who committed suicide"

"Omar Kebe"

"Momar Massa"

"Gana Mbaye" from Dakar

"Abdoulaye Ndiaye" from Louga

"Djobe Ndiaye"

"Mor Ndoye" from Pout

"Mbaye Niang" from Saint Louis

"Massamba Sarr" from Louga

"Assane Seye" from Ouakam

"Demba Sow" from Pout

"Mamadou Sow" from Ouakam

"My two elder brothers, [who were] killed at the Dardanelles."

And remember, too, the unborn child of Seydou Amadou Thiam's sister, who perished from her mother's grief.[24]

NOTES

[1] Sickh Yero Sy: 2A.

[2] The attitudes of this group of Senegalese veterans are probably indicative of the vast majority of *tirailleurs* recruited elsewhere in A.O.F. before 1918, whose experiences were similar but who have left no testament. Significantly, their views were also shared by nearly all the women interviewed. Even more than the soldiers, Senegalese women were disposed to interpret the meaning of the war in profoundly negative terms, with the death of their loved ones as its only abiding legacy. See: Aminata Ngom: 1B; Coumba Kebe: 2B; Coumba Niane: 1A.

[3] Sambu Ndiaye: 3A. This self-appraisal was not always shared by those at home who witnessed their return. Most women felt that the soldiers had been altered in subtle ways by their experience—either by their acquisition of *"Tubab"* habits" or through their increased nervousness. See: Gamou Wade: 1A and 1B; Aminata Ngom: 1A; Coumba Kebe: 2B.

[4] Nouma Ndiaye: 3A. The acquisition of knowledge was referred to in a positive context by nearly half (47.8 percent) of the pre-1918 *tirailleurs*.

[5] Sera Ndiaye: 6A.

[6] Yoro Diaw: 3A; Malal Gassala: 3A; Abdou Karim Gaye: 1B.

[7] Bara Seck: 3A. This reference is to the French massacre in 1944 of Senegalese veterans at the training camp of Tiaroye. The soldiers, predominantly returning prisoners of war angry at the refusal of the French to award them back pay, were demonstrating in the camp when French soldiers opened fire on them. See Myron Echenberg, "Tragedy at Thiaroye: The Senegalese Soldiers' Uprising of 1944," in *African Labor History*, eds. Robin Cohen, Jean Copans, and Peter Gutkind (Beverly Hills: Sage Publications, 1978), pp. 109–28. See also Ousmane Sembene's critically acclaimed film, *Camp de Tiaroye*.

[8] Momar Khary Niang: 3A.

[9] Soudou Leye: 2B. Like rates of pay during the war, the pensions subsequently received by *tirailleurs* were substantially less than those given to French citizens. In 1996, *tirailleurs* with major physical disabilities (i.e., loss of an arm, leg, or both legs) still received only about 25 percent of the disability pensions allocated to their metropolitan counterparts. See "Etude comparative des tarifs de pension pour certaines infirmités graves," septembre 1996, Ministère des anciens combattants et victimes de guerre, Paris.

[10] Alassane Kane: 5A.

[11] Samba Laga Diouf: 2A.

[12] Yoro Diaw: 2B; Nar Diouf: 6A; and Amar Seck: 4A.

[13] Thiam Nding: 4A.

[14] Mbaye Khary Diagne: 5B.

[15] Yoro Diaw: 2B; Nar Diouf: 6A.

[16] Abdoulaye Ndiaye, 6B. Abdoulaye Pierre Diaw: 3B; Demba Mboup: 13A.

[17] Nar Diouf: 6A.

[18] Blaise Diagne was a highly controversial figure among veterans; opinions of him ranged from unabashed hero worship to the most scathing allegations of moral corruptness. Though on the whole positive, for the range of variation, see: Amar Seck: 4B; Ndiaga Niang: 2B; and Abdoulaye Gassama: 2B.

[19] Ibrahima Thiam: 2B and 3A.

[20] For other interpretations explicitly linking the soldiers' wartime contribution (often in the form of deferred French promises) with the acquisition of independence, see: Abdoulaye Ndiaye: 6B; Thiam Nding: 4B; and, significantly, the son of Nar Diouf (6A).

[21] Masserigne Soumare: 5A.

[22] Mahmout Demba: 2A.

[23] Anthony Clayton, *France, Soldiers and Africa* (London: Brassey's Defence Publishers, 1988). In marked contrast to the monuments found in villages and towns all over Europe, no names of the Africans who perished are inscribed on the three monuments to the Great War in Senegal.

[24] See, in order of sequence: Mamadou Ndiaye: 1A; Seydou Amadou Thiam: 1A; Diouli Missine: 2B; Ousmane Diagne: 2A; Alassane Kane: 3B; Makhoudia Ndiaye: 1A; Aliou Dioama: 1B; Ousmane Diagne: 2A and 2B; Sera Ndiaye: 5A; Abdoulaye Gassama: 2A; Makhoudia Ndiaye: 1A; Diouli Missine: 2B; Ousmane Diagne: 3B; Abdoulaye Ndiaye: 6A; Demba Mboup: 9B; Sera Ndiaye: 5A; Ndiaga Niang: 2B; Demba Mboup: 12A; Momar Candji: 2B; Sera Ndiaye: 5A; Alassane Kane: 3B; Samba Laga Diouf: 1B; Seydou Amadou Thiam: 1A.

GLOSSARY

Bataillon d'étapes: Communications or labor battalion.

Bourba: Title of the rulers of Jolof, one of the major precolonial Wolof states.

Bur Sine: Title of the rulers of Sine, one of the two precolonial Serer states.

Ceddo: Originally slave warriors in the service of Wolof kings; the word has also acquired the connotation of adhering to pre-Islamic religious precepts.

Cercle: Normally the smallest territorial unit headed by a European in the French administrative system.

Certificat d'hébergement: Lodging certificate necessary for a soldier to obtain authorization for a furlough.

Chef de canton: African chief designated by the French who commanded the smallest jurisdiction in the French administrative system; responsibilities included the collection of taxes, control of forced labor, and recruitment of soldiers.

Chef de village: African chief responsible at the local level for collecting taxes, providing forced laborers, and recruiting soldiers for the *chef de canton*.

Commandant: French administrative officer heading a *cercle*; possessed wide powers, especially judicial.

Communes de plein exercice: Cities in which Senegalese residents held (after 1916) the legal status of French citizens and had the right to vote for local officials, as well as for a Deputy to represent them in the French Chamber. St. Louis, Gorée, Rufisque, and Dakar constituted the Four Communes in Senegal.

Communes mixte: Cities in which African residents could elect local officials but, not being French citizens, could not vote for a Deputy.

Conseil général: Council composed of 20 members elected by *originaires* of the communes, which possessed deliberative, advisory, and some budgetary prerogatives; superseded by the *conseil colonial* in 1920.

Coupe coupe: Large heavy knife used in hand-to-hand combat; issued to *tirailleurs* in the Colonial Army.

Coups de main: Surprise raids.

Creole: A person of Eurafrican ancestry.

Croix de guerre: Military cross commemorating soldiers for heroism and those who received individual citations from their units.

Dag: Armed retainers of the *chef de canton.*

Damel: Title of the rulers of the precolonial Wolof state of Kayor.

Dara: A community of disciples who gathered for religious instruction and labored for the teacher; under the Mourides, these communities became important in the colonization of eastern Senegal after the First World War.

État civil: Civil status.

Force noire: Term used by French prewar proponents of expanded recruitment in West Africa to designate the force they would raise for use—if necessary—in a European war.

Gamelle: Soldier's mess tin.

Gardes de cercle: Paramilitary force used to back up authoritarian rule of the *commandant de cercle*; usually recruited from among ethnic groups alien to the locale where they were stationed and noted for their brutality.

Goumbala: Fulbe song normally sung before the shedding of blood.

Griots: Caste of musicians, historians, and praise-singers.

Habitants: Indigenous residents of the Four Communes.

Haut-Sénégal et Niger: French administrative territory to the east of Senegal; included all or part of the present states of Mali, Burkina Faso, and Niger.

Hivernage: Winter period (normally between November and April) when West African troops were withdrawn from the Front and stationed in the south of France (or North Africa).

Indigènat: Colonial law code that gave wide and arbitrary powers to French administrators over African subjects.

Jugements supplétifs: Special court decisions after 1916 confirming Africans as *originaires* of the Four Communes.

Khassidas: Form of poetry, or ode, recited by Senegalese Muslims.

Lat Dior: Damel of Kayor who resisted the French for more than 25 years before being killed in battle against them in 1886.

Marabout: Muslim cleric.

Marraines de guerre: Young women who befriended soldiers on active service. Relationships between couples varied, ranging from pen-pals to lovers.

Mawahibou: Incantation sung by Senegalese Muslims stressing Allah's promise of paradise.

Médaille militaire: Military decoration recognizing soldiers wounded one or more times who distinguished themselves by an act of courage during combat.

Métis: Persons of Eurafrican ancestry.

Mourides: A Sufi fraternity founded by Amadou Bamba; the second largest Muslim brotherhood in Senegal.

Mutilés de guerre: Disabled veterans.

Navetaans: Seasonal migrant workers.

Originaire: Originally a person from the Four Communes; later applied to any Senegalese with French citizenship.

Poste de police: Police station or guardhouse.

Profession de foi: Campaign platform statements of candidates for elective office.

Rog: High god of the Serer, who created the world and continued to act in its affairs through supernatural beings.

Spahi: French colonial cavalry composed largely of African troopers.

Sujet: Subject. During the colonial period, all Africans who were not *originaires* were in point of law "subjects."

Talibe: Students or disciples of a marabout.

Tidjaniya: A Sufi fraternity founded in North Africa; the largest Muslim brotherhood in Senegal.

Tirailleurs: Riflemen. French West African infantry (regardless of their origins) were known as Senegalese *tirailleurs*.

Travaux forcés: Compulsory labor—ostensibly not exceeding 12 days per year, but sometimes abused—performed at the behest of the colonial authorities by African subjects.

Tubab: A European.

Sources

ORAL HISTORIES:

Key: The following list of respondents with whom oral histories were conducted is divided into three sections: "veterans," "witnesses," and "unrecorded interviews and oral traditions." A final section lists interviews conducted with French veterans. Entries are arranged alphabetically within each category.

The code at the end of an entry (e.g., [T: 28 (N) 1A–6A]) provides the following information. The first letter indicates the general category (out of six) of the respondent: T (*tirailleur*), O (*originaire*), B (*Banlieue de Dakar*), W (witness), OT (oral tradition), and UI (unrecorded interview). The number that follows (e.g., 1–35 in the case of *tirailleurs*) indicates the listing assigned to them in the biographical ledger. In the case of witnesses, the letter and number following in parentheses after their broader designation (e.g.: W: (FO 6)) subdivide the respondents into more specific categories—FO (Female Observer), MO (Male Observer), PR (Potential Recruit), and V (postwar veteran who entered the army in 1920 or 1921)—and gives their numerical assignment. The letter in parentheses following thereafter indicates who served as translator (i.e., (N) (William Ndiaye), (F) Daouda Fall, (O) other). The symbol "+" appearing within the bracket (i.e., (N+)) indicates the use of a second translator speaking in the respondent's primary language through Ndiaye or Fall to me. The final designation (e.g., 1A–6B) indicates the length of the interview. Recorded on 60-minute cassettes, "1A (Tape 1, Side A)" indicates a 30-minute interview; alternatively, "1A–13A" indicates a twelve-and-a-half-hour interview.

Copies of the tape recordings and transcripts are available through the Archives of Traditional Music and Folklore, Indiana University, Bloomington; and the Archives Nationales du Sénégal, Dakar.

Veterans:

[*Tirailleur* (T); *Originaire* (O); *Banlieue de Dakar* (B)]

Bokar, Mamadou	[T: 12 (N+) 1A–2A.]
Camara, Ibrahima	[T: 24 (N) 1A–3A.]

Candji, Momar	[B: 5 (N and F) 1A–3A.]
Cisse, Momar	[T: 19: (N) 1A–1B.]
Diaw, Yoro	[T: 10: (N) 1A–3B.]
Demba, Mahmout	[T: 8 (N+) 1A–2A.]
Dembele, Daba	[T: 5 (N) 1A–6A.]
Diagne, Mbaye Khary	[O: 6 (N) 1A–6A.]
Diagne, Ousmane	[O: 5 (N) 1A–6B.]
Diakhate, Aliou	[O: 9 (N) 1A–2B.]
Diallo, Giribul	[O: 7 (O) 1A–2B.]
Diallo, Thiecouta	[O: 4 (N) 1A–2B.]
Diaw, Abdoulaye	[O: 12 (N) 1A–3B.]
Diop, Samba	[T: 20 (N) 1A–3A.]
Diouf, Antoine	[T: 23 (N) 1A–2A.]
Diouf, Nar	[T: 28: (N) 1A–6A.]
Diouf, Samba Laga	[T: 14 (N) 1A–2A.]
Djigo, Mamadou	[O: 15 (N and O) 1A–6B.]
Gassala, Malal	[T: 3 (N+) 1A–3A.]
Gassama, Abdoulaye	[T: 32 (N+) 1A–2B.]
Gaye, Abdou Karim	[T: 7: (N) 1A–5A.]
Gueye, Abdoulaye	[O: 10 (N) 1A–2A.]
Gueye, Boubacar	[O: 8 (N) 1A–2B.]
Gueye, Daour	[B: 1 (F) 1A–4B.]
Gueye, Galaye	[T: 15 (F) 1A–3A.]
Gueye, Niaki	[B: 3 (N) 1A–6B.]
Kane, Alassane	[B: 6 (N and F) 1A–5A.]
Leye, Mousa	[T: 33 (N and F) 1A–2A.]
Mbange, Ishmale	[B: 4 (N and F) 1A–4B.]
Mbaye, Kamadou	[O: 1 (O) 1A–1B.]
Mbaye, Mandaw	[B: 2 (N) 1A–2A.]
Mbaye, Ndematy	[O: 14 (N) 1A–2B.]
Mboup, Demba	[O: 3 (F and N) 1A–13A.]
Missine, Diouli	[T: 31 (N+) 1A–2B.]
Ndao, Doudou	[T: 6: (N) 1A–4B.]
Ndiaye, Abdoulaye	[O: 11 (N) 1A–6B.]
Ndiaye, Lebasse	[T: 34 (F) 1A–1B.]
Ndiaye, Makhoudia	[T: 18 (F) 1A–2B.]

Ndiaye, Mandiaye	[T: 26: (N) 1A–2B.]
Ndiaye, Nouma	[T: 16 (N) 1A–3A.]
Ndiaye, Sambou	[T: 9 (N) 1A–2A.]
Ndiaye, Sera	[T: 27: (N) 1A–6A.]
Ndiaye, Souleye Sama	[T: 30 (N+) 1A–2A.]
Nding, Thiam	[T: 21: (N) 1A–4B.]
Ndoye, Lattyr	[B: 7 (F) 1A–3A.]
Niang, Momar Khary	[T: 13 (F) 1A–3A.]
Niang, Ndiaga	[O: 13 (N) 1A–3A.]
Seck, Amar	[T: 4: (F) 1A–4B.]
Seck, Bara	[T: 22 (F) 1A–3A.]
Soumare, Masserigne	[T: 2 (N) 1A–5B.]
Sow, Mody	[T: 35 (F) 1A–4B.]
Sy, Sickh Yero	[T: 29 (N+) 1A–2A.]
Thiam, Ibrahima	[T: 17: (F) 1A–3B.]
Thiam, Seydou Amado	[T: 11 (N+) 1A.]
Tine, Biram Mbodji	[T: 25 (N) 1A–3A.]
William, Jacques	[O: 2: (N) 1A–2B.]
Yassin, Amadou	[T: 1 (N) 1A–2A.]

Witnesses (W) and Oral Traditions (OT)

Cisse, Karamako	[W: (PR 3) (F+) 1A–2B.]
Diatta, Souan Gor	[W: (PR 2) (N+) 1A–2A.]
Dioama, Aliou	[W: (MO 2) (F) 1A–2A.]
Ditta, Allou	[W: (MO 3) (N+) 1A–1B.]
Fati, Malang	[W: (MO 1) (N+) 1A–1B.]
Kebe, Coumba	[W (FO 5) (N+) 1A–3A.]
Laye, Soudou	[W: (V 3) (F) 1A–2B.]
Loum, Saer Anta	[W: (V 1) (N) 1A–1B.]
Ndiaye, Abdoulaye (Z)	[W: (V 2) (N) 1A–2A.]
Ndiaye, Adiouma	[W: (FO 4) (N+) 1A–1B.]
Ndiaye, Coumba	[W: (FO 3) (N) 1A.]
Ndiaye, Mamadou	[W: (PR 1) (N+) 1A–1B.]
Ngom, Aminata	[W: (FO 2) (F) 1A–1B.]
Niane, Coumba	[W: (FO 1) (N) 1A.]
Niang, Issap	[OT 1 (N) 1A.]

Souka, Birane   [W: (PR 4) (N) 1A.]
Wade, Gamou   [W: (FO 6) (N) 1A–1B.]

Unrecorded Interviews (UI)

Ba, Memoudou   [UI 4 (N).]
Bayo, Moussa   [UI 6 (N).]
Dia, Mamadou   [UI: 1 (N).]
Diene, Mathioro   [UI 3 (N).]
Diop, Fatou   [UI 11 (F).]
Diop, Mamadou   [UI 8 (N).]
Magaye, Bandia   [UI 7 (N).]
Mbengue, Baye   [UI 10 (N).]
Sall, Oumar Ousman   [UI 9 (N).]
Sow, Makhtar   [UI 5 (N).]
Thiaw, Abdou   [UI: 2 (F).]

French Veterans Interviewed

Lapierre, Henri   [F: 1, UI.]
Rougière, Nicolas   [F: 2, 1A–1B.]

ARCHIVAL SOURCES

In Senegal
ANS: Archives nationales du Sénégal, Dakar

Archives du gouvernement général de l'A.O.F.

1. Série D, Affaires militaires

    4 D 19: Recrutement des originaires, 1907–1919

    4 D 24/25: Recrutement des originaires: Application de la loi du 19 octobre 1915

    4 D 31: Recrutement indigène: Mission des études du Colonel Mangin pour le recrutement des troupes noires, 1909–1910

    4 D 32: Recrutement indigène, 1911

    4 D 35: Recrutement indigène, 1912

    4 D 43: Recrutement indigène, 1914–1916

    4 D 49: Recrutement indigène de 50,000 hommes: Rapport du 28 janvier 1916

4 D 54: Recrutement indigène de 50,000 hommes: Questions diverses, 1915–1916

4 D 55: Recrutement indigène de 50,000 hommes: Sénégal, 1915–1916

4 D 65: Recrutement indigène: Rapport de l'Inspecteur-Général Picanon sur le recrutement, 1916

4 D 68: Recrutement indigène: Nouveau recrutement, 1916–1917

4 D 69: Recrutement indigène, 1916–1917

4 D 70: Recrutement indigène: état d'esprit des tirailleurs en France, 1916–1917

4 D 71: Recrutement indigène: Questions diverses, 1916–1917

4 D 72: Recrutement indigène: Rapport du Gouverneur-Général J. Van Vollenhoven, 1917

4 D 73: Recrutement indigène: Rapport et correspondance du Ministère des colonies et du Ministère de la guerre. Reprise du recrutement; mission Diagne, 1917–1918

4 D 74: Recrutement indigène: Préparation, 1917–1918

4 D 76: Recrutement indigène: Rapports d'ensemble et statistiques, 1918

4 D 77: Recrutement indigène: Correspondance avec le Sénégal et le Haut-Sénégal et Niger, 1918

4 D 80/81: Recrutement indigène, 1918

4 D 82: Recrutement indigène, 1918–1919

4 D 83: Recrutement indigène: Sénégal et Mauritanie, 1918

4 D 87: Recrutement indigène: Fils de chefs, 1918–1920

4 D 88: Recrutement indigène: 1918

4 D 89: Recrutement indigène: Santé et assistance, 1918

4 D 139: Décès, 1915–1919

2. Série 2 G, Rapports périodiques (politiques, économiques, administratifs)

2 G 15 (44): Rapport général sur l'épidémie de peste au Sénégal, 1914–1915

2 G 17 (4): Gouverneur Général au Ministère des Colonies (n.d.) [1917]

3. Série 17 G, Affaires politiques, A.O.F.

17 G 15: Déplacements et activités de Deputé Diagne, 1914–1919

17 G 39: Politique indigène, 1908–1920

17 G 233 (108): Triptyque Diagniste; Blaise Diagne, 1919–1931

17 G 234 (108): Blaise Diagne [1914–1924]

4. Série 20 G, Élections

20 G 69 (23): Sénégal: élections municipaux de décembre 1919

20 G 70 (23): Sénégal: élections législative, 1919

5. Série 21 G, Police et sûreté

21 G 27 (17): Notes de l'Agent Désiré, 1925–1926

21 G 30 (17): Documentation relative à Lamine Senghor, 1925–1927

21 G 38 (17): Individus suspects, 1928–1939

21 G 111 (28): Propagande révolutionnaire dans l'armée, [1927–1935]

Archives des cercles, Sénégal

2 D 5 (2), Casamance: Administrateur supérieur, correspondance, 1896–1917

2 D 8 (6), Sine Saloum: Rapports divers, 1893–1917

2 D 9 (20), Louga: Affaires des déserteurs Peuls du cercle, 1918

In France
AG: *Archives de la Guerre, Service Historique de l'Armée, Château de Vincennes*

EMA: État-Major de l'Armée

7 N 144: Pièces de principe au sujet des troupes indigènes, 1915–1919

7 N 440: Effectifs, décembre 1915–janvier 1919

7 N 441: Infanterie coloniale et armée noire, 1918

7 N 444: Les Troupes noires, 1914–1915 (hivernage)

7 N 1990: Camps de sénégalais, 1916–1919

7 N 1991: Camps de sénégalais, 1916–1919

7 N 2120: Troupes indigènes coloniales, recrutement, transport, dépôts, pertes, 1914–1918

7 N 2121: Troupes indigènes coloniales, recrutement, transport, dépôts, pertes, 1914–1918

Fonds Clemenceau

6 N 96: Troupes coloniales et indigènes, 1916–1918

6 N 97: Troupes coloniales et indigènes, 1916–1918

GQG: Grand Quartier General

16 N 85: L'Offensive Nivelle

16 N 100: Reorganisation de l'emploi des Bataillons de tirailleurs sénégalais

16 N 196: Organisation Maroc et Afrique du Nord: utilisation sur les fronts des troupes indigènes, sénégalais

16 N 525: Statistiques sur les pertes, contingents indigènes sénégalais, 1917

16 N 2094: "Hivernage" des sénégalais, 1917–1918

Unités

22 N 2481: 2*e* Corps d'Armée colonial

24 N 3027: 10*e* Division d'Infanterie coloniale, 1917

26 N 869/873: Journaux de marche et d'opérations des régiments et bataillons des tirailleurs sénégalais, [1911–1919]

AN: *Archives nationales, Paris*

Série AP: Archives privées

110 AP 2 7-8: Papiers Galandou Diouf. Album photographique concernant une mission militaire en A.O.F. (n.d.); tournée de Diagne, recrutement de l'armée noire en 1914 [1918]

149 AP 11: Papiers Charles Mangin. "Troupes Noires," emploi, 1912–1919

149 AP 12: Papiers Charles Mangin. "Troupes Noires," emploi, 1919–1924

ANOM: *Archives nationales, Section d'outre-mer, Aix-en-Provence (formerly in Paris)*

Série: Affaires politiques

170 (5): Rapport sur la loi Diagne, 1916

595 (1): Sénégal, élections 1919

3034 (3, 4): A.O.F., Affaires militaires: Recrutement des tirailleurs pendant la guerre: Mesures à prendre contre la dépravation féminine, 1915–1916; Comité d'Assistance aux Troupes Noires

3035 (1): Recrutement de "50,000 hommes" (1916)

3036 (2, 3, 11): A.O.F., Affaires militaires: Recrutement des tirailleurs pendant la guerre: Mission d'inspection Picanon, 1916; propagande Islamique en France; Mission Diagne

Série: Affaires militaires

14 MI 323: Recrutement 1912

14 MI 346: Recrutement des originaires, 1907–1919

Série: Affaires politiques

14 MI 1091: Élections legislatives au Sénégal, 1914

14 MI 1110: Statistiques: Colonie du Sénégal, 1915–1916

14 MI 2356: État civil indigène, 1914–1920

14 MI 2877: Élections legislatives et municipales du Sénégal, 1919–1920

14 MI 2880: Élections legislatives au Sénégal, 1928

CMIDOM*: Centre militaire d'information et de documentation sur l'Outre-Mer, Versailles*

A.O.F. INT-CIII-27-B: Manuel tactique pour le Groupe de l'A.O.F.: Notions générales (1910)

A.O.F. INT-CIII-27-C: Rapport sur les opérations militaires en A. O. F. pendant la guerre, 1914–1918

Publications: "Notice sur les Sénégalais et leur emploi au combat," (n.d.) [May 1917–November 1918]

IF*: Institut de France, Bibliothèque, Paris*
Fonds Auguste Terrier

MS 5919: Troupes noires

MS 5920: Troupes noires

MS 5925: Gouverneurs Généraux

Ministère de l'Économie et des Finances, Paris

"Administration des finances pendant l'année 1917: dépenses publique"

OFFICIAL PUBLICATIONS

Annales de la Chambre des Députés.
Annuaire du Gouvernement Général de l'Afrique Occidentale française (Annuaire du Sénégal). Saint Louis: Imprimerie du Gouvernement.
Annuaire du Gouvernement Général de l'Afrique Occidentale française, 1913–1914. Paris: Emile Larose, 1914.
Annuaire du Gouvernement Général de l'Afrique Occidentale française, 1917–1921. Paris: Emile Larose, 1921.
Annuaire du Gouvernement Général de l'Afrique Occidentale française, 1922. Paris: Emile Larose, 1922.
Les Armées Françaises d'Outre-Mer. Paris: Imprimerie national, 1931–1932.
Employment contrary to International Law of Colored Troops upon the European Arena of War by England and France. Berlin: Foreign Office, 1915.
Le Français tel que le parlent nos tirailleurs. Paris: Imprimerie Libraire Militaire Universelle L. Tournier, 1916.
Histoire militaire de l'A.O.F. Paris: Imprimerie national, 1931.
Journal Officiel de la République Française. Documents Parlementaires.
  Débats de la Chambre
  Chambre des Députés
  Débats
  Comités Secrets
  "Rapport Marin," *Journal Officiel de la République Française. Documents Parlementaires*, Chambre, 1920, tome 2, annexe 633, pp. 32–78.

"Rapport . . . sur les pertes en morts et en blessés . . . par le baron des Lyons de Feuchins . . .," *Journal Officiel de la République Française. Documents Parlementaires*, Chambre, 1924, annexe 335, pp. 1275–1321.

Procès verbaux des déliberations du Conseil Général. Paris: Imprimerie national, 1919.

Les Troupes coloniales pendant la Guerre 1914–1918. Paris: Imprimerie national, 1931.

PERIODICALS

L'A.O.F. (Dakar)
Les Continents (Paris)
Le Courrier Colonial (Paris)
La Démocratie du Sénégal (Dakar)
La Dépêche coloniale Illustrée (Paris)
L'Illustration (Paris)
L'Independent Sénégalais (Dakar)
Le Journal (Paris)
Le Midi colonial et maritime (Marseille)
Le Petit Var (Marseille)
La Presse coloniale (Paris)
La Race nègre (Paris)
Le Temps (Paris)
Union coloniale, Bulletin de la Section A.O.F. (Paris)

PAMPHLETS

Les Troupes noires. (Le Parlement: Rapports. Commissions. Séances. L'Opinion militaire et colonial. La Presse. Les Conférences.) Paris: Edition du Journal "L'Armée Coloniale," 1911.

SECONDARY SOURCES

Adenaike, Carolyn Keyes, and Jan Vansina, eds. *In Pursuit of History: Fieldwork in Africa.* Portsmouth, NH: Heinemann/Oxford: James Currey, 1996.

Ageron, Charles-Robert. "Clemenceau et la question coloniale." In *Clemenceau et la Justice* (Actes du Colloque de décembre 1979 organisé pour le cinquantenaire de la mort de G. Clemenceau.). Paris: Publications de la Sorbonne, 1983.

Alexandre, Pierre. "Chiefs, *Commandants* and Clerks: Their Relationship from Conquest to Decolonisation in French West Africa." In *West African Chiefs: Their Changing Status under Colonial Rule and Independence.* Edited by Michael Crowder. New York: Africana Publishing Corporation, 1970.

d'Almeida-Topor, Helen. "Les populations dahoméennes et le recrutement militaire pendant la première Guerre mondiale," *Revue Française d'Histoire d'Outre-Mer* 60 (1973): 196–241.

Ba, Oumar. *Amadou Bamba face aux autorités coloniales (1889–1927).* Abbeville: L'Imprimerie F. Paillart, 1982.

Balesi, Charles. *From Adversaries to Comrades-in-Arms: West Africa and the French Military, 1885–1918.* Waltham, MA: Crossroads Press, 1979.

Ballard, John. "The Porto Novo Incidents of 1923: Politics in the Colonial Era." *Odu: University of Ife Journal of African Studies* 1 (1965): 52–75.

Barry, Boubacar. *Senegambia and the Atlantic Slave Trade*. Cambridge: Cambridge University Press, 1998.

Becker, Charles. "Les Effets demographiques de la traite des esclaves en Sénégambie: Esquisse d'une histoire des peuplements du XVIIᵉ à la fin du XIXᵉ siècle." In *De la Traite à l'esclavage. Actes du Colloque international sur la traite des Noirs, Nantes 1985*. Vol. 2: *XVIIIᵉ–XIXᵉ siècles*. Edited by Serge Daget. Paris: L'Harmattan, 1988. Pp. 70–110.

———, and Martin, Victor. "Kayor et Baol: Royaumes sénégalais et traite des esclaves au XVIIIᵉ siècle." *Revue Française d'histoire d'Outre-Mer* 62 (1975): 278–83.

Becker, Jean-Jacques. *The Great War and the French People*. Leamington Spa/Heidelberg/Dover, NH: Berg, 1993.

Bernard, Philippe, "Le dernier de la 'Force Noire,'" *Le Monde*, 12 novembre 1998.

Betts, Raymond F. "The Establishment of the Medina in Dakar, Senegal, 1914." *Africa* 41 (1971): 143–52.

Bocquet, Léon, and Hosten, Ernest. *Un fragment de l'épopée sénégalaise: Les tirailleurs noirs sur l'Yser*. Brussels and Paris: G. Van Oest, 1918.

Boutillier, J. L. "Les captifs en AOF (1903–1905)." *Bulletin de l'Institut Fondamental de l'Afrique Noire*, Sér. B, 30 (1968): 528–29.

Brunschwig, Henri. *French Colonialism, 1871–1914: Myths and Realities*. Translated by William Glanville Brown. London: Pall Mall Press, 1966.

———. "French Expansion and Local Reactions in Black Africa in the Time of Imperialism (1880–1914)." In *Expansion and Reaction: Essays on European Expansion and Reactions in Asia and Africa*. Edited by H. L. Wesseling. The Hague: Martinus Nijhoff; Leiden: Leiden University Press, 1978.

———. *Noirs et Blancs dans l'Afrique noire Française, ou comment le colonisé devint colonisateur (1870–1914)*. Paris: Flammarion, 1983.

Buell, Raymond Leslie. *The Native Problem in Africa*. 2 vols. New York: Macmillan, 1928.

Calvet, M. J., and Ragon, C. *Aperçu des origines et du développement de Dakar*. Dakar: Ambassade de France, 1982.

Campion-Vincet, Véronique. "L'image du Dahomey dans la presse française (1890–1895): Les sacrifices humains." *Cahiers d'études Africaines* 25 (1967): 27–58.

Charbonneau, Jean. *Les contingents coloniaux: du Soleil et de la Gloire*. Paris: Imprimerie national, 1931.

Charles, Uyisenga. "La Participation de la Colonie du Sénégal à 'l'effort de guerre,' 1914–1918." Mémoire de Maîtrise: University of Dakar, 1978.

Clark, Andrew F. "Slavery and Its Demise in the Upper Senegal Valley, West Africa, 1890–1920." *Slavery and Abolition* 15 (1994): 51–71.

———. "Freedom Villages in the Upper Senegal Valley, 1887–1910: A Reassessment." *Slavery and Abolition* 16 (1995): 311–30.

Clayton, Anthony. *France, Soldiers and Africa*. London: Brassey's Defence Publishers, 1988.

Cohen, William. *Rulers of Empire: The French Colonial Service in Africa*. Stanford: Hoover Institution Press, 1971.

———. "Literature and Race: Nineteenth Century French Fiction, Blacks and Africa, 1800–1880." *Race and Class* 16 (1974): 181–205.

————. *The French Encounter with Africans: White Response to Blacks, 1530–1880.* Bloomington: Indiana University Press, 1980.

————. "French Racism and Its African Impact." In *Double Impact: France and West Africa in the Age of Imperialism.* Edited by G. Wesley Johnson, Jr. Westport, CT, and London: Greenwood Press, 1985.

Conklin, Alice L. *A Mission to Civilize: The Republican Idea of Empire in France and West Africa, 1895–1930.* Stanford: Stanford University Press, 1997.

————. "Colonialism and Human Rights, a Contradition in Terms? The Case of France and West Africa, 1895–1914." *American Historical Review* 103 (1998): 419–42.

Cooper, Frederick. *Decolonization and African Society: The Labor Question in French and British Africa.* Cambridge: Cambridge University Press, 1996.

Coquery-Vidrovitch, Catherine. "French Black Africa." In *Cambridge History of Africa.* Volume 7: *1905–1940.* Edited by A. D. Roberts. Cambridge: Cambridge University Press, 1986.

Cornevin, Robert. "Du Sénégal à la Provence: Lamine Senghor (1889–1927), pionnier de la négritude." In "Mélanges André Villard." *Provence historique* 25 (1975): 69–77.

Cousturier, Lucie. *Des inconnus chez moi.* Paris: La Suene, 1920.

Cros, Charles. *La parole est à M. Blaise Diagne.* Paris: Aubenas, 1961.

Crowder, Michael. *Senegal: A Study of French Assimilation Policy.* 2d rev. ed. London: Methuen & Co., 1967.

————. "West Africa and the 1914–1918 War." *Bulletin de l'Institut Fondamental d'Afrique Noire,* Sér. B, 30 (1968): 227–47.

————. "The Administration of French West Africa." *Tarick* 4 (1969): 59–71.

————. "Blaise Diagne and the Recruitment of African Troops for the 1914–1918 War" (1967). In *Colonial West Africa: Collected Essays.* London: Frank Cass, 1978. Pp. 104–21.

Curtin, Philip D. *Economic Change in Precolonial Africa: Senegambia in the Era of the Slave Trade.* Madison: University of Wisconsin Press, 1975.

————. "The Abolition of the Slave Trade from Senegambia." In *The Abolition of the Atlantic Slave Trade: Origins and Effects in Europe, Africa, and the Americas.* Edited by David Eltin and James Walvin. Madison: University of Wisconsin Press, 1981.

Davis, Shelby Cullom. *Reservoirs of Men: A History of the Black Troops of French West Africa.* Chambry, 1934; rpt. ed., Westport, CT: Negro Universities Press, 1970.

Demaison, André, and Mille, Pierre. *Amour d'une blanche pour un noir.* Paris: Editions de France, 1924.

Dewitte, Philippe. *Les Mouvements nègres en France, 1919–1939.* Paris: Editions L'Harmattan, 1985.

Diallo, Bakary. *Force-Bonté.* Paris: Rieder, 1926.

Dieng, Amody Aly. *Blaise Diagne: Député noire de l'Afrique.* Paris: Editions Choka, 1990.

Diouf, Mamadou. *Le Kajoor au XIXe siècle: Pouvoir, ceddo et conquête coloniale.* Paris: Karthala, 1990.

Drescher, Seymour. "The Ending of the Slave Trade and the Evolution of European Scientific Racism." *Social Science History* 14 (1990): 415–50.

Duroselle, Jean-Baptiste. *Clemenceau.* Paris: Rayard, 1988.

Dutreb, Maurice. *Nos Sénégalais pendant la Grande Guerre.* Metz: R. Ferry, 1922.

Dyer, Gwynne. *War*. New York: Crown Publishers, 1985.

Echenberg, Myron. "Tragedy at Thiaroye: The Senegalese Soldiers' Uprising of 1944." In *African Labor History*. Edited by Robin Cohen, Jean Copans, and Peter Gutkind. Beverly Hills: Sage Publications, 1978.

———. *Colonial Conscripts: The "Tirailleurs Sénégalais" in French West Africa, 1857–1960*. Portsmouth, NH: Heinemann/London: James Currey, 1991.

Fall, Mar. *Des Tirailleurs Sénégalais aux . . . Blacks: Les Africains noirs en France*. Paris: Editions L'Harmattan, 1986.

Fussel, Paul. *The Great War and Modern Memory*. Oxford and New York: Oxford University Press, 1975.

Gaillet, Léon. *Coulibaly: Les Sénégalais sur la terre de France*. Paris: Jouve, 1917.

———. *Deux ans avec les sénégalais*. Paris: Berger-Levrault, 1918.

Gamble, David. *The Wolof of Senegambia: Together with Notes on the Lebu and Serer*. London: Hazel, Watson & Viney, 1957.

Ganier, Germaine. "Lat Dyor et le chemin de fer de l'arachide 1876–1886." *Bulletin de l'Institut Fondamental d'Afrique Noire*, Sér. B, 32 (1965): 223–81.

Garcia, Luc. "Les mouvements de résistance au Dahomey (1914–1917)." *Cahiers d'Etudes Africaines* 37 (1970): 144–78.

Geggus, David. "Sex Ratio, Age and Ethnicity in the Atlantic Slave Trade: Data from French Shipping and Plantation Records." *Journal of African History* 30 (1989): 23–44.

Geiss, Imanuel. *The Pan-African Movement*. Translated by Ann Keep. London: Methuen & Co., 1974.

Gellar, Sheldon. *Structural Changes and Colonial Dependency: Senegal, 1885–1945*. Beverly Hills and London: Sage Publications, 1976.

Glinga, Werner. "Ein Koloniales Paradoxon–Blaise Diagne und die Rekrutierungsmission 1918." In *"Tirailleurs Sénégalais": Zur Bildlichen und Literarischen Darstellung Afrikanischer Soldaten im Dienste Frankreichs— Présentations Littéraires et Figuratives de Soldats africains au Service de la France*. Edited by János Riesz and Joachim Schultz. Frankfurt am Main: Peter Lang, 1989. Pp. 21–37.

Gnankambary, Blamy. "La révolte bobo de 1916 dans le cercle du Dedougou." *Notes et études Voltaïques* (July–September 1970): 56–87.

Görög-Karady, Veronika. *Noirs et Blancs: Leur image dans la littérature orale Africaine: Étude—Anthologie*. Paris: Centre National de la Recherche Scientifique et du Conseil International de la Langue française, 1976.

Guerre, John Gaffar la. *Enemies of Empire*. St. Augustine, Trinidad: College Press, 1984.

Gueye, Lamine. *Itinéraire Africain*. Paris: Présence Africain, 1966.

Guinard, Pierre, Devos, Jean-Claude, and Nicot, Jean. *Inventaire sommaire des Archives de la Guerre. Série N 1872–1919*. Troyes: Imprimerie La Renaissance, 1975.

Guiraud, Xavier. *L'Arachide sénégalais: Monographie d'economie coloniale*. Paris: Librairie Technique et Economique, 1937.

Haine, W. Scott. *The World of the Paris Cafe: Sociability among the French Working Class, 1789–1914*. Baltimore: Johns Hopkins University Press, 1996.

Herbert, Jean. "Révoltes en Haute-Volta de 1914 à 1919." *Notes et études Voltaïques* (July–September 1970): 3–54.

Hopkins, A. G. *An Economic History of West Africa*. London: Longmans, 1973.

Hosten, Ernest. *Un fragment de l'épopée sénégalaise: Les Tirailleurs noirs sur l'Yser*. Brussels and Paris: G. Van Oest, 1918.

Ingold, Francois. *Les Troupes noires au combat.* Paris: Berger-Levrault, 1940.

Jennings, Eric T. "Monuments to Frenchness? The Memory of the Great War and the Politics of Guadeloupe's Identity, 1914–1945." *French Historical Studies* 21 (1998): 561–92.

Johnson, G. Wesley, Jr. "Blaise Diagne: Master Politician of Senegal." *Tarikh* 1 (1966): 51–57.

———. *The Emergence of Black Politics in Senegal: The Struggle for Power in the Four Communes, 1900–1920.* Stanford: Stanford University Press, 1971.

———. "The Senegalese Urban Elite, 1900–1945." In *Africa and the West: Intellectual Responses to European Culture.* Edited by Philip D. Curtin. Madison: University of Wisconsin Press, 1972. Pp. 139–87.

———, ed. *Double Impact: France and West Africa in the Age of Imperialism.* Westport, CT, and London: Greenwood Press, 1985.

Kanya-Forstner, A. S. *The Conquest of the Western Sudan: A Study in French Military Imperialism.* Cambridge: Cambridge University Press, 1969.

———. "Mali-Tukulor." In *West African Resistance: The Military Response to Colonial Occupation.* Edited by Michael Crowder. London: Hutchinson, 1971.

———. "French Expansion in Africa: The Mythical Theory." In *Studies in the Theory of Imperialism.* Edited by R. Owen and B. Sutcliffe. London: Longman, 1972.

———, and Andrew, C. M. "France, Africa and the First World War." *Journal of African History* 19 (1978): 11–23.

Keegan, John. *The Face of Battle: A Study of Agincourt, Waterloo and the Somme.* Harmondsworth: Penguin Books, 1976.

———. *The Second World War.* London: Hutchinson, 1989.

Klein, Martin A. *Islam and Imperialism in Senegal: Sine-Saloum, 1847–1914.* Edinburgh: Edinburgh University Press, 1968.

———. "Traditional Political Institutions and Colonial Domination." *African Historical Studies* 4 (1971): 659–60.

———. "Colonial Rule and Structural Change: The Case of Sine-Saloum." In *The Political Economy of Underdevelopment: Dependence in Senegal.* Edited by Rita Cruise O'Brien. Beverly Hills: Sage Publications, 1979.

———. "Studying the History of Those Who Would Rather Forget: Oral History and the Experience of Slavery." *History in Africa* 16 (1989): 209–17.

———. "The Impact of the Atlantic Slave Trade on the Societies of the Western Sudan." *Social Science History* 14 (1990): 231–53.

———. "Slavery and Emancipation in French West Africa." In *Breaking the Chains: Slavery, Bondage, and Emancipation in Modern Africa and Asia.* Madison: University of Wisconsin Press, 1993. Pp. 171–96.

———. *Slavery and Colonial Rule in French West Africa.* Cambridge: Cambridge University Press, 1998.

Langley, J. Ayo. "Pan-Africanism in Paris, 1924–1936." *Journal of Modern African Studies* 7 (1969): 69–94.

Lasnet, Dr. "Notice concernant l'état sanitaire des divers contingents Européens et Indigènes de l'Armée du Rhin." *Annales de Médecine et de Pharmacie coloniale* 20 (1922): 273–89.

Lawler, Nancy Ellen. *Soldiers of Misfortune: Ivoirien Tirailleurs of World War II.* Athens: Ohio University Press, 1992.

Leed, Eric J. *No Man's Land: Combat and Identity in World War I.* Cambridge: Cambridge University Press, 1981.

Lovejoy, Paul E. "The Volume of the Atlantic Slave Trade: A Synthesis." *Journal of African History* 23 (1982): 473–501.

———. *Transformations in Slavery: A History of Slavery in Africa*. Cambridge: Cambridge University Press, 1983.

Lunn, Joe Harris. "Kande Kamara Speaks: An Oral History of the West African Experience in France, 1914–18." In *Africa and the First World War*. Edited by Melvin Page. London: Macmillan, 1987.

———. "Memoirs of the Maelstrom: A Senegalese Oral History of the First World War." Ph.D. dissertation, University of Wisconsin–Madison, 1993.

———. "'Les races guerrières': Racial Preconceptions in the French Military about West African Soldiers during the First World War," *Journal of Contemporary History* 34, 4 (1999).

Lüsebrink, Hans-Jürgen. "'Tirailleurs Sénégalais' und 'Schwarze Schande': Verlaufsformen und Konsequenzen einer deutsch-französischen Auseinandersetzung (1910–1926)." In *"Tirailleurs Sénégalais": Zur Bildlichen und Literarischen Darstellung Afrikanischer Soldaten im Dienste Frankreichs– Présentations Littéraires et Figuratives de Soldats Africains au Service de la France*. Edited by János Riesz and Joachim Schultz. Frankfurt am Main: Peter Lang, 1989. Pp. 57–73.

Ly, Abdoulay. *Les Mercenaires noirs: Notes sur une forme de l'exploitation des Africains*. Paris: Editions Présence Africaine, 1957.

McCloy, Shelby T. *The Negro in France*. Lexington: University of Kentucky Press, 1961.

Manchuelle, François. *Willing Migrants: Soninke Labor Diasporas, 1848–1969*. Athens: Ohio University Press; London: James Currey, 1997.

Mangin, Charles. "Troupes noires." *La Revue de Paris* 4 (1 and 15 July 1909): 61–80; 383–98.

———. *La Force Noire*. Paris: Libraire Hachette, 1910.

———. "L'Utilisation de troupes noires." *Bulletins et Mémoires de la Société d'Anthropologie de Paris* 2 (1911): 95–100.

———. *Comment finit la Guerre*. Paris: Plon, 1920.

———. *Lettres de guerre à sa femme, 1914–1918*. Edited by Antoinette Cavaignac Mangin. Paris: Fayard, 1950.

Mangin, Louis-Eugene. *Le Général Mangin*. Paris: Editions Fernand Lanore, 1986.

Marseille, Jacques. *Empire coloniale et Capitalisme française. Histoire d'un Divorce*. Paris: Albin Michel, 1984.

Martinbus-Zemp, Ada. *Le Blanc et le Noir: Essai d'une description de la vision du Noir par le Blanc dans la littérature française de l'entre-deux-guerres*. Paris: A-G Nizet, 1975.

Maupassant, Guy de. "Tombouctou." In *Contes du jour et de la nuit*. Paris: L'Edition d'art H. Piazza, [1885].

M'Bokolo, Elikia, "Peste et société urbaine à Dakar: l'épidémie de 1914." *Cahiers d'Etudes Africaines* 22 (1982): 13–46.

Mettas, Jean. *Répertoire des expéditions negrières Françaises au xviiiᵉ siècle*. Edited by Serge Daget. 2 volumes. Paris: Société Française d'histoire d'outre-mer, 1978–1984.

Michel, Marc. "La genèse du recrutement de 1918 en Afrique noire Française." *Revue Française d'Histoire d'Outre-Mer* 58 (1971): 433–50.

———. "Citoyenneté et service militaire dans les quatre communes du Sénégal au cours de la Première Guerre mondiale." In *Perspectives nouvelles sur le passé de l'Afrique noire et de Madagascar: Mélanges offerts à Hubert Deschamps*. Paris: Editions de la Sorbonne, 1974.

————. "Un mythe: la 'Force Noire' avant 1914." *Relations Internationales* 1 (1974): 83–90.

————. *L'Appel à l'Afrique: Contributions et réactions à l'effort de guerre en A.O.F. (1914–1919)*. Paris: Publications de la Sorbonne, 1982.

————. "Les troupes coloniales arrivent." *Histoire* no. 69 (1984): 116–21.

————. "'Memoire Officiel': Discours et pratique coloniale le 14 juillet et le 11 novembre au Sénégal entre les deux Guerres." *Revue française d'histoire d'outre-mer* 77 (1990): 145–58.

Midiohouan, Guy Ossito. "Le Tirailleur Sénégalais du fusil a la plume: La fortune de *Force-Bonté* de Bakary Diallo." In *"Tirailleurs Sénégalais": Zur Bildlichen und Literarischen Darstellung Afrikanischer Soldaten im Dienste Frankreichs–Présentations Littéraires et Figuratives de Soldats africains au Service de la France*. Edited by János Riesz and Joachim Schultz. Frankfurt am Main: Peter Lang, 1989. Pp. 133–51.

Mosse, George L. *Toward the Final Solution: A History of European Racism*. London: J. M. Dent, 1978.

Nelson, Keith L. "The 'Black Horror on the Rhine': Race as a Factor in Post-World War I Diplomacy." *Journal of Modern History* 42 (1970): 606–27.

O'Brien, Donal Cruise. *The Mourides of Senegal: The Political and Economic Organization of an Islamic Brotherhood*. Oxford: Clarendon Press, 1971.

————. *Saints and Politicians: Essays in the Organisation of a Senegalese Peasant Society*. Cambridge: Cambridge University Press, 1975.

O'Brien, Rita Cruise. *White Society in Black Africa: The French in Senegal*. London: Faber and Faber, 1979.

Page, Melvin E. "Malawians in the Great War and After, 1914–1925." Ph.D. dissertation, Michigan State University, 1977.

————. "Malawians and the Great War: Oral History in the Reconstruction of Africa's Recent Past." *Oral History Review* 8 (1980): 49–61.

Pedroncini, Guy. *Les Mutineries de 1917*. Paris: Presses Universitaires de France, 1967.

————, ed. *Histoire Militaire de la France*. Vol. 3: *1871–1940*. Paris: Presses Universitaires de France, 1992.

Pheffer, Paul Edward. "Railroads and Aspects of Social Change in Senegal, 1878–1933." Ph.D. dissertation, University of Pennsylvania, 1975.

————. "The African Influence on French Colonial Railroads in Senegal." In *Double Impact: France and West Africa in the Age of Imperialism*. Edited by G. Wesley Johnson, Jr. Wesport, CT, and London: Greenwood Press, 1985.

Richardson, David. "Slave Exports from West and West-Central Africa, 1700–1810: New Estimates on Volume and Distribution." *Journal of African History* 30 (1989): 1–22.

Robinson, David. *Chiefs and Clerics: Abdul Bokar Kan and Futa Toro, 1853–1891*. Oxford: Oxford University Press, 1975.

————. *The Holy War of Umar Tal: The Western Sudan in the Mid-Nineteenth Century*. Oxford: Clarendon Press of Oxford University, 1985.

Roche, Christine. *Histoire de la Casamance: Conquête et résistance, 1950–1920*. Paris: Editions Karthala, 1985.

Sanneh, Lamin. *The Crown and the Turban: Muslims and West African Pluralism*. Boulder, CO: Westview Press, 1997.

Schneider, William H. *An Empire for the Masses: The French Popular Image of Africa, 1870–1900.* Westport, CT, and London: Greenwood Press, 1982.

Searing, James F. "Accommodation and Resistance: Chiefs, Muslim Leaders, and Politicians in Colonial Senegal, 1890–1934." Ph.D. dissertation, Princeton University, 1985.

———. *West African Slavery and Atlantic Commerce: The Senegal River Valley, 1700–1860.* Cambridge: Cambridge University Press, 1993.

Séché, Alphonse. *Les Noirs d'après des documents officiels.* Paris: Payot, 1919.

Seck, Assane. *Dakar Métropole Ouest-Africaine.* Dakar: IFAN, 1970.

Senghor, Léopold Sedar. "René Maran, précurseur de la négritude." In *Hommage à René Maran.* Paris: Présence Africaine, 1965.

Shepperson, George. "Pan-Africanism and 'Pan-Africanism': Some Historical Notes." *Phylon* 23 (1962): 355–56.

Soumah, Moussa. "Population." In *Atlas du Sénégal.* Edited by Paul Pélissier. Paris: Editions Jeune Afrique, 1980. Pp. 26–29.

Spiegler, James S. "Aspects of Nationalist Thought Among French-speaking West Africans, 1921–39." D.Phil. thesis, Oxford University, 1968.

Stein, Robert. "Measuring the French Slave Trade, 1713–1792/3." *Journal of African History* 19 (1978): 515–21.

Stepan, Nancy. *The Idea of Race in Science.* London: Macmillan, 1982.

Stovall, Tyler. *Paris Noir: African Americans in the City of Light.* Boston: Houghton Mifflin, 1996.

———. "The Color Line behind the Lines: Racial Violence in France during the Great War." *American Historical Review* 103 (1998): 737–69.

Summers, Anne, and Johnson, R. W. "World War I Conscription and Social Change in Guinea." *Journal of African History* 19 (1978): 25–38.

Tharaud, Jérôme, and Tharaud, Jean. *La randonnée de Samba Diouf.* Paris: Plon, 1922.

Thompson, J. Malcolm. "Colonial Policy and the Family Life of Black Troops in French West Africa, 1817–1904." *International Journal of African Historical Studies* 23 (1990): 423–53.

Vaillant, Janet G. *Black, French, and African: A Life of Léopold Sédar Senghor.* Cambridge, MA, and London: Harvard University Press, 1990.

Vansina, Jan. *De la tradition orale.* (Sciences de l'homme, Annales no. 36.) Tervuren: Musée royal de l'Afrique centrale, 1961.

Venema, L. B. *The Wolof of Saloum: Social Structure and Rural Development in Senegal.* Wageningen: Center for Agricultural Publishing and Documentation, 1978.

Zuccarilli, François. *La Vie politique Sénégalaise (1789–1940).* Paris: CHEAM, 1987.

INDEX

ABOUT THE AUTHOR

JOE LUNN is currently Assistant Professor of History at the University of Michigan-Dearborn. His publications include articles in *Africa and the First World War* and the *Journal of Contemporary History.* He is presently working on a second book entitled *African Voices from the Great War: An Anthology of Senegalese Soldiers' Life Histories,* which will further explore the First World War's impact on the lives of the Senegalese.

ISBN 0-325-00139-1

90000>

EAN

9 780325 001395

HARDCOVER BAR CODE